Routledge Revivals

Economic Planning in France

When it was originally published in 1963, this was the first full study in English of French economic planning in the 20th century and appeared at a time when the UK was beginning a similar experiment. The book is an extensive source of information on the 20th century structure of the French economy, economic and governmental institutions and post-war French economic history that until this publication, was not conveniently available to English readers. The book will appeal to economic historians, and anyone concerned with French banking, taxation, government and agriculture. The book discusses the relations between the various public departments, in particular the Ministry of Finance, local government, the political parties, the consultative bodies, Parliament and the Plans as well as the attitudes of the trade unions, of French business and farmers.

Economic Planning in France

John Hackett and Anne-Marie Hackett.

Routledge
Taylor & Francis Group
ROUTLEDGE REVIVALS

First published in 1963 by George Allen & Unwin Ltd.

This edition first published in 2026 by Routledge
4 Park Square, Milton Park, Abingdon, Oxon, OX14 4RN

and by Routledge
605 Third Avenue, New York, NY 10158

Routledge is an imprint of the Taylor & Francis Group, an informa business

For Product Safety Concerns and Information please contact our EU representative GPSR@taylorandfrancis.com. Taylor & Francis Verlag GmbH, Kaufingerstraße 24, 80331 München, Germany

ISBN: 978-1-041-32680-9 (hbk)
ISBN: 978-1-003-78394-7 (ebk)
ISBN: 978-1-041-32682-3 (pbk)

Book DOI 10.4324/9781003783947

ECONOMIC PLANNING IN FRANCE

JOHN HACKETT
AND
ANNE-MARIE HACKETT

with a Foreword by
PIERRE MASSÉ
Commissaire Général du Plan

London
GEORGE ALLEN & UNWIN LTD
RUSKIN HOUSE MUSEUM STREET

FIRST PUBLISHED IN 1963

PRINTED IN GREAT BRITAIN
in 10 on 11 point Times Roman type
BY SIMSON SHAND LTD
LONDON, HERTFORD AND HARLOW

TO OUR PARENTS
IN FRANCE AND ENGLAND

FOREWORD

The foundation of the French Plan is a collective reflection on the future. It leads to conclusions which are concerted between the representatives of the various groups in society and correspond to a middle way between the traditional liberal market economy and the detailed, centralized and authoritarian type of planning which existed, and still exists, in the Eastern European countries.

Extreme solutions are always more pure from a doctrinal point of view than those intermediate solutions expressing compromises which, in turn, vary from one period and from one country to another. And they are consequently easier to explain and to defend. But life itself imposes a compromise. Thus there is no such thing as a 100 per cent liberal economy. Everywhere the State has had conferred upon it a more or less wide range of responsibilities in the economic field. Doubtless, a 100 per cent imperative type of planning does not exist either. It is universally recognized that a measure of individual initiative is a factor generating economic progress. Being realistic, French planning is less a theory than a practice, less a codified charter than a set of usages in constant evolution. It is, above all no doubt, a state of mind.

The experiment which has been carried on in France for the last fifteen years merits to be more widely known. But its complexities and varying shades of meaning call for penetration in their analysis and for a considerable effort in marshalling the available information. We have cause to be particularly grateful to John and Anne-Marie Hackett for the systematic and exhaustive study they have made of it for the benefit of an Anglo-Saxon audience.

They begin by describing in a precise and lucid manner the institutional framework of planning in France. This framework has been built up and enriched progressively since the creation by M. Jean Monnet of the Planning Commissions, whose rôle is to provide a meeting-place for the representatives of the public departments, business enterprises and the trade unions, enabling them to concert their decisions. In their turn, and at successively higher levels, the High Planning Council, the Economic and Social Council and the Parliamentary Assemblies provide for concerted discussions whose technical content becomes less pronounced. And, today, this effort of collective reflection is acquiring a regional dimension which is likely to impose itself increasingly during the years ahead.

The book then goes on to deal with the methods used in drafting the Plan, first at the outline stage and then as to the final detailed preparation. It shows how the objectives of the Plan are more or less firm according to whether basic activities with large-scale production units or highly diversified sectors, such as the secondary industries, are concerned. There is no doubt that the success of the Plan calls for the achievement of the production targets set-up for steel or electric power. Conversely, if changes in prices or in consumers' tastes lead to more refrigerators being sold and less washing machines the Plan is in no way compromised. When it is realized that, in France, the production of electricity is vested in a public corporation whilst the steel industry remains in private hands, it will be appreciated that the economic characteristics of productive activities are at least as important for the rôle they play in the Plan as their legal status.

A third part of the book deals with the execution of the Plan. Indeed, a question arises here. A Plan, which is not an obligation, is nevertheless implemented within acceptable limits. The heart of the matter is that French planning is active; it tends to ensure that the State budget conforms to the Plan and it regulates the stimuli and aids at the disposal of the public departments in such a manner that the objectives assigned to the private sector are achieved, notably as regards regional development. These day-to-day aspects of policy-making, with which the Ministry of Finance has had the wisdom to associate the General Planning Commissariat, add to the specific virtues of the internal coherence of the Plan and of the feeling of participation which comes from working together during its preparation.

After having analysed the present, the authors turn their attention to the future with the problems surrounding the Fifth Plan. We live in a world of rapid change and the French planners are acutely conscious at one and the same time of what has been achieved already and of the considerable distance which still separates us from a more rational and democratic system of planning. Moreover, rationality and democracy are linked. For the first without the second would be powerless to create the required ardent adhesion to the goals of the Plan. And the second without the first would deprive the expansion of the economy of its full fruits.

The law approving the Fourth Plan decided that Parliament will be called upon to give its views on the major economic and social choices to be made in future Plans. For this debate, at the stage of the preliminary outline of the Plan, to be both rewarding and coherent, the General Planning Commissariat will have to put forward alternative sketches as a guide to choice. These sketches will have to be both lucid and simple whilst sufficiently precise and significant. In this way, the work of the General Planning Commissariat has received a new impetus in the fields of statistics, methodology and the informing of public opinion.

During the same period, the French Plan is acquiring a social dimension, a regional dimension and, it should be added, a European one. In a growth process, obstacles of human origin are more important than technical ones. The imbalances between social groups and between regions as to income levels attest the existence of these human obstacles which it will not be possible to surmount in a climate of freedom without a notable effort to improve information and understanding. Also, planning is more difficult and more uncertain in a country whose frontiers are open to the world outside than in one whose frontiers are closed. Happily, the spirit of the Plan is spreading.

But its diffusion abroad does not mean the adoption of uniform solutions. The methods used in one country cannot be transposed to another without adaptation. The British genius differs from the French and will know how to find an original expression in the field of flexible planning methods. Beyond the differences, however, there are likenesses which must be stressed as well. Our two countries have in common their democratic traditions, an advanced state of economic development and a sophisticated sociological milieu. The participation in drawing up the Plan of all the economic and social forces of the nation which has been achieved by successive French governments, seems to be just as necessary in the United Kingdom and just as attainable. In the less-developed countries, on the contrary, the needed 'intermediary tissue' which is required for the communication of information, conception and decision would be lacking no doubt.

For these reasons the experiment which is beginning in the United Kingdom is an encouragement of exceptional value for the French planners. It brings them the assurance that the spirit, if not the letter, of their methods will continue to gain ground. Few writers would have been as qualified as John and Anne-Marie Hackett to contribute to its diffusion. The one British but having completed his university training in France where he has published economic studies whose value is generally recognized, is now working with the Organization for Economic Co-operation and Development in Paris. The other, born in France, and having grown up in the tradition of public service and the respect for the spirit of French syndicalism, is now Conseiller Référendaire at the French Cour des Comptes. I am convinced that their book will be, like themselves, a link between their two countries.

PIERRE MASSÉ
General Planning Commissariat

Paris, December 1962

ACKNOWLEDGMENTS

We are indebted to M. Pierre Massé, Commissaire Général du Plan, who encouraged us to undertake this study and has greatly facilitated our task in writing it.

We should like to thank all those who were good enough to assist us with advice and criticism and, in particular, the following:

MM. R. Barre, Professor of Economics at the Faculté de Droit et des Sciences Economiques of Caen; J. Bénard, Professeur at the Faculté de Droit et des Sciences Economiques of Poitiers, and Director of the CEPREL; L. Blanc, Directeur des Synthèses Economiques at the INSEE; F. Bloch-Lainé, Directeur Général of the Caisse des Dépôts et Consignations; J. F. Breton, Chargé de Mission at the Commissariat Général du Plan; M. Caradet, Administrateur Civil at the Ministère des Finances; F. Chapel, Inspecteur de l'Industrie, Adjoint au Directeur de l'Expansion Industrielle at the Ministère de l'Industrie and General Rapporteur of the Commission des Industries de Transformation; F. de Clinchamps, Président Directeur Général of the Papeteries Navarre and Chairman of the Commission des Industries de Transformation; G. Fournier, Ingénieur des Mines at the Direction des Carburants, Ministère de l'Industrie and General Rapporteur of the Commission des Carburants; Mme Gay, Chef du Service de la Documentation at the Commissariat Général du Plan; MM. L. Gouni, Ingénieur en Chef des Mines, Chargé de Mission at the Commissariat Général du Plan, and General Rapporteur of the Commission de l'Energie; C. Gruson, Directeur Général of the INSEE; J. P. Guinot, Administrateur at the Conseil Economique et Social; P. Huvelin, President of the Société Générale d'Exploitations Industrielles, member of the Bureau of the Conseil National du Patronat Français; A. Laure, Ingénieur en Chef des Ponts-et-Chaussées, Chargé de Mission at the Commissariat Général du Plan; P. Le Brun, Secrétaire Confédéral of the CGT and Vice-Chairman of the Section des Investissements et du Plan of the Conseil Economique et Social; F. Le Guay, Head of the National Accounts Division at the OECD, Paris, and sometime member of the SEEF; P. Lemerle, Inspecteur des Finances, Chargé de Mission at the Commissariat Général du Plan; G. Levard, Président of the CFTC; D. Lewandowski, Inspecteur des Finances; E. Lisle, Directeur Adjoint of the CREDOC; J. Mamert, Maître des Requêtes at the Conseil d'Etat and Secrétaire Général of the Conseil Economique et Social; G. Maugars, Inspecteur des Finances, Chargé de Mission at the Société Centrale d'Equipement du Territoire, Directeur des Programmes; H. d'Ormesson, Inspecteur des Finances, Directeur des Services Financiers et Juridiques of Electricité de France; G. Pallez, Inspecteur des Finances, Directeur, Adjoint au Directeur Général des Collectivités locales at the Ministère de l'Intérieur; G. de la Perrière, Inspecteur des Finances,

Chargé de Mission at the Commissariat Général du Plan; P. Rappello, Chargé de Mission at the Commissariat Général du Plan, Secretary-General of the Commission des Transports; J. Ripert, Conseiller du Plan, Chef de la Division Economique at the Commissariat Général du Plan; G. Van Den Plas, Conseiller du Plan and Secretary-General of the Commission des Industries de Transformation; V. Ventejol, Secrétaire Confédéral of the CGT-FO, Vice-Chairman of the Section des Investissements et du Plan du Conseil Economique et Social; A. Verret, Président du Conseil d'Administration of the Charbonnages de France and Chairman of the Section des Investissements et du Plan of the Conseil Economique et Social; M. Vienot, Inspecteur des Finances; P. Viot, Conseiller Référendaire at the Cour des Comptes, Chargé de Mission at the Commissariat Général du Plan.

M. P. Lemerle, Inspecteur des Finances, Chargé de Mission at the Commissariat Général du Plan; and Prof. Brian Tew, of the University of Nottingham, who also read the manuscript for us and made many valuable suggestions.

Our friends, M. P. Questiaux, Inspecteur des Finances, and Madame Questiaux, Maître des Requêtes at the Conseil d'Etat, showed great patience in bearing with our requests for information and guidance whilst never failing to accede to them.

We were able to appreciate once more the qualities of intelligence and method of Madame Gudrun Couturier, our former student, who did research for us on a number of topics.

We are entirely responsible for the opinions expressed in this book. In particular, they in no way represent either the official position of the French Government or of the Organization for Economic Co-operation and Development.

CONTENTS

INTRODUCTION

Economic planning has at last acquired an honourable status as a branch of theoretical and, even more, of applied economics. Indeed, in the present decade, after a period of isolated experiments in the post-war years, it seems likely to become the dominant theme of national and international economic policy. At the same time, planning is moving out of the arena of purely political passions. The respective virtues of 'socialist' and 'capitalist' varieties will continue to evoke lively debate, but it is more and more evident that such polemics cover a large measure of common ground. This is particularly the case where the techniques of drawing up plans are concerned. But the same is true of the methods of executing them; whilst on the left, opinion has come to recognize that market mechanisms, decentralized decision-making and indirect controls have their value, on the right there is increasing willingness to envisage forms of control and public action formerly felt to be anathema.

It is not the intention of this book to deal with these broader issues *in vacuo*, nor to attempt a synthesis of planning techniques. Its object is more limited and more concrete. Whatever may be the virtues or shortcomings of the French system of planning—a subject which *inter alia* this book attempts to deal with—it is the most advanced example of such a system in an industrially developed economy whose essential structures remain capitalistic. Also it is one which has a comparatively long history behind it as the current four-year Plan, when it ends in 1965, will complete two decades of planning since the war. The French experiment is naturally one which attracts interest from abroad now that a number of countries are initiating similar efforts themselves. But it should be emphasized that the authors have not sought to write a recipe for other countries, though it would be less than frank not to admit their conviction that the French system does contain valuable lessons for them when faced with the multiple problems of growth; if these lessons appear implicitly in the course of this book, they are left to the reader to draw or not as he thinks fit.

In France as well the advent of the Fifth Republic has coincided with a burst of interest in planning for which there is no precedent since the war. Although the Plan had become a permanent feature of the economic landscape, whose existence was not seriously contested, and although the final publication of a new Plan, or the appearance of the annual report by the Commissaire General, was in the past the occasion for newspaper articles, and other comment of short duration, neither the day-to-day process of planning nor the theoretical and technical issues it raised had been the object of much study until recently.[1] But since 1959, there has probably been more written on planning than in the whole preceding fifteen years. Each stage in the process of elaboration of the Fourth Plan was widely discussed in public. General de Gaulle himself referred to the Plan in a broadcast speech as an 'ardent obligation', a phrase which lent itself to various interpretations. Ministers refer to the Plan frequently. Professional associations have discussed it, and the planning mechanism, at length. The trade unions also have debated the subject at their annual congresses, and various left-wing associations have devoted special meetings to the problems raised by planning. Strangely enough, it is the political parties who seem to have shown least interest in the Plan, a phenomenon which will merit closer examination later on. Despite, or perhaps because of, this, the Plan represents for many people a way of infusing a new spirit into the democratic process in France.

Alongside these signs of an awakening interest in the Plan in many circles, work on improving the technical aspects of planning has received a new impetus. This first became apparent during the preparation of the Fourth Plan, from 1959 onwards, when a number of important changes were introduced compared with the approach used for the first three Plans. And work on the Fifth Plan, which is now proceeding actively, is carrying this process a step further.

These two new elements—a greater degree of interest in planning on the part of the public, and improvements in the methods of planning at the technical level—are not independent. Rather, they are two aspects of a dialogue between the planners and those whom the Plan is designed to serve. The outcome of this dialogue, upon which the future of planning in France largely depends, is still uncertain, and the problems which will call for solutions over the next few years are as difficult as any of those met with since the end of the war. Those responsible for planning in France are acutely aware of this, as the concluding passage from the Commissaire General's speech to Parliament during the ratification debate on the Fourth Plan in May 1962 shows:

'This Plan corresponds to a particular moment in our economic history and it is normal, and in conformity with democracy, that it should be the object of your remarks, suggestions, criticisms and, finally, your sanction. But the French system of planning, which I have received from my predecessors, and which I endeavour to

[1] The only book on the Plan until quite recently was: P. Bauchet, *Experience Française de Planification*, Editions du Seuil, 1958.

advance further, is something more lasting and more valuable than a Plan. I hope it will not emerge from your debates with diminished stature for it is an asset for France, and the interest it evokes in neighbouring countries is one of the avenues open at one and the same time to the influence of French thought and to a common conception of European development.'[1]

I. OUTLINE OF THE BOOK

Such are the considerations that have dictated the choice of the method of exposition adopted in this book. The progressive evolution and transformation of the planning mechanism can only be seen in an historical perspective, and an extended treatment of this subject would call for a different kind of book from the one we have tried to write. A compromise was necessary. Consequently, the historical record, and the major characteristics of the first three Plans (1946-61), have been sketched in broadly in the following section of this introduction. The indispensable background to present institutional arrangements and policies is given when these topics are discussed in the course of the book where we have tried consistently to bear in mind the needs of the non-French reader who may not possess a sufficient knowledge of the structure and working of the French economy.

Part One is devoted to institutional questions. We describe the nature of the various bodies which intervene in the Plan during its elaboration and execution. The treatment here is static, and the main emphasis is on structure and functions. This enables later references to institutions to dispense with explanatory details, and the reader is referred back to this Part when he needs elucidation. There have been a number of innovations in this field in France in recent years, notably concerning the consultative bodies, the arrangements for regional planning, and the technical units which play an important rôle in drafting the Plan. It is hoped that this Part will also be of interest to the reader who is already acquainted with the French economy.

Part Two describes the process of drafting the Plan. The method is to follow the Plan through its stages, from the first tentative projections to the final version as approved by Parliament. In view of what was said earlier of the changes which have taken place, and are still continuing to take place, in the techniques of planning, a problem of selection arises here also. The solution adopted has been dictated by the writers' intention to concentrate on French planning

[1] A full translation of the text of this speech is given in Appendix 2.

today, and the details of the elaboration of the first three Plans have been excluded. On the other hand, the way in which the most recent completed example of a four-year Plan, the Fourth (covering the period 1962-65), was drafted, will not be repeated in all respects for the Fifth, for example, as regards the choice of chief objectives, and the methodological approach used at the technical level. These changes are themselves a response to problems met with during the process of drawing up the Fourth Plan. So what is said in Part Two refers to the state of affairs prevailing for the Fourth Plan which was voted by Parliament in July 1962. Developments since the drafting of the Fourth Plan are examined in Part Four.

Part Three follows the career of the Plan after its final adoption by Parliament, and discusses the ways in which the authorities seek to ensure that the objectives laid down in the Plan are achieved. In this Part the institutional framework described in Part One is seen from a dynamic point of view. In these chapters also some important items of unfinished business will be met with, but any extended treatment of them will be reserved for Part Four.

Part Four attempts to grasp what is essential in the changes which are taking place now in the Plan. The changes spring from the lessons of the Fourth Plan and from the requirements of the Fifth. In many instances what is said is, in the nature of things, only a provisional progress report. But the scale of the problems involved, and the fact that no industrial country has yet found a satisfactory solution for them,[1] give a particularly topical interest to such developments in France at the present time.

II. ECONOMIC TRENDS SINCE 1945 AND THE FIRST THREE PLANS

1 *Growth since 1945*

The growth of the economy has been rapid since the end of the war; at least twice as fast as the best rate achieved since the end of the nineteenth century and among the fastest in Western Europe. The average rate of growth of total output (GNP) has been rather more than 4.5 per cent annually. The rise in the active population being very small, the increase in output per head has been about 4.5 per cent per year also. Expansion has been fairly regular and the pauses in growth short-lived on the whole. The investment effort has been intense; in 1948 the percentage of the GNP invested in gross fixed capital formation with 20.5, compared with only 13 in 1938. By 1953, however, it had fallen to 16.2, at a time when the external deficit was

[1] Many indeed are only now becoming aware of their existence.

FRANCE, 1938-62

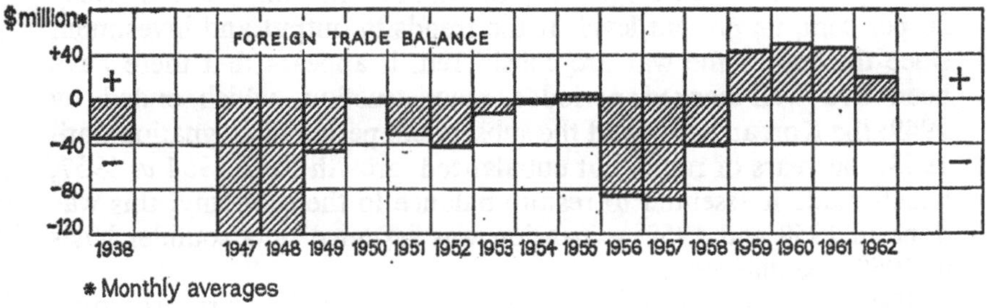

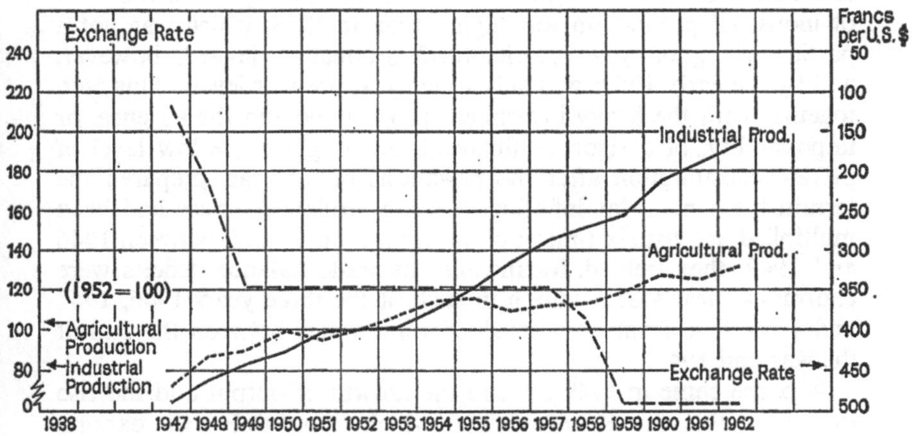

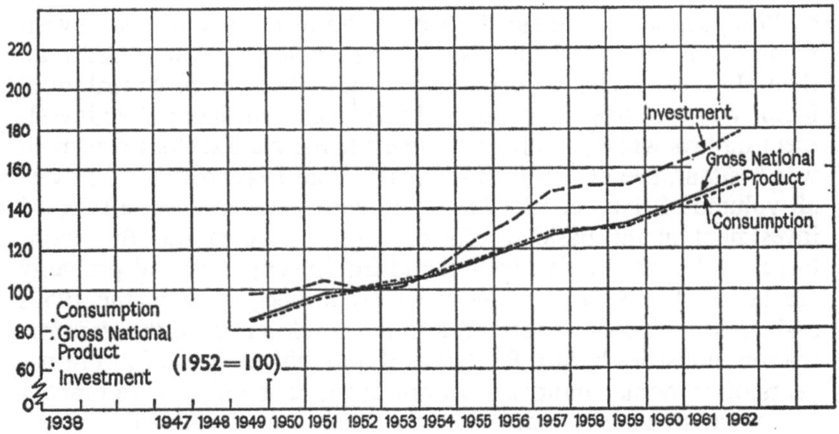

practically nil, but rose again rapidly in the following years to nearly 20 per cent, its present level. If the trends in output and investment since the end of the war are considered, it appears that there have been five well-marked periods: reconstruction, which ended by 1949; the Korean boom and the subsequent period of stagnation until 1953; the years of rapid, but unbalanced, growth from 1954 to 1957, which made it essential to restore balance to the economy; this was done in 1958 and 1959; expansion was resumed on a sounder basis in 1960 (see diagram).

The reconstruction period lasted some five or six years, according to whether industry or agriculture are involved. By 1948, the level of industrial production was higher than in 1938, which was not a particularly good year. Agricultural production lagged, however, and by the early 1950s was only roughly at pre-war levels. This fact, together with the heavy investment programme and the absence, or impossibility, of a rigorous financial policy, given the low level of private consumption after the privations of the war, prepared the terrain for a post-war inflation of some virulence. Prices had been multiplied at least six times during the war years and, between 1946 and 1949, they trebled. Meanwhile the trade balance deficits were enormous; nearly $1.5 billion in each of the three years 1946, 1947 and 1948. The franc was devalued three times between the end of the war and 1949.

A pause came in 1949 both in the growth of output and the rise in prices. But the Korean crisis, which boosted French exports phenomenally, although it wiped out the trade deficit by 1950, set off a fresh rise in prices which lasted until the stabilization measures of 1952. These accompanied a stagnation of production and investment which contrasted sharply with the whole post-war period until then. Its reasons still appear somewhat obscure. A contributory factor was certainly the policy of budget economies in public investment outlays which, coming at a time when private sector investment was hesitant, meant that for four years, from 1949 to 1953, the overall volume of fixed capital formation hardly increased at all. Fixed investment in the basic sectors of industry, which was the major target of the first Modernization and Equipment Plan, had probably reached its limits for the time being by the beginning of the 1950s and could not progress further until the development of the transformation industries began. Be that as it may, the early 1950s were not years of economic optimism in France; the economists were practically unanimous in condemning the 'malthusian' character of the French economy, the family structure of its industry, the restrictive attitude of the large firms towards production and investment, and the general tradition of protectionism. The fact that, by 1952, the rise in prices had come to an end was considered a mixed blessing by many people and the statement 'the French economy can expand only when prices are rising' was widely accepted.

Nevertheless, the basic sectors of the economy had been transformed since 1945. The railways and the mines had been modernized and were improving their productivity rapidly. The electricity industry had carried out a large-scale investment programme. Outside the nationalized sector, the steel industry had modernized and regrouped its production units, and its output level was one-third higher than in 1938. But it was still only fractionally higher than over twenty years earlier, in 1929. Other indices told the same story and gave weight to the opinion of those who, taking 1929 as the peak year of French prosperity between the wars, maintained that, the task of immediate post-war reconstruction being achieved, the French economy was stuck and could not proceed further. The production of passenger-cars exceeded a quarter of a million in 1950 but had already reached 212,000 in 1929 and, in 1951, the index of production in the mechanical and electrical industries was only 3 per cent higher. This line of reasoning missed the real significance of what was happening; a structural imbalance had been built up as a result of the development efforts in the basic sectors of industry and transport which had expanded ahead of the secondary sectors. But even in these sectors, the achievement of output levels comparable with those of 1929 had accompanied a revolution in techniques and managerial practices. Consequently, the ground had been prepared for what was to follow. The years after 1953, until the next period of restrictions in 1958, transformed the structure and outlook of French industry.

For four years, from 1954 to 1957, the annual rate of growth of the economy (GNP) was nearly 5½ per cent and, what was more remarkable in the light of experience in previous years, the trade balance was in equilibrium until 1956 and prices were stable until 1957. Fixed capital formation rose by nearly 10 per cent annually and private consumption increased by 6 per cent. These years were the watershed in French post-war economic development; afterwards nothing was ever really the same as before. Attitudes towards growth changed completely as a mystique of expansion appeared so that, even in 1957 and 1958, when it became clear that the economy was roaring ahead at a rate that could not be sustained, given the growing trade deficit, it was considered heretical to suggest that the need to restore balance required a pause. The awful warning of the United Kingdom's experience was often invoked in this connection.

But attitudes were not the only things to change. These years witnessed the break-through to mass consumption habits by the French population as home market sales of automobiles rose from 290,000 per year in 1953 to 540,000 in 1954, and the textile industry, after the recession of the early 1950s, increased its output by one-third, mainly in the new branches of synthetic fibres. The basic sectors also went ahead; steel production increased from 10 to 14.7 million tons, the chemical industry doubled its output and production of crude oil and natural gas increased fourfold.

There remained, though, the problem of the trade balance. This had been practically in equilibrium in 1953, 1954 and 1955. But, in 1957 and 1958, there were annual deficits of over $1 billion, a fact which serves to illustrate the excessively 'inward-looking' character of the growth of the French economy during these years, when export demand was only a minor factor in the growth of output, and all major sectors were orientated towards the satisfaction of the home market. This situation was probably, it is true, more the result of an exchange rate which had not been devalued since 1949, so that it took no account of the appreciable price rise between then and 1952, than of any innate lack of initiative by French industry. But, as the external payments position continued to deteriorate, and it became necessary to restrict imports more and more by going back on all previous liberalization measures, home production was protected from foreign competition, and exports had to be facilitated by a series of fiscal subterfuges tantamount to subsidies.

The restrictive credit and fiscal measures which began to be applied early in 1958, and a rise in prices which was more rapid than the rise in incomes, produced their effects gradually during that year. There was a marked slowing down in the rate of advance of fixed capital formation and production, and private consumption did not increase during the year as a whole. At the end of December 1958, the franc was devalued by 17.5 per cent, imports were liberalized and, on January 1, 1959, the first tariff reductions of the Common Market came into operation. These external measures accompanied a number of internal policy measures designed to hold the price level and restrict the growth of nominal incomes. But, at the same time, a vigorous policy of expanding investment activity in the public sector was adopted in order to palliate the slackening of private investment, which showed that the lesson of 1952 had been taken.

The results of this policy were spectacular. Whilst the rise in prices did not exceed the increase expected from the devaluation, the trade balance became sharply positive—and the capital account also benefited from large-scale receipts, of French capital coming back from abroad in the first instance, of foreign capital subsequently. In 1959, for the first time since the 'freak' boom in 1950, exports were the main growth-point in the economy. Gross fixed investment did not rise, nor did private consumption, yet the index of industrial production rose by over 10 per cent. The stagnation of investment and consumption was short-lived, however, and since 1960 both have grown rapidly without impairing the favourable trade balance.

In retrospect, improvement in the foreign trade balance in 1959 seems less surprising than it appeared to many economists who were, on the whole, critical of what they considered to be, at one and the same time, a too restrictive and a too liberal policy. The industrial base of the economy had been strengthened and diversified during the boom years after 1953, building upon the foundations laid in the early post-war period. Technically and managerially, French industry had transformed itself, at least in the more dynamic sectors. Also, preparation for the Common Market had begun to exercise a powerful influence long before January 1, 1959, so that, despite the last minute protests which proliferated from French industry, the generous devaluation at the end of 1958 found French manufacturers prepared to take advantage of the opportunities opened up to them.

2 *The first three Modernization Plans from 1947 to 1961*

(a) *The First Plan 1947-52.* The First Plan was expected to cover the four years 1947-50; in fact it was prolonged until 1952 but, despite this, four-year planning periods have been maintained since then.[1] The decree issued in January 1946 decided both the drafting of the Plan and the creation of a technical body—the General Planning Commissariat—to do the work of planning. The decree was signed by General de Gaulle as head of the Provisional Government. The First Plan was approved by the Cabinet a year later, in January 1947. However, already in 1944, an emergency programme, or plan, had been drawn up to deal with the most urgent problems raised by the liberation of metropolitan France. It was co-ordinated by M. Jean Monnet in relation to emergency post-war aid from the United States and, in 1945, a further tranche of this programme was drawn up by the Ministry of the National Economy, which created a special department to take care of the work. The idea of planning was, of course, in the air in France at the Liberation. Not only was the administration attuned to the controlled economy of the war years, but the members of the Government (which was the most

[1] But the Fifth Plan, which will begin in 1966, will be a five-year Plan.

left-wing post-war France has known, comprising as it did numerous Communist ministers), were favourable to planning. Also, the programme of the National Liberation Committee, the central organization of the resistance movement, called for the elaboration of a Plan. Such ideas were inseparable from the large-scale programme of nationalization, notably in gas, coal, electricity, transport, banks, insurance, which was carried through immediately after the war.

The First Plan did not, and could not in the circumstances of the time, envisage the balanced development of the whole of the economy—although the decrees of January 3, 1946, spoke of an 'overall Plan'. A general objective of achieving the level of total output in 1929 by 1948-49 was adopted. But, in practice, six priority sectors were selected—coal, electricity, steel, transport, cement, fertilizers and agricultural machinery, the last two being grouped together as agriculture. Production targets were set up and investment needs calculated. Subsequently, credits, building permits and import licences were allocated according to the priorities thus set up.

The First Plan was promulgated by administrative decision and was not submitted to Parliament. Its objectives and duration were subject to revision: the prospect of American aid, and the appearance of certain bottlenecks, made it both possible and necessary to revise some of the output objectives and to prolong the Plan for two years until 1952. Fresh targets were added to the original ones; sulphuric acid, non-ferrous metals and raw materials for the textile and paper industries were put on the list of production targets and shipping and tourism became priority sectors as foreign currency earners.

It is difficult to say whether the First Plan was achieved insofar as the production targets fixed were reached or not. The targets were revised periodically and new products were added from time to time. That this should have been so is not a proof of the inefficacy, or inefficiency, of the Plan; given the economic situation in France, an empirical approach was the only sensible one. A target set up in 1946 for 1950 or 1952 could, in the nature of things, be no more than an informed guess as to future needs subject to revision in the light of events. Also, the economic climate of the early 1950s was, as has been seen earlier, quite different from that of the immediate post-war years; the worst shortages had been overcome, the Korean crisis had released a spate of inflationary demand which had upset the fragile price stability achieved in 1949, and defence expenditure began to loom larger as a drain on available resources. The objectives of the First Plan, seen as a crash programme for reconstruction, were reached by 1949, except in agriculture. In 1952, the end-year of the Plan, a policy of deflation, to correct the inflation and a mounting external deficit, was the prime objective of the Government, not the increase in production and the achievement of ambitious planning targets. But the task of reconstruction had been accomplished, basic sectors of the economy had been modernized and their production facilities increased, so that the foundations for further growth, which subsequent Plans were to build on, had been laid. Moreover, the institutional structure and procedures of planning had been firmly implanted in French life. These were the real claims to success of the First Plan.

(b) *The Second Plan 1954-57.* A difficult phase opened in the early 1950s for French planning. The problems met with—rearmament, balance of payments deficits, the need to favour the growth of other sectors of the economy than the key-sectors—were manifestly different from those to which the First Plan had addressed itself. Furthermore, the political and economic climate of those years was not particularly conducive to the adoption and, even less, to the application of high growth targets. These considerations explain why the second Modernization and Equipment Plan did not see the light until 1954. It was to run until 1957. When it did appear, its objectives were ambitious and certainly attested to a determination to break with the stagnation of the years 1952 and 1953. Total output was to rise by 25 per cent by 1957 compared with 1952, as a result of a growth of 25 to 30 per cent in industrial production, of 20 per cent in agriculture and of 60 per cent in construction. Given the fact that growth had been extremely modest in 1953, these targets implied an annual growth-rate of 6 per cent from 1954 to 1957. Living standards, measured by private consumption, were to rise by 20 per cent or by less than total output but nevertheless by a substantial amount.

Yet the decision to draft a Second Plan had been taken a year before the official end-date of the First Plan, by a decree published in December 1951. Parliament was not associated with its preparation any more than in the case of the First Plan, and although the Plan was submitted to Parliament in June 1954, that is six months after it had begun to operate, it was not voted until March 1956, a delay which would appear to reflect Parliament's interest for matters of planning at that time.

The primary preoccupation of the planning authorities in the Second Plan seems to have been the implementation of a certain number of reforms. It has been said that the 'basic sectors' of the First Plan were followed by the 'basic actions' of the Second. These actions were: the development of scientific and technical research and of improved agricultural production methods; the encouragement of industrial efficiency (notably specialization between firms); the improvement of productivity and reduction of costs; the reform of agricultural marketing techniques and modernization of the commercial sector in general; the granting of assistance to firms reconverting their production or modernizing their equipment; the expansion of facilities for training skilled workers.

The mere enumeration of these objectives calls to mind the typical, and usually ephemeral, 'programme' so current in many countries, and so devoid of real content. That this aspect of the French Plan was more solid than its counterparts elsewhere is not easy to establish. Certainly efficiency in industry rose during the period 1954-57 and the authorities facilitated regrouping of firms as they had already done in the steel industry. Agricultural production began to increase rapidly—partly as a reflection of the investments carried out earlier—but marketing arrangements, except for a few pilot projects, have remained a perennial source of discontent for consumers and farmers alike. The process of modernization of commercial distribution circuits began to produce some results, and fiscal policy, although continuing to discriminate against integrated concerns, was amended to reduce the grossest handicap deriving from the indirect transactions tax. On the other hand, much more than by public policy, the decline of the small shopkeeper, so entrenched in French economic life, particularly in the provinces, was precipitated by the economic decline of certain regions (Pierre Poujade was a shopkeeper in the poorest region of the Massif Central) and by the growing affluence of consumers, which made modernization of commerce possible for those firms who could afford it. However, it should not be lost sight of that these general, less precise objectives are an integral part of a planning process. They do not supplant output targets but they do supplement them. Indeed the system of French planning, with its insistence upon the rôle of the Planning Commissions—tripartite consultative bodies representing employers, workers and the administration—institutionalizes the drawing up of policy measures and programmes to improve the functioning of the economy. Each time a Plan is drawn up, the Commissions draft reports which enumerate the policy measures considered to be desirable. No doubt such a procedure can, and often has, led to the presentation of mere lists of grievances. But to dismiss them all as such would be to ignore the numerous significant examples of reforms whose origin has been the General Planning Commissariat and a Planning Commission.

Still the Second Plan did not content itself with drawing up a few overall objectives, leaving their achievement to the spontaneous working of the economy. The development of the basic sectors of the First Plan (coal, electricity, gas, liquid fuels, steel and cement, the last two having by then a long history of close association with the Plan although they remained in private hands) was again given priority. In addition, house building was planned to reach 240,000 units annually in 1957. For these sectors, the authority of the planners was sufficiently real, especially as regards providing finance, for the output objectives to have a guarantee of being realized. The Second Plan went further than this, and drew up a list of output targets in the form of indices for a dozen or so other branches of industry (machine-tools, automobiles, textiles, paper, etc.). In the case of agriculture, the overall output target of 20 per cent was broken down into a list of about ten specific products. It would be unfair to the planners to suppose that these very detailed targets were expected to be achieved 100 per cent. Neither the techniques for drawing up such programmes, nor the possibilities for implementing them existed. They were at best projections of likely, and desirable, trends which seemed to correspond with the intentions of the entrepreneurs in the Planning Commissions.

In the event, as has been seen earlier, the growth-rate of the economy during the period of the Second Plan was more rapid than the ambitious target had laid down. Total output in 1957 was 30 per cent higher than in 1954, industrial production having risen by 46 per cent instead of 30 per cent although agricultural output was only 19 per cent higher instead of the planned target of 20 per cent. Production objectives in the key-sectors were approximately respected but the transformation industries had overshot theirs very substantially. Output in the mechanical and electrical industries rose by 55 per cent compared with the Plan figure of 30 per cent. But some capital goods industries, on the contrary, had not responded to demand as had been hoped; production of machine-tools rose by only 9 per cent between 1952 and 1957 instead of an expected rise of 40 to 50 per cent. The heavy demand for capital goods to sustain the investment boom in these years overspilled into demand for imports, and was one of the factors aggravating the balance of payments problem, the more so as French mechanical industry was not yet very export-minded. The construction industry reached its target of 240,000 housing units annually by 1956 and, in 1957, 274,000 units were completed. But this progress of output was accompanied by a substantial rise in prices of nearly 40 per cent. Perhaps the major policy lesson of the experience of the Second Plan was the need for close co-ordination between day-to-day policy making and the medium-term Plan. It was applied painfully during the Third Plan, and has not been forgotten since.

(c) *The Third Plan 1958-61.* The unbalanced growth of the economy, and the critical state of the external balance in particular, had to be taken into account in drafting the Third Plan (1958-61). Consequently, one of the primary objectives of the Plan was to achieve a small surplus on the balance of payments of the franc area by 1961, as a result of a rise of 40 per cent in exports and 13 per cent only in imports. This was the first time that the foreign trade balance was the object of such detailed projections. Despite this, the target set for the expansion in total output was an ambitious one; a rise of 27 per cent by 1961 over 1956, or a marginally faster rise than for the Second Plan. Industrial production was to increase by 30 per cent and agricultural production by 20 per cent, or the same rates as for the Second Plan. To achieve this, fixed investments were expected to rise by 28 per cent and private consumption by 24 per cent, that is by less than the rise in total output whereas, in the years 1952-57, it had gone up faster than GNP.

The Third Plan marked a considerable advance on the technical level compared with the two previous Plans insofar as its objectives were specifically directed to balanced growth and covered the whole economy in a more systematic fashion. With these in view, the Plan figures were drawn up in the framework of the national accounts, of which a complete breakdown by major sectors for the terminal year (1961) was set up. The main production targets concerned once more the basic sectors (energy, steel, non-ferrous metals, cement, and the principal agricultural products). But the manufacturing industries too were expected to contribute heavily to the growth of output (+33 per cent) and, especially, to exports (+70 per cent). Agricultural policy was discussed in some detail, and a number of reforms were proposed dealing with price-fixing and the improvement of marketing, the latter by now having become a perennial theme. As for industrial competitiveness, the Plan did not fail to point out all the implications of the entry into force of the Rome Treaty on January 1, 1959, at the end of the first year of the planning period, and productivity measures—for which there now existed a national productivity agency—were stressed. Finally, the social side of the Plan was more developed than previously. In addition to a fresh housing target of 300,000 units annually by 1961, programmes for school and university building and for hospital construction were written into the Plan.

The Third Plan remained extremely vague as to the annual rhythm for achieving these four-year objectives. Yet it was clear by 1958 that this was the key problem. The first restrictive credit and fiscal measures recently taken, spontaneous trends in demand aiding, were beginning to have an effect. However, 1958 was a particularly full year on the political scene, and it was only in the second half of the year, the Fifth Republic being meanwhile instituted, that the Government returned to economic affairs. At the end of 1958, as a result of the advice tendered by a committee of experts headed by M. Jacques Rueff, the measures outlined earlier were accepted.

In 1959, the preparation of the Fourth Plan for the period 1962-65 started. Meanwhile, a major problem was to see whether the changes induced in the rhythm and structure of the growth of output and demand since the Third Plan entered into application rendered the latter invalid or not. The first task of the newly-appointed Commissaire General, M. Massé—M. Hirsch, his predecessor, having been appointed head of Euratom—was therefore to decide on the policy to be followed by the planning authorities in the remaining half of the Third Plan.

The solution adopted was called the Intermediate Plan for 1960 and 1961. This document set out resolutely to achieve the overall growth targets of the Third Plan. This entailed a faster rate of growth of 5.5 per cent in GNP and of 7.4 per cent in industrial production, in each of the remaining two years of the Plan, in order to compensate for the relative stagnation during part of 1958 and in 1959. Stress was laid on the need to increase investments, and the public sector's investments were reinforced, including those of the nationalized industries.

The troubled history of the Third Plan could not be expected to lead to the fulfilment of targets in all respects and yet both the main output targets and the criteria of external balance and relatively stable internal prices[1] were in fact achieved by 1961. (See table on page 32.)

The growth of output in the period 1958-61 was practically the same as the target. The rise in imports was much higher than planned but, as the objective for exports was also surpassed, the external surplus was even more important than the Third Plan had forecast. The chief internal demand factor making this adjustment possible was the slower rise in private consumption. Investment expenditure, on the other hand, was up to planned levels.

It would be doing less than justice to the French planning system not to recognize the rôle of the Third Plan in these achievements. In

[1] After allowing for the effects of the devaluation.

THIRD PLAN (1958-61)
SUPPLY AND USE OF RESOURCES
(volume indices, 1956=100)

	1961 *Planned*	1961 *Actual*
Resources: Total	125	123.5
Production*	127	123.4
Imports	110	123.7
Uses: Total	125	123.5
Private consumption	124	119.1
Public consumption	112	110.8
Investment	128	128.1
Exports	135	156.4

Source: Fourth Plan, p. 19.

* Gross internal production, excluding notably the service rendered by the Government sector.

particular, the fact that important objectives such as halting inflation and restoring balance to the external accounts were reached with such a short phase of stagnation in overall growth must be attributed in no small part to the 1959 and 1960 policy which was fixed resolutely in the framework of the growth objectives of the Third Plan and its complement, the Intermediate Plan. But the need to halt inflation, and to ensure that the devaluation at the end of 1958 did not have the ephemeral success of previous devaluations since the war, led the authorities to abstain from any expansionist policies as regards private consumption until the rise in exports was an accomplished fact, as it was clear that securing external balance could not be achieved without some sacrifice in terms of the growth of home demand. The choice between private consumption and investment was made resolutely in favour of investment, however, and specific measures were taken to ensure this. Looking back over the economic history of those years, it would be difficult to deny that this order of priorities was the right one. But the consequences, in terms of a temporary halt to the growth of private consumption, were not without influence on attitudes towards the Fourth Plan, as will be seen later.

A significant innovation of the period was the introduction of the Intermediate Plan in 1960-61. The previous period of stagnation in the post-war period had also been marked by the appearance of an 'eighteeen-months Plan' at the end of 1953. But the 1960-61 Intermediate Plan was a more systematic attempt to review the objectives of the Third Plan in the light, both of the new situation created by the reforms at the end of 1958, and of the Fourth Plan then in the process of elaboration. There is no doubt that the objectives of these two Plans—the one in force and the other in preparation—gave the general tone to the Intermediate Plan as has been mentioned. The final decision to try to achieve the Third Plan in 1960-61 by a process of catching up was only taken, though, because it seemed reasonable and desirable to do so. The possible use which might be made of such a comprehensive review of the medium-term Plans during their implementation will be referred to again later.

PART ONE

THE INSTITUTIONAL FRAMEWORK OF PLANNING

The set of institutions used in France to carry through the Plan is an original one in several respects. The most novel element is the General Planning Commissariat itself whose motto could well be 'power through persuasion'. Its self-effacing policy has led the Commissariat to keep its own staff very lightweight, whilst seeking systematically to work through other administrations, rather than taking over their functions, and it has paid handsome dividends. It is also in keeping with the French concept of planning that the Commissariat's links with the private sector should be organized mainly through the Planning Commissions which have a considerable degree of latitude in organizing their work.

All this implies that a great deal of the work on the Plan is done outside the Commissariat. This is true of both the technical preparation of the Plan and its implementation. A number of specialized bodies do the backroom job of forecasting and making economic projections, the most important of them being a part, until recently, of the Ministry of Finance which also assumes the main burden of execution.

Alongside the flexible methods of the General Planning Commissariat, the more traditional tendencies in French administration continue to assert themselves. Centralization has a long history in France and it is not surprising to find that the control of the central administration in Paris over the local units of government and the nationalized industries is a strict one.

But changes seem to be under way here since the Fourth Plan which extended the consultation procedures when the Plan was being drawn up, and stressed, as one of its objectives, regional development. For the first time since the Plans started, Parliament received the text of the Fourth Plan before it entered into application. More important was the pre-consultation with the Economic and Social Council, at the end of 1959 and early in 1960, before the major options of the Fourth Plan were taken. Later on, in 1961, the top-level consultative body, called the High Planning Council, which had been set up after the war but had been allowed to become moribund, was resuscitated. For the Fifth Plan, consultation procedures will be more elaborate still.

The biggest potential change in French administrative practices may come from another direction, however. Regional development policy has been respected more in the breach than in the observance until quite recently, but now it is being taken very seriously indeed, and is leading to a thorough shake-up of local government which means, among other things, a loosening of the control of Paris over what goes on in the provinces.

Clearly then, the institutional structure of planning is evolving in France at the present time. We shall reserve an examination of the problems thrown up by that evolution for a later chapter. Here we shall be concerned with a description of the main institutional features of the Plan. We begin with the General Planning Commissariat itself, and the Planning Commissions, before going on to look at the two consultative bodies, the Economic and Social Council and the High Planning Council. We then turn to the administration of the public sector, including the nationalized industries. Regional development policy is sufficiently novel to merit a chapter to itself. Finally, we review the work done on the technical level by a number of specialized bodies.

CHAPTER I

THE GENERAL PLANNING COMMISSARIAT

The General Planning Commissariat, set up in 1946[1] by the decree which ordered the drafting of the First Plan, is no doubt the least of the administrations of the French Government from the point of view of size, but certainly not according to the influence it exerts. That this should be so is due in no small measure to the efforts of the three men who have held the post of Commissaire General since the war. Otherwise this newcomer to French administration would in all probability have been absorbed by a larger department, or have been relegated to a purely consultative rôle with no real influence. The policy adopted by each successive Commissaire General of refusing systematically the temptations of empire building has paid handsome dividends. A corollary of this policy is that the work of the General Planning Commissariat calls for the skills of the diplomat, as well as the knowledge of the economist. Indeed, the technical work behind the drafting of the Plans has been done mainly by another specialized service which, until 1962, was part of the Ministry of Finance. Today there is perhaps more unity at the top as regards the technical and policy aspects of the Plan than at any time since the war, because the present Commissaire General is himself one of the leading French experts on planning techniques.

The period when the diplomatic qualities of the staff of the Commissariat are most fully stretched is probably during the eighteen months or so when the various Planning Commissions are engaged in putting flesh on the skeleton outline of the medium-term Plan. This period includes, in its final phases, an arduous series of negotiations leading to the last version, which then has to be steered through the ultimate consultations and over the final hurdle of parliamentary approval. Of course, the General Planning Commissariat's task has never stopped there. The work of seeing that, as far as possible, the objectives of the Plan are reached has always been incumbent on it. Now, however, this task is the more absorbing as the Government is making the achievement of the Plan the cornerstone of economic policy much more than in the past. As a result, although there is no official post of economic adviser to the Government, the Commis-

[1] Decree No. 46, January 2 and 3, 1946.

saire General is called upon to advise on an increasing number of questions concerning general economic policy.

The place of the Commissariat in the French Government machine and the nature of its duties can best be seen by looking in turn at: the status of the Commissariat; the personalities of the men who have headed it; the internal structure; the nature and rôle of the Planning Commissions.

I. STATUS OF THE COMMISSARIAT

In 1946, the General Planning Commissariat came under the Prime Minister's Office. In 1954, when M. Mendès-France was Prime Minister, it was attached instead to the Ministry of Finance and Economic Affairs, although in a rather loose and imprecise manner. According to the 1954 Decree, the Minister of Finance exercised the Prime Minister's authority over the work and administration of the General Planning Commissariat. But, being attached to the Ministry of Finance was not the same thing as being integrated into the Ministry. Also, the General Planning Commissariat has always kept its own administration extremely light and has sought to work in liaison with the rest of the Government rather than to supplant other public departments. Consequently, the transfer, in 1962, of responsibility for the Commissariat back to the Prime Minister's Office did not call for any notable changes in previous administrative arrangements. A more important change in the situation of the Commissaire General had already occurred in 1959, after the establishment of the Fifth Republic and the vote of the new Constitution which gave greatly increased powers to the President of the Republic in the conduct of Government. The President has, in fact, taken an active and personal interest in planning matters, and the Commissaire General often reports directly to him.

In the beginning, the Commissariat was intended to be the key organ for co-ordinating the Government's economic policy. The 1946 Decree, modified in 1947, made the Commissaire General the 'permanent delegate of the head of the Government *vis-à-vis* the ministerial departments for all matters concerning the setting-up of the Plan'. And Article 4 of the same Decree stated that all public offices and competent ministers should assist him in his tasks.

In practice the functions of the Commissaire General have grown steadily since that date. He was charged at first only with the basic sectors of the economy; then he became responsible for the agriculture, the overseas territories, housing and secondary industries, whilst his activities in the sphere of general economic policy were widened within the pattern of the long-term overall balance of the economy. But he has never fulfilled entirely the mission of co-ordination given to him by the texts, and has not always participated in the work of the various interministerial committees organized for that purpose.[1] Moreover, the ministries have often set up their own economic sections whose work was sometimes parallel to that of the General Planning Commissariat. The Service for Economic and Financial Studies, created in the framework of the Ministry of Finance in 1950 and charged initially with preparing the national accounts and the annual economic budgets, has since then come to occupy the rôle of brains trust for the Commissariat, particularly as concerns the initial projections of the Plan.

This state of affairs was deplored by many observers for some time after the war.[2] There were good reasons for their fears that the action of the Commissariat would be nullified by the passive, or active, resistance of other sections of the administration. The story which attributes to a former Finance Minister a preference for 'plans which do not commit future action' may be apocryphal, but it corresponds to an attitude which took a long time to overcome. Its final demise—as will be seen in later chapters, in particular Chapter XII—did not come about in the way foreseen by the protagonists of a policy of more power for a central co-ordinating body—preferably the General Planning Commissariat and, in any case, not the Ministry of Finance—but by a double evolution of the Plan and of the rest of the public departments. The Plan has tended to become more all-embracing notably in problems of general economic balance,

[1] The functions of the General Commissariat were recently enlarged in two directions—productivity and regional development. By a decree in 1959, the Productivity Commissariat, set up as a separate body in 1954, was merged with the General Planning Commissariat, whose full title became: General Commissariat for the Equipment Plan and for Productivity. But productivity activities have remained distinct from the planning work proper of the Commissariat and will not be examined here in detail. Regional planning has come to assume such importance that it merits a separate chapter (see Chapter IV).

[2] For example, writing in 1958, Professor Bauchet, who had worked with the General Planning Commissariat, felt that: 'The extreme suspicion of the various ministries, each jealous of its own prerogatives, and the privileges of the nationalized industries, have done more to prevent the General Planning Commissariat from playing a vital rôle of initiator and have threatened its existence more than the hostility of political groups to planning. In order not to antagonize the public departments, the Commissaires General have followed a policy of conciliation, and not one of authority and of co-ordination. Unless there is a far-reaching administrative reform it is to be feared that the idea of a body charged with co-ordinating the economic policy of the country will remain an idea only.' *Op. cit.*, p. 56.

and its objectives are therefore more operative concepts from the point of view of the financial and credit authorities, and more relevant to their day-to-day preoccupations than isolated objectives. At the same time the progressive winning over of senior officials to the idea of planning, and pressure from the highest government circles in the same direction, have facilitated the strengthening of collaboration in planning matters inside the administration.

The General Commissariat's rôle is twofold. It concerns both the drafting and the execution of the Plan. At the drafting stage, the Commissariat has to prepare the work of the Planning Commissions and to co-ordinate their activities in the framework of the directives issued by the Government to the Commissariat when the process of drawing up the Plan commences. Subsequently, the Commissaire General is responsible for the first draft of the Plan, which then goes through the last stages of consultation to the final approval by Parliament. The Commissariat has also to follow through the execution of the Plan and to prepare an annual report. With the Fourth Plan this side of its work is due to develop considerably. The High Planning Council, of which the Commissaire General is the Executive Secretary, will meet twice a year and Parliamentary debates and those of the Economic and Social Council will be more extensive than in the past.

As already mentioned, the Commissariat has never been given the specific rôle of economic adviser to the Government on current economic policy, the technical aspects of this task being performed normally by the economic directorates in the Ministries, or by the Service for Economic and Financial Studies of the Ministry of Finance.[1] However, as the action of the Commissariat in the execution of the Plan is being considerably reinforced, it is inevitable that it will be called upon increasingly to give its opinion when economic policy is being discussed. This process should be two-sided, insofar as the Government also intends to view economic policy-making more than previously in the light of the Plan and its objectives.

Even before that, the Commissariat was charged with advising the Government on measures to facilitate the execution of the Plan, particularly those which had been thrown up as a result of the work of the Planning Commissions. In this way the Commissariat has initiated over the years a number of policy measures, especially in the tax field. The Commissariat has also come to play a co-ordinating rôle as between different ministries and other bodies. Although interministerial committees were set up for this purpose, in fact the different departments are finding it a useful habit to meet on the

[1] Described in Chapter V.

neutral ground the Commissariat can provide. There the rôle of the Commissariat, although discreet, is nevertheless important, and the small size of the Commissariat and its consequent freedom from accusations of domination is of great use. In the same way, private interests often like to use the services of the Commissariat.

The influence of the Commissariat is further enhanced by its representation in practically very body having a voice in economic policy-making. The Commissaire General is a member of the National Credit Council (the supreme advisory body on matters of credit policy) and of the board of directors of the Economic and Social Development Fund and its committees.[1] He and his representatives belong to a large number of other committees, such as the interministerial committee of the European Economic Community, the Committee for the Co-ordination of Statistics, the board of the Centre for Documentation and Study of Consumption.[2] Three recent examples of the participation of the Commissariat in *ad hoc* official bodies give some idea of the breadth and scope of the Commissariat's influence. The Commissaire General himself was a member of the Rueff-Armand Committee in 1960, on the obstacles to economic expansion, and the Government's directives for setting-up the Fourth Plan requested the Planning Commissions to take account of the conclusions of this Committee in drawing up their reports—which several of them did, the Housing Commission for example. The Deputy Commissaire General, M. Vergeot, served on the Commission for the Study of the Problems of the Family in 1961 (the Prigent Commission) and on the Commission for the Study of the Problems of Old Age in 1962 (the Laroque Commission). The conclusions of both of these Commissions have been used in drafting the 'social' chapter of the Fourth Plan and in drawing up concrete policy measures to implement it.

The full range of the rôle of the Commissaire General and of the General Planning Commissariat will only become apparent later when the procedure for the Fourth Plan is examined in detail. It is clear, however, that the Commissaire General, whilst being less than a Minister, is in a position to influence policy which is unequalled by any other civil servant. He is received regularly by the President of the Republic. He also appears before the National Assembly, the Senate and their Commissions, and before the Economic and Social Council. His contacts with the Prime Minister and the Minister of Finance are frequent and regular. He attends Cabinet meetings when requested. Thus, the impact of the General Planning Commissariat

[1] These two bodies are described in Chapter III.
[2] Described in Chapter V.

is the result of a complex of representation, advice, conciliation and co-ordination which has grown up through the years in an unexpected way, not least thanks to the personalities of the men who have successively occupied the post of Commissaire General.

II. THE PERSONALITY OF THE COMMISSAIRE GENERAL

It would be surprising if a post of such originality and complexity in the framework of French administration had not come to bear the imprint of the men who have occupied it. Very likely, if they had not been what they were, the General Planning Commissariat would have long since become an appendage of one of the ministries. Another fact of practical importance is that there have been only three Commissaires General so far, whilst there have been twenty-two Finance Ministers. M. Jean Monnet, the first incumbent, was Commissaire General from 1946 until 1950. His successor, M. Hirsch, served until early 1959. The present Commissaire General is M. Pierre Massé. This continuity gives the Commissaire General added authority *vis-à-vis* Ministers whose terms of office are often measured in months.

The institutional aspects of the planning mechanism owe most to M. Monnet.[1] It was he who decided that the only way of carrying out the reconstruction programme after the war to get all interested parties to participate in drawing up the programme. This system found its concrete expression in the tripartite Planning Commissions, which are described in the next section. The structure of these Commissions remains essentially the same as in 1946, although they are much more numerous, despite the changes in emphasis and in the scope of planning since that time.

M. Monnet's successor in 1950, M. Hirsch,[2] was already Deputy

[1] Born in Cognac in 1888, M. Monnet was a member of the organization charged with co-ordinating supplies to the allied armies during the First World War. In 1919, he became Deputy Secretary-General of the League of Nations. Subsequently, he directed the making of the reconstruction and development programmes of Poland and Rumania, and, in 1932, was responsible for drafting a plan for industrial investment for the Government of China. Just before the outbreak of the Second World War, he became head of the French Purchasing Commission in the United States and, during the war, was a member of the British War Supplies Council. In 1950, when he left the General Planning Commissariat, M. Monnet became the first President of the European Coal and Steel Community.

[2] M. Hirsch is an engineer by training and had been a member of the board of directors of the Kuhlman Group before becoming Deputy Commissaire General. During the war, he had been head of the French purchasing mission with the Supreme Allied H.Q. In 1959 he became the President of Euratom, a post he occupied until 1962.

Commissaire General. There was, therefore, no break in continuity. But the period from 1950 to 1959, which included the drafting of the Second and Third Plans, was a difficult transition for the General Planning Commissariat. The tasks facing the Plan were changing rapidly and called for new techniques. Also, by 1950, the position of the Commissariat was not yet sufficiently solid to ensure that it would be able to survive once the most urgent tasks of reconstruction were complete. That planning did not suffer an eclipse, but managed to consolidate its position, was due in no small measure to the personal influence of the Commissaire General.

The appointment of M. Pierre Massé[1] as Commissaire General in February 1959 was made soon after the setting-up of the Fifth Republic. It was also the time when the initial work of preparing the Fourth Plan (1962-65) was beginning. As was seen earlier, the Fourth Plan is a much more ambitious project than its three predecessors; the growth-rate, already high by historical standards, is only one of the objectives of the Plan. It has, in addition, a distinctly normative character, notably as regards public expenditure, and will be called upon to operate in a national and, particularly, international context very different from the earlier Plans. Important innovations, both technical and institutional, have accompanied the drafting of the Plan, whilst others are being applied for its execution. In all these fields the influence of the present Commissaire General makes itself felt.

III. INTERNAL STRUCTURE

The internal structure of the General Planning Commissariat is characterized by the limited numbers of the staff; for many years there were some twenty-five professional staff and a hundred clerical and other personnel. Today, total numbers have risen to about 140 due to the integration of the Productivity Commissariat, but

[1] M. Massé, born in Paris in 1898, is a Polytechnician and Doctor of Science, and an engineer by profession. He became Deputy Director-General of the nationalized French electricity industry (EDF). M. Massé played a leading rôle after the war in the drafting and execution of the equipment programmes of Electricité de France and was the main influence behind the considerable progress in planning in the EDF, sponsoring especially the introduction of linear planning techniques. Always interested in economic problems, M. Massé has written a large number of articles of an economic and technical nature, and published in 1959, a remarkable book on the choice of investments: *Le Choix des Investissements,* Dunod, Paris. An English translation has been published under the title *Optimal Investment Decisions,* Prentice-Hall, 1962.

these activities remain relatively distinct from the planning work of the Commissariat.

The origins of the professional staff are extremely diverse and this is another feature of the structure of the Commissariat. Out of a total of thirty-five, rather less than half have been engaged directly by the Commissariat. Of the remainder, some are seconded to the Plan by their own department and are paid by the Commissariat, the others are put at its disposal, and they continue to be remunerated by their own administration. It is not easy to determine just how long they remain with the Plan, but periodic changes are not infrequent, as was the case in the last two years during which a certain number of new members arrived. The more senior members of the staff have the title of 'Conseiller du Plan', the others being denominated 'Chargés de Mission'.

The administration of the General Planning Commissariat is highly flexible—a characteristic in keeping with its methods of work. There is no agreed administrative organigram which all members of the staff would accept unequivocally. In general, however, a threefold division exists which may be summarized as: the central directorate; the divisions; and the sections.

(a) The Central Directorate is composed of the Commissaire General, his Deputy and the Secretary-General.

(b) The Divisions, of which there are three, have what may be called 'horizontal' responsibilities as compared with the sections which, dealing with individual branches of activity, are 'vertical'.

The Economics Division employs five professional staff—an agronomist, an 'Inspecteur des Finances', an official from the Ministry of Finance, a University economist and an official from the Post Office. The Financial Division has three members, of whom two are 'Inspecteurs des Finances' and one a professional archivist. A newcomer is the Regional Division which also has three members, a Counsellor at the Court of Audit, a member of the Ministry of Industry and an international civil servant on loan.

There are ten 'vertical' sections: Agriculture has two members (a member of the farmers' professional association and an engineer agronomist) and was formerly larger; Energy (three engineers, of whom one is a Polytechnician); Water (an engineer); Transport (two engineers, of whom one is at the same time Chairman of the Transport Commission of the Plan); Industry (four members, of whom two are engineers); Fisheries and Artisans (one member); Construction, Housing and related industries (one engineer lent half-time by the Ministry of Construction); Urban Development (two engineers); Overseas Territories (a jurist); Algeria (one member).[1] Some of the professional staff are only employed part-time.

Despite the varied character of the professional origin of the staff, there is a certain preponderance of those having a 'scientific' background (twelve have passed through the Grandes Ecoles Scientifiques) and a sprinkling of members of the 'Grands Corps de l'Etat' (four in number). The number of professional economists appears surprisingly low, but it should be recalled that, in France—and contrary to what the foreigner might be led to expect—planning in practice has preceded planning in theory up to now, and many men have acquired their professional competence on the job. This was even more necessary in view of the paucity of qualified economists in France until recently. More important, perhaps, is the fact that the Commissariat relies heavily for the technical aspects of planning and projections, either on the qualified staff of specialized groups such as the Service for Economic and Financial Studies of the Ministry of Finance (SEEF), the National Institute of Statistics and Economic Studies (INSEE), the National Demographic Institute (INED) and the Centre for the Documentation and Study of Consumption (CREDOC), or on the members of the Commissions and their numerous working groups.

IV. THE PLANNING COMMISSIONS[2]

Two points will be examined here: the composition of the Commissions and their methods of work. A study of the work the Commissions did in drafting the Fourth Plan, and the projects at present under discussion for giving them a rôle in the control of the execution of the Plan, will be left over for later chapters.

Until 1962, these representative, non-permanent bodies were called together each time a new four-year Plan was prepared and were then dissolved. Since then, the Commissions hold annual meetings. This change is part of the new follow-up procedure for the Plan. Their creation was foreseen in 1946, in the same decree (Article 5) which set up the General Planning Commissariat, and they constituted the principal innovation in French planning. Their structure is tripartite—employers, workers and civil servants. The Commissions are of two types: vertical and horizontal.

Vertical Commissions specialize in different sectors of activity. Their number has increased steadily from seven, for the First Plan,

[1] This was the position before Algeria became independent.
[2] A list of the Commissions and their membership is given in Appendix III.

to seventeen for the Third and twenty-two for the Fourth. There has been a tendency for requests to set up Commissions to be made by the interested parties themselves in the public sector in particular. The motives for this are various, but the realization that the Plan was becoming the real point of convergence of Government policy was no doubt a contributory factor and having a Commission was a way of improving one's chances of securing budget allocations.

Horizontal Commissions, of which there were only two for the Third Plan but five for the Fourth, exercise more general functions. They are called General Economic and Financial, Manpower, Productivity, Scientific and Technical Research and Regional Plans.

Each Commission has a number of working parties, each being left free to organize its work as it thinks fit in this respect. One working party is of sufficient importance to be mentioned immediately: this is the Equilibrium Working Party of the influential horizontal General Economic and Financial Commission which has the task of co-ordination, which means, among other things, assessing the compatibility of the individual programmes of the Vertical Commissions. The Vertical Commission with the widest scope—the one for the Transformation Industries—which covers 240 separate branches, formed sixty working parties for the Fourth Plan.

An analysis of the composition of the Commissions gives the following results. The Chairman, general rapporteurs, and members, are all appointed by decision of the Minister of Finance after they have been proposed by the General Planning Commissariat. The background of the Chairmen shows the preponderance of members of the Grands Corps de l'Etat (Counsellors of State, Counsellors of the Court of Audit, Inspecteurs des Finances). If university professors are included, ten of the twenty-one Vertical Commissions' Chairmen belong to this group. Some Chairmen are also engineers, but only four can be considered as really representing a branch of private industry. This is the case for Chemicals, Secondary Industries, Steel and Tourism. The Vice-Chairmen are nearly all senior civil servants representing a specific administration and most of the time they are designated by their title and not their name. Among the general rapporteurs, a few represent the private sector. As a result, few employers' representatives, and no trade unionists, have served as Chairmen, Vice-Chairmen or general rapporteurs. But employers' representatives make up the majority of the ordinary members of the Commissions dealing with directly productive private sectors (fifteen to fifty-five, according to the Commissions). Each Commission has a few trade union members, usually four of them, or one representative of each of the Confederations—CGT,

CGT-FO, CFTC, CGC.[1] In some cases (Energy), the number of trade unionists is greater than four. The trade union representation was reinforced for the Fourth Plan at the instigation of the General Planning Commissariat, but the situation is still not felt to be satisfactory by many people, and first and foremost by the trade unions themselves.

Each Commission has a certain number of ex-officio members. They are all civil servants and vary according to the Commission, but there is a small group whose members are found on the ex-officio list of practically all the Commissions. This is the case for the Director of the Budget, the Director of the Treasury, the General Director of Prices and Economic Studies, the Director of External Economic Relations, the Head of the Service for Economic and Financial Studies and the General Director of the INSEE.

For the Fourth Plan there were 980 members of the Commissions, excluding the ex-officio members. If the members of the numerous working parties are included, the total number of persons who collaborated in the work of the Commissions was over 3,000 (see table).

The working methods adopted by the Commissions are not a matter for rigid rules. But their tasks imply a certain common approach. Thus the Vertical Commissions have to complete for the General Planning Commissariat a statistical questionnaire which is used in constructing the provisional synthesis of the Plan. Later on, each Vertical Commission drafts a report.

MEMBERS OF COMMISSIONS AND WORKING PARTIES

Employers (including the nationalized industries)	715
Farmers	107
Employers' professional associations	562
Trade unionists	281
Civil servants	781
Other (university teachers and other independent experts) ...	691
Total	3,137

The replies to the questionnaire are based upon the objectives of the Plan for the terminal year. The data filled in by the Commissions are only provisional when they are supplied (some six to eight months after the first meeting) and are adjusted subsequently in the light of new information, or following policy decisions and arbitre-

[1] The structure of French trade unionism is summarized briefly in Chapter XVII.

ments by the Commissaire General. This aspect of the work of the Commissions is still important, but perhaps less so than in the early years, when the paucity of statistics made it an indispensable way of securing data.

The reports, which were all published for the Fourth Plan, have a fairly standard pattern.[1] They give firstly, an up-to-date survey of the situation in each sector as regards production, employment, relations with other sectors and foreign trade. Then come the projections for the sector during the period of the Plan. Questions of production goals and investment expenditures receive particular attention here. The 'social' Commissions adopt a rather similar procedure, except that their projections are founded upon needs rather than firm policy commitments and can, therefore, differ from the text of the Plan. This problem does not arise as a rule in the case of the productive sectors, as the discrepancies between the objectives of the Commission and the targets put into the Plan are ironed out beforehand as far as possible. Still, divergences do remain sometimes, and are recorded in the report of the Commission. Just how this co-ordination is done is an important aspect of the Plan and we shall return to it again. Finally, the reports usually devote a chapter to suggestions for policy changes which, in the opinion of the members of the Commission, are called for if the goals set by the Plan are to be reached. Naturally, this sometimes leads to special pleading but, as will be seen later, this is by no means the general rule.

The object in publishing the reports is essentially educative. They are a way of informing individual firms of the general problems of their branch and they bring specific economic and social problems to the notice of public opinion. A well-documented report can have great influence when questions of economic policy are being discussed, and when it represents a sort of specialized appendix to the main text of the Plan and is used as a reference document by the Administration. An advantage of this system is that ideas can be ventilated in this way without being considered as expressions of official policy.

[1] We study some examples of Commission reports in Chapter IX.

CHAPTER II

CONSULTATIVE BODIES

'Planning by Consent' has been, and remains, a fundamental principle of the French system of planning. For a long time this principle found its main expression in the work of the Planning Commissions (which was discussed in the last chapter) as, otherwise, consultation procedures were rather sketchy until the Fourth Plan. A High Planning Council was set up in 1946 with consultative responsibilities, but it rapidly became moribund and the Economic and Social Council had to fight to obtain recognition as a consultative assembly for the Plan.

Today, in view of the great revival, or more accurately, the sudden upsurge, of interest in planning in France, such a situation could not endure. Indeed, the authorities themselves[1] must be given credit for taking the initiative in extending the field of consultation procedures for the Fourth Plan. For the first time, the opinion of a consultative assembly—the Economic and Social Council—was sought on the general objectives of the Plan before its preparation began and, at the end of 1961, the completed Plan was again submitted to the Council before going to Parliament. The High Planning Council was resuscitated in 1961 and was consulted on the main lines of the completed Fourth Plan. There is no doubt that the Economic and Social Council, and the High Planning Council, will play at least as active a rôle as regards the Fifth Plan as they did for the Fourth. Both these bodies are also being called upon to participate in the follow-up procedure of the Plan.[2] This chapter discusses the structure and work of the Economic and Social Council and the High Planning Council.

I. THE ECONOMIC AND SOCIAL COUNCIL

The existence of consultative assemblies to advise on economic and social problems goes back quite a long way in French history. Under the Ancien Régime there was a 'Conseil du Commerce' which could

[1] And the present Commissaire General in particular.

[2] This extension of consultation procedures should be seen against the general background of the debate now proceeding in France on the theme of economic democracy which we discuss in Chapter XVIII.

be called upon by the King to advise him. A more direct predecessor of the post-war councils is the 'Commission Consultative du Travail' set up by the provisional Government of the Second Republic in 1848. The Commission held its meetings in the Luxembourg Palace, was composed of delegates from the various professions, with a sprinkling of intellectuals, and was charged with the study of economic problems and with advising the Government.

Between the two world wars, a further experiment along the same lines took place when, in 1925, a National Economic Council was created to 'study the major questions affecting the economic life of the country' and to 'bring together, in close solidarity, all French social and productive forces'. This body, of 47 members, represented three main groups: labour (30 members); the population and consumers (9 members); capital (8 members). It was purely consultative, and reported directly to the Prime Minister. With the formation of a Popular Front Government in 1936, the Council's membership was increased and it was given the novel task of arbitrator in industrial conflicts. Also, the Council became a consultative body for Parliament (either the Chambers or the Parliamentary Commissions) as well as for the Government.

These precedents have strongly inspired the post-war history of the Economic Council, as it was called in 1946, or of the Economic and Social Council, as it became in 1958. However, the differences between the two post-war councils are sufficient to make it useful to examine them separately.

1 *The Economic Council 1946-59*

An Economic Council was provided for in the first post-war constitution in 1946, which created the Fourth Republic, and a law passed in October 1946 gave effect to this. The functions and composition of this Council, and its responsibilities towards economic planning, were not without influence when the present Economic and Social Council was formed.

(a) *Functions.* The consultative character of the Economic Council was clearly marked, and the arbitration functions of the inter-war Council were not continued. The consultative rôle was a double one; to advise Parliament and to advise the Government.

As for legislation, the Council was authorized to examine all texts and draft laws of an economic or social character, except the budget and international agreements. This limitation has been retained since then. The Council could either be asked for an opinion by Parliament or the Government, or take up a question on its own initiative. As far as decrees and administrative orders were concerned, initially the Council had to be consulted, but the scope of this rather sweeping measure was reduced in 1951 to decrees and administrative orders taken by virtue of laws which themselves expressly provided for such a consultation.

According to the law of 1946, the Council had to be consulted 'on the setting-up of a national economic Plan'. In 1951, this reference was enlarged to refer to the 'Plans', in the plural, and it was decided that the 'Council would report annually on the working-out of these Plans, and would suggest any changes which the facts of the situation seemed to call for'. The law of 1951 was important also insofar as it made more precise the type of work the Council was to do, by mentioning specifically regular reporting on the economic situation and on the official national accounts data. These two innovations were a reflection of the steady spreading and deepening of knowledge of economic facts in France after the war.

The double consultative function led to the creation of official channels of communication between the Council and Parliament and the Government. The authors of legislative proposals could be heard by the Commissions of the Council. All members of Parliament could attend sessions of the Council. Its recommendations and resolutions were published in a special series of the Official Gazette, together with a summary of the discussions. These documents had to be sent to Parliament and the Government within a delay of five days. In 1951, it was further decided that the studies, resolutions and minutes of the Economic Council should be sent to the members of the corresponding Parliamentary Commissions, and this increased the interpenetration of the work of the two types of Commission.

Before seeing how the Council did in fact fulfil its mandate between 1946 and 1958, it is necessary to see how it was composed.

(b) *Composition.* The Economic Council of 1946 was a considerably larger body than its pre-war predecessor. There were 169 members in all and the number of 'interest' groups represented was much broader. The three largest groups were the 40 delegates representing 'workers, employees, civil servants, technicians, engineers and administrative staff'. Agriculture had 33 members and the employers' side of industry 20, some of them from the nationalized sector, however. Commerce and artisans had 10 members each, the co-operative movement (not to be confused with the British type of co-operation) and family associations, which are very powerful in France, nine each. Eight seats were reserved for non-representative intellectuals with special competence in economics or science, thus preserving the tradition of 1848. With fifteen representatives from the overseas territories—which were still very considerable in population and territory at that time—and various smaller groups, the Council was complete.

The internal structure of the Council comprised a general assembly of all members, a president and an elected bureau, and several Commissions, among the latter being an Economic Affairs and Planning Commission.

(c) *The Council and Planning*. As was seen earlier, the Council received a specific mandate in 1947 to study the Modernization and Equipment Plans. In fact it had some difficulty in carrying out its mandate. Consultations took place very tardily and could hardly have had much influence on policy.

The Council having been set up only in 1947, it was not consulted at all on the draft of the First Plan which was approved before that. Between 1947 and 1950 the Council passed at least five resolutions requesting the Government to comply with the terms of the Constitution, and the law of 1946, and to submit the Plan, and/or its annual programmes, for examination. In the event, this activity does not seem to have had the desired effect, and the first opportunity given to the Council to discuss the Plan was in 1950, when a report by the Commissaire General (M. Monnet) on achievements from 1947 to 1949 and targets for 1950 to 1952 was submitted by the Government.

During these years the Council endeavoured to overcome this reluctance of the authorities by other means. It took up itself each year the investment programme in each Finance Act and was able, in that way, to discuss certain aspects of the Plan. The Council was also active in particular sectors touching the Plan, for example, in housing and the repercussions of the European Coal and Steel Community on the two French industries which were key sectors in the Plan.

The pressure exercised by the Council bore fruit with the Second Plan (1954-57). The Government submitted the text of the Plan which was discussed in July, 1954, and the law voted by Parliament approving the Plan contained the phrase 'after consultation with the Economic Council'. It went on to stipulate that any subsequent revision of the Plan would also be submitted to the Council. As the date of the consultation indicates, the Council was faced with a *fait accompli* insofar as the Second Plan had not only been drafted, but it had been applied already since the beginning of the year. In these circumstances it was of little use to suggest any major amendments.

Its discussion of the Third Plan (1958-61) was practically the last act of the post-war Economic Council. Indeed, by the time the debate took place (February 1959), the texts creating a new Economic and Social Council had already appeared. Once more, the Council was consulted by the Government on a text which was already finalized and had been in operation for over a year. The troubled history of the previous twelve months in France is a sufficient explanation why this delay should have occurred. Taken in conjunction with the profound shock to the economy administered by the devaluation at the end of 1958, and the economic policy associated with it, it is not surprising that the Council's debates should have had a rather unreal character. It did not discuss the objectives of the Plan in any detail, but reserved its comments for the changed circumstances in which the French economy would have to operate from then on, as a result of the Common Market and trade liberalization, and for the consequent need, firstly, to take an overall view of the problem of economic balance in future and, secondly, to link the carrying-out of the Plan to shorter-term economic policy. At that time, these points were certainly more relevant than criticism of the Plan itself.

2 *The Economic and Social Council since 1959*

The constitution of the Fifth Republic (October 1958) provided for an Economic and Social Council (Articles 70 and 71) and the first meeting of the Council in its new form took place in July 1959.

The Economic and Social Council differs from its predecessor in a number of respects. Its composition is broader, and its rôle as regards the planning process larger. These two points are studied first before examining the methods of work of the Council.

(a) *Composition.* Originally, the members had a double origin—professional and geographical—and a large place was made for representatives from Algeria, the Sahara, the Overseas Territories and Départements and the Independent States of the French Community. More recently, the evolution of the relations of Metropolitan France with the ex-Overseas Territories and with Algeria has rendered most of these provisions inapplicable.

The representation of the various activities of Metropolitan French life was fixed at 175. Of these, 45 represent workers, employees, technicians, engineers and administrative personnel. The three Trade Union Confederations (CGT, CGT-FO and CFTC), have 13 members each, the professional group 4 (Confédération Générale des Cadres) and the teachers' and an independent trade union federation 1 each.

Industry, trade and the artisans have 41 seats. Among these, 6 come from the nationalized sector. Another 16 represent private firms; they are chosen by the Conseil National du Patronat Français (the employers' federation) and the Confederation for Small- and Medium-Sized Firms, according to a formula which allows representation for firms employing more and less than 100 workers. Commerce has 9 members and the artisans 10. Agriculture has 40 seats with provision for representation of all the important agricultural organizations: the Agricultural Chambers, the National Federation of Farmers' Unions, Agricultural Co-operative and Credit Organizations and so on.

Fifteen members are appointed by the Government by reason of their competence in economic, social, scientific and cultural fields. In this group are found ex-Ministers, professors of economics, engineers, a lawyer and an accountant. Another fifteen members are delegated by a number of social organizations concerned with health, housing, etc., including not less than eight delegated from the National Union of Family Associations. Ten members are appointed by the Government because of their special knowledge of the problems of the countries of the old Overseas Territories. Nine others come from a variety of activities such as tourism, exports and regional development bodies. Besides these full members, the Government can appoint experts for a period not exceeding one year—the mandate of the Counsellors being for five years—who sit on the internal committees of the Council, but who do not participate in the general assemblies.

Counsellors are paid salaries of one-third the usual Parliamentary salaries. But as they are nearly all delegates, they usually pay back these sums to the bodies they represent.

The mode of appointment of members makes it clear that there is no question of election. The groups, and the numbers of their representatives, are fixed by the Government. The groups delegate members to the Council who have, therefore, no personal mandate. The only exceptions to this are the individual nominations made by the Government. Nevertheless, it would be a mistake to consider the members of the Council as simple executants of their mandates. On the contrary, a real *esprit de corps* has been created over the years, and a substantial number of Counsellors have held their mandates for a long period, since 1947 in many cases. The Council is the scene of real discussions, conducted in an atmosphere fairly free from slogans and propaganda. It is not difficult to understand that, in these circumstances, Counsellors are not only informing the Government and public opinion on economic problems but are also informing each other. The practice of cohabitation in the same assembly and working groups favours the inter-penetration of ideas, and a greater degree of reciprocal understanding, even in cases where fundamental positions are unchanged. This is perhaps why the Council is at its best in questions of a more specialized character. Among them planning has been particularly important as will be seen in Chapters VII and VIII.

(b) *The Council and the Plan.* The Constitution of 1958 was explicit on this point. Article 70 stated that all economic plans are to be submitted to it. But for the first time a mention was made of the rôle of the Council in preparing the Plan. The ordonnance of December 29, 1958, noted that the Council 'could be associated with the drafting of the Plan' independently of the obligation for the Government to consult it on the final text.

But the Economic and Social Council loses its double rôle of adviser to the Government and to Parliament. Henceforth, it is solely the Government's adviser and all members of the Government can attend any meetings of the Council, but members of Parliament no longer have this privilege. Another difference from the previous Economic Council is that the debates of the new Council are no longer published although the reports and resolutions still are, and they continue to provide a means of informing public opinion about the work of the Council on the economic and social questions of the day. The Press usually devotes space to reporting on these activities and, particularly when a subject like the Plan is being discussed, full-page articles are by no means rare.

So much for the legal structure. As regards its methods of work in connection with the Plan, no major change has taken place since the war, and so the following description can be taken as valid, save in questions of detail, for the whole post-war period.

The practical work of the Council is done through permanent committees called 'Sections'. The Section responsible for the synthesis of all work on the Plan is the Investment and Planning Section. At the time of the preparation of the Fourth Plan, the membership of the Section consisted of 20 full counsellors and 6 members appointed by the Government as experts. The 20 full members were divided as follows:

5 Trade Unionists—CGT (1); CGT-FO (1); CFTC (2); CGC (1)
4 Employers' representatives

2 representatives from agriculture
1 member each to represent the nationalized industries, artisans, co-operatives, Overseas Territories, family associations, the middle classes and others
3 independent members (all specialists in economics)

The Chairman of the Section was the representative of the nationalized industries and the two Vice-Chairmen the representatives of the CGT and the CGT-FO respectively. The Section has only a limited technical staff of two persons to assist it in its work. This fact is not without its importance as will be seen in Chapter VII.

It is the task of the Section to prepare work for the General Assembly by submitting a report and a draft resolution on the question it has been asked to examine. Sections can also carry out studies at the request of the Government, or on their own initiative, and these are submitted directly to the Government without going to the General Assembly.

The procedure for preparing reports is for the Section to choose one of its members as rapporteur. The rapporteur, with the help of the Secretariat and any other assistance he can obtain, drafts the first version of the report which is finally agreed by the Section as a whole. As regards the drafting of the resolution, or other matters, the principle of the majority vote is applied. This means that, as in the General Assembly, no single group is sufficiently numerous to carry a vote or to defeat a motion without joining with other groups. A Section can request others to assist it in carrying out its work. This procedure was widely used for the Fourth Plan.

When the Section has completed its work, its report and draft resolution go to the General Assembly which meets, as a rule, four times a year. As noted earlier, the members of the Government can attend the General Assembly and intervene in debates—but this is of rare occurrence. It is significant, however, that the final session on the Fourth Plan in 1961 was attended by the President of the Republic, General de Gaulle, in person.

At the General Assembly, the rapporteur summarizes the Section's report and reads the draft resolution. After debate, a vote is taken, and this furnishes the opportunity for members to propose amendments. The resolution having been voted, it is sent to the Government together with a copy of the Section's report and the Minutes of the General Assembly. The report is then published in the Official Gazette.

II. HIGH PLANNING COUNCIL

After a period of eclipse following its creation in 1946, this body is called upon to play an important and new rôle in connection with the Fourth Plan.

In the past, and until 1953, the Planning Council was made up of Ministers interested in various aspects of the Plan, and of eighteen representatives of the economic life of the country—industry, agriculture, Overseas Territories, scientific research and so on. The Chairman was the Prime Minister. It was supposed to present to the Government the Plan 'and the means for ensuring its execution'.[1] At that time, the Council was rather in the position of a super Planning Commission—the present Horizontal Commissions not yet having been set up—*vis-à-vis* the Vertical Commissions. It was left to the Planning Council to discuss the general orientation of the Plan, a task which it accomplished for the first two Plans until it was replaced by the High Planning Council in 1953. But the Planning Council did not meet very frequently between 1946 and 1953 and its contribution to planning was small.

In 1953, the Planning Council was split into two bodies—the High Planning Council and the Inter-Ministerial Planning Committee. Neither of these bodies had more than a shadowy existence. The High Planning Council only met once in connection with the Second Plan and not at all for the Third. Composed solely of representatives of the major economic activities of the country—many of whom were already members of Horizontal or Vertical Planning Commissions—there seemed to be little point in submitting the Plan to its examination.

The Inter-Ministerial Planning Committee was supposed to coordinate the work of the various Government departments on the Plan during its drafting and execution. At that time, it was the only body with such a task, outside the General Planning Commissariat itself. But quite quickly its functions were absorbed by the Ministry of Finance and Economic Affairs and the Inter-Ministerial Planning Committee ceased to meet.

With the Fourth Plan the High Planning Council was resuscitated by a Decree published in July 1961. Its Chairman is the Prime Minister and it has some 60 members.[2] The list of their names

[1] Decree January 6, 1946.

[2] Among them are: Vice-Presidents: Minister of Finance and the President of the Economic and Social Council. Members: Governor of the Bank of France, Chairman and two Vice-Chairmen of the Planning and Investment Section of the Economic and Social Council. Eight members chosen from the members of the National Accounts Commission. Seven Chairmen of

shows that the Council is a pretty high-powered assembly, more so than the Economic and Social Council, a fact that seems to have helped to determine the division of labour established between these two bodies.

According to the 1961 Decree, the Council intervenes at two stages in the planning process—during drafting and during execution. It is supposed to be kept informed of the progress in drafting the Plan and to draw up a report on it before the final version is submitted to the Government and the Economic and Social Council. It is also called upon to examine the execution of the Plan each year and to report on the results obtained compared with the targets fixed. It is asked to propose any measures which seem to be required to execute the Plan, particularly about its social objectives. For that reason it is the body which was used for the first annual consultation on the distribution of the fruits of expansion, in 1962, which is the French approach to the problem of elaborating an incomes policy.

regional expansion Committees who sit for one year and are replaced by other Chairmen of similar Committees. (In fact, nearly all these members are parliamentarians.) The Chairmen of the Chambers of Commerce and Industry, the Chambers of Trades and the Chambers of Agriculture. Two members of the Council of the Constantine Plan (for Algeria). One representative of each of the following bodies: the French Employers' Federation, the Small- and Medium-Sized Firms' Federation; the three representative agricultural bodies, the Cadres' Trade Union and the three workers' Confederations. A number of delegates, not more than a third of the Council, are chosen by the Government in view of their personal qualifications. One finds in this group some Chairmen of Planning Commissions, a few senior civil servants, university professors, members of Parliament, industrialists. M. Jean Monnet is a member of the Council in this category.

CHAPTER III

THE PUBLIC SECTOR

The public sector is the basic element in the Plan both for drafting and implementation. We discussed the General Planning Commissariat previously and devote the last chapter of this Part to the various technical bodies which collaborate with the Commissariat in drawing up the Plan. Here we shall consider, in the first place, the Ministries. Among them, one is supreme from the point of view of our subject—the Ministry of Finance—and we deal with this first. As regards the rest of the public sector, the fact that two Ministries exercise wide tutelary powers over the nationalized industries makes it more convenient to study these industries at the same time as their respective Ministries. We then turn to the social sector, the banking sector and, briefly, to the Ministry of Agriculture.

I. THE MINISTRY OF FINANCE[1]

We saw in Chapter I that the General Planning Commissariat, though occupying a rather special position, was for some years attached to the Ministry of Finance. Since 1962, it has been moved back to the Prime Minister's Office. But this has only modified in a formal way the relations of the Commissariat with the Ministry of Finance. The organic links remain and are by far the most important. The Ministry of Finance really comes into its own, however, when the four-year Plan is implemented.

1 *Functions and Powers*

The Ministry is responsible for preparing the budget, accounting for public receipts and expenditures, taxation and customs, public debt management, assuring the finance of the State's activities and for overseas financial relations. These are the classic functions of Ministries of Finance. What this enumeration does not indicate is the wide powers the Ministry exercises over the rest of the public sector—Ministries, local authorities and nationalized industries—and the private sector.

[1] In drafting this section we have consulted with great profit the lectures by Mr Pallez (Inspecteur des Finances and Director at the Ministry of the Interior) at the Institut d'Etudes Politiques, Paris, 1961-62.

The counter signature of the Minister of Finance is required for each draft law or decree which concerns in one way or another—sometimes very indirectly—the public finances. This rule increases the occasions when the Ministry of Finance is invited to participate in preliminary discussions with other Government departments or in inter-departmental committees where the final stage is likely to be a text requiring the counter signature of the Minister of Finance. The control of the Ministry over expenditure is highly developed and means that contacts are permanent and far-reaching with the rest of the public sector. In French public finance, there is a sharp distinction between the agent who decides the amount, or opportunity, of a receipt, or an expenditure, and the agent who handles the funds. The second function has given rise to a corps of public accountants at every echelon of the administration, who are responsible to the Minister of Finance, and are really only a decentralized part of his department. Moreover, in each Ministry and nationalized industry, there is an official belonging to the Ministry of Finance, called the financial controller—who may have one or more deputies—and who must be informed of important decisions relating to undertakings to spend public moneys. The financial controller has to deal strictly with the correctness of an operation but this influence often goes beyond that to include an appreciation of its expediency also.

The Ministry of Finance controls its own external agents through the corps of the Inspecteurs des Finances. The latter's importance in French administrative life is much greater than this, however. The Inspecteurs des Finances—recruited today through the National School of Administration—are an elite whose members are to be found occupying senior posts in all branches of public administration. At the present time, two Ministers, of Finance and Foreign Affairs, are Inspecteurs des Finances as well as the Governor of the Bank of France, the Directors of the Budget and the Treasury in the Ministry of Finance, and many directors in other Ministries and in the nationalized sector. A not inconsiderable number of ex-members of the corps are to be found in private business.

The Minister of Finance is the arbiter of personnel problems in the public sector, and all questions of grading, recruitment and remuneration in the civil service have to be approved by him. In fact, though not in principle, he takes the final decision on remunerations in the nationalized industries. Collective bargaining between the trade unions and the representatives of each of these industries was accepted at the time of the nationalization acts, with powers of arbitration being given to the tutelary Ministers (Industry and Transport and Public Works). But quite soon this system was modified as part of the general trend towards an increase in the control of the State compared with the initial legislation, so that effective power of decision now lies with an inter-ministerial committee, where the Minister of Finance has the last word. No agreement for increases in wages or salaries can be implemented, although it can be concluded, by the management of a nationalized industry until the approval of this committee has been obtained.[1]

The control of the Ministry of Finance over investment is considerable and its importance for the Plan calls for a fairly detailed examination in a later chapter.[2] It is sufficient to note here that, besides controlling direct investment through the budget, the Ministry of Finance has acquired the right to examine the investment programmes of the nationalized industries through the working of the Economic and Social Development Fund.[3] This Fund also enables it to pass judgment on a great variety of investment programmes of the local authorities and of private firms who solicit loans or fiscal exemptions. Besides, the Ministry controls access to the capital market by the private sector.

Finally, what remains of authority to control prices—in the public and private sectors—adds another weapon to its armoury.

2 *The Minister of Finance*

The result of this situation is to reinforce many people, inside and outside the public sector, in their opinion that the 'financiers' have the upper hand in the affairs of Government and that a wider appreciation of economic and social problems is lacking. That the 'rue de Rivoli'[4] has refused a credit, or insists on a reduction, is a common journalistic phrase which appears every day in the Press to give substance to this belief. This hankering after a solution which would loosen the hold of the Ministry of Finance has often led to proposals for an 'Economics Ministry' distinct from the Ministry of Finance. The only post-war experiment was at the Liberation, when M. Mendès-France was Minister of the National Economy and M. Pleven Minister of Finance. The divergencies between the two men on a whole range of financial and economic problems led to the departure of M. Mendès-France and the experiment of two such Ministers was not repeated. The idea that there are specific economic tasks which are carried out by the Minister of Finance, but which

[1] There are some exceptions to this. The Renault motor-car firm is left outside this system to all intents and purposes, and the banks and insurance companies also have a fair degree of freedom.

[2] See Chapter XII.

[3] See later, page 65.

[4] The address of the Ministry of Finance.

ought not to be, is encouraged by the existence of a service called Economic Affairs which is attached to his Ministry. This service's responsibilities which were very important during the early post-war years, with their network of controls, have been very much a withering asset since policy began to rely more and more on financial and credit instruments, and less on direct controls.

The rôle of the Minister of Finance in the Government, as his functions indicate, is a very important one. Although no formal distinction is made in any texts between him and his colleagues he is very much a *primus inter pares* despite the legal equality of the various Ministers.

He is assisted by several Secretaries of State. Their titles have varied over the years. There have been Secretaries of State for Economic Affairs, but, because of the reduced importance of the Service of Economic Affairs already noted, this post has been abolished. What remain of his functions have been brought under the authority of a Secretary of State for Internal Trade who is concerned with prices and internal commercial structures. The work done previously by the Secretary for Economic Affairs as regards external economic relations has been placed directly under the Minister of Finance himself. For the detailed work of preparing the budget and, in particular, of steering the latter through Parliament, the Minister of Finance is assisted by a Secretary of State for the Budget.

3 *Structure of the Ministry of Finance*

The organigram of the Ministry of Finance can be represented as seen on page 63.[1]

4 *Rôle of the Ministry of Finance in the Plan*

The two key Directorates here are the Budget and the Treasury.

The Budget Directorate. The staff of the Directorate is not large—it consists of about sixty persons—partly because of the decentralized network of agents of the Ministry of Finance in all the spending departments which has already been mentioned.

It is convenient to examine the rôle of the Budget Directorate in relation to the Plan from two points of view: the preparation of the four-year Plan; the preparation of the annual budget.

For the *four-year Plan,* collaboration between the Budget Directorate and the General Planning Commissariat is indispensable but has not always been fully achieved. The Director of the Budget is an

[1] We borrow this useful organigram from the *Cahiers Français* published by the Documentation Française, May 1962.

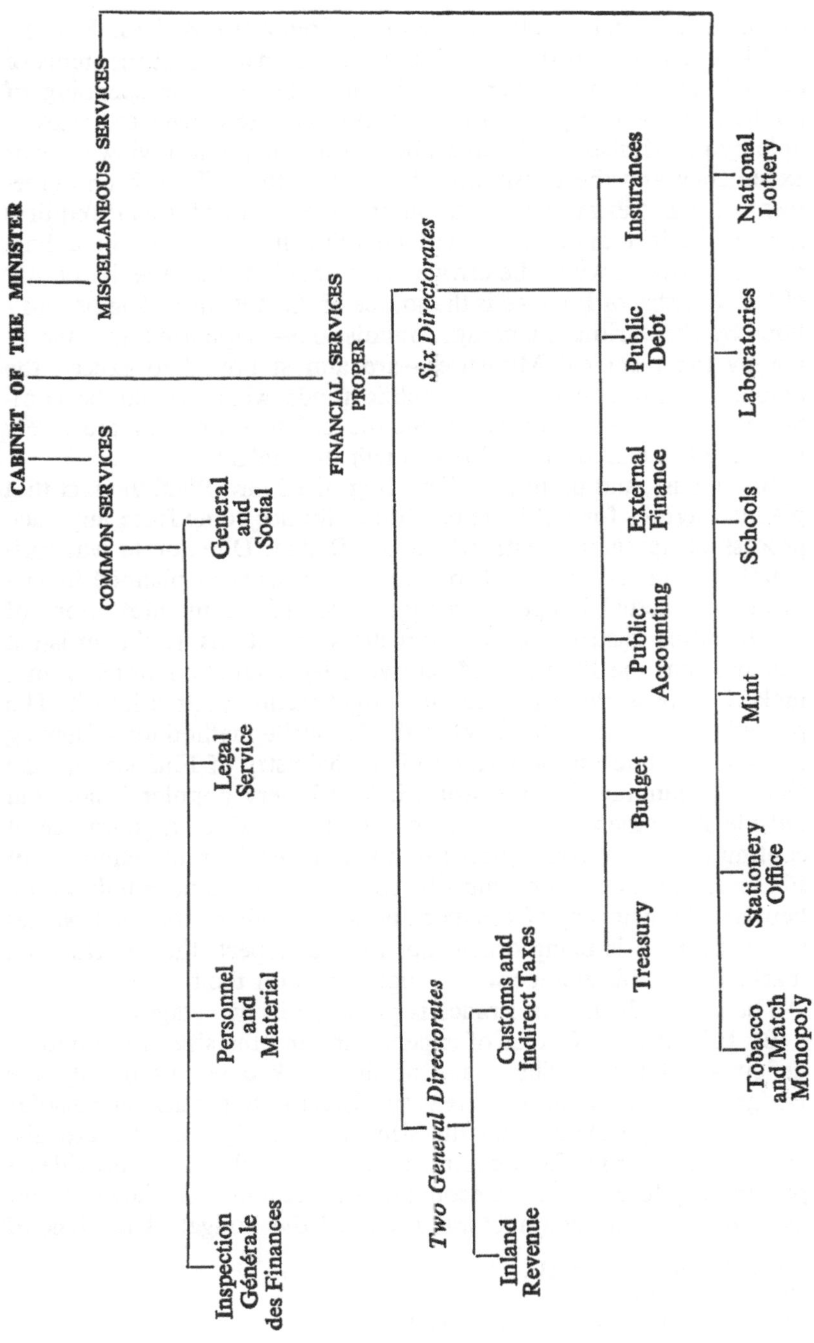
CABINET OF THE MINISTER
COMMON SERVICES
FINANCIAL SERVICES PROPER
MISCELLANEOUS SERVICES
General and Social
Legal Service
Personnel and Material
Inspection Générale des Finances
Six Directorates
Two General Directorates
Customs and Indirect Taxes
Inland Revenue
Insurances
Public Debt
External Finance
Public Accounting
Budget
Treasury
National Lottery
Laboratories
Schools
Mint
Stationery Office
Tobacco and Match Monopoly

ex-officio member of all the Planning Commissions, both Vertical and Horizontal. But this is not sufficient to ensure that the items of expenditure calling, either directly or indirectly, for spending of public funds which get written into the Plan are considered reasonable by the Ministry of Finance, both from the point of view of their expediency and the possibility of financing them. If such an agreement does not exist, the execution of the Plan, insofar as it requires specific budget allocations, will be difficult to achieve in a harmonious way. It would be erroneous to conclude that the 'bad faith' of the Ministry of Finance is the source of the difficulty. The propositions by the various Planning Commissions—supported as often as not by the technical Ministries—are almost bound to exceed the amount of investment out of public funds which would be compatible, either with general economic balance, or with the likely volume of resources available through the budget.

In the past, and up to (and including) the Third Plan, the fact that planned figures for public expenditure did not come from any such process of agreement with which the Budget Directorate was intimately associated often led to divergences between planned investments and actual budget allocations. One of the manifestations of the resulting distrust of the Ministry's intentions is the insistent demand that the Plan should receive a legal sanction which would make it impossible to reduce the budget credits written into it. The procedure of programme laws[1] is the favourite method for achieving this and, despite the opposition of the Ministry of Finance and the General Planning Commissariat, it is still very popular inside and outside Parliament. This is not to deny the need for a guarantee of continuity by exerting pressure upon a recalcitrant Ministry of Finance. But the solution must be sought in a genuine collaboration between the Ministry of Finance and all the other interested parties when the Plan is being drawn up. In this respect, the Fourth Plan marked a notable change which augurs well for the future.[2]

The *annual budget* in France is prepared in two stages:

By July, the chief items of expenditure and the size of the budget deficit are known.[3] This stage of the work concerns mainly the Budget Directorate but the Treasury Directorate participates insofar as financing problems, and the size of the budget deficit, are discussed. The Service for Economic and Financial Studies provides a preliminary forecast of the economic situation in the following year as a guide to the conjunctural needs of the budget. The General

[1] Described in Chapter XII.
[2] See Chapter XII.
[3] The budget year begins on January 1.

Planning Commissariat is consulted about the main investment categories. Consequently, by the summer, the key decisions as to the shape and intentions of the next budget have been taken. The detailed preparation follows and lasts until about November, when the Government's proposals are submitted to Parliament. We return to these questions in Chapter XII.

The *Treasury Directorate* has a less detailed rôle to play in drafting either the Plan or the annual budgets than the Budget Directorate. Nevertheless, its influence in implementing the Plan is considerable. It intervenes in the field of investment in an original way through the working of the Economic and Social Development Fund for which it provides the Secretariat. It should be recalled that not all investment funds are included in the general budget. Part of them are found in annexed budgets or in special Treasury accounts. The ESDF is by far the most important of the latter, and the amount of its annual budget allocation is included in the Finance Act each year. The uses of the ESDF credits are various but the major slice is for loans to the nationalized industries, the rest being used to make loans directly, or indirectly, to local units of Government, other semi-public bodies and private firms. As the nationalized industries have to obtain a favourable decision from the Council of the ESDF before final approval by the Minister of Finance, it has become established practice for the ESDF to examine each year the whole investment programme of these industries. We return to this procedure in a later chapter as well as to the other activities of the ESDF which have an important rôle in relation to the Plan.[1] Meanwhile we shall describe briefly the history and structure of the ESDF.

The first Fund of this kind was set up in 1948 under the name of the Modernization and Equipment Fund (MEF), a name it was to retain until its reorganization in 1955. Its main source of credits in the early years was the counterpart of American aid, although Treasury grants, receipts of interest, and repayment of loans became progressively more important. The beneficiaries of loans from the Fund were fixed at the same time. They were most of the nationalized industries,[2] local authorities and firms in the private sector undertaking investments in conformity with the Plan. The last category was obviously, theoretically, unlimited, although in practice few sectors benefited from really substantial credits. The 1948 law further specified that the loans approved by the Fund would be granted in

[1] See Chapters XII and XIV.

[2] Electricité de France, Gaz de France, Charbonnages de France, SNCF (French Railways), Air France; thus the Renault firm was excluded, for example.

two ways, either by the MEF itself directly, or by specialized credit institutions (Crédit Foncier, Crédit National, Caisse des Dépôts et Consignations, Caisse Nationale de Crédit Agricole) and this is still the case today.

The direction of the Fund was entrusted to a Committee called the Investment Commission, under the chairmanship of the Minister of Finance. The Commissaire General was also a member from the beginning. Although, strictly speaking, the Fund was called upon to intervene only when its approval was required for the use of its own resources, or those of the specialized credit institutions to which it could refer prospective borrowers, in practice it was consulted on all aspects of the investment policy laid down in the Plan as the need for financing arose.

Between 1950 and 1955, five other investment Funds were created, either outside or in the framework of the MEF. The most important were the National Territorial Investment Fund (Fonds National d'Aménagement du Territoire) in 1950, the National Productivity Fund in 1953, the Fund for Conversion, Decentralization and Re-employment of Labour in 1954. Then, in 1953, the MEF itself was changed to the Fund for Construction, Rural Equipment and Economic Expansion. The main reform, however, which gave the Fund the form it still retains, came in 1955.

In that year a Decree was published which grouped all the existing Funds in one to be called the Economic and Social Development Fund. Its powers were to extend to all investments comprised in the National Plan and in the regional plans. The ESDF is controlled by a board of directors whose chairman is the Minister of Finance and which includes the Commissaire General.[1] The Secretariat of the ESDF is provided by the Treasury Directorate.

The most important part of the work of the ESDF is carried out in a number of specialized committees which have wide powers of decision. Any matter decided unanimously by a Committee is considered to have received the approval of the ESDF governing body.

[1] Other members are: Vice-Chairman: the Secretary of State for Economic Affairs. Members: the Financial Secretary of State, the Minister of Industry and Commerce, the Minister of Agriculture, the Minister of Public Works, the Minister of Transport and Tourism, the Minister of Labour and Social Security, the Governor of the Bank of France, the Governor of the Crédit Foncier, the President Director General of the Crédit National, the Director General of the Caisse des Dépôts et Consignations, the Director of the Budget, the Director of the Treasury, the Director-General of the Caisse Nationale de Crédit Agricole, and several other senior civil servants. Other Ministers attend meetings when they are directly concerned by the question being discussed.

For historical reasons, which it is not necessary to go into here, there are twelve specialized committees but only Nos 1, 2, 3, 4, 5, 6, 8, 12 still operate, and among them No. 3 is dormant for the moment. These committees are by no means of equal importance.

An influential committee is No. 1, which has also created two sub-groups, 1a and 1b. Its chairman is the Commissaire General and its functions extend to all actions in favour of investments of an industrial or commercial character, regional development, productivity and scientific research. Committee No. 1 acts as a court of appeal to its two sub-groups and as a source for establishing the jurisprudence for their activities. Group 1a looks after investments in industry, commerce, tourism and scientific and technical research. It is headed by the President Director General of the Crédit National. Group 1b is responsible for regional development, decentralization, reconversion and productivity. Its chairman is the Director General of the Caisse des Dépôts et Consignations.[1] The General Planning Commissariat is represented on both committees.

Committee No. 2 deals with the financing of local authority investments and is chaired by a Counsellor of State. Here again two working groups, 2a and 2b, have been set up, the first for urban development projects, including housing schemes in the Paris area, the second for the same activities in the provinces.

Committee No. 4 is responsible for the energy sector, which means the nationalized industries and the oil industry.

Committee No. 5 approves the granting of the State guarantee to issue bonds by overseas areas (départements, territories and independent territories). It acts as a branch of the Treasury.

Committee No. 6 has a general mandate for agriculture matters. It is chaired by the Commissaire General.

Committee No. 8 is the transport committee (railways, canals, shipping and airways). Its rôle is similar to that of Committee No. 4 for the energy sector.

Committee No. 12 studies questions of finance for the cinema industry.

The framework for the functioning of the Fund was laid down by Decree in 1960. This Decree set up a special Treasury account called 'Loans by the Economic and Social Development Fund'. Article 1 of the Decree states that the account 'registers the payment of loans granted to establishments, enterprises or collectivities undertaking equipment projects designed, either to achieve objectives set out in the Modernization and Equipment Plans, or to inaugurate specific policies, notably as regards productivity, regional develop-

[1] Cf. page 83.

ment, conversion and decentralization'. Article 2 adds that decisions to allocate funds—either directly by the Treasury or by specialized agencies—are made by order of the Minister of Finance, taking account of the division of loans proposed by the managing board of the ESDF. The Minister of Finance also determines the terms on which loans are made. Besides its credit-granting activities, the ESDF gives its opinion as to authorizing various guarantees. The distribution of the ESDF's loans in recent years is shown in the following table:

LOANS BY THE ECONOMIC AND SOCIAL DEVELOPMENT FUND
(million NF)

	1960	*1961*	*1962*
I. *Public Sector*			
Coal	150	150	65
Electricity	1,680	1,650	1,400
Compagnie Nationale du Rhône	130	110	145
Atomic Energy	170	180	170
Gas	180	—	190
Railways	—	150	—
Air France	150	60	190
Paris Airport	50	—	—
Total	2,510	2,300	2,160
II. *Private Sector*			
Agriculture	160	180	205
Navigation	88	110	139
Tourism	38	75	109
Industry	222	285	247
Overseas	125	137	183
Miscellaneous	12	3	8
Total	644	790	890
III. GRAND TOTAL (I+II)	3,154	3,090	3,050

Source: Annual Report of ESDF, 1961, p. 5.

II. THE PUBLIC SECTOR IN ENERGY, INDUSTRY AND TRANSPORT

It is not easy to determine the precise extent of the enterprises owned wholly, or partly, by the State. A recent study suggests that the largest enterprises in this sector account for 35 per cent of gross fixed capital investment by firms, half of it in the energy sector and 30 per cent in transport and communications.[1] However, there are a large number of enterprises where the State is only a minority shareholder. The annual Finance Act contains a list of 496 enterprises of an industrial and commercial character where the State holds 30 per cent or more of the capital, but there are many others where the share is below that figure. Many minority shareholdings have been created by the participation of the nationalized industries in private firms. Up to now the State has not used this situation in order to facilitate the achievement of the four-year Plans although it has often been suggested that it should do so.[2]

Control over the nationalized sector is exercised in the first instance by the various technical ministries, especially the Ministry of Industry and Commerce and the Ministry of Transport.

1 *Nationalization*

There were examples of nationalization in France before the war, notably the railways, but the big wave came after the Liberation.

The motives behind the movement were various. From the point of view of post-war reconstruction, the large amounts of capital required were not easy to reconcile with the existing structure of basic sectors such as coal, electricity and gas where the heritage of low levels of capital renewal and of technical innovation made it difficult to apply a dynamic policy of modernization. At the political level, there was a strong current of opinion in favour of nationalizing the 'key sectors' of the economy. The first post-Liberation Government of General de Gaulle was the most left-wing of all French Governments and included several Communist ministers. On the other hand, the National Council of the Resistance had drawn up, in 1944, a programme which included a policy of nationalization. All the political parties left of centre, that is the Communists, Socialists and the new Catholic party known as the Mouvement Républicain Populaire, were favourable to such a policy.

The main laws were not passed until after the vote of the Constitution of the Fourth Republic in 1946 and, although the Constitution contained the principle of nationalization, by then the political scene was already changing. It is highly probable that, if the nationalization legislation had been voted earlier, it would have been more extensive than it turned out to be. It was nevertheless considerable. We shall look at three sectors: energy, transport, in-

[1] P. Bauchet: *Propriété Publique et Planification*, Editions Cujas, 1962, p. 31.
[2] Cf. Chapter XVIII, p. 349.

dustry, and shall reserve the banks and insurance companies for a later section.

(a) *The Energy Sector*. Nationalization here concerned coal, electricity and gas. In the oil industry also the share of the public sector's participations is important.

The situation in the coalfields after the war was not so much that they had suffered material damage, but that their equipment was worn out and obsolete. The operation of price control had led already to large subsidies being paid to the mines to keep prices down and, as it was clear that they would not be able to find the big sums required to finance the needed investments, the case for nationalization was considerably reinforced. This took place in two stages—on a provisional basis by an ordinance issued in December 1944 and definitively by the law voted in 1946. In 1944, the most important coalfield—the Nord and Pas de Calais—was nationalized, and seven working groups were created out of the previous twenty individual concessions. In 1946, all the coalfields in France were finally nationalized, and a number of regional public enterprises, the Houillères de Bassin, were set up under the central authority of the Charbonnages de France. The tripartite character of the boards of these regional areas—Government, workers, consumers—has been maintained in principle since then but, in practice, the authority of the Directors General and the Government nominees has become predominant in the coal industry as in the other nationalized industries.

The nationalization of electricity and gas was also voted in 1946. The production of electricity had already become subject to State control over the years, but the multiple companies in existence were still largely owned by some ten financial groups responsible for over 90 per cent of production. For years, these companies had been criticized for their short-sighted policy of restricting investments to thermal power stations, to the neglect of hydraulic power, and, in view of the very large electricity needs of the post-war reconstruction programme, public financial aid appeared inevitable. In the political climate of the time, this was unthinkable without a transfer to public ownership. The nationalization of gas was considered as a necessary complement to that of electricity which was the chief object of debate. Two central bodies—Electricité de France and Gaz de France—were set up to control these industries.

The oil industry remained in private hands, however. In the immediate post-war period there was practically no production in Metropolitan France and the major distribution networks were owned by the big international oil companies. But the State held a 35 per cent share in the Compagnie Française des Pétroles, which at that time was mainly concerned with the Middle East. An initiative which turned out to have far-reaching consequences was taken in 1945 when a public body called the Bureau de la Recherche de Pétrole (BRP) was created with public funds to organize the search for oil. Subsequently, the Régie Autonome des Pétroles, and its subsidiary the CREPS, were established to undertake prospecting also. The success of these efforts, along with those of the older companies, either French or foreign, in finding oil and natural gas in Metropolitan France and in the Sahara is well known. It has completely transformed the energy balance in France over the last few years.

With the discovery of these deposits, it became necessary to organize the refining and distribution of their output—a task for which the prospecting groups were not equipped. Under the influence of the Minister of Industry at the time (M. Jeanneney), a body called the Union Générale des Pétroles was formed in 1960. Its capital was divided into three equal parts among the Groupement des Exploitants Pétroliers (formed by the subsidiaries set up by the Bureau de Recherche du Pétrole), the Régie Autonome des Pétroles and the REPAL (an association between the BRP, the Government General in Algeria and various finance companies specializing in oil prospecting). The Union Générale des Pétroles is a refining company in which the State has a majority interest.

It should be noted that there is also an Atomic Energy Commissariat but its activities have not yet reached a commercial scale.

(b) *Transport*. The railways were nationalized in 1936. Since 1945, further nationalization measures have taken place in maritime and air transport. The term 'nationalization' is perhaps too strong, though, to be applied to the case of the two shipping companies (the Compagnie des Messageries Maritimes and the Compagnie Générale Transatlantique). The State possesses only a majority of their share capital, but it appoints both the Chairman and Directors General. As regards air transport, practically the entire share capital of the three existing companies—Air France, Air Bleu and Air-France Transatlantique—was transferred to the State by ordinance in 1945. In 1948, the three companies were merged into one called Air France, but there remained two private air companies, the UAT and the TAI.

It is worthy of notice that, apart from public transport in large towns—notably Paris—there has been no attempt to nationalize road transport in France.

(c) *Industrial Nationalization.* The examples of nationalization in this sector are not numerous, and can usually be explained by special circumstances rather than by the application of a doctrine of public ownership. Two sectors where there have been instances of public ownership are aircraft and motor-cars. The aircraft industry came under public ownership in 1936, when the Société Nationale de Constructions Aéronautiques was set up. In 1945, the manufacturers of aircraft engines, Gnôme et Rhône, were nationalized as a result of collaboration with the enemy and the Société Nationale d'Etudes et de Construction de Moteurs d'Avions (SNECMA) was created with the State as sole shareholder and major client. The most notable example of a nationalization measure decided as a reprisal for acts of collaboration was the taking-over of the Renault automobile firm. It remains subject to private law and follows broadly the same methods of management as its private competitors.

2 *The Tutelary Ministries*

There are two Ministries which exercise wide powers of control over the nationalized sector of the economy—the Ministry of Industry and the Ministry of Public Works and Transport.

(a) *The Ministry of Industry.* The task of the Ministry of Industry can be considered from two points of view—its technical mission and its relations with the Ministry of Finance and the General Planning Commissariat.

Various technical directorates carry out the work of the Ministry *vis-à-vis* the public and private industrial sectors. For the public sector, there are two directorates: mining, and electricity and gas. A number of other specialized directorates are responsible for the private sectors of industry (liquid fuels, steel, chemicals, mechanical and electrical industries, miscellaneous and textiles). There is also a Directorate for Industrial Expansion whose work is of a more general character.

The mandate of the technical directorates for the nationalized industries is very comprehensive. For example, in the case of coal, it comprises all questions of an economic and social nature relating to production and trade, both home and foreign, as well as the surveillance of the technical aspects of production, including safety measures. The mandate of the Gas and Electricity Directorate is similar. This implies that price changes have to be approved by the Minister, and wage and salary questions are dealt with in the way already described. The Minister of Industry is not alone in taking such decisions, as prices, wages and salaries interest the Ministry of

Finance as well, and are indeed usually questions of high policy, decided at Cabinet level.

The rôle of the Ministry of Industry as regards investment policy in the public enterprises can best be seen when it collaborates with the General Planning Commissariat and the Ministry of Finance. The resources of the technical directorates are used to a considerable extent when the first projections for the four-year Plan and beyond are being made. The SEEF called upon these directorates not only through 1960 and 1961, when the Plan was being drafted in detail, but also in 1959 when the first alternative models were built up. The Ministry of Industry also intervenes when the annual investment plans are drawn up for each nationalized industry, notably through the work done in Committee No. 4 of the Economic and Social Development Fund. The responsibilities of the Ministry of Industry are particularly far-reaching as to the investment programme of Electricité de France. Besides the detailed scrutiny of investment projects in liaison with Committee No. 4 of the ESDF, the Minister of Industry has to notify Electricité de France of his agreement with its general operating proposals as well as with its investment budget before the approval of the Minister of Finance is given. As Electricité de France benefits from a programme law voted by Parliament for its investment programme, the Ministry of Industry also prepares the necessary draft legislation for this law.

The Ministry's staff are therefore very active at several stages in drafting and applying the Plan. Collaboration is all the more close as a few senior civil servants from the Ministry occupy key posts in the committees dealing with planning. For example, the Director of Gas and Electricity is also the Chairman of Committee No. 4 of the Economic and Social Development Fund and, at the same time, the Chairman of the Vertical Planning Commission for Energy set up under the Fourth Plan. The two Directors of Mines and Liquid Fuels were the two Vice-Chairmen of the Energy Commission. These personal links exist also in the non-nationalized sector. The Chairmen of the three Vertical Planning Commissions for Steel, Chemicals and Transformation Industries are businessmen, but the Vice-Chairman of the Chemicals Commission is the Director of Chemicals and two of the Commission's rapporteurs come from his directorate. A member of the Steel Directorate is Vice-Chairman of the Vertical Planning Commission for Steel and the two Vice-Chairmen of the Commission for Transformation Industries are the Directors of Mechanical and Electrical Industries and of Miscellaneous Industries and Textiles respectively. The General Rapporteur of this Commission and his two assistant rapporteurs are also civil servants from the Ministry of Industry. Finally, the rapporteur of the Vertical Planning Commission for Liquid Fuels is an engineer from the Liquid Fuels Directorate.

(b) *Ministry of Public Works and Transport*. This Ministry does a great deal of direct investment in addition to exercising control over the investment expenditures of the nationalized transport industries.

In the public works sector, two Directorates are particularly important: Roads, and Ports and Inland Waterways. The Directorate of Roads implements the road-building programmes, manages the Road Fund and is responsible for bridges. The activities of the Directorate for Ports and Inland Waterways are self-explanatory. Thus this Ministry, unlike the Ministry of Industry, is a big spending administration on its own account, whose programmes have to be discussed in the Planning Commissions as regards the four-year Plans, and each year by the Ministry of Finance and the General Planning Commissariat when the annual State budget is being prepared.

The tutelary powers of the Ministry are quite extensive. They include the French railways, the Paris transport system, Air France and the Paris Airport. The last two bodies are not attached directly to the Ministry but come under the General Secretariat for Civil Aviation.[1] The rôle of the Ministry *vis-à-vis* these four nationalized bodies resembles that exercised by the Ministry of Industry both as concerns general surveillance, participation in the drafting of the four-year Plan and the fixing of annual investment programmes. The corresponding Committtee of the Economic and Social Development Fund is No. 8.

For a long period after the war, the Ministry's links with the planning mechanism, and its own work in relation to the enterprises for which it was responsible, suffered from a lack of unified control of general economic problems. This situation was corrected after 1958 by the creation of a special service for Economic and International Affairs attached directly to the office of the Minister and headed by an Inspecteur des Finances. Apart from the International Section, this Service comprises three divisions. A Programme and Co-ordination Division co-ordinates the investment programmes of the public departments and nationalized enterprises. A Studies Division does research on long-term transport problems as well as on specific projects. It is now studying the building of a second airport in the north Paris region and the proposal for a Channel tunnel or

[1] There is also a General Secretariat for the Merchant Navy.

bridge. The third division is concerned with the collection and publication of statistics.

As in the case of the Ministry of Industry, relations with the Plan are achieved not only through administrative arrangements but also as a consequence of the rôle played by certain senior officials of the Ministry. One of these is at the same time Chairman of the Vertical Planning Commission for Transport, head of the 'Transports' section of the General Planning Commissariat and Chairman of Committee No. 8 of the ESDF. One of the vice-chairmen of the Planning Commission for Transport is the Inspecteur des Finances who heads the Service for Economic and International Affairs in the Ministry of Public Works and Transport. The other vice-chairmen of the Planning Commission for Transport are the Secretary-General for Civil Aviation, the Director-General for Railways at the Ministry of Transport, and the Director for Sea Ports and Inland Waterways. One of the rapporteurs of the Commission is the head of the Studies Division in the Service for Economic and International Affairs.

III. THE SOCIAL SECTOR

This is a very wide field which includes the activities of several government departments: the Ministries of Labour and Social Security, Public Health and Population, Construction, Education, War Veterans. Clearly a choice is necessary to avoid fastidious details. In line with the rest of this chapter, we shall limit ourselves to those departments having particularly close relations with the Plan, which in turn means that we shall be concerned with spending administrations having the responsibility for large investment programmes.

There are three of these: Construction, Education, Public Health and Population, each having a special importance for the Plan in respect of housing, school building and university building, health and social establishments.

1 *Housing*

The place of the State in the house-building programme is a capital one. During the post-war reconstruction period, when a large volume of war-damaged housing had to be replaced, the Government had to intervene more and more in this field and its influence has persisted since then. But the action of the State has remained indirect and limited to supplying financial assistance to other administrations or to private individuals.

Three procedures are used by the Central Government.[1] For some types of building the State contributes funds directly. Elsewhere, incentives are offered to private investors. A category of tenants receive financial assistance from public funds.

The Treasury's direct participation profits the organisms known by their initials as HLM (Habitations à Loyer Modéré) which operate as public offices usually at the level of the département. There are some 14,000 of them at present. The annual credits are included in the budget and are released in the form of long-term loans at low interest rates of 1 to 2 per cent. The HLM offices are responsible for executing the building programmes. Part of the accommodation is rented and the rest sold to private owners. In principle, HLM's are reserved for families with limited means but, over the years, this has suffered a growing number of exceptions.

The second method of intervention is less direct still. The State uses the services of the Crédit Foncier[2] and its subsidiary, the Sous-Comptoir des Entrepreneurs, in the framework of a policy for encouraging private building, called 'aide à la pierre'.[3] The Crédit Foncier grants 'special loans' for the pre-financing of an economy-type of family flat called 'logécos' from the full title which is 'logements économiques et familiaux'. Some loans outside of this special procedure are also made. No repayment is called for during the first five years and, in practice, after that the Treasury assumes part of the 'consolidation' of the loans with the Crédit Foncier through a budget grant.

When a special loan is made, its recipient automatically becomes eligible for premia to reduce the interest cost of the building and which are paid during twenty years. The amount of these is calculated in relation to the size of the housing unit and is at present 10 new francs per square metre for logécos and 6 new francs for other types. Whereas all loans give the right to an interest premium, the latter can be granted without a loan. The recent change in this system whereby interest payments themselves are reduced directly does not alter the end result of the previous premia arrangements.

The data in the table on page 77 give an idea of the relative importance of these two types of State aid.

Taking HLM building and war-damage reconstruction together, the share of total house-building in 1960 financed directly by the

[1] On all these points, the reader who wishes to have fuller details can consult the chapter on housing by M. Morisot in *Succès et faiblesses de l'Effort Social français*, Colin, 1961.
[2] Described in Section 4 of this chapter.
[3] See Chapter XI for the Plan's suggestion for a reassessment of this policy.

HOUSES COMPLETED IN 1960

Type	*Number (in thousands)*
War damage reconstruction	12.7
HLM total:	95.8
of which: 77 rented, 19 sold	
Units qualifying for premia	176.7
of which: 89 logements économiques et familiaux	
Units without premia	31.3
Grand total	316.5

Source: Bulletin Statistique du Ministère de la Construction, May 1961, quoted by M. Morisot, *op. cit.*, p. 129.

Treasury is over one-third. Only 10 per cent of houses built did not benefit from State assistance in one form or another.

The attractive level of State aid to prospective owner-occupiers has, no doubt, stimulated demand for this type of assistance whereas the number of houses for renting is comparatively small. But there are signs that this situation is changing and the Ministry of Construction is taking steps to meet the increased demand for rented accommodation.

The third type of State aid was instituted in 1948 and is designed to reduce the effective cost of rent for families with limited means and the aged, by direct allocations from public funds. Its scope has been extended greatly by the system of the 'housing indemnity' paid at present to 600,000 families, whether tenants or house owners, who are buying their houses through one of the State schemes.

2 *Education*

A few words on the structure of the French educational system, and on the status of teachers, are called for before turning to the methods for implementing investment programmes.

Education is in France more uniform than in Great Britain. School programmes are fixed by the Ministry of Education for all State schools and, although the private schools—which can qualify for a subsidy from public funds since 1951—are not obliged to follow suit, they usually do so as their pupils sit for State examinations.

The various types of teaching establishment, whether State-owned or private, fall into three traditional categories—primary, secondary, higher. The primary stage covers infant and elementary classes, usually to the age of eleven. Secondary education has become more diversified and, alongside the traditional lycée, a number of technical colleges have been created. Besides, at all three levels, provision of sporting and holiday facilities now comes under a High Commissioner for Youth and Sports, whose department is attached to the Ministry of Education.

All the staff of State-owned schools and establishments for higher education are employed by the Ministry of Education directly and not by the local authorities. Questions of salaries and conditions of work are therefore settled directly between the teachers' unions and the central government departments.

Given this centralized system, it is not surprising to find that investment programmes as well are implemented from the centre, that is from Paris, by a special Direction of the Ministry of Education set up in 1956, called the Direction for School, University and Sporting Equipment. But these arrangements have been subject to growing criticism as part of the lag incurred in recent years between the receipt of budget allocations and their expenditure is attributed to them. Moves to decentralize the procedures for carrying out investment programmes have been decided recently.

Before 1962 already, a part of primary and secondary school-building was decentralized but large projects, and higher education building, were dealt with in Paris. As an effect of the suggestions put forward by the Planning Commission for Education in 1962, all preparatory study and implementation of primary school building up to 1 million New Francs have been turned over to the local authorities. The administrative and technical preparation for secondary education projects costing less than 2½ million New Francs have also been decentralized.

3 *Public Health and Social Policy*

A single Ministry, for Public Health and Population, is responsible for both these matters. Rather paradoxically and contrary to experience in education, the consensus of opinion in the Planning Commission on Public Health was that investment programmes were lagging because there was too much decentralization and local autonomy.

Most hospitals are publicly owned but, due to their history, they are nearly all managed by the local authorities, generally the communes. The Ministry has powers of supervision and awards subsidies, of up to 40 per cent for investment programmes, but does not intervene directly in their execution. The management of other social establishments—children's homes, rest homes and so on—is largely private and the only weapon at the disposal of the Ministry is the encouragement offered by subsidy policy.

Some reforms have been introduced to overcome the defects of this situation, for example in sanitary matters with the creation of a central technical service to assist local authorities in drawing up and implementing building programmes. But the state of things is still not one which gives entire satisfaction, particularly as the intention of the Government is to increase credits for these purposes very considerably during the Fourth Plan.

IV. THE BANKING SECTOR

We shall not set out to describe French banking and credit structure in this section but only to indicate which credit institutions in the public sector play, or could be called upon to play, a rôle in implementing the Plan.[1] We shall consider the Bank of France and the National Credit Council, which are placed at the summit of the banking and credit hierarchy, the deposit banks and the very important public or semi-public specialized credit institutions.

1 *The Bank of France and the National Credit Council*

The post-war wave of nationalization did not stop at the industrial and transport sectors but included the Bank of France and four of the biggest deposit banks.[2] The Act of Parliament nationalizing the banks was among the first to be passed—December 1945—and it included as well an important organizational reform of the banking system.

The nationalization of the Bank of France had begun in fact before the war. In 1936, the Conseil de Régence, the governing body of the Bank, where private banking interests predominated, was replaced by a Conseil Général with a wider representation and some State nominees. The Bank was still privately owned until 1945, when its share capital passed into the hands of the State and the private shareholders' representatives disappeared from the Conseil Général. Today the Governor of the Bank and his deputy are appointed by the Government. There have been occasions since the war when the Governor has objected publicly to the Government's policy, notably when the Treasury was in need of special advances. In the last analysis, though, it is beyond dispute that the Bank of France is subservient to the Government.

The influence of the Governor of the Bank can be considerable nevertheless when policy is being decided. One of the channels through which this influence is exercised is the National Credit

[1] The reader who wishes to have more details can consult with profit J. G. S. Wilson: *French Banking and Credit Structure*, London, 1958.

[2] And a number of insurance companies.

Council. To appreciate the rôle of this body, it is necessary to recall the history of banking in France under the Vichy régime, and the passionate debates in the nationalization period on the question of who should be responsible for monetary policy. The general philosophy of Vichy was the controlled economy of a corporatist type and, in 1940, a whole series of professional bodies called Organization Committees were set up in all sectors, including banking, with the object of putting these ideas into practice. The 1945 Act kept certain of the organizational principles of this wartime legislation.

Hence a classification of all banking institutions into three categories—deposit banks, banques d'affaires, and long- and medium-term credit banks. The credit institutions had to opt for one or other of these groups; the major effect was that the banques d'affaires left the deposit banking business proper. The definition of deposit banks was the maximum length of time for which they could accept deposit accounts (two years), and restrictions were placed upon their participations in the share capital of other enterprises. The four nationalized deposit banks belong to this group. The banques d'affaires became specialized in taking-up participations in other firms and in granting credits to them. Their sources of funds are their own capital and deposit accounts with at least a two-year life. There are forty-one banks of this type, among which thirty-two only are public limited liability companies. Two of them dominate the others by the size of their capital—the Banque de Paris et des Pays Bas and the Banque de l'Indochine. The non-limited liability companies include such firms as Lazard Frères and Rothschild. It is certain that these banks, through the specialized activity they exercise in financing industry and trade and promoting new companies, help to reduce the obstacles met with by the small firm in obtaining capital.

The medium- and long-term credit institutions under the 1945 Act were bodies created, usually by the deposit banks, in order to grant medium-term credit which the deposit banks themselves could not undertake to do. But, since then, the growth of the specialized credit institutions in the public and semi-public sectors has lessened their importance.

In relation to this classification of the banks, a central body called the Banking Control Commission was formed in 1945 with powers of decision as regards the technical surveillance of the banks. Its chairman is the Governor of the Bank of France. More important was the National Credit Council instituted by the same Act. This Council was designed to bring together representatives of the economic life of the nation and to give them a voice in deciding monetary and credit policy. It has certain powers of a technical character and is the tribunal of appeal for the Banking Control Commission. It is essentially a consultative body, however. Its forty-three members include the Minister of Finance, who is ex-officio chairman, the Governor of the Bank of France (vice-chairman), eighteen representatives of industry, trade and agriculture (from both the employers' and workers' sides), seven delegates from the major economic ministries, seven from the public or semi-public credit institutions and nine members chosen for their personal competence. Besides, the Director of the Treasury attends meetings as does the Commissaire General. It is significant of the 1945 debates that nowhere is it said in the Act who the National Credit Council is to advise. Indeed, at the time, it was even suggested that it should be the President of the Republic. In fact, as was inevitable, the Minister of Finance's authority is predominant, although the position of the Governor of the Bank of France on both the Council and the Banking Control Commission gives him influence. He instructs the banks by letter of policy measures finally decided by the authorities. Also the Bank of France is in a strong position for the surveillance of the other banks because it manages the Service Central des Risques, set up in 1946 to centralize all information on credits granted by banks so as to avoid, in particular, bad debts due to multiple credit applications by private borrowers. This Service is informed of some 80 per cent of all credits granted. Of course, too, the Bank of France is the last resort for credit for the other banks through its re-discount facilities.

2 *Deposit Banking*

Deposit banking is less centralized in France than in the United Kingdom and there is an important network of regional banks. So the nationalization of the four largest deposit banks in 1945 left a large field open to the private deposit banks.[1] With two privately owned banks, the Crédit Industriel et Commercial and the Crédit Commercial de France, the four nationalized banks make up the group of six big nation-wide banks based on Paris. But together they represent only about half the total value of the balance sheet of all registered deposit banks in France. In addition, there are some twenty regional banks, of which the largest is the Crédit du Nord, and a large number of 'local banks' (over 200) which operate in a single town only. This group is continually subject to pressure to

[1] The four banks are: Crédit Lyonnais, Société Générale, Comptoir National d'Escompte, Banque Nationale pour le Commerce et l'Industrie.

join with larger units and the total number of banks in France is declining, although slowly.

All commentators agreed that the nationalization of the four deposit banks has not changed much as regards the way they conduct their activities. They actively compete with each other and with the other private banks. Indeed, the existence of these competitors is probably the chief reason why the nationalized banks have continued to act as they do. Moreover, the personnel of the banks remained practically unchanged after 1945. It follows that although the presence of the nationalized banks makes it easier on the whole for the authorities to apply monetary policy measures, they do not appear to be used very actively to achieve planned objectives. Of much greater importance in this respect are the specialized credit institutions.

3 *The Specialized Credit Institutions*

All these institutions existed before the war, and one at least since the beginning of the nineteenth century. But they have been adapted progressively in the post-war period to deal with the urgent need to find finance for investment. The institutions in question are diverse, some are banks and others not. But, as a common feature, they tend to specialize in one or a few lines of activity. It will be useful to consider the two banking institutions first.

These are the Crédit Agricole and the Crédit Populaire, both of which work on co-operative principles, the former in agriculture, the latter in industry. The Crédit Agricole spread to France from Germany and Italy in the second half of the nineteenth century. Two sectors in agricultural credit grew up—an official one which, besides the capital of its members and its deposits, served as a channel for the distribution of government credits, and a private credit sector which is in a minority today. The official sector is headed by the Caisse Nationale de Crédit Agricole controlled by the Minister of Agriculture. It distributes available funds (authorized by the ESDF as a rule) in the first instance to the regional caisses who, in turn, supply the needs of the local caisses. There are some 4,000 local caisses in the official agricultural credit movement and some 2,000 in the independent movement. The total of their sight deposits is about one-tenth of all sight deposits in the country.

Popular credit also began at the end of the nineteenth century and was designed to assist small industrial firms on a co-operative basis similar to agricultural credit. In 1917, an Act of Parliament foresaw two forms of co-operation: mutual guarantee societies which would group small industrialists so as to increase the available guarantee when making requests for credit, and 'popular banks' constituted on a co-operative basis and receiving State subsidies. The activities of the Popular Banks have increased considerably since the war. There are about sixty of them now with some 350 offices, and they hold about 5 per cent of total sight deposits. Since 1929, they have been subject to public control through the Chambre Syndicale des Banques Populaires, which receives advances from the State.

The other specialized credit institutions in the public sector are much less banks than the Agricultural and Popular Banks. We shall mention the five main ones, which are: the Caisse des Dépôts et Consignations, the Crédit National, the Caisse Nationale des Marchés de l'Etat, the Crédit Foncier de France, the Banque Française du Commerce Extérieur.

The Caisse des Dépôts et Consignations has been described as the biggest banque d'affaires in France, which is somewhat of a misnomer in view of the source of its funds and the multiple uses it makes of them, although there is some truth in the remark. The quantitative importance of the Caisse is, in any case, undeniable when it is realized that its total deposits are equal to those of all the sight deposits of the deposit banks combined. It is noteworthy also that the Director General is a member of the important Horizontal Planning Commission for the General Economy and Finance.[1] The origin of the Caisse goes back to 1816 when it was formed to act as a public depository for funds confided to the State such as unclaimed inheritances, funds in legal dispute and so on. Hence the name 'consignations'. The desire to give the Director General a large measure of independence entailed the creation of a board composed of members of Parliament, the Conseil d'Etat, Court of Audit, the Bank of France, Treasury and the Paris Chamber of Commerce. The Director General is appointed by the President of the Republic and can only be dismissed following a motivated request by the board.

Today the main resources of the Caisse come from the Savings Banks which re-deposit their funds with it, from the social security funds and various pension funds. The investments open to the Caisse differ with the type of its deposits, but it can, and does, invest in the whole range of financial instruments, from Treasury bills and medium- and long-term bonds of the State and the local authorities or specialized institutions, like the Crédit Foncier de France, to industrial debentures and shares. The Caisse has participated also in many common ventures with private capital. With the social security funds, it is authorized to build and rent houses, and has built a

[1] The present holder of this office, M. Bloch-Lainé, an Inspecteur des Finances, is well known as a writer on planning problems. See Chapter XVIII.

great deal since the war in the Paris region on its own account as well as lending for the construction of low-rent accommodation. The Caisse also lends to local authorities to finance all types of public works. The more liquid of its funds are used in part to assist the 'mobilization' of medium-term credit, either by direct re-discount or, more usually, by adding a signature making the paper re-discountable with the Bank of France. The mere enumeration of these activities is sufficient to show the influence the Caisse can exercise on the finance of investment.

The mission of the Crédit National is also of importance in relation to the Plan, but in a different way from the Caisse des Dépôts et Consignations. The origin of the Crédit National was the settlement of war damage after 1919. It still remains a public company, registered under private law, and its shares are quoted on the Paris Bourse but its Director General and two Directors are appointed by the Government. The Crédit National played a similar rôle after the Second World War as after the First as concerns war damage settlements. Another pre-war activity was to facilitate payment by the State for its debts to contractors by allowing them to draw bills upon it, but this was suspended in 1955. Also during the early post-war years, the Crédit National acted as the channel for distributing credits contracted abroad and Marshall Aid. A new, but permanent, post-war function is the distribution to private industry of a part of budget credits for investment. The Crédit National is used by the Economic and Social Development Fund for this purpose. A special activity has been to allot State aid to the film industry. But the Crédit National too makes long-term loans to the private sector out of its own resources, which it procures largely from making issues of debentures on the capital market.

The growth of medium-term credit which supplies over 10 per cent of total investment finance constitutes a stable feature of the banking system in France since the war. The rôle of the Crédit National is preponderant here, although the other semi-public institutions such as the Crédit Foncier, the Crédit Agricole and, especially, the Caisse des Dépôts et Consignations, also grant such credits. Briefly the mechanism is as follows. The borrower applies to his own bank which makes the credit available for a period up to five years, but, as this period is too long for ordinary deposit bank resources, the borrower signs three-month bills which are discounted by his bank and renewed automatically at each maturity. Two further procedures may thereupon be utilized. Firstly, such paper can be rediscounted with the Crédit National, whose agreement to this is usually sought beforehand by the deposit bank. Hence the system, referred to in Chapter XIV, according to which the Crédit National consults the General Planning Commissariat on applications for medium-term credit exceeding 1 million New Francs. Secondly, a safety-valve has, since 1944, been provided by the Bank of France which thereafter has been prepared to re-discount such paper on condition that it carries at least four signatures. This implies the interposition of another public credit institution—the Caisse des Dépôts et Consignations. The four signatures are then: the borrower, his banker, the Crédit National, the Caisse des Dépôts et Consignations. For housebuilding, the Crédit Foncier takes the place of the Crédit National, in agriculture the Crédit Agricole and in foreign trade the Banque Française du Commerce Extérieur.

Access by small and medium-sized firms to this medium-term credit mechanism is facilitated by the Caisse Nationale des Marchés de l'Etat, which gives its signature in cases where firms group together to grant each other a mutual guarantee. The Caisse is a purely public body of fairly recent date. Since 1936, it has acted as a means of prefinancing Government contracts by giving its name. After the war, it diversified its activities to include local units of Government and nationalized and private industry. A characteristic of the Caisse Nationale is that it never lends funds directly.

Founded in 1852, the Crédit Foncier was designed to support agriculture through mortgage loans and loans to rural local authorities, and only progressively moved over to urban property. Its present vocation is essentially the financing of housebuilding, which it does with the assistance of a subsidiary called the Sous-Comptoir des Entrepreneurs. But the bank remains in private hands although the control of the State is strict, and the Government appoints the Governor and the two Deputy-Governors. The growth of the post-war housebuilding programme made it necessary to use medium-term finance here also. The Sous-Comptoir des Entrepreneurs is authorized to grant loans up to 70 per cent of the total cost of construction for a limit of five years against first-class mortgages. The Crédit Foncier discounts this paper and can in turn re-discount it with the Bank of France. The funds of the Crédit Foncier come from its own capital, deposits, issues of debentures on the market, and budget credits.

We shall not enter here into the long discussions which have occurred since the war as to the possible inflationary effects of this system.

The Banque Française du Commerce Extérieur was set up in 1946 at the same time as the Compagnie Française d'Assurance pour le Commerce Extérieur which fulfils functions similar to those of the

Export Credits Guarantee Department in the United Kingdom. The Banque Française du Commerce Extérieur is a semi-public institution but its Director General is appointed by the Minister of Finance and the bank is subject to Government control. As its name implies, it intervenes in the finance of French foreign trade, either directly or by giving its signature to deposit bank paper in the same way as the other specialized credit institutions discussed in the previous paragraphs.

V. THE AGRICULTURAL SECTOR

The agricultural sector in France, so profoundly individualistic despite a *de facto* dependence on State aid and protection, is undergoing a transformation which we describe in a later chapter.[1] In this process, a great many long-established attitudes are being called into question.

Since the end of the war, the State has been led to define a policy for agriculture, either through the four-year Plans or in special legislation. The rôle of the Ministry of Agriculture in this respect has tended to be less than would have been expected until quite recently, with the consequence that the General Planning Commissariat has been more active than would otherwise have been the case. We do not consider here policy as regards agriculture, but only the structure of the Ministry of Agriculture in relation to the Plan.

Chronology is particularly important as, up to 1961 and the arrival of M. Pisani at the Ministry of Agriculture, the Ministry had few economic preoccupations and few links with the Plan. Since 1961 a new trend has begun, however.

Until November 1961, the Ministry had little interest in the economic problems of agriculture and, perhaps as an effect of this, its personnel showed a marked lack of new and younger elements. The Ministry of Agriculture was traditionally in the hands of the Radical Party in France. In 1945, the Socialist Party took over, but this did not bring any permanent change in the attitude of the Ministry to the economic problems of agriculture after the brief passage of the first Socialist Minister of Agriculture (M. Tanguy Prigent). Parallel with this situation, the influence of certain farming elements was preponderant. Until recently, only one member of the Ministry had passed through the National School of Administration—which recruits since 1946 for the administrative class of the civil service—and all the other administrators were over forty years of age.

[1] See Chapter XV.

At the same time, the administrative structure of the Ministry was cumbersome, and contained a large number of directorates each having little contact with the others. It must be noted, though, that there was an Economic Affairs Directorate—headed by an Inspecteur des Finances—with an office for Studies and Plans under the responsibility of the sole recruit from the National School of Administration. This office was charged with drafting an annual report on the situation in agriculture, with preparing general economic studies and with maintaining relations with the General Planning Commissariat.

This timid beginning of an interest in the economic problems of agriculture has been reinforced since 1961 and the present Minister has announced his intention of making his Ministry 'an instrument for planning' and 'for the renovation of life in the countryside'.

The internal structure of the Ministry has been simplified and the number of directorates reduced to five: studies and general questions; production and markets; teaching and professional and social affairs; rural engineers and water questions; rivers and forests.

The last four of these directorates can be called 'technical', and, if they are compared with the main lines of agricultural policy described in a later chapter, it will be seen that they have to deal with implementing special aspects of that policy.[1] The first directorate has a 'horizontal' function to prepare the long-term policy for agriculture and to establish liaisons with the others. It comprises a study and planning service responsible, in particular, for relations with the General Planning Commissariat and for long-term agricultural problems, the study of which is an innovation in the Ministry.

These changes will probably reduce the work for the General Planning Commissariat, which had to develop its own agricultural activities more than would have been the case if the Ministry of Agriculture had been in a position to assume the tasks performed by other Ministries—notably the Ministry of Industry—for the sectors for which they are responsible. There is an encouraging sign of the wind of change that is now blowing through the Ministry of Agriculture; in 1962, three recruits to the administrative class from the National School of Administration chose to enter the Ministry of Agriculture in preference to the other Ministries.

[1] 'L'espace, le produit, l'homme' as the Minister has defined them.

CHAPTER IV

THE REGIONAL FRAMEWORK

A characteristic which is common to all national planning efforts at the present time, whether in developed countries or in undeveloped ones, is the addition of regional and urban planning considerations to the overall Plan, thus giving the latter a 'third dimension' it lacked previously.

The reasons why questions of regional and urban planning have come to occupy the important rôle they do are numerous and need only be mentioned here in a summary fashion. The rise and decline of regions is a basic fact of economic history as far back as we can trace records of human activity, but the appearance of a sense of national solidarity on the economic and social level and the idea that the State is responsible for the fate of all the citizens and, consequently, of all the regions is more recent. Besides, the natural tendency for political representatives is to press the interests of their electors upon the central Government. More than this, the concept of welfare, and of the distinction between private and social costs, when once admitted to economics, gives an intellectual respectability to regional and urban development which an intense liberalism denied for a long period. It is therefore possible to discuss problems of this kind in terms of costs, including social costs, and outputs, including reductions of social tensions, without being accused of sentimentalism.

The facts of regional imbalance in France are well known. Modern industrial development, powerfully aided by administrative and social factors, has led to an ever greater concentration of population and activity in certain areas. The most spectacular manifestation of this is the growth of the Paris region which, with over 8 million inhabitants, now groups more than one-sixth of the total population. In the present century, Paris has been the centre of modern industries—mechanical, electrical, chemical—whilst provincial centres based on older traditional industries—textiles and leather in particular—went into decline. Thus there is a marked difference in development and income levels between the North and North-East of France—all the territory to the north of a line running from Belfort to the Mont St Michel—and the West and South. Also, the regular fall in the agricultural population, and the general internal migratory trend towards the towns means that some of these are growing very fast indeed, which gives rise to considerable problems of urban development outside Paris, whilst many rural areas are losing their populations.

The French situation is different from the British. In France, the main regional problem is after all one of agricultural regions with either a low population density due to past and present emigration—as is the case with much of the South-West or Centre—or a high population density, despite emigration, and consequent unemployment—as in Brittany. In both instances the problem is one of creating new non-agricultural activities in areas where industry has never had much importance—except occasionally on a handicraft basis. The British problem has been dominated since the war by the declining traditional industries dragging whole regions in their wake.

The turning point in the history of regional development in France is the application of the Fourth Plan. This Plan has among its chief objectives the setting up of a coherent regional policy within the scope of the national Plan. Examination of the means by which this policy is being put into practice belongs to a later chapter of this book (Chapter XIII) but three aspects of the question find a place here. Firstly, regionalism has not appeared solely with the Fourth Plan, but has built upon the numerous, if dispersed, efforts of the post-war period and the intentions of the Fourth Plan can only be understood in the light of their history. Secondly, the Fourth Plan has created a coherent scheme for a policy of regional development which, whilst it does not represent a *tabula rasa*, does change fundamentally the institutional structures which existed until now. Thirdly, urban development is a necessary complement to regional development and neither can be considered in a comprehensive way separately from the other.

I. REGIONAL PLANNING BEFORE THE FOURTH PLAN

Although the first steps inspired by similar preoccupations to those which have led to a full-blown regional development policy today can be found even before the Second World War, the first notable efforts which secured Government support appeared with the Second Plan in the early 1950s. The Third Plan carried this process further. Our history of the subject during those years deals with the definition of a geographical framework, the creation of institutions for implementing a policy of regional development and the drafting of regional plans.

1 *The Geographical Framework*

The traditional basis of French local government was laid down early in the nineteenth century by the establishment of ninety départements. The strong centralizing flavour of French local administration is much older than that, and was perpetuated by the creation of the system of the préfet who is the senior official in the département and the direct representative of the central Government. The powers of supervision and of intervention of the préfet in the life of the département and its component parts—the communes—are great.[1] For that reason, among others, local government in France is only a shadow of what it is in Anglo-Saxon countries, or many other countries of Western Europe, despite the centralizing tendencies which have sapped the bases of local autonomy everywhere during the present century. This aspect of local government in France is of importance now that official policy is resolutely fixed on the objective of regional development. For it is clear that this, whilst it depends upon the assistance of the central Government, is not something that can be implanted in the region from outside but must, on the contrary, grow from local roots. We shall have to return to this problem in Part Four of this book when we discuss the problem of democracy and planning. For the moment, it must suffice to note that two converging currents of opinion can be discerned in thinking on the subject of regional planning; one is the realization that the traditional system of local administration does not favour the growth of local initiative, which is an indispensable prerequisite for a successful regional policy, and the other is the wider problem envisaged by some influential groups of seizing the opportunity of regional planning to transform the conditions of political democracy itself.

As concerns the administrative framework of French local government, the traditional basis of the département has been shown progressively to be inadequate and has led gradually to the concept of the region. This is not the concept of the old regions of the Middle Ages of the great French provinces although, insofar as these did correspond to geographical entities—echoes of them can be found in the current use of the names of the old provinces. Thus regional courts of appeal, regional university academies and regional military structures have been organized. During the war, the Vichy régime created the first regional préfets, whose mission survived after the war, firstly with the emergency system of the Commissaires de la République created in 1944, followed, in 1948, by the establishment

[1] The financial aspects of local government in France are noted in Chapter XII.

of a corps of super-préfets known as the inspecteurs généraux de l'Administration en mission extraordinaire (IGAME) with responsibilities over areas wider than the département.

These isolated examples of a widening of the traditional structure of local government left practically intact the organization of the département and, the policy of regional development having finally gained respectability, it soon became necessary to define a new geographical framework for it, and by a Decree in 1956, the creation of twenty-one 'programme regions' was decided.

Each of these regions is larger than a département; the number of départements they contain varies from two to eight and their average population is 1½ million—with the exception of the Paris region which has over 8 million. 'In drawing the limits of these regions their geography, history and demographic and employment trends have been taken into consideration. They follow the external limits of the départements they cover and take account, as far as possible, of the extent of the large agricultural tracts, the industrial and commercial networks and, in particular, the zones of influence of the large towns.'[1] (See map on page 92.)

The fact that the existing limits of the départements have been respected at the frontier of each programme region has made it possible to begin to bring the administrative structures of the départements into harmony with the new regions. This was the task outlined in the 1960 Decree, which intends to eliminate any overlapping between the regions and other administrative areas. A beginning has been made for the meteorological services, the fiscal services, defence areas, the university academies among others.

2 *Regional Planning Organization*

The first to see the light of day were isolated examples, such as the regional committees created in Rheims in 1943 and the Moselle in 1947, followed in 1950-51 by further committees for regional development inspired by the Minister of Construction. Most of these committees were created afterwards, however, under the name of Committees for Economic Expansion, foreshadowed in various decrees in 1954, 1955 and 1956. The area of the committees was sometimes the département, sometimes a group of départements having strong local affinities. Essentially local study and advisory groups, they comprised representatives of the communes and other local administrations as well as of private industry, commerce or agriculture.

In order to bring these bodies into line with the programme

[1] M. Viot, *La planification régionale—Commissariat Général du Plan.*

REGIONAL DEVELOPMENT AREAS

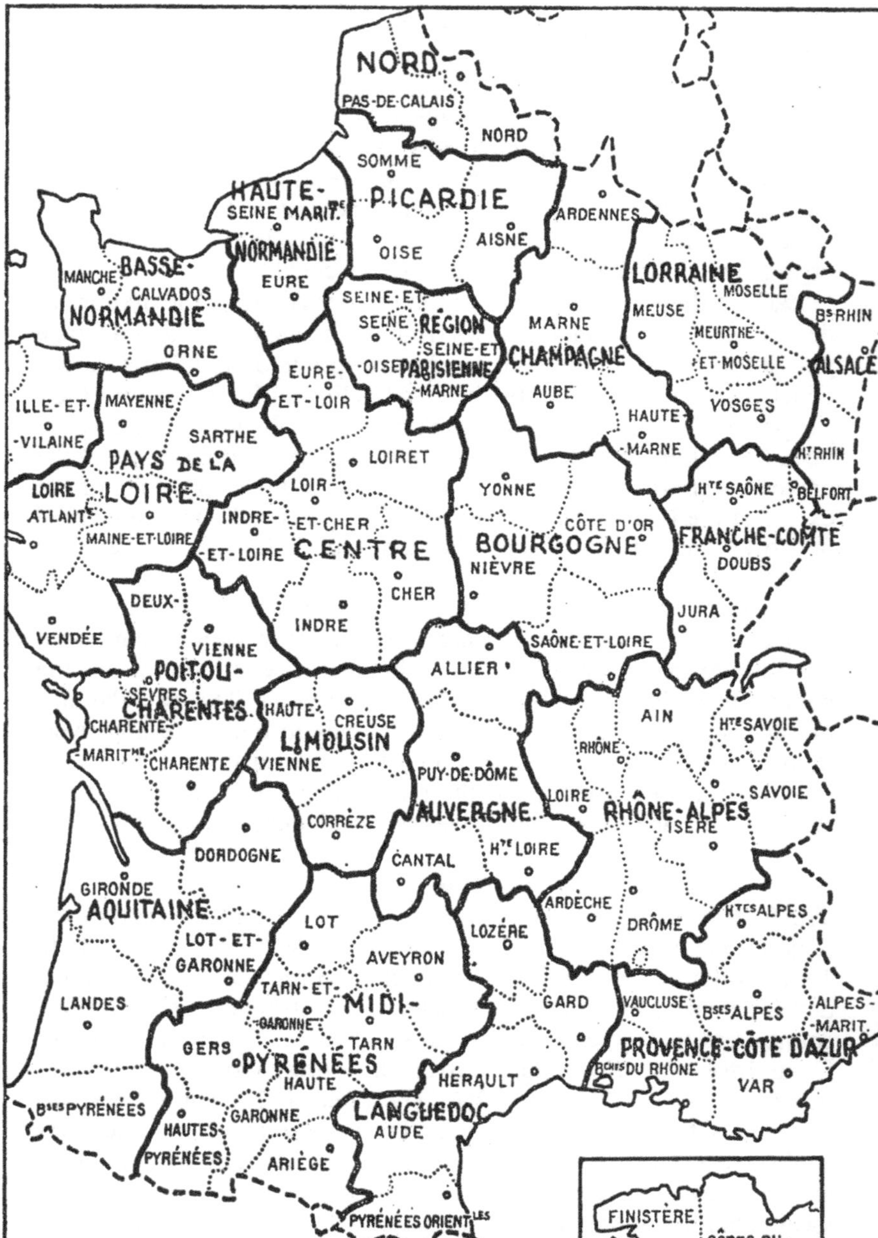

The thick lines denote the limits of regional areas and the dotted lines the limits of existing départements.

regions, a decree issued in 1961 provided for the creation of regional committees for regional expansion, grouping several committees for economic expansion, whose area corresponds with the limits of the former. They are approved by the Ministry of Finance which can grant them an operational subsidy. Their task is mainly to advise on the drafting of regional development plans. They are destined to play the rôle of a motor in stimulating regional development and their membership is prescribed by the central Government so as to ensure their representativeness. Numerous groups must be represented; agriculture, trade, industry, artisans, trade unions, universities, banks, consumer groups and family associations.

At the official level, these private groups have been joined by what are called 'interdepartmental conferences', which were first mooted in 1959 but did not come into being until 1960 and 1961. Their functions in the immediate future is to act as the principal agents for the application of the Fourth Plan, although eventually they will also draw up the regional plans. The chairmanship of the conferences is held by one of the préfets of the region and all the préfets are also participants. Members of the private sector can be invited to attend meetings on a consultative basis.

Of particular importance for the Plan is the provision that, in future, all programmes for public investment expenditure, which are drafted at present at the departmental level, must be brought together for confrontation in the conference. Also the conference will report each year, beginning in 1962, on the execution of the regional plan. For this task the regional committee must be consulted. Thus the conference will have the opportunity to propose amendments to the Plan.

A Ministerial circular published in December 1961 fixed the rôle of the interdepartmental conferences in three respects: *vis-à-vis* the national Plan; as regards the regional plans; in connection with the annual public-works budgets. The circular recognizes that no decentralized consultations took place for the drafting of the Fourth Plan but lays down the rule that they will be organized for the drafting of the Fifth. Their mission in relation to the regional plans is a double one. Their first task is to draw up such plans for regions which do not yet possess one and to bring existing plans up to date. The second is to help to prepare the 'operational tranches' of the regional plans, that is the part of each regional plan which will be executed during the period of the Fourth Plan (1962-65). (See next section.) The equipment budgets will give the interdepartmental conferences the opportunity to intervene when investment decisions are taken by any Ministries. In brief, the interdepartmental conferences must be informed of all programmes having a regional interest and must advise the central administrations as to the order of priority for public investments in their regions.

A link between the traditional département and these new bodies is provided by the Departmental Equipment Commissions (December 1961) which serve as two-way channels for passing work up to the inter-departmental commissions and translating, at the departmental level, the decisions of the latter into action.

3 *Regional Plans*

Alongside these efforts to define an appropriate geographical and administrative framework for the policy of regional development, the 1950s saw the drafting of a number of regional plans for development. But, until the Fourth Plan, these plans contained neither a timetable for their execution nor provision for their finance. They were documents whose use was rather to serve as an outline for the general orientation of the development of each region.

The Plans, of which thirteen had been fully approved by the end of 1962, were the result of merging, in 1958, two earlier types of regional development projects—the programmes for regional action and plans for regional development. The former were created in 1955 under the co-ordination of the General Planning Commissariat. The latter, dealing more particularly with public investment, were the responsibility of the Ministry of Reconstruction and Housing.

The entry into force of the Fourth Plan and its intention to make the regional plans more precise through the procedure of operational tranches have changed the character of regional planning as it had existed until then. A further factor is the intention of the Government, as an effect of pressure from Parliament during the debate on the Fourth Plan, to submit a programme law for the underdeveloped Western regions to Parliament at the end of 1963.[1]

II. REGIONAL PLANNING AND THE FOURTH PLAN

The fundamental approach of the Fourth Plan to the problem of regional disparities in development was through the repercussions of such disparities on the employment situation. This analysis facilitated the definition of certain priorities. Furthermore, the Fourth Plan has set up a new procedure for implementing regional development plans—the operational tranches.

1 *Employment Trends*

The analysis of the future trends in employment was carried out by

[1] See Chapters X and XVI.

one of the Horizontal Commissions of the Plan—the Manpower Commission. Although, eventually, more detailed regional projections are intended, the present lack of adequate statistics made it necessary to take as an index of overall regional trends the evolution of the manpower situation.

A comparison between the estimated supply of manpower and the evaluations made by the Vertical Commissions of the Plan of the demand for labour in each region, led to the conclusion that a marked insufficiency of manpower was to be expected in the Paris region (some 200,000 persons from 1960 to 1965) and manpower surpluses in some ten or so other regions, particularly in the West.

This analysis of employment trends enabled the experts to define one of the main orientations of the Fourth Plan which is to stress the development of the regions where excesses of manpower relative to demand are forecast. The action of the State has been defined as a propulsive policy[1] in the latter, whereas in the regions where the rate of development will be sufficiently rapid to lead to manpower shortages a complementary policy[2] will be sufficient.

2 *Operational Tranches*

The innovation of the Fourth Plan in the field of regional planning is to bring closer together the methods of national and regional planning, methods which, as has been seen, were notably different before that.

The regional plan is intended to constitute a projection on the regional level of the objectives of the national Plan. In other words, the regional aspect of planning consists of localizing the objectives of the National Plan. Ever since there have been national plans, this aspect of the application of the Plan has existed. But, up to the Fourth Plan, the concrete application of national objectives had not been envisaged in the light of its impact upon regional economies. In future these will be studied systematically and the results of the analysis may, in turn, influence the decisions taken at the national level.

The system of operational tranches is designed to make this linking of national and regional plans a practical proposition by giving the regional plans two of the characteristics of the national Plan which they lacked up to now, that is a timetable for the achievement of their objectives and a prospect of financing. A procedure for drawing up the operational tranches has been laid down by the General Planning Commissariat. This was explained

[1] *Politique d'entraînement.*
[2] *Politique d'accompagnement.*

in a note addressed by the Commissaire General to all the Interdepartmental Conferences in March 1962.

The framework and contents of the operational tranche are as follows. It must trace the general prospects of the region during the four years of the national Plan, taking into account both the long-term orientations of the regional plan and the sectorial objectives of the national Plan, with particular stress on the manpower situation. The second aspect of the operational tranche is the rôle of public investment. The object here is to insert in the operational tranche all the public investments envisaged for the four years of the national Plan. This involves translating as far as possible the national Plan's public investment programmes in terms of geographical location.

The General Planning Commissariat is responsible for organizing the work of drawing up the operational tranches. At the regional level the major responsibility is given to the Interdepartmental Conferences. A first step is the communication to them of a set of basic documents drawn up by the Commissariat and containing the text of the Fourth Plan, the results of the Manpower Commission's employment studies and data concerning those public investment expenditures which have already been individualized and localized. The Interdepartmental Conferences, in conjunction with the regional expansion committees and the regional representatives of the Ministry of Finance, have then to draw up a draft operational tranche. This document must contain a synthesis of the work of the Conference and details, in a standard form, of the main public investment projects for the period 1962-65.

In February 1963, a Délégation à l'Aménagement du Territoire et à l'Action Régionale was created to provide the secretariat of the interministerial committee and to co-ordinate the activities of the various public departments (see the *Journal Officiel*, February 15, 1963). This new body will also collaborate with the General Planning Commissariat in drafting the operational tranches of the National Plan.

At the same time, the task of laying down the guide-lines of a long-term policy for regional and urban development was given to a permanent National Territorial Development Commission. The basis for the Commission's work will be provided by the 'prospective' studies now under way at the General Planning Commissariat (see Chapter XVI).

III. URBAN DEVELOPMENT

Paris and the French Desert is a justly well-known study of the undesirable consequences of the ever-increasing concentration of population in the Paris region.[1] Since its publication in 1948, it has become commonplace to denounce the phenomenon of the Paris region and/or the traditional centralizing tendencies of French life —administrative, intellectual and cultural—which favour the continued growth of Paris and the asphyxia of the provinces. At times indeed, as often happens with new ideas, the anti-Paris campaign seems to have left the world of reality to join the lunatic fringe of the regional development school. So the Commissaire General himself has been obliged to point out that, things being as they are, the Paris region is the greatest industrial zone France possesses and it would be madness, faced with the competition from other similar zones such as the Ruhr today and the Home Counties and the Midlands tomorrow, to adopt a policy which would weaken the dynamism of Greater Paris.[2]

This is one aspect of the problem which a policy of urban development has to solve in present-day France. It is clear that it can only be solved if such development is seen as part and parcel of the problem of regional development. The link with decentralization and the implanting of new industries in the provinces is particularly evident.

Another aspect is that the growth of towns—and not only the growth of the Paris region—since the war has raised appreciably the percentage of the population living in urban conditions. The growth of urbanism has been estimated to be about 2 per cent a year and although Paris does not appear to be expanding any faster than the national average, the very size of the existing population is sufficient to class Paris apart from the rest of the country. It is worth recalling that, for the moment, urban conditions are less widespread in France than in many European countries as the following table shows:

	United Kingdom	*Germany*	*Italy*	*France*
Percentage of population in towns with more than 5,000 inhabitants	80	63	74	50
Percentage of population in towns with more than 100,000 inhabitants	50	32	20	17

Source: Rapport Général de la Commission de l'Equipement Urbain, 1961, p. 15.

[1] See *Paris et le désert français,* by J. Gravier, Paris, 1948.
[2] See his speech to Parliament quoted in Appendix II, p. 394.

Finally, so far since the war, housebuilding programmes have been at the centre of efforts to meet the urban problem and successive Plans have pushed the annual rate of construction up from 71,000 in 1950 to 320,000 units today. But, as the Fourth Plan points out, the time has come when it is necessary to correct the imbalance which has grown up between the progress of the housing programme and the progress, or lack of progress, of urbanism.[1] This entails both policy towards the old and still-growing urban agglomerations, and policy designed to equip the regions chosen for development efforts with adequate urban centres.

Mention should be made also of the policy of increasing expenditure on 'collective' consumption at the expense of 'individual' consumption.[2] An important part of such collective consumption expenditure—health, education, leisure—will be made in urban centres. A correct urban development policy is therefore at one and the same time the framework for solving a problem which had become urgent—the anarchic spread of urban conditions—and for giving a first, if mild, touch of the brake to the headlong rush of the French consumer towards the delights of the affluent society.

How are these results to be achieved in practice? Leaving aside, for the moment, the question of the financial implementation of the Fourth Plan's intentions in this field, there was, firstly, an administrative problem similar to the one met with in connection with regional planning, namely the inadequacy of the traditional form of local government and the need to find a newer, and more appropriate one. Secondly, the plans for urban development have to be drawn up and to be approved in some way by the central authorities. A special case which arose under both these heads is that of the Paris region.

1 *The Administrative Framework*

The basic unit of local government in France is the commune. In towns the commune is ideally responsible for the whole area of urban development. But, as has happened in other countries also, the growth of towns has increasingly upset the initial correspondence between the area of the commune and that of the town. Only five of the existing 72 large towns in France with more than 50,000 inhabitants are still mono-communal. In other towns, a large number of communes are found within the limits of urban areas. Lyons with 850,000 inhabitants includes Lyons plus 31 communes, Marseilles (800,000 inhabitants) the original Marseilles plus 5 communes, the

[1] See Fourth Plan, p. 75, and Chapter XI.
[2] See Chapter XI.

Bordeaux area (460,000 inhabitants) Bordeaux and 13 communes. This situation makes the application of a unified policy for urban development practically impossible and, in addition, the spread of towns into what were previously rural communes leads to conflicts of interest between the Ministry of the Interior and the Ministry of Agriculture for the provision of services such as roads and water supply.

Before 1959, when two administrative orders were issued to facilitate inter-communal co-operation, it was extremely difficult for communes to participate jointly in any but specific and limited ways. Since 1959, the object of co-operation can be much broader and the rule of unanimous voting suspended. Also it has become possible to create new units of local government called urban districts. However, according to the Commission for Urban Equipment—one of the Planning Commissions created by the Fourth Plan—little was achieved between 1959 and 1961 because of a variety of causes of a political and financial nature.

The solutions put forward by the Commission are, in the first instance and wherever possible, a complete fusion of all communes in the same urban area. This can be done by the Ministry of the Interior, under the 1959 legislation, even when a unanimous decision of the communes cannot be secured. Where this solution is not practicable, the Commission suggests a reinforcement of the powers of the urban district with, in particular, provision for adequate financial resources. The district can be given any of the functions of the communes, in which case its substitutes itself for them in those instances, but in those only. As a necessary complement to these reforms at the local government level, the Commission proposes that central Government activities should be harmonized with the new urban areas it is hoped to create. Finally, the Commission considers that the practice of working together inside the urban areas, and of seeing the town's problems as a whole, can be greatly stimulated by the task of drawing up an overall plan for urban development. But local resistance to these ideas is considerable.

2 *Plans for Urban Development*

For most of the post-war period, town planning was the responsibility of the Ministry of Construction but the plans which were drawn up suffered from the fact that their finance was not foreseen and they had no obligatory character. During the Third Plan (1958-61), the problem was taken up by the General Planning Commissariat for the first time, but the work that was done remained limited to a census of the investments qualifying for State subsidy by the Ministry of the Interior. In practice, the efforts of the Commissariat during that period were far from yielding spectacular results. The amount of investment accomplished for urban development, as then defined, was no higher from 1958 to 1961 than it had been during the previous four years despite an initial hypothesis given by the Plan of an increase of 25 per cent. With the Fourth Plan, the scope of town planning was widened considerably. The general Government directives (see Appendix I) contained quite specific instructions on this point. To implement them, a new Commission—the Commission for Urban Equipment—was created in 1960 along with the other Vertical Commissions. Its Chairman is the General Director of the Caisse des Dépôt et Consignations—the powerful State banking authority which, among other things, receives the resources of the postal savings system and supplies practically all the long-term borrowing requirements of the local authorities.[1] The task given to the Commission was a broad one; not only to inquire into the investment needs of towns, but also to begin to study problems raised by their rational and harmonious development. The long-term character of this task was recognized by giving the Commission a mandate of indefinite duration.

The Commission organized its research on the basis of two resources of documentation which existed already: firstly, the work being done by the Fourth Plan by other Vertical Commissions (Transport, School Building, Sanitary and Social Equipment, Cultural Equipment, Agriculture, etc.) and, secondly, studies made by two Committees (Nos 2a and 2b) of the Economic and Social Development Fund.[2] These two committees had begun to examine, in 1958, problems of town planning, one in the Paris region, the other in a few large provincial cities. Besides this, the Commission was able to use the findings of the more traditional inquiries made by the Ministries of the Interior, Construction and Public Works, on specific needs as regards water supply, drainage and main roads.

But, as the members of the Commission point out in their first report, the results of this type of inquiry do not lend themselves easily to incorporation in a coherent plan for urban development. Defining a doctrine in this field is still a task for the future, but the methodological notes given by the Commission show that the problem is now envisaged as a whole. These principles are being applied in the studies financed by the Economic and Social Development Fund—part of them being confided to specialized institutes, among

[1] See Chapter III.
[2] *Ibid.*

them the CREDOC.[1] Working groups have been created for this purpose under the Chairmanship of the Mayor and with the participation of the various technical services of the local and central Government. But the acceleration of this work is likely to be slow owing to the limited number of available specialists for preparing the technical aspects of the work.

Meanwhile, the programmes are presented for approval to the Committee 2b of the ESDF[2]—whose Chairman is the Deputy-Governor of the Crédit Foncier. The standard form required for the plans is as follows: the main lines of a twelve-year programme must be indicated, centred upon the projected development of the area. The tasks to be accomplished are enumerated together with an indication of their cost. Finally, a more detailed plan for four years (1962-65) is drawn up, based upon a thorough analysis of the financial situation of the local authority.

The object of this procedure is to make it possible to fill in the operational tranches of the national Plan, as in the case of regional development plans, the two often being inseparable. However, this does not imply that approval by Committee 2b confers an absolute guarantee that the Plan will, in fact, be implemented. Such a procedure would confer on urban development plans a privileged status that the national Plan itself does not possess. The approval by Committee 2b is not an idle gesture either. On the one hand, the Ministries who will be called upon to support the Plan in one way or another can give their views on it during the discussions thanks to their membership of the Committee. On the other, the road from the drafting of a plan to its final insertion in an operational tranche of the national Plan leads obligatorily through Committee 2b.

A follow-up procedure has been instituted under the responsibility of the préfet of the département who must submit an annual report to the Committee. There is also provision for a fresh examination by the Committee if important changes in the Plan appear necessary.

By the end of 1962, nine urban plans had been approved by Committee 2b according to the full procedure outlined above and others are in the process of being drawn up, most of them for areas with

[1] See Chapter V. The CREDOC prepared a special study on the principles which should be applied in drafting plans for urban development. 'Etude Méthodologique sur les Programmes d'Equipements Urbains réalisés à ce jour', 1961. See also a communication by the Deputy Director of the CREDOC: E. Lisle, 'Planification Régionale et Développement urbain', Communication to the International Congress on Economic Development, International Economic Association, Vienna, September 1962.

[2] cf. Chapter III.

over 100,000 inhabitants.[1] An emergency procedure has been applied to two cities (Marseilles and Bordeaux). The town council of Marseilles has been a pioneer in this field as, in 1955, the Mayor (M. Defferre) submitted to the General Planning Commissariat the first plan for urban development for the period covered by the Third Plan. For the time being, four-year programmes for these two cities have been approved by Committee 2b so that they can be used for the current Fourth Plan.

3 *The Paris Region*

The importance of the Paris region for any programme of regional development or town planning has already been noted. It is sufficient to recall here that the two problems of defining a coherent local government area and of drafting a plan for that area were inseparable.

The total area constituting the Paris region comprises Paris proper, 326 communes and three départements (Seine-et-Oise and Seine-et-Marne, and, in a special category, Seine).

The most ambitious effort to date to solve the administrative complexities of the region is the creation of the Paris District in February 1959 on the same lines as the urban districts already described. The District associates the départements and communes of the region and aims firstly at the study of the problems raised by town planning for the area as a whole and, secondly, at the eventual taking-over of the services which have been the object of such studies. The scope of the District's activities is, therefore, extremely wide, at least in theory. The Paris District is headed by a Delegate-General—at present M. Delouvrier—who is directly responsible to the Ministers of Finance and the Interior. An assembly exists which groups representatives of the various local government units in the District.

The first overall plan for the Paris region was initiated in 1958, before the creation of the District. It was drawn up by the Commissariat for Construction and Urbanism in the Paris Region, which depended upon the Ministry of Construction, and was published as a decree in 1960. This plan, called PADOG[2] after its initials, was for a period of ten years, during which time 1 million new inhabitants—most of them migrants—were allowed for. PADOG was a framework which laid down general principles and lines for policy rather than

[1] This represents practically all towns with over 100,000 inhabitants as the latter number only thirty-four, according to the 1954 census, excluding the Paris region.

[2] *Plan d'Aménagement et d'Organisation Générale de la Région Parisienne.*

detailed proposals. The latter were contained in an emergency three-year plan drawn up at the end of 1959 and early in 1960 by the General Planning Commissariat, that is, by a different authority from the author of PADOG, at the request of the Government. It was approved by Committee 2a of the Economic and Social Development Fund in the same year. The scope of the plan is wide: housing, green belts and parks, traffic problems, public transport, water, sanitation, schools, universities, sports facilities, public health. Detailed estimates of expenditure on each of these objects were also drawn up.

Meanwhile, under the initiative of the General Planning Commissariat, work began on a twelve-year plan, as for other urban areas. A first draft of this plan, for the period 1964-75, was published in February 1963.[1] In order to ensure that the Paris region is integrated into the Fourth Plan, a new four-year plan is being prepared for the period 1960-65, the first year being, in fact, the terminal year of the earlier 1960-62 plan. This will also be submitted to Committee 2a.

[1] See 'Avant-Projet de Programme Duodécennal pour la Region de Paris', *Imprimerie Nationale*, 1963.

CHAPTER V

TECHNICAL BODIES

The deliberate policy adopted by the General Planning Commissariat of keeping its own administration extremely light-weight has implied that the Commissariat chooses to work through other bodies rather than to supplant them. This policy is met with at every turn in the consultation procedures with the Planning Commissions, in the execution of the Plan with the Ministry of Finance, and, in the technical procedures of forecasting and planning, with the bodies described in this chapter.

There are six of them in fact: the SEEF,[1] the CREDOC,[2] the CEPREL,[3] the CERMAP,[4] the INSEE,[5] the INED.[6] Their functions and the scope of their contribution to the planning process vary notably. Broadly speaking, the first four carry out analyses whereas the other two supply basic data needed by the planners in the form they require. The SEEF is the organization with the most general mission; the CREDOC's contribution is more specialized although it has widened in the last few years; the CEPREL and CERMAP are of more recent origin and played no part in the Fourth Plan.

I. THE SERVICE DES ÉTUDES ÉCONOMIQUES ET FINANCIÈRES (SEEF)

The administrative structure of the SEEF underwent a profound transformation during the summer of 1962 following the appointment of its head (M. Claude Gruson) as Director-General of the INSEE. As a result, the SEEF was split into two parts. Before describing the present position, we recall the history and functions of the SEEF as it existed until 1962.

1 *History*

The SEEF was officially created in 1952, but it had been in gestation for several years before that.

[1] *Service des Etudes Economiques et Financières.*
[2] *Centre de Recherche et de Documentation sur la Consommation.*
[3] *Centre d'Etudes de la Prospection Economique à Moyen et Long Termes.*
[4] *Centre d'Etudes et de Recherches Mathématiques sur la Planification.*
[5] *Institut National de la Statistique et des Etudes Economiques.*
[6] *Institut National d'Etudes Démographiques.*

Since 1877, there had been a Statistical Office in the Ministry of Finance which had come progressively to undertake certain tasks of economic analysis of a financial character. In the early post-war years, a small working group was set up inside the Treasury Directorate[1] of the Ministry of Finance by M. Claude Gruson, who is an Inspecteur des Finances, to study national accounting problems. There was an acute consciousness among some senior civil servants in those years of the backwardness of French statistical apparatus and analysis compared with the Anglo-Saxon countries, and the problem of planning and of post-war economic management in general meant that the lack of a national accounting apparatus was cruelly felt. A decree in 1950 set up a group of experts to examine this problem, and the advice of this committee was behind the mission given to M. Gruson's working group to provide detailed retrospective national accounts and annual economic budgets to serve as a framework for economic policy-making.[2]

The pioneer research done by the experts—on the basis of a national accounting model drawn up by M. Gruson[3]—called for an enlargement of the resources of the working group. This finally led to the creation of a special service—the SEEF—of the Treasury Directorate by a fusion of the group and the Statistical Office of the Ministry of Finance.

2 *Functions*

The functions of the SEEF derived from its double origin. Its rôle was always to act as a general source of information for the whole of the Ministry of Finance and to issue all published statistical data prepared by the financial services, notably in the review 'Statistiques et Etudes Financières'. It has special responsibility for economic analysis on current problems as they arise and then works directly at the request of the Cabinet of the Minister.

In a different sphere, corresponding more to the tasks initiated by the old Working Group, the SEEF has produced the economic budgets, a summary of which now has to be presented to Parliament annually at the time of the budget. The SEEF draws up two economic

[1] See Chapter III.

[2] A pioneering work in this field in France was Prof. Perroux's *Les Comptes de la Nation*, PUF, 1949. Subsequently Prof. Perroux became chairman of the 'Methods' Group of the National Accounts Commission.

[3] For the early work see: 'Note sur les conditions d'établissement d'une comptabilité nationale et d'un budget économique national': *Statistiques et Etudes Financières*, No. 19, July 1950. For the most recent work see: *Les Comptes de la Nation pour 1959*, Vol. II—*Méthodes*. Imprimerie Nationale 1961.

budgets each year. The first is drafted in July and is used in conjunction with the preparation of the first outline of the financial budget.[1] The economic budget is revised in the autumn in the light of the most recent data which have come to hand and following the major policy decisions taken by the Government in the meantime as regards the State budget.

The work of the SEEF on national accounts is also submitted for discussion twice a year to a body called the National Accounts and Economic Budgets Commission set up in 1952. At present and since 1960, the chairman is *ex-officio* the Minister of Finance. In the early years this was not the case, and M. Mendès-France presided over the Commission for a long time. There are 32 members of whom 16 are civil servants from the Ministry of Finance and other Ministries, 8 are members of the Economic and Social Council and 8 are independent members appointed because of their competence in the field. The first meeting takes place before the summer when the SEEF produces the national accounts for the previous year, the revised economic budget for the current year and the first outline of the economic budget for the following year. The second meeting is held at the end of each year, after the Finance Act, or budget, has been submitted to Parliament, and the agenda includes the first provisional accounts for the year which is reaching its close, as well as a new version of the economic budget for the coming year. Now that the SEEF is beginning work on quarterly national accounts, it may be that this procedure will be modified somewhat.

Also in the range of national accounting is the task of establishing the final national accounts for past years, as the work of the SEEF just described deals essentially with forecasts and very provisional data. This was confided to the INSEE by the 1952 decree organizing the National Accounts Commission. In fact, the INSEE has never received the resources, human and other, enabling it to fulfil its task, and indeed, in view of the paucity of qualified national accountants in France which still exists today, it is difficult to see how things could have been otherwise. Consequently, the SEEF has made itself responsible for this work.[2]

Given the type of work being done by the SEEF, and the fact that practically all available talent had been concentrated there, it is only natural that the General Planning Commissariat should have turned to the SEEF for technical assistance as soon as it was created. The SEEF has thus become a technical bureau for the Commissariat for

[1] See Chapter XII for the procedure used for drafting the budget.

[2] See, for example, the 1960 volume of national accounts which contained long series since 1949.

all problems connected with economic forecasting and many others as well. The methodological approach to planning problems described in Chapter VI is due to the work of the SEEF in large part. It should be noted that this is a field in which the present Commissaire General has himself a profound experience, both practical and theoretical, and the new departures in the researches of the SEEF as well as the setting up of two other bodies (the CEPREL and the CERMAP), bear the mark of his influence.

For the Second Plan (1954-57), the contribution made by the SEEF was still rather slight as its creation was too recent, but for the Third Plan, it was more considerable. It was at this time that a first attempt at long-term forecasting was made.[1] The contribution of the SEEF was much more substantial again for the Fourth Plan as will be seen in a later chapter.[2]

3 *The 1962 Reform*

The change, in 1962, in the structure and functions of the SEEF and the INSEE is an illustration of the importance now being given to the Plan in the formation and execution of economic policy.

The INSEE has had its previous responsibility for establishing the retrospective national accounts series confirmed, and in addition is now specifically charged by the Minister of Finance to assist on the technical level in drafting prospective national accounts destined either for the annual economic budgets or the pluri-annual plans. In order to carry out these tasks, M. Gruson, the present Director General of the INSEE, has taken with him part of his team of collaborators from the SEEF.

It will be seen from the above that the development of work on national accounting and forecasting in France has been accomplished by a relatively small group of people working together in the old SEEF. One finds that the methods of work and of recruitment of the SEEF resemble those adopted by the General Planning Commissariat in the early days, and for much the same reasons. The very great lack of trained economists and statisticians in France after the war was only filled progressively by such institutions as the Ecole d'Application of the INSEE or the CEPE[3] set up by the SEEF and, more recently, it is to be hoped, by the universities. This meant that, when the SEEF was created in 1952, sufficient talent did not exist either in the public departments or in the universities. So the personnel policy the SEEF was allowed to pursue was quite different from the

[1] See 'Les Perspectives de l'Economie Française pour 1965', SEEF, 1956.
[2] See Chapters VI and VII.
[3] *Centre d'Etudes des Programmes Economiques.*

policy of the administration in general. Staff were given responsibilities according to their capacities, specialists were persuaded by hook or by crook to come to the SEEF regardless of whether they possessed any previous experience in government service. The hierarchy of the SEEF was, therefore, less rigid than in the Ministry of Finance. Before the change to the new structure, the SEEF employed about 140 persons in administrative grades, of whom not more than a third were working more or less directly on forecasting and national accounts. The origins of the staff remain extremely varied and a great number are employed on a contractual basis without being incorporated in the permanent civil service. Thus one finds civil servants—amongst them a good sprinkling of Inspecteurs des Finances—statisticians, engineers who have acquired a taste for econometrics, post-graduate economics students and mathematicians.

II. THE CENTRE DE RECHERCHES ET DE DOCUMENTATION SUR LA CONSOMMATION (CREDOC)

1 *History*

Created in September 1953, on the initiative of M. Dumontier, Director at the INSEE, the CREDOC was attached to the Productivity Commissariat—which was an independent body at that time before being absorbed by the Plan. Its mission at the beginning was to study consumption in France, notably from the point of view of distribution and with the object of contributing to improved productivity in that sector. There was no connection with the Plan at that time, but the CREDOC was soon led—due in large part perhaps to the preoccupations of its team of research workers with forecasting problems—to enter the field of economic projections.

On January 1, 1962, the status of the CREDOC was changed as it had become clear that the range of its work had gone well beyond the initial objective; moreover the Productivity Commissariat had been absorbed by the General Planning Commissariat. The present legal status of the CREDOC is that of a non-profit-making association created and controlled by the State. The board of directors is in fact appointed by the Ministry of Finance. The Chairman is M. Gruson, the Director General of the INSEE, so the reform of the status of the CREDOC is in line with the general policy of rationalizing the structure of the technical services concerned with drafting the Plan, which was noted above in the case of the reform of the SEEF (1962). This reform will increase the importance of public moneys in the budget of the CREDOC through grants from the Ministry of Finance or the General Planning Commissariat. In the past, the work done on contract for private clients had been about half total resources.

2 *Functions*

Three functions are assumed by the CREDOC. The changes introduced in 1962 leave them intact. They are:

establishing data on consumption in France for use in the national accounts. The CREDOC works in co-operation with the group 'households' of the SEEF for this;
carrying out research into consumer behaviour;
making forecasts of consumer demand.

The CREDOC employs a professional staff of some thirty persons, among them doctors and engineers as well as economists and statisticians.

3 *Activities*

The CREDOC was called upon to contribute to the Third Plan but its major work for the General Planning Commissariat came with the Fourth Plan. The CREDOC's work was of three kinds: a contribution to the 1975 long-term prospective, a more summary contribution to the three 1965 variants, participation in the work of a number of Planning Commissions.

The activities of the CREDOC have increased since the end of the 1950s. The problems surrounding long-term projections of consumer demand have been studied intensively and incorporated where necessary in the projections of the Plan. The 1950-60 series of consumption according to 200 groups of goods and services was revised[1] and a number of studies of individual categories undertaken (energy, automobiles, textiles, medical expenditure, food and non-food products, etc.). These studies often form the object of articles published in the Centre's review called *Consommation*.[2]

An important and original new departure in the work of the Centre concerns urban development. This work is done on a contract basis for local authorities in the framework of their development plans.[3] Thus economic and demographic projections and the equipment needs of Marseilles, Aix-en-Provence, and the Western Area

[1] See J. Albert: 'L'évolution de la consommation en France de 1950 à 1960', in *Consommation*, Nos. 3 and 4, 1961.

[2] For example: M. Chassenet, 'Une enquête sur les dépenses médicales des ménages', *ibid.*, No. 1, 1961; H. Faure, 'Les perspectives à long terme de la demande de textile', *ibid.*, No. 2, 1961.

[3] See an article by the Director of the Centre, G. Rottier: 'Développement Economique et équipements urbains', *Consommation*, No. 1, 1960.

of the départements of the Bouches-du-Rhône and the Somme had been completed by 1961. At the same time an empirical study of demand for housing was done for the Housing Commission of the Fourth Plan.

The current programme of work of the CREDOC is of particular importance for the preparatory work now going on for the Fifth Plan and we return to it in Part Four.

III. THE CEPREL AND THE CERMAP

These two small study groups were set up in 1961 with government support so as to pursue methodological and long-term researches on planning questions. Their contribution to the changes now taking place in planning procedures will be discussed later in Part Four. It is sufficient here to note their existence and status. Both are small units—the CEPREL has about seven members and the CERMAP rather less. The CEPREL is headed by a university economist—Prof. Bénard—who has worked with the SEEF and was responsible for the first long-term projection undertaken by that body.[1] The CERMAP is led by M. Nataf, who is a mathematician.

The CEPREL has three tasks to perform: to develop the methodological study of general long-term problems, to explore limited areas in this field at the limit of methodological and empirical researches, to collaborate with similar bodies abroad. The work of the CEPREL is centred on the problems of 'prospective' research.[2] Of these, a study of the possibilities of applying to France the growth model for non-agricultural production drawn up by a group of experts for the European Coal and Steel Community has been completed.[3] A long-term demand study of foreign trade trends for the main industrial countries, both exports and imports, and their compatibility is still under way, as is an analysis of the impact of technical progress and its insertion in growth models. Finally, a task to which we shall have to refer again, consists of a systematic comparison of the first three French Plans and the results actually achieved. The period of the Third Plan is receiving priority. The object of the work is to draw lessons for the future from the experience of planning in the post-war period.

The work of the CERMAP is of a more limited kind and is directed essentially towards the application to the Plan of mathematical

[1] See 'Les Perspectives de l'Economie Française pour 1965', SEEF, 1956.

[2] The importance being given to this aspect of planning is underlined in Chapters VI and XVI.

[3] See: 'Méthodes et prévision du développement économique à long terme', *Informations Statistiques*, Nov.-Dec. 1960.

computable models, that is models which can be used on electronic computers. This work will be of capital importance for the pre-consultation of Parliament in the choice of the main objectives of the Fifth Plan which will take place early in 1964.[1] We return to this later in Part Four.

IV. THE INSTITUT NATIONAL DE LA STATISTIQUE ET DES ÉTUDES ÉCONOMIQUES (INSEE)

The new structure of the INSEE since 1962 can be summarized in the following organigram:

DIRECTOR GENERAL

General Services, Service of the Inspection Générale, Documentation, National School of Economic Statistics and Administration

FIRST DIRECTORATE	SECOND DIRECTORATE	THIRD DIRECTORATE
Regional work Co-operation Overseas Statistics	Statistics (consumption, production, trade, prices, incomes) Theoretical Studies	Economic Syntheses (medium- and long-term programmes). National Accounts and short-term projections. Conjuncture Theoretical Studies

The part of the old SEEF transferred to the INSEE has been used to form the Third Directorate.

The INSEE was set up in 1946 as a public body attached administratively to the Ministry of the National Economy and grouped a number of smaller services scattered throughout the public sector. It soon came to play a big part in the general raising of the level of statistical knowledge in France which has been quite marked since the war although much still remains to be done.[2]

The work of the INSEE has always included a great deal of direct collection of statistics as, for example, prices and employment samples. And the eighteen regional offices facilitate this. At the same time, the regional offices issue specialized statistical bulletins for their areas. The publication at the national level of statistical

[1] The head of the group has published an article on the introduction of price changes in a model of growth. See: 'Le modèle à moyen terme à prix variables SEEF, *Etudes de Comptabilité Nationale*, No. 3, 1962.

[2] The programme of statistical inquiries at present being organized by the INSEE is included in the preparatory work for the Fifth Plan. (See Chapter XVI.)

bulletins represents the main source of statistics on prices, employment and production. The INSEE possesses the most complete set of mechanical and electronic processing equipment and carries out the work of processing the results of large inquiries, such as the census data, as well as material for other public departments.

The INSEE has traditionally done short-term economic forecasting by conjuncture test methods.[1] There does not appear to have been any very close co-operation in the past between this section of the INSEE and the SEEF, charged with preparing the economic budgets. Since 1962, the conjuncture service is part of the Third Directorate with most of the old SEEF so that the liaison should be closer in future.

Finally, the work of the INSEE in training statisticians and econometricians in France has been of capital importance in view of the lack, until recently, of facilities for this in the universities. The Ecole Nationale de la Statistique et de l'Administration Economique—whose director is M. Malinvaud—counts among its former students several members of the staff of the SEEF and the INSEE.

V. THE INSTITUT NATIONAL D'ÉTUDES DÉMOGRAPHIQUES (INED)

The INED was another post-war creation designed to improve knowledge of economic and social questions in France. Since its foundation in 1945 the INED receives a subsidy from the Ministry of Health and Population, and its Director (M. Alfred Sauvy) is appointed by decree. Nevertheless, the INED is not a public service like the INSEE.

We shall not attempt to describe the extent and variety of the work done by the INED. They are sufficiently well known outside France through the publications of the Institute.[2]

As regards the Plan, the INED collaborates in supplying demographic projections of various kinds—population by age groups, by regions and so on. It is also the body which bears the major responsibility for the population censuses—the last of which took place in 1962.

[1] The results are published in the monthly review of the INSEE: *Etudes et Conjoncture*.

[2] The INED publishes a monthly review called *Population* and full-length studies in its collection 'Travaux et Documents'.

PART TWO

DRAFTING THE PLAN

Just as the scope of the Plan, and the nature of its objectives, have changed over the years, so the methods used in drafting the Plan are being improved continuously. This was especially true of the Fourth Plan, and further changes are being envisaged for the Fifth. In this Part we shall be dealing mainly with the Fourth Plan as it is possible to follow through the whole process from the initial technical work on long-term projections to the final version which was approved by Parliament. The method of exposition is chronological. This makes it possible to appreciate the problems which arose at each stage, and the ways in which they were dealt with.

At the beginning, as with any plan, there is a phase during which the specialists give their imagination a rather free rein, if only because they are setting out deliberately to bring into evidence major choices and what they imply. The Plan acquires solidity later on. This first stage in France concerns the small group of technicians in the SEEF and in the General Planning Commissariat. We discuss this work in Chapter VI.

Quite soon in the process, however, other groups intervene and, as choices get made, the general objectives of the Plan become more precise. This enables the technicians to proceed further and to elaborate on their initial projections. Among these new elements in the planning process is the work of a consultative body—the Economic and Social Council—and that of the Planning Commissions (Chapter VII), the latter being rather astride the two fields—technical and policy. As was explained in Part One, they assist the planners on the technical level, notably through their replies to the questionnaire leading to the provisional synthesis. But they are also the meeting ground for interest groups and for a discussion of policy problems. Some specific examples are examined in more detail in Chapter IX. A last round of consultations on the final synthesis of the draft Plan involves the Economic and Social Council for the second time and the High Planning Council (Chapter VIII).

There remains the final sanction by Parliament. We look at this in the next chapter (Chapter X). In the past, it was a subject which would hardly have called for extended treatment. But this time, the passage of the Plan through Parliament was the object of more elaborate debate. Moreover, given the fact that the rôle of Parliament is now under active discussion, the treatment of the Fourth Plan is not without significance as a possible pointer for the future.

The Plan being approved by Parliament, it appears a logical point in the exposition, before going on to discuss in Part Three how the Plan is implemented, to summarize the main aspects of the definitive version. This is done in Chapter XI.

The planning calendar, which is the basis of the following chapters, was the following:

First half 1959:	First Projection 1975.
September 1959-February 1960:	First projection 1965.
December 1959-April 1960:	First consultation of Economic and Social Council.
May 1960:	Government's directives issued.
July 1960:	Projection for 1965 on basis of Government's directives ready.
July 1960:	Planning Commissions start work.
February 1961:	Commissions reply to General Planning Commissariat's questionnaire.
March 1961:	First provisional synthesis for 1965 on the basis of a 5 per cent growth-rate submitted to Government.
April 1961:	Government decision to adopt 5½ per cent growth-rate and total and major breakdown of public investments approved.
May 1961:	Final synthesis 1965 ready and first draft of Plan prepared.
September 1961:	Government approves Plan.
October 1961:	Plan submitted to High Planning Council.
November 1961:	Second consultation of Economic and Social Council.
December 1961:	Final draft of Plan submitted to Parliament.
June 1962:	Final vote by National Assembly approving the Plan with small changes.
July 1962:	Final approval by the Senate.
August 1962:	Fourth Plan published in the Official Gazette.

CHAPTER VI

PLANNING TECHNIQUES

Planning techniques in France have evolved largely through practice. This is certainly not to say that theory plays no rôle in French planning.[1] But, as theoretical economists in France have been but little attracted to planning problems until recent years, the principal advances have been due to non-academic economists mainly in Government service. This situation, and the fact that, until recently, neither the statistical basis for a general model approach, nor the possibility of using it in conjunction with electronic computors, was present, imparted a strongly empirical flavour to planning. This showed up notably in the preference for iterative, or step-by-step, methods which were used up to the Fourth Plan, although a more formal mathematical approach is now being prepared for the Fifth, which will supplement the traditional one. But we reserve a discussion of this for Part Four. Meanwhile, we examine the general framework of planning methods, the long-term horizon and the methodology of projections.

I. GENERAL FRAMEWORK

The characteristics of the planning exercise at the technical level can be classified under three heads. They are:

1 the use of iterative or discretionary methods rather than a simultaneous solution with a formalized general model;[2]

2 the predominance of demand as the initial starting point for the projections;

3 the degree to which the Plan can be considered to be a normative document.

[1] As one observer seems to have concluded apparently under the effect of a preference for econometric model-building and an erroneous belief that such proofs of logical rigour were the *sine qua non* of any self-respecting plan. But, perhaps the article in question carries heavy traces of the date when the research was done, i.e. presumably before work on the Fourth Plan, cf. S. Wellisz: 'Economic Planning in the Netherlands, France and Italy', *Journal of Political Economy*, June 1960.

[2] We return to this distinction in Part Four, cf. P. Massé, 'Discretionary and Formalized Planning', communication to the Conference on Economic Development, International Economic Association, Vienna, September 1962.

1 *Iteration or Simultaneity?*

To introduce the problem in this form is to risk an error of interpretation. The absence, so far, of a general model in French planning is not the consequence of a 'parti pris', but is to be explained by a number of theoretical and practical considerations. The fact that the introduction of such a procedure is now being investigated is sufficient proof of this. The Commissaire General has summarized in three points the reasons why great precautions are needed before 'making the jump' to a full-scale computor model. They are: the influence on results of initial errors in constructing the model; the contrast between the precision of the methods and the indeterminate character of the matter treated; the problem of the difference between orientation and actual prices.[1]

More important is to determine the exact content of the term 'iterative'. Its general implication is that work proceeds by successive approximations, from the simpler to the more complex or from one aspect to another and back again. The final breakdown of the economy into 65 branches in the 1965 projection for the Fourth Plan was the result of three earlier stages using respectively 3, 17 and 28 sectors or branches. Also, final production and projections of manpower needs and resources are derived by a to-and-fro process of checking and cross-checking. The decision of the planner is implied continually throughout the process and initial balances of production and consumption can be 'corrected' later on by other balances such as manpower or financing factors.

A consequence of this approach is that the technicians are continually called upon to exercise their own discretion in making adjustments so as to keep the results of their analysis in contact with the 'real world'.

2 *Final Demand*

One difference between the Fourth Plan and its predecessors is frequently said to be that the point of departure for the Fourth Plan was final consumption. Production and investment were considered as means for achieving final consumption objectives. This aspect of the Plan is related to the question of its normative character but is best dealt with separately. The First Plan was seen to have been in essence a set of production targets for a limited number of sectors of fundamental importance whose reconstruction was a prerequisite for any durable increase in final consumption (private or collective). Similar considerations prevail today in less-developed countries

[1] Colloquium in London, at the National Institute for Economic and Social Research, April 1961.

where the initial objective of policy is to raise the percentage of total output devoted to investments and, as a corollary, to restrain the growth of consumption. Or, again, the immediate problem facing the United Kingdom's planning effort is to ensure a notably faster growth of output and of exports.

France's problem is different. Since 1959, the external balance is positive and, after a pause, growth has been resumed at a high rate. No agonizing choice, implying sharp changes in economic trends, is therefore called for. So, the logical approach to the determination of output targets is to start from the likely trends in demand. In other words, output, and the ways in which it is achieved, appear as means, not ends.

3 *The Normative Character of the Plan*

A strict application of this approach would imply that the Plan contains no normative elements at all. It would be a generalized market research project, whose success would depend upon the degree to which policy measures facilitated the working out of spontaneous demand trends. The basic equilibria of savings and investments, employment and external payments being supposed to be satisfactory in the starting year, policy would have the task of preserving them within the growth trend set down by spontaneous forces. This view of economic policy is a figment of the imagination if only because today's 'spontaneous' trends are themselves, in part, the product of yesterday's policy actions. Nevertheless, it does contain an element of truth in the current French situation where, after a very considerable shaking-up from 1958 to 1960, the Fourth Plan did not have to set out to achieve a real change in trend of either output or the trade balance, for example. It is this situation, more than any conscious choice of policy, which enabled the French planners to start their projections in principle from the demand side. We say in principle because in some cases, notably agriculture, the output trend had to be taken as an ineluctable fact. But we return to this point later.

The same situation also provided the opportunity, which the French authorities seized eagerly, of extending the breadth of choice of economic aims to include the social sector, through planning a big increase in 'collective consumption'.[1] A consequence is that the growth of private consumption is estimated to be one point less than the rise in GIP[2] (23 per cent instead of 24 per cent) during the Fourth

[1] Defined as expenditure on education, sporting equipment, health, scientific research, cultural equipment, urban and rural equipment and public works by the State.

[2] Gross internal production. See p. 32.

Plan and the rise in collective consumption 50 per cent. This is no doubt only a small beginning in a policy which is likely to become more marked in future Plans, but it does mean an important new departure in the objectives of the Plan. Thus, far from the present economic situation in France leading to a projection of existing trends, the contrary would be nearer the truth, that is the margin of choice has widened, potentially at least. The fuller potentialities of the new situation will be more accentuated with the Fifth Plan.

Together with the decision to raise collective consumption by a very substantial amount, the choice of a high growth-rate, and of the localization of growth where possible in the least developed western areas, represent the major normative aspects of the Fourth Plan. There is no reason to believe that the high rate of growth would result from the spontaneous working out of economic forces; it will require specific policy measures to achieve it. The preoccupation with regional imbalance in France has led the authorities to seek to determine, in addition to the rates of growth of each sector, the relation between them and the growth of the different regions. Work is not yet very advanced on the construction of regional national accounts but partial indicators, in particular the employment projections by regions, have shown that, without appropriate action, the existing disparities between the growth of the North and East and that of the West and South-West would continue. Hence the policies called 'propulsive' and 'complementary' for public sector investment already analysed in the chapters on regional development policy.

II. THE LONG-TERM HORIZON

Several types of projection are made in the process of drafting the Plan. As mentioned above, the general approach is from the simpler to the more complex, from the more to the less general. The methods used at each stage do not always differ in essence but only in the amount of material analysed or the width of the circle of persons who contribute to the work. This will make it possible to consider forecasting techniques as such under one head when the various types of projection have been enumerated. One distinction between these is, however, important. The four-year French Plans have 'a terminal year and an horizon'.[1]

Which horizon and why? Certain economic decisions take much more time than others either to implement or to bear their fruits. A decision to build a steel mill or a dam which is written into a four-year Plan will be unlikely to raise output of steel or electricity

[1] P. Massé: 'Prévision et Prospective', *Prospective*, No. 4, 1959.

before some time during the following Plan.[1] Again, a decision to raise the school-leaving age, or to increase the numbers of university students, has to be taken now and prepared for over a number of years whilst its effects on the total of technicians or engineers qualifying will take even longer to appear. This is only to say that some sector plans cannot be squeezed usefully into a medium-term time-period which is, nevertheless, appropriate for the majority of economic policy issues. Decisions relating to demographic trends are usually in this category. Energy problems are also a field where long-term forecasts and plans are appropriate, due to the inelastic supply and the heavy investments involved.

But there is another sense in which long-term forecasts and plans are of value—say for periods of fifteen to twenty years ahead. 'The Fourth Plan will have above all to initiate, with flexibility, the future trends which are the most obviously necessary, and to try not to close any of the doors of the future (basic investments, formation of human capital, long-term research). Prospective studies, which are divorced from the constraints imposed by action, can be an essential feature of medium-term plans, not only by supplying reasons for choice but also by aiding public opinion to look towards the future . . .'[2]

The major impact of 'prospective' studies of this kind will not be felt until the Fifth Plan and we do not discuss them here. But two systematic long-term forecasts have already been completed in France. The first was designed as part of the work on the Third Plan and was prepared in 1956 with an horizon 1965.[3] The second attempt was made in 1959 for the Fourth Plan and took as its horizon 1975.[4]

III. METHODOLOGY OF PROJECTIONS

The object of work at this stage is to reduce policy options to a limited number of coherent variants which can serve for the consultations and the choice of the Government. The final product is thus a set of accounts for the terminal year of the Plan (1965). The variants used for the 1975 prospective work, which preceded the drawing-up of the 1965 projections, were the same, so the two can be discussed together.

[1] See the example of Electricité de France quoted in Chapter XII.
[2] P. Massé: *op. cit.*, p. 120.
[3] *Perspectives de l'Economie Française en 1965, Commissariat Général du Plan and SEEF*, March 1956.
[4] *Les perspectives à long terme de l'économie française. Commissariat Général du Plan and SEEF*, Roneotyped, 1959.

In view of the time available and the calls being made upon the technical staff, and in view also of the unsolved methodological problems associated with such a task, about which more will be said in a later chapter, it was decided to use only three variants, and to take as a criterion of choice the rate of growth of total output. The three growth rates analysed were 3, 4½ and 6 per cent, corresponding to three types of growth—slow, average and fast—and they were chosen in order to illustrate the types of policy problem each gives rise to.

A set of hypotheses was admitted implicitly in the model, such as the absence of an armed conflict, of a serious economic recession in a foreign country, or of social or other upheavals in France. More explicit hypotheses concerned the continuation of the trend towards freer international trading conditions and the need for France to contribute to the financing of development plans overseas.

For this stage of the work, and for both the terminal years, a highly aggregative model was used with three sectors of production only (agriculture, industry, services). On the demand side were distinguished: fixed capital formation by enterprises—including those in the public sector—housing, administrative investments and consumption, foreign trade and private consumption.

This stage led to the construction of a second model with seventeen productive branches for the last year of the Plan only (1965) according to each of the three growth rates studied. This model, with supplementary material on particular aspects, notably private consumption and social investments, provided the starting point for the Government's final choice of options and, before that, for the first consultation with the Economic and Social Council. The model is at constant prices.[1] It was expanded later to twenty-eight branches and, eventually, to sixty-five. But the methodological problems met with can be illustrated from the seventeen-branch model.

The framework of the analysis is the national accounts. In France these cover five groups of 'agents' in the economic life of the nation: households, non-financial enterprises, financial institutions, public administrations, the foreign sector.[2]

The activity of each agent is described in a series of three double-entry accounts—production, appropriation, capital; the first shows

[1] Some work has been done since on the problem of introducing the effects of price changes into the model. See M. Nataf: 'Le Modèle à Moyen Terme à Prix Variables du SEEF', *Etudes de Comptabilité Nationale,* No. 3, 1962, Imprimerie Nationale.

[2] On all these points see: National Accounts: *Methods,* Vol. II, published by the SEEF in 1961; and J. Marchal: *Comptabilité Economique Nationale,* Presses Universitaires, 1962.

the formation of income where it exists, that is for the productive sectors only, essentially the enterprises; the second, the distribution and use of incomes generated in the production account; the third, the balance between savings and investment. Each of these three types of account, for each group of agents, was projected forward to 1965. At the same time, three types of operations are defined and all the activities concerning them grouped in a single double-entry table. They are: goods and services, incomes and transfers, financial operations. As the first table (goods and services) includes both final and intermediate products, it is in fact a complete table of inter-industrial exchanges. The three types of account can be grouped further in a single table called the general economic table.

The method employed is a set of balance equations for the three types of equilibria studied, *viz.* production, manpower, finance. One other equilibrium is used—the regional balance—but was still in its infancy when the Fourth Plan was being drafted.

The three balance equations are represented as follows:

1 *Goods and Services* (for each category studied):
Production = Private consumption + Public consumption + Fixed capital formation + Exports *less* Imports + Stocks change + Intermediate consumption. [Production = GIP, see p. 32.]

2 *Manpower:*
Available manpower (taking account of demographic trends, immigration, retirement, school-leaving age, activity rates for women)
= Manpower required in agriculture + other productive branches + administration + financial institutions + domestic service.

3 *Finance* (taking account of the external balance):
Financing needs of firms and public administrations = Financing capacity of households.

The value of these equations is that they provide an exhaustive reference pattern which avoids both double-counting and omissions. The three equations are not used simultaneously. The first balance studies are carried out in constant prices from the production point of view. Equations 2 and 3, the last being an innovation of the Fourth Plan, are studied afterwards, but the backward and forward checking and adjusting that accompanies their establishment implies that the production balance can be called into question later on by the results of the other two equations.

The methods used to set up these three equations are described in the following paragraphs, beginning with the production balance. It will be seen that they are eclectic and imply no rigid methodological choice.

1 *The Production Balance*

As has already been mentioned, the approach to production problems has been to start from the demand side and work back to the supply. It assumes a sufficient elasticity of supply. This condition is relaxed after the preliminary studies and certain considerations regarding production levels intervene. The most important example of this, during the preparation of the Fourth Plan, was the output of agriculture whose rate of increase was taken as given very largely by the previous trend, so that the main problem became one of finding outlets for it.

From the common standpoint that demand determines production, two types of demand factors can be distinguished:

independent factors;
dependent factors.

Going back to the list of demand factors on the right-hand side of the production balance equation given earlier, we can group these factors under two heads as follows:

Independent	*Dependent*
Private consumption	Intermediate consumption
Public consumption	Fixed capital formation of enterprises
Public investment	Imports (in part)
Exports	Stocks (in part)

Let us examine each item of these two lists in turn, beginning with the independent factors.

(a) *Independent demand factors—private consumption.* The most important part of the technical work was done by the CREDOC.[1] The growth-rate of private consumption per head was derived from the initial studies of development in the three-sector model. This provides the starting point for the projections of consumer demand for each category of goods and services taken separately. The general assumption used was that income distribution would be unchanged. This assumption facilitates considerably the task of projecting demand. Moreover, it reflects a characteristic of the whole planning procedure which is that no major changes in the existing structure of society and its institutions are envisaged.

[1] See Chapter V.

The main groups of goods and services analysed were: food, clothing, housing, health, transportation and communications, leisure, hotels, cafés, and restaurants. Sub-groups were distinguished for each of the principal categories. The statistical data used were of three kinds: a long-term series of consumption at constant prices 1950 to 1958;[1] a family budget inquiry carried out jointly by the CREDOC and the INSEE in 1956-57—the results of this study were only given progressively in 1959 and 1960 as the planning work proceeded; international comparison, notably for the United States and the United Kingdom. Some special studies on rent, consumer durable goods and medical expenditure were also available.

There were two stages in making the projection. Firstly, the projections of consumption by major consumption function, based on the preceding data, were extrapolated to cover the whole population. In a second stage, the total demand under each function was distributed among the products covered by the function according to the standard production nomenclature. This second stage was done using a 'function-product' matrix for the year 1956. The problem of substitution was dealt with empirically in the absence of valid data on price changes and of price elasticities.

These projections for the year 1965 could be studied against the background of the more rudimentary 1975 projections which made it possible to see more clearly the trends at work. The initial 1965 projections were perfected as new data became available, in particular as a result of the work of the Planning Commissions (durable consumer household goods, clothing, services).

Public consumption. In part, public consumption is fixed by the level of output, but the margin of choice is, nevertheless, considerable and it is here that problems arise. What is implied, in fact, is a projection of the budget for 1965. This was done for the first time by the SEEF and the Ministry of Finance jointly (see Chapter XII).

At the beginning, the experts have only the estimates submitted by the various administrations (national defence, education, health, public works, etc.). But the projections are co-ordinated by the Ministry of Finance before they are used.

Public investment. These considerations apply even more to public investment where a particularly important element is housing, given the important contribution by the State to financing of house-building.

[1] Published jointly by the SEEF and the CREDOC in 1958 and 1959. See *Consommation*, No. 2, 1958, and No. 3, 1959.

These two sectors of final demand—public consumption and public investment—are the ones where the work of the planner at the technical stage is, at one and the same time, simpler than elsewhere and more difficult. It is simpler because the levels of expenditure envisaged depend upon decisions made by the State and they can, in principle, be known with certainty. Nevertheless, the chief options in this respect are taken only progressively as the planning procedure advances, the last intervening when the Plan is ratified by Parliament. Before that, the Planning Commission phase is a very active one as it is here that the largest number of real options, or arbitrements, occur.

Still, despite all this, it is necessary to make projections of public sector expenditure from the beginning. What happened is that the best estimate possible was made at the technical level on the basis of data supplied by the administrations and of the major known long-term policy intentions of the Government. The result was a set of projections for 1965 which already showed a certain policy tendency, such as the desire to increase 'collective consumption' and, incidentally, to keep defence expenditure relatively stable. But this second objective must be viewed with reserve because it has never really been a topic for debate.

Exports. Export projections are notoriously difficult to make and, from the planning point of view, are different from most others in that their achievement escapes very largely from the influence of national policy, except insofar as it should ensure price competitiveness and a sufficient degree of adaptation of production to foreign demand.

In drawing up the Fourth Plan, some special problems had to be solved, or the best possible approximations to solutions found for them. They were: the effects of the devaluation at the end of 1958, and of the trade policy of the Common Market. Several policy constraints had to be taken as given: the desired amount of the trade surplus both with the rest of the franc area and with foreign countries, and the need to allow for a substantial aid to the underdeveloped countries. An important consideration at the time the Plan was being drawn up was the Constantine Plan for the development of Algeria, although this Plan was kept separate from the Fourth Plan for Metropolitan France.

Once these factors have been introduced, the projections are based upon two further hypotheses: the overall growth of external markets and the share of French exports in each market, or in the total sales of each product on each market. The growth of GNP in the rest of the Common Market was supposed to be 3.5 per cent annually, and in other industrial countries 3 per cent. The growth of demand in the French franc area was similarly fixed. Exports from France were expected to hold their share of these markets, by and large, but a number of special studies were made of particular products, notably agricultural products and textiles. In the case of agriculture, the major uncertainty remained the Common Market, and it became necessary to revise the initial forecasts as the work of the Commissions proceeded. In other cases, the Commissions' forecasts were revised by the technicians of the Plan. Examples of this were the lower export estimates for motor-cars and farm equipment which were finally adopted.

Export projections and, more important, Government export strategy could not be studied separately from imports as the current balance of payments surplus is mainly determined by the net results of trends in both exports and imports. But imports called for different forecasting techniques.

(b) *Dependent demand factors—fixed capital formation of enterprises.* The method is to situate the level of productive investment in the general growth trend of the economy so that gross fixed capital formation (GFCF) in 1965 is independent of output in 1965 but is dependent upon the level of output it is desired to maintain early in the Fifth Plan. A problem could arise here if a notable acceleration of output was projected during the period 1961-65, but this was not the case in the projection phase of the Plan although it may be so today (early 1963). The volume of investment is broken down firstly by branches of productive activity, and then by types of product. This second step is necessary as the demand for productive investment is satisfied by a limited number of industries.

For the first step—investment by branch—the main analytical tool is the relation between the level of output and the level of investment required to achieve it, in other words, the capital coefficient, used as a rule in a marginal form. These coefficients are derived in a variety of ways: past experience in France or abroad, the opinion of experts and by taking account of technological changes. This last element is an important part of the contribution of the Planning Commissions.

In some sectors, a more direct method is possible, even at an early stage in the projections, as the sectors themselves (energy, railways, steel and aluminium) can provide estimates of investment needs according to the output level fixed. In the case of agriculture, the fact that the link between the level of investment and the level of output is not very close, makes it indispensable to take the advice of specialists.

The overall results of these various estimates at the branch level are compared with past experience as a cross-check. For the Fourth Plan the capital-output ratio for the economy as a whole was 2.5, i.e. each £100 addition to annual output was assured to require an investment of £250.

For the breakdown of investments by products, the same two procedures are used—direct inquiry or indirect evaluation—or both. The main conceptual problem here is the influence of a technical change, for example, a switch between thermal and hydro-electric power or the likely higher percentage of electrical equipment in the capital goods purchases of most branches of industry. As happens for projections of private consumption, it is usual to find that the degree of uncertainty is greater at the branch level than at the product level due to the effect of mutual compensations between the different types of demand. More generally, the same phenomenon appears in the case of projections of demand for basic products such as steel, energy and cement which enter into the production of a wide range of products. They can be treated with a much higher degree of confidence than projections of secondary products.

Intermediate productions. The SEEF possesses an inter-industrial matrix for 1959 that is used for these projections. It is adjusted to take account of all foreseeable technological changes to the extent that they are not a response to relative price changes which are not taken into account at this stage.[1] The main exceptions to this procedure are electricity and transports, two sectors whose production is linked closely to the general level of output of the economy. For 'energy' as a whole, an additional problem is raised by the possibilities of substitution between different types of energy.

Imports. The very substantial changes which took place in French import policy with the devaluation at the end of 1958 and the opening of the Common Market on January 1, 1959, and which will continue to operate during, and beyond, the Fourth Plan, made the forecasting of imports a particularly delicate task.

The amount of imports of raw materials and semi-finished products was considered to the sufficiently closely related to the volume of total output for the projections to be based essentially on that relationship. But the problem of relative prices, and all the other

[1] See Fr Le Guay: 'Les projections à long terme en France', International Conference on Input-Output Techniques, Geneva, September 1961.

factors of competitiveness, together with the reactions of consumers and firms to higher availabilities of imported consumer and investment goods, made it difficult to establish any valid trends to judge the likely evolution of import demand for these two types of goods. The Planning Commissions provided some assistance, although, in practice, they tended to be too optimistic about the likely low import demand, at least in the view of the technical services of the Plan.

In the last analysis, the projections of foreign trade were made in order to leave a certain margin of security for the trade balance, taking account of all available relevant material. So this is a field where the degree of uncertainty is great. As a result, the need for flexibility is also great.

Stock change. Given the comparative paucity of statistical data, the simple hypothesis was used that the level of stocks in 1965 would bear the same relation to output as in 1959, after correction for any abnormal movements.

2 *The Manpower Balance*

Supply of, and demand for, manpower were projected separately, the general assumption being that mobility was high as between comparable employment. But the problems of regional imbalance and requirements for professional qualifications received particular attention. The comparison of availabilities and needs—according to each of the three growth projections—was a valuable cross-check which made it possible to see, for example, that not only a growth-rate of 3 per cent but of 5 per cent also did not provide for full employment, unless a reduction in working hours was envisaged.[1] Debate on this point, which began during the first consultation with the Economic and Social Council early in 1960, is still going on. The terms of the problem have been modified somewhat by the increase in the number of immigrants from Algeria in 1962, which is greater than that initially calculated by the Commissariat.[2] The studies of needs for professional qualifications showed that demand for engineers and technicians would probably press hard on available resources.[3] The likely changes in manpower needs and resources were used for the regional development policy, but this is a field where a great deal of work remains to be accomplished.

[1] Chapter VII gives more details of the horizontal Manpower Commission which did most of the demographic work for the Fourth Plan.

[2] At present, over 500,000 persons.

[3] This problem is seen from another angle in the forecasts of the Planning Commission for Education.

3 *Financial Balance*

The study of the financial aspects of the Plan was the principal innovation introduced with the Fourth Plan.[1] Two stages in the analysis are involved: the examination of the conditions required so that the 'physical' output targets can be financed; the ways in which savings are channelled to their various uses.

It is at this stage that the projections of the three types of accounts for each of the five groups of 'agents' which have been described on page 120 are used.

For the first step, the mutual compatibility achieved between 'physical' output and demand (i.e. goods and services in constant prices), and manpower availabilities and requirements may not be compatible, in turn, with the financial conditions prevailing. This aspect is all the more important in a market economy where profitability is the main criterion which determines production and investment decisions.

A number of constraints are introduced by the general policy objectives laid down by the Plan, viz. price stability and a certain limit to the rise in public sector receipts. In addition, as with the other projections, the permissible degree of variation in the behaviour attributed to the economic agents—income distribution, savings, self-financing norms—limit the solutions which can be envisaged by the physical balance, or the extent to which financial conditions can be adapted to ensure their achievement. In this way a further stage of mutual adjustment between the physical objectives and financial conditions is called for.

The logical framework of these projections is the balance equation on page 121. The accounts of households, firms and administrations in the national accounts are projected for the terminal year of the Plan and a balance is established between financing needs and financing possibilities, after allowing for the level of the external balance. This equality between saving and investment is defined according to the levels of self-financing existing in the base year. This implies that the price system has to be adjusted to achieve balance. The extent of these adjustments should serve to bring out the financing difficulties likely to arise in executing the Plan. This being done, it would then be necessary to envisage the changes in the fiscal system, or the distribution of incomes, which are called for by the implementation of the physical objectives. In practice, for the Fourth Plan, it was not possible to do this, and recourse was had to a

[1] The methodology used was described in *Rapport Introductif aux Travaux du Groupe de l'Equilibre de la Commission de l'Economie Générale et du Financement du Plan,* December 1960.

simpler set of projections of the net financing capacity of households and the net financing needs of firms and of the public sector.

Household savings were projected on the basis of the average saving propensity which was taken, as a first hypothesis, to be equal to the highest rate found in the past—13.2 per cent in 1955. Other items of the capital account of households are the importance of direct taxation, the incomes of artisans (which are not separated from those of households in the capital account) and social transfers. The net result, after taking into account consumption and investment by households in housebuilding, is a net lending capacity of households.

As for firms—including the nationalized sector—a number of elements of their financial situation are known from the previous steps in the analysis. They are: the volume of production, wages and salaries paid, and incomes of artisans. With an assumption as to taxation, a net need for finance can be defined as a rate of indebtedness, i.e. the relation between net new indebtedness and the amount of investments to be financed. The rate actually used was 29 per cent, equal to the 1958 rate, the highest found in the past.

The Government sector's financial situation is found to have been determined already (current and capital expenditure and tax revenues) and its net financing needs also. It is possible to go further and to allow for the participation of the public sector in financing housebuilding and the activities of the local authorities. In this way, the budget deficit proper is defined.

Various measures for achieving the overall balance between saving and investment which respect the possibilities of adaptation of the financial behaviours of households, firms, the State and the financial institutions can then be envisaged. At one end of the scale are high personal savings and a high level of borrowing by enterprises. This alternative suggests paying particular attention to the ways in which the access of firms to the capital market can be facilitated, and to the mobilization of private savings. At the other extreme, a low level of private saving and a high level of self-financing can be considered. Such a solution implies finding means of influencing the level of incomes which do not upset the physical balance of goods and services previously obtained. In sum, an unlimited number of intermediary solutions can be examined by combining different values of the three variants—net savings of households, indebtedness of firms and the deficit of the public sector—and then making explicit the instruments of policy which each of them calls for.

This leads on logically to an analysis of the ways in which the flows between these three variables are organized. A first effort to project the accounts of the financial intermediaries was made for the Fourth Plan. The institutions chosen for this purpose were the Treasury, the Central Bank, the rest of the banking sector, and the Stock Exchange. A study of the structure of the financial holdings of households and firms and of the attitude towards their liquidity was also carried out. This work, although it is only at an early stage, seems to be exercising an influence on current financial policy which has sought to reduce short-term interest rates in order to encourage savers to invest in longer-term debt. More generally, the financial aspects of the Fourth Plan are receiving much more attention than was the case in the past.

CHAPTER VII

STAGES OF ELABORATION

We have seen in the previous chapter what are the techniques used in making the projections of the Plan considered as a coherent and comprehensive set of quantified objectives. It is an essential part of the French concept of planning that this technical work should proceed as soon as possible in the form of organized exchanges between the technical staff, the private sector and the decision-making branches of Government. In the past, that is until the Fourth Plan, the Planning Commissions were the sole channel of communication with the private sector. The Fourth Plan has set in motion a more elaborate process of consultation which is only at its beginning and whose final term it is difficult to see at present.

Preparation for the Fourth Plan started early in 1959. During most of that year the work done corresponded to the description in the previous chapter, so that by November 1959 the authorities were ready for their first experiment in initial consultation with the Economic and Social Council on the basis of a seventeen-sector projection for each of the three growth-rates for the terminal year 1965.

Following the Economic and Social Council's debates, the Government's directives gave the final word as concerns the main objectives of the Plan, and the Planning Commissions were set up. We devote a separate chapter to the Planning Commissions and shall not deal systematically with their work here. We pick up the Plan again at the stage of the first synthesis, which is the first time any single document which could be called the Plan appears. Subject to amendments, it is the preliminary draft of the Plan. We break off the story in this chapter at this point and discuss the final round of consultations in the following chapter.

I. FIRST CONSULTATION WITH THE ECONOMIC AND SOCIAL COUNCIL

The body which assumed the work of this consultation was the Investment and Planning Section of the Council.[1] It took place in two stages. In December 1959, the Commissaire General sent in a document entitled 'Projections of Consumption in 1965'. The auditions

[1] See Chapter II.

and debates in the Section lasted until February 1960, when a report was approved based on a document drawn up by a trade unionist who had been appointed rapporteur. Early in February 1960, a second document, 'Prospects of the French Economy in 1965', was submitted to the Council and a report, with M. Charvet, a member of the employers' group, as rapporteur, was approved by the Section in May 1960. Both these documents were then sent to the Prime Minister, in accordance with the procedure of the Council.

1 *The Consumption Study*

The President of the Economic and Social Council was seized of this question by a letter from the Prime Minister dated December 7, 1959. In his letter the Prime Minister described the object of the consultation as follows: 'The Section[1] will firstly comment on the basis of, and methods used in, the technical researches which, starting from the observation of past trends in France and abroad, describe the likely future spontaneous evolution of consumption. Secondly, the Section will have to say if it considers it desirable, for reasons over which it will be the judge but which will, of course, have to be made explicit, to bring about an inflexion of this evolution in certain respects. If this were so, the Section's study would also have to take into consideration the means to be used by the authorities, in the framework of the Plan, to direct consumption in the required manner. In this part of the report, the term "consumption" should be used in the widest sense to include, in particular, the provision of collective services whose supply is incumbent on the State, notably as regards health, education and housing.'

Three points in this letter fix the nature of the work required from the Section: firstly, a technical appreciation of the forecasts; secondly, a judgment on the desirability of making changes in the likely trend in consumption and in policy towards public expenditure of a social character; thirdly, concrete proposals for achieving these objectives.

The Commissariat's forecasts set out to estimate private consumption, according to major types of expenditure, in 1965.[2] The base year chosen was 1956, i.e. a year preceding even the beginning of the Third Plan. Indices for 1965 only were given without intermediate dates, although it transpired during the course of the discussions with the technicians that some assumptions had been made concerning the growth of consumption that had occurred since 1956

[1] That is, the Investment and Planning Section of the Economic and Social Council.

[2] They were drawn up by the experts of the SEEF and the CREDOC.

and was likely by 1961, the terminal year of the Third Plan. This choice of a base year was determined largely by statistical considerations as it was the year for which the CREDOC had carried out an extensive inquiry into family budgets, the first of its kind in France.

The study was built round the three hypothetical annual rates of growth of consumption in the period 1962-65; 3.9, 5.1 and 6.2 per cent, its authors having no illusions as to the utility of their decimals which were simply derived from the three overall growth-rates. Two assumptions were made from the beginning: that the existing structure of income distribution would remain unchanged, and that relative prices would be stable. The second assumption was necessary for very different reasons from the first, namely the technical problems raised by substitution effects when price changes are allowed for. The methods used in drawing up the forecasts were described in Chapter VI.

The main groups of products and services analysed were the following: food, clothing, housing, health, transport, culture and leisure. The final estimate of private consumption in 1965 was given under sixteen different heads. These groups were commented on individually by the experts in order to highlight certain aspects of the likely changes in demand. Although the growth of demand for food was estimated to rise less rapidly than incomes,[1] the increase was expected to be particularly large in the case of good quality beef, and fruit and vegetables. Demand for passenger cars would be buoyant, corresponding to 6.3 million cars in use in 1965 compared with 2.8 million in 1956.

Data on 'collective' consumption, i.e. housing, education, social services, etc., were not inserted in the document but were supplied by the Commissariat at subsequent meetings. During these, the Section was assisted by two officials from the General Planning Commissariat and the SEEF. This enabled a number of technical points regarding the estimates to be cleared up.

In writing its report, the Section decided to leave aside any detailed comments on the forecasts, as it was not in a position to supply any better ones. But this did not prevent the report stressing the importance of further work on the subject where, it was suggested, such factors as price changes, socio-professional differences, changes in income structure and regional trends should explicitly be taken into account. This being said, the Section concentrated upon 'the inflexions it appears necessary to bring about in the spontaneous

[1] By 36 per cent at the middle growth-rate compared with a growth of incomes of 41 per cent.

growth of demand and, with them, the more general considerations relating to the final objectives of the Fourth Plan'.[1] Its remarks fell into two groups—on individual products and on types of consumption.

As for individual products, they ranged over such problems as ensuring a rise in meat production concomitant with the forecast of the increase in demand—an understandable preoccupation in the light of French post-war experience in this field, encouraging consumption of non-alcoholic drinks as part of a campaign against alcoholism, and abstaining from any measures to stimulate demand for motor-cars, given the strong upward trend in spontaneous demand. This last point led on to the problems of urban development and of collective consumption in general.

Faced with a choice between 'individual' and 'collective' consumption, most members of the Section appear to have been ready to support a faster rise of the latter even if it was at the expense of individual consumption. The Section strongly supported the rise in such expenditure implied by the data communicated by the General Planning Commissariat. But, going beyond this initial judgment, the Section envisaged two other aspects of the consumption objectives, that is leisure time and income distribution.

A debate thus began on the desirability, and possibility, of a reduction in working hours during the Fourth Plan, which has been reopened whenever a consultative body has been asked for an opinion on the Plan's targets. Admittedly, the question could not be divorced from the study of the growth process as a whole—which the Section was not discussing at that time. The Commissariat's view, which remains in the final version of the Plan,[2] was that the labour market situation was likely to be too tight, at least until the second half of the Plan, for a general reduction to be envisaged for the time being. But it is a significant fact that allusions to the problem in Plan documents became more qualified.

The preoccupations of the Section as regards incomes were threefold: to ensure a more than average increase in the wages of the lowest paid workers, to adopt a more generous scale of family allowances, and to attenuate the discrepancies in income levels between sectors, in particular between agricultural and other pursuits and between poor and rich regions. This is the problem of income distribution which, in a wider context, has become an important point for the success of the Plan at the present time.

The final report was adopted unanimously by the Section.

[1] *Report of the Investments and Planning Section,* p. 4.
[2] See Fourth Plan, p. 5.

2 *The General Growth Study*

As with the consumption study, the Economic and Social Council was seized of the question by a letter from the Prime Minister in February 1960, which referred to the need for an opinion as to the 'objectives of the French economy during the period 1962-65'. The nature of the problem raised by the consultation was defined more specifically in the General Planning Commissariat's background document.

There was, first of all, a question of presentation. Given the need to choose between the claims of rival demands on production, a large range of alternative models could be built up. This not being practicable, the problem was simplified and presented against the choice of a rate of overall growth.[1] To illustrate the issues involved, a central rate (4½ per cent) was given together with two rates at the extremes of what could be considered to be practical propositions (3 per cent and 6 per cent). The view of the Commissariat was that the real choice should be between 4.5 and 5 per cent. As in the case of the consumption study, the Section was invited to give its opinion not only on the choice of ends but also on the ways of achieving them.

The General Planning Commissariat's background paper—a document of some sixty pages—did not content itself with an exposition of likely trends but drew a number of provocative conclusions of a policy nature from them to which it expected the Section to react. An initial section explained the assumptions behind the exercise which was that there would be no radical change in existing social structures and no significant change in the range of policy instruments available to the State (with the very important exception that foreign trade policy had already changed radically and would continue to do so under the influence of the Common Market). The document went on to comment on the methods used to make the projections, and the main results obtained for production, consumption, investment and foreign trade. The final conclusions were: as regards manpower, that there would be enough for a fast rate of growth but no slack until 1963 at the earliest; foreign trade forecasts showed a serious risk of a deficit with a 6 per cent growth-rate, despite certain favourable factors, such as price competitiveness since the devaluation and the prospect of big economies in foreign currency expenditures on oil imports; production goals were reasonable on the whole, even with a high rate of growth, but problems would arise in specific sectors such as agriculture, energy, steel, chemicals, automobiles and textiles; investment, with a 3 per cent

[1] This is the key problem in an exercise of this kind. We shall see in Part Four what solutions are envisaged for the Fifth Plan. The figures refer to GIP.

growth-rate, could rise less than in the past, but the two higher rates would call for its growing share in total output; consumption, due to a likely fall in the export surplus and a diminished part of public sector expenditure, notably defence, could be allowed to increase at only a slightly slower rate than output.

The conclusion the General Planning Commissariat drew from its projections was that the need for a fast growth-rate existed. The numbers of young people arriving on the labour market would swell very substantially in the decade and jobs had to be created for them. Moreover, there was an almost irresistible pressure in all groups of the population in favour of improved standards of living. The State had obligations to fulfil at home and abroad which would absorb available resources. Nevertheless, the risks of a 6 per cent growth-rate seemed considerable, particularly for the external balance and the effort required from the steel, metal-working and electrical industries. These considerations finally brought the Commissariat to recommend a growth-rate of between 4.5 and 5 per cent.

Completed at the beginning of May 1960, the Section's second report was also approved unanimously. It was undoubtedly a document which influenced thinking about the Fourth Plan and its problems, both in Government circles and elsewhere. As in the case of the consumption study, the members of the Section decided not to attempt to scrutinize the statistical details of the projections but set out to examine the broader issues raised by the Plan.

A caveat was introduced from the beginning relating to the way the Third Plan—due to close at the end of 1961—was going to be carried to its term. The break in trend during 1958 had been sufficiently sharp to make the Government decide to hold a general stock-taking—which led later, in 1960, to the Intermediate Plan[1]—and attitudes to the projected pattern of growth from 1962 to 1965 could not abstract from this.

As regards the Fourth Plan, the Section felt that it was necessary to adopt an ambitious output-target. The dangers this implied for the external balance in particular would mean that the Plan would not only have to be a conscious effort by everyone in the drafting stage, but that it would need the same effort in implementation. As for sectors of production, the Section noted that the agricultural problem was one of markets and could not be solved by a reduction in the rate of growth.

Three major types of problem were felt to be possible obstacles to achieving a higher growth-rate—the foreign balance, the balance between savings and investment, and manpower needs and resources.

[1] See Introduction, p. 31.

The Commissariat's export estimates were thought to be excessively prudent concerning the growth of foreign markets and the prospects for agricultural exports. The equipment goods industries would have to bear the brunt of the export drive, and the Planning Commissions should be asked to pay particular attention to them. The Section also had some doubts as to the high savings rate. It considered that some encouragement to savings might be needed to achieve it and, more important, some adaptations in the supply of credit for investment, if self-financing margins fell with increased competition from abroad as tariffs came down. The view taken was that it should become a general rule to specify, as far as possible, desirable investment projects in the Plan, so that they could receive preferential treatment from the credit institutions. At the limit, the Section envisaged that the State could be led to step in directly if there was a problem of 'finding an entrepreneur'.[1] On the manpower question, the Section noted the need to improve training and mobility but did not go beyond recording the opinion, of its trade union members in particular, that the Commissariat's statement on working hours was too categorical.

A general conclusion by the Section was that the problems raised by the Fourth Plan were different from those the previous Plans had had to deal with, in particular regarding the increasingly open character of the French economy. The necessity for more international co-ordination of development policies was clear.

Finally, the Section recommended a 6 per cent growth-rate on an average during the four years 1962-65, to be achieved progressively over the period, starting from the rate actually reached in 1961.

The preceding paragraphs have dealt with the first consultation with the ESC in some detail, firstly because it seems to contain some lessons on both the extension of the consultation process, which is to play such a big part in the Fifth Plan, and the technical difficulties it gives rise to, and, secondly, because the consultation undoubtedly influenced policy for the Fourth Plan in certain important respects.

It is rather remarkable that an assembly such as the Investment and Planning Section should have decided unanimously in favour of a high growth-rate despite the warnings of the experts.[2] Ten years earlier, or some would say five years, such a unanimous decision would have been well nigh unthinkable.[3] Effects of the planning

[1] An idea which is included in the text of the Plan: p. 15. See also p. 348.

[2] As the Commissaire General pointed out, there are reasons why this should be so, and which the authorities will seek to avoid next time. But this does not detract from the fact itself. See Chapter XVI.

[3] The same phenomenon was observed in the Vertical Planning Commissions.

process? The lesson of experience? We shall have to return to this point later. Meanwhile, it is sufficiently noteworthy to be highlighted. The Section's justification for its choice certainly skated over some delicate problems—not least the income/price relationship—but it would be unfair to conclude that no explanation was offered for its choice. Serious arguments were put forward, some of which found sufficient merit in the eyes of the authorities to receive a mention in the final text of the Plan.

Nevertheless, the Section did tend to adopt a policy of eating its cake and having it too, as concerns the preferences it expressed for more collective consumption and a very high growth-rate. The question of the correct formulation of problems, so as to make it less easy to avoid awkward questions such as this, is one of the big items on the agenda of the planning authorities at the present time. One incidental aspect of the discussion must be allowed for in any case in assessing the results of the exercise. It is the date of the consultation and the fall in private consumption levels for some social groups after 1958. As, between 1958 and 1962—the first year of the Plan, an important economic readjustment had taken place, it was very difficult to jump to 1962 as if nothing had happened. To the extent that the Fourth Plan ensures overall balance, this problem should not arise for the Fifth. However, more generally, there are obvious drawbacks to asking for opinions and judgment on projections whose starting point is still two years away and this illustrates the need to speed up the drafting phase if possible. The suggestions by the Section in favour of much closer co-operation with the private sector and its representatives in following-up the Plan have a relevance here, and seem now to be accepted Government policy.

Turning to the statistical aspects of the consultation, it would appear that it is not really practicable to ask a body such as the Investment and Planning Section to examine figures with a view to suggesting different ones. This does not imply that the Section cannot criticize the technical work which lies behind them, or suggest improvements for the future. On the contrary, the discussions with the experts were fruitful for all and the encouragement given by the Section in its reports to further research was a welcome one for the technicians *vis-à-vis* the spending administrations. But the Section could not change estimates in the sense of substituting its own figures for those of the experts.

Finally, the Section's reports were rather weak when it came to policy measures to implement the desired objectives. This was particularly so for the problem of adjusting the growth of private consumption—and hence of private incomes—so that the desired expansion of 'collective' consumption could take place as planned without danger for the overall balance of the economy. This problem is, of course, only one facet of the more general one of 'sharing the fruits of expansion'. The economic climate, early in 1960, which has already been referred to, made any spectacular progress here difficult. But the debate was launched. It was the big item on the agenda for economic policy in 1962 as will be seen in Part Four.

II. THE GOVERNMENT'S DIRECTIVES

The issue by the Government of its directives to the General Planning Commissariat represents a watershed in the process of elaborating the Plan. Before that, work is essentially one of forecasting and of facilitating the choice of ends and means by the competent bodies who have either to advise on the choice or to make the final decisions. Afterwards, the technicians have a specific set of objectives to which they must work and the contacts they have in increasing number with other bodies, in particular with the Planning Commissions, lead them to envisage problems from a policy angle. This distinction has to be qualified to take account of the fact that the work on projections is a continuing process in many cases, and also that operational planning does not wait for the Government's directives before it begins. Nevertheless, the change in purpose and content with the issue of the directives is marked.

The directives were dated June 8, 1960, and occupied some thirteen roneotyped pages. As the document is given in full in Appendix 1, it is not necessary to do more here than to note the main points. Their object is to enable the Planning Commissions to carry out their work in a common perspective of the economic development of the country. Beginning with an enumeration of the chief national tasks (overseas development, adaptation of economic structures to freer trading conditions, modernization of the military forces, and increased well-being of the population), the directives go on to expand on the last point of improved welfare. The present position is analysed in the light of a number of special problems (regional disparities, housing conditions in large towns, large families, the aged and so on) and a general one (the halt to the rise in living standards after 1957). The stress on collective consumption (health, education, town planning, leisure, etc.) is considerable and gives one of the major notes of the final Plan. Turning to the rate of growth, the overall goal fixed for the Plan is to be 5 per cent a year of gross internal production. But the directives specify that the work of the Planning Commissions will show whether it is possible to move up to 5½ per cent, a concession to the view expressed by the Planning and Investment Section of the Economic and Social Council. A qualification is introduced, however, as regards the length of working hours when the directives note that such a rate of growth makes it difficult to envisage a reduction in hours 'which should not be an aim of the Fourth Plan but the final criterion of its success'.[1] In this connection a warning is added on the need to keep the external accounts in balance and to maintain stable prices.

A third section is devoted to an enumeration of what the overall growth-rate requires as a response from each of the main sectors of the economy.

The last section contains a number of considerations grouped around the idea of maintaining the 'basic balances' during the four years of the Plan. Each Planning Commission has a job to do here in its own sector and specific mention is made of the Rueff report prepared early in 1960 on the obstacles to expansion.[2] But the major tasks are wider ones. They concern maintaining balance as regards manpower, external transactions, savings and investment, and regions. The directives expanded on each of these points in turn.

Finally, the Government recalled the timetable for the Fourth Plan, and in particular the need to consult Parliament before the beginning of the Plan period.[3] This meant that the Planning Commissions would have to start work in a few weeks so as to make it possible to establish the first synthesis at the beginning of 1961, and to complete their reports during the summer of 1961.

III. THE FINAL STAGES

This phase, which lasted practically during the whole of 1961, is one of intense activity. The circle of persons engaged in the planning process widens from a few dozen to over three thousand as the Planning Commissions enter the scene. The technical staff of the Commissariat, the SEEF and, to a less extent, the CREDOC, find their work taking on a more normative, policy character at the same time as it becomes more detailed and precise. The Ministry of Finance, most of the spending Ministries and the General Planning Commissariat, are called upon to take the thousand and one decisions, some of them important policy actions, others concerning points of detail,

[1] See Directives, page 6.

[2] Due to the wide publicity it received, this report's reputation has gone beyond its real content. It should not lead the reader to lose sight of the work being done in the same direction through the General Planning Commissariat and the Planning Commissions.

[3] Which had never been done before.

which are called for as the details of the Plan are filled in.

It is not easy to make any sharp divisions into phases at this stage of the work. Technical refinements are going on all the time even when the document containing the Plan has been submitted to Parliament at the end of 1961. Policy decisions are similarly spread out over the year. The characteristics of this phase can best be seen by examining first of all the work of the Planning Commissions, distinguishing the work of the Vertical from the Horizontal Commissions. This being done, the stages leading to the drafting of the final synthesis of the Plan for submission to the High Planning Council and the Economic and Social Council can be seen more clearly.

1 *Vertical Planning Commissions*

As explained elsewhere,[1] there are twenty-two Vertical Commissions which can be grouped according to social and productive activities. This distinction is important both for the type of work done by each, and the way in which it is incorporated into the Plan. We devote Chapter IX to a more detailed examination of the Planning Commissions. Here we shall be concerned solely with their contribution to the Plan viewed as a set of coherent objectives describing in a quantitative manner the evolution of the economy from 1962 to 1965. This contribution is made essentially through the submission of statistical data to the General Planning Commissariat.

When the Planning Commissions were constituted in the summer of 1960 they, and their rapporteurs—nearly all civil servants—were supplied with a certain number of documents. These serve a double purpose; they inform the Planning Commissions of the main lines of Government policy and they contain a detailed request for information. Each member of the Commissions received a copy of the Government's directives, accompanied by a short statistical paper prepared by the SEEF called 'Economic Prospects for 1965 corresponding with the Government's directives', which included a breakdown of production into three sectors and of expenditure by main categories (consumption, investment, etc.). A brief note described the methods of drafting the Fourth Plan with particular reference to the work of the Commissions.

The rapporteurs of each Planning Commission received a more precise documentation. It consisted of the national accounts for the year 1965 (base year 1959) giving resources and expenditures by major categories, employment projections according to twenty-eight branches and similar data for investments and production, a summary forecast by sectors of productivity trends, a breakdown of

[1] See Chapter I.

consumer expenditures, imports and exports and investments by sectors in 1965. In practice it was found necessary to give more details to some working parties who were unable to use the twenty-eight branch classifications. Later on, two technical notes were sent to each rapporteur, one giving the hypotheses lying behind the forecasts for foreign trade, the other dealing with changes in prices. The second was an attempt by the planning authorities to overcome the distortions introduced by projections at constant prices, due either to anomalies in the price structure in the base year or, more important, to changes in relative prices over the period of the Plan. The rapporteurs of each Commission were asked to comment on the trends in prices indicated in the note.

Besides these working documents, each rapporteur received the relevant papers enabling him to comply with the first task set to each Commission which was the completion, by February 1961, of the questionnaire. From the point of view adopted in this chapter, this was the key task of the Commissions.

The field covered by each Commission is defined according to a certain number of products and services for which each one studies the outlets and general prospects. This standard inter-administrative nomenclature, called the 'SH system', can be contracted or expanded; the full system uses sixty-five categories of goods and services, but the problems of aggregation of the results for each Commission were too great and the replies requested were based on twenty-eight groups only, even where working groups had used the more detailed classification.

The questionnaire itself consisted of seven statistical tables dealing with:

production and consumption of the branch concerned by major categories for the period 1956-61 and the year 1965;

foreign trade by regions in 1959 and estimates for 1965;

production of the branch concerned consumed by other sectors as intermediary products in 1959 and estimates for 1965;

consumption by the branch of raw materials and intermediary products in 1959 and estimates for 1965;

investments by purpose and type, and means of financing of total investment, in 1959 and estimates for 1965;

data on employment (numbers, hours worked, productivity, qualifications) in 1959 and estimates for 1965;

location, by regions, of manpower employed by the branch in 1954 and 1965 (1954 being the last census year in France).

A detailed note to all rapporteurs explained how the tables should be filled in. It was stated that all Vertical Commissions were expected to complete them, as far as they were able to do so. The Commissions were not to limit themselves to supplying statistical data, but were requested to supplement them wherever possible with information concerning the likely trend in production techniques, prices and geographical location of production. The General Planning Commissariat also asked for full notes explaining how the estimates in the tables had been made, as well as for copies of the detailed studies done by each Commission's Working Parties.

The first replies by the Vertical Commissions, in February 1961, bore the traces of the tight timetable to which they had been working, and also of the difficulties met with by many Commissions in filling in the tables. Replies were sometimes rather summary and others inconsistent. A very big task of adjustment therefore fell to the staff of the SEEF through consultation with the rapporteurs and cross-checking with other Commissions. It is possible that this experience will lead to a remodelling of the questionnaire so as to make it more immediately intelligible to the Commissions, even though the strict conformity with national accounting concepts may have to be sacrificed somewhat. The final versions of the questionnaires were not ready until the summer, after completion of this process of harmonization.

The value of the statistical work appears to have been variable from one Commission to another.[1] In general, the Commissions still represent a useful source of data, not least as regards the ex-post performance in their respective sectors up to the most recent year. Statistical information in France is still subject to lacunae and the Commissions help to fill them. Concerning the projections, experience seems to have shown that a few highly concentrated productive sectors (energy, transport, steel) are able to supply aggregate data on investment schemes and related aspects of development as there exist fairly well-known, and not too numerous, projects established by each company. There are exceptions to the degree of precision in reporting. In the public sector, the Atomic Energy Commission's projects are much less well-known than those of the rest of the energy group. In the case of a concentrated, essentially private, industry, like the motor-car industry, where national and international competition is intense, the development plans of the firms are much less well-known and this is true of the nationalized firm (Renault) as well.

[1] We are not referring here to the wider aspects of the system of the Planning Commissions which are discussed elsewhere.

The procedure used by the 'social' Vertical Commissions (health, housing, education) is rather different from that of the Commissions dealing with productive sectors. The former start from a concept of needs and, although some tentative projections of these have been made by the General Planning Commissariat, following the Government's directives, the Commission's figures more often than not exceed what is possible; they have to be submitted to further arbitrement inside the Government during the preparation of the final synthesis which we describe below.[1]

The work of the Commissions dealing with sectors where there are a large number of small- and medium-sized production units, is different again. They are not in a position to build up aggregate projections from plans of individual firms. This is the case of agriculture, most transformation industries, and trade and services. The projections made in these sectors are, therefore, heavily dependent upon past trends corrected for a few major influences thought likely to be important. In the last analysis, the process is one in which the forecasts made by the General Planning Commissariat are checked by the representatives of the branch, or at least commented upon, often after consulting other branches, and then adjusted in discussions between the Plan and the Commission. In some sectors, now that so many transformation industries have achieved representation in the Commissions, statistics are almost entirely lacking and, even where they exist, their aggregation in a useable form is difficult. As for the manpower and financial aspects of the objectives and their realization, there was a considerable paucity of data in most sectors. In general, however, the rôle of the Plan in stimulating industries to improve their self-knowledge has been a constant factor since the war, and great progress has been made in gathering, and analysing, statistical data. Attitudes towards figures have changed also; they are no longer seen as secrets to be guarded jealously from prying eyes at all costs, although this does not mean that the 'secret des affaires' is a thing of the past.

2 *Horizontal Commissions*

As explained in Chapter I, there are five Horizontal Commissions (General Economic and Financial, Manpower, Regional Development, Productivity, Research). The main task of preparing the final version of the Plan falls upon the first—the General Economic and Financial Commission—assisted by the Manpower Commission.

(a) *The General Economic and Financial Commission.* In fact, as

[1] This problem is referred to again in Chapter XII.

for the Vertical Commissions, the spadework is done by a series of working parties. The General Economic and Financial Commission had six of them: Private Funds, Public Funds, Statistics, Fiscal, External Accounts, Equilibrium. The last is the key working party —its Chairman was M. Gruson—and can be considered as the testing ground for the final synthesis before it is passed up to the Commission as a whole.

The task of the Equilibrium Working Party was defined as follows: '... to check the compatibility of the propositions put forward by the various Planning Commissions and to lay down an overall economic balance in conformity with the Government's directives. It is also charged with pointing out the risks likely to upset such a balance, to indicate how they can be overcome and, if necessary, to propose changes in the objectives of the Fourth Plan. To this end, the Working Party will carry out, in the first quarter of 1961, a first synthesis of the proposals put forward by the Vertical Planning Commissions. The final synthesis will be done during the third quarter of 1961.'[1]

The mandate of the group was, therefore, an extremely wide one. It embraced two aspects of the Plan where the contribution of the Vertical Commissions was particularly weak—finance and manpower, the second being carried out in close collaboration with the Manpower Commission.

It has already been noted that the systematic search into the financial aspects of the Plan was one of the innovations of the Fourth Plan.[2] The Equilibrium Working Party was used by the SEEF to try out its suggested conceptual approach for the study of these problems before it became absorbed in the task of collating the data submitted by the Vertical Commissions. This was the object of the report submitted in December 1960, and which has been summarized in Chapter VI.[3]

During 1961, however, the work of the Commission and its Working Parties became inseparable from the preparation of the Plan itself and we shall discuss the two together later in this chapter.

(b) *The Manpower Commission.* As the Manpower Commission's work was more specialized than that of the General Economic and Financial Commission, it can best be considered as a whole although, in practice, collaboration with the General Economic and Financial

[1] *Rapport Introductif aux Travaux du Groupe de l'Equilibre de la Commission de l'Economie Générale et du Financement du Plan,* December 1960.
[2] See Chapter VI.
[3] Cf. Footnote 1.

Commission in the preparation of the final synthesis was continuous.

Manpower problems were studied much more extensively for the Fourth Plan than previously. In addition to the traditional analysis of overall employment and its distribution between chief sectors of activity, which was entrusted to a special committee, two others were set up by the Manpower Commission to examine, respectively, needs for professional qualifications and the manpower situation by regions.

(i) *Employment by major sectors.* This was of capital importance in determining the objectives of the Plan. As was explained in Chapter VI, the technicians of the SEEF 'tested' their projections of production against the likely manpower balance, the data for the latter being supplied mainly by the Manpower Commission. The conclusions reached during this stage of the work contributed to the Government's decision to raise the overall growth target from 5 per cent a year to 5.5 per cent.

The basic data at hand were various. The results of the last population census, taken in 1954 and kept up to date by the INED and the population forecasts made by that body, enabled the Commission to project manpower availabilities.[1] On the demand side, the Ministry of Labour carries out three-monthly employment inquiries and the General Planning Commissariat and the SEEF had made some initial estimates by sectors of activity. Then, during 1961, it became possible to study the replies by the Vertical Commissions to the questionnire. But, despite the improvement over the years in the popula-

MANPOWER AVAILABILITIES, 1959-65

(*Thousands*)

	1959	*1961*	*1965*	*Change 1961 to 1965* '000	*Change 1961 to 1965* %
Total active population with constant activity rates ...	19,640	19,770	20,370	+600	+3.0
Effect of raising the school leaving age	—	−140	−460	−420	—
Effect of lower activity rates in older age groups ...	—		−100		
Net immigration	—	+130	+420	+290	—
Total available active population	19,640	19,760	20,230	+470	+2.4
Armed Forces	550	550	360	−190	—
Total civilian availabilities ...	19,090	19,210	19,870	+660	+3.4

Source: Rapport Général de la Commission de la Main d'Oeuvre, 1962, p. 15.

[1] The results of the 1962 census are only now becoming available.

tion and employment statistics, which has been due in no small part to the work of the Manpower Commission, the Commission felt it necessary to put readers of its report on their guard when interpreting the statistics used.

The results of the projections of manpower availabilities are summarized in the table on page 146.

Estimates of manpower needs using the first synthesis based on the replies of the Vertical Commissions to their questionnaire were the following:

MANPOWER NEEDS, 1959-65
(*Thousands*)

			Changes	
	1959	*1965*	*'000*	%
Agriculture and forestry	4,540	4,100	−440	−10
Industry	7,092	7,460	+368	+ 5
Other	7,208	8,060	+852	+11
Total	18,840	19,620	+780	+ 4

Source: Op. cit., p. 18.

These forecasts depend on the correctness of the estimates of the growth of productivity. Overall, the annual rate used was about the same as the one achieved during the period 1949-59, that is, 4.8 per cent a year. In sectors such as agriculture, chemicals and mechanical and electrical industries, some acceleration of the rate of growth of productivity is expected. In others, especially transport, where the big post-war modernization programme has been completed, progress will be slower than in the past.

(ii) *Professional Qualifications.* The Committee dealing with this study decided quite early in its work that the terminal year of the Fourth Plan, 1965, was too close to be suitable because of the necessarily long-term nature of programmes for education and professional training. However, as precise recommendations had to be made for the Fourth Plan, the Committee chose two end-dates for its studies, 1965 and 1975.

For the 1965 projection, the replies by the Vertical Planning Commissions early in 1961 to the standard questionnaire furnished certain elements. Others were available in two inquiries carried out by the Ministry of Labour in 1952 and 1957 into the distribution of the industrial labour force according to professional qualifications. Moreover, the Committee sent two special questionnaires to the Vertical Planning Commission. The first dealt with the qualifications, and professions, likely to experience a rapid expansion in the future and for which special measures were called for. The second was designed to collect information on the changes being induced in professional qualifications by technical progress and by transformation in job specifications.

A number of separate studies were made for the 1975 projection. The Chairman of the Commission submitted one paper[1] and the INED a second one carried out by other methods. The SEEF's 1975 projection, which was described in Chapter VI, was used in both papers for the estimates of production. Professor Fourastié's study contained two parts: the first set out to estimate the distribution of professional qualifications divided into six groups between primary, secondary and tertiary activities; the second was more detailed and dealt with six types of professional qualifications for each of twenty branches of activity. The methodology used was similar to that adopted by the Italian Institute SVIMEZ.[2]

The results of these studies are given in the table:

DISTRIBUTION OF PROFESSIONAL CATEGORIES IN 1959, 1965 AND 1975

(*Thousands*)

	1959	*1965*	*1975*
Engineers	105	121	155
Senior administrative personnel	67	80	99
Technicians and draughtsmen ...	222	275	377
Foremen	231	256	344
Employees	660	717	839
Skilled workmen	2,165	2,401	2,794
Unskilled workers	3,060	3,170	3,282
Total	6,510	7,025	7,890

Source: Rapport Général de la Commission de la Main d'Oeuvre, 1962, p. 20.

The Commission was at pains to point out the provisional and tentative character of all its work in this field. Much of the data remain incomplete as the Vertical Commissions were unable to supply the figures, either because they did not exist, or because they did not have the time to compile them as well as the other data requested by the General Planning Commissariat. Other difficulties arose due to the absence of any necessary, or rigid, correlation between the needs of the productive sector and the degree of professional qualification of the active population. 'Even a good estimate

[1] Professor Fourastié: *'Essai sur une image de la population active française en 1975 et sur ses niveaux de qualification désirable'.*

[2] Cf. 'Trained Manpower Requirements in the Next Fifteen Years', SVIMEZ, Rome, 1960.

of the needs of firms does not make it possible to deduce exactly the level and type of investments required in teaching staff, in buildings and material for the various types of education, as there is no rigid relationship between a man's training and the function he exercises. Finally, it should be stressed that the needs of the economy are not the only ones to be taken into account. The needs for instruction, the aspirations to culture of a large part of the population, must be among the constant preoccupations of a social policy for education."[1]

(iii) *Regional trends.* Three main factors must be considered when estimating manpower availabilities at the regional level: demographic trends, disparities in employment levels and the decline in agricultural employment. These 'availabilities' can then be confronted with estimates of demand for manpower in each region. The resulting differences, positive or negative, give a picture of the regional pressures likely to manifest themselves. They indicate the size and direction of the regional movements of population, after allowing for the effect of immigration from abroad.

Demographic trends by regions were established for the period 1954 (the date of the last census) to 1975 by members of the INED and INSEE. An important statistical problem here was to account for the influence of internal migrations between 1954 and 1960. Also each regional projection had to be corrected along the same lines as the national projection to allow for the effect, on the active population, of a higher school-leaving age, a lower activity rate among older workers and changes in the participation rate of women. The statistics on unemployment which are currently available in France underrate the actual numbers of unemployed which are only known when a population census is taken. In line with the objective of the Plan of achieving full employment, the Commission used an unemployment rate of 1.75 per cent of the active population available and seeking work. This method therefore implied that existing unemployment—small at the national level, but less so in some regions—would be absorbed in each region during the Fourth Plan.

Taking account of the extent of the future decline in the agricultural population raised more arduous problems. A member of the Vertical Agricultural Planning Commission had prepared estimates of the theoretically 'required' agricultural population in each region if the techniques of cultivation reached in a few advanced regions were generally used. Other evaluations were made by extrapolating migrations from agriculture observed in the past. Finally, the Commission took the figure of 80 per cent of farmers' sons leaving

[1] *Op. cit.*, p. 87.

GROWTH OF NON-AGRICULTURAL MANPOWER AVAILABILITIES, 1960-65
(in percentages)

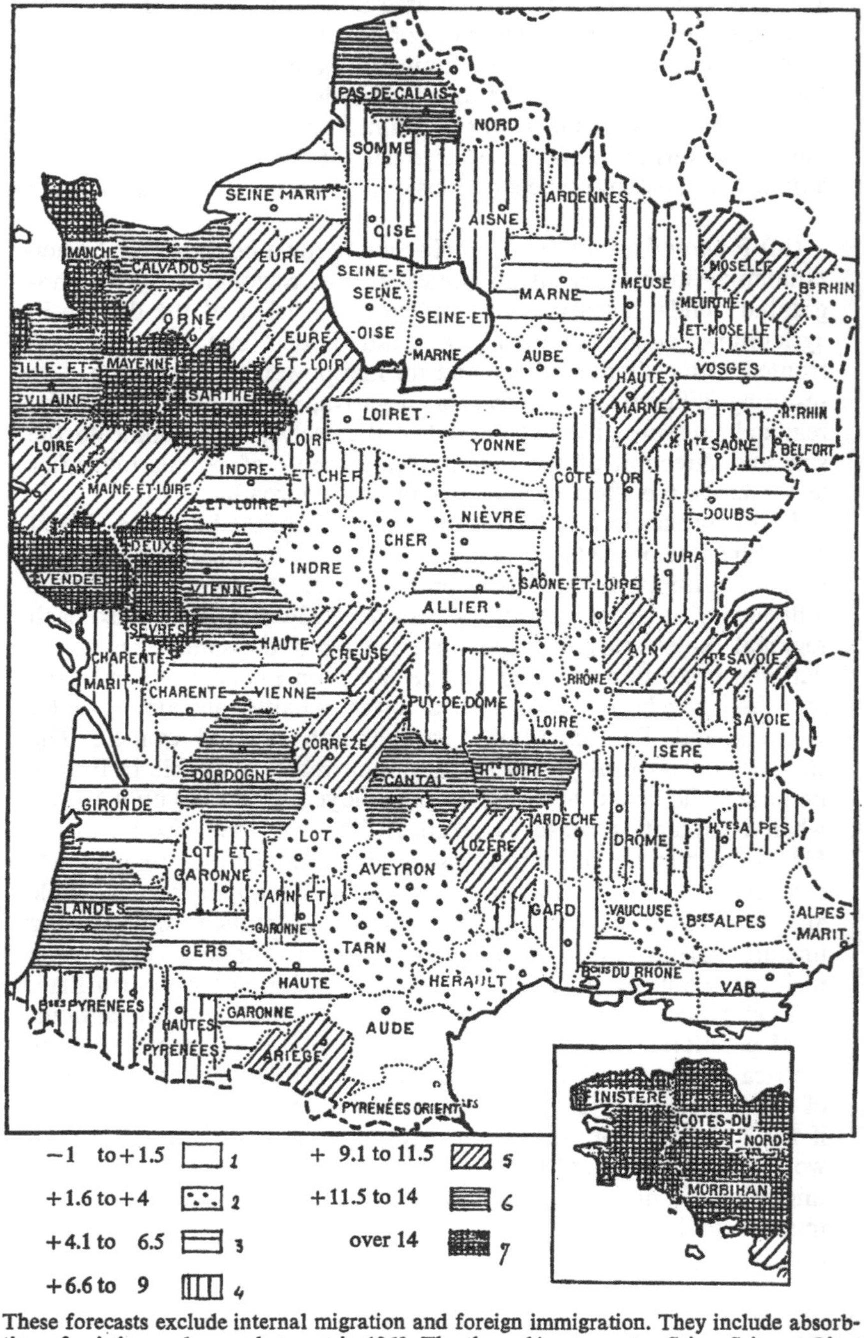

These forecasts exclude internal migration and foreign immigration. They include absorption of existing under-employment in 1960. The three départements—Seine, Seine et Oisse and Seine et Marne—have been treated as a single unit. Data for Corsica not available.
[*Source:* Fourth Plan.]

agriculture between 1959 and 1965 as a maximum for areas such as Brittany, parts of Normandy and the Loire region. Migration rates out of agriculture for the other regions were adjusted in accordance with special considerations applicable to each.

Manpower needs by region up to 1965 were even more difficult to define. The Vertical Planning Commissions had been asked to give evaluations, but their replies were of inequal value. The highly concentrated branches probably gave the most reliable estimates. But trade and other service sectors, where it was known from the calculations made at the national level, that the biggest relative increases were to be expected, remained largely unknown territory.

FORECASTS OF REGIONAL MANPOWER AVAILABILITIES AND REQUIREMENTS 1960-1965

(*Thousands*)

	Increase in non-agricultural employment requirements (*1*)	*Increase in manpower availabilities (including immigration from abroad)* (*2*)	*Difference* (*3*)
North	+ 57	+ 81	+ 24
Paris Region	+298	+124	−174
Picardy	+ 36	+ 37	+ 1
Champagne	+ 26	+ 27	+ 1
Centre	+ 35	+ 35	0
Haute Normandie	+ 40	+ 37	− 3
Basse Normandie	+ 24	+ 42	+ 18
Loire Region	+ 49	+ 80	+ 31
Brittany	+ 34	+ 73	+ 39
Lorraine	+ 55	+ 64	+ 9
Alsace	+ 37	+ 19	− 18
Franche-Comté	+ 27	+ 23	− 4
Bourgogne	+ 28	+ 26	− 2
Rhône-Alpes	+ 98	+100	+ 2
Auvergne	+ 18	+ 26	+ 8
Limousin	+ 7	+ 12	+ 5
Poitou-Charentes	+ 22	+ 31	+ 9
Aquitaine	+ 38	+ 56	+ 18
Midi-Pyrénées	+ 24	+ 45	+ 21
Languedoc	+ 12	+ 26	+ 14
Provence	+ 73	+ 74	+ 1
Total	+1,038	+1,038	—

(Corsica excluded)

Source: Rapport de la Commission de la Main d'Oeuvre, 1962, p. 171.

The Commission exercised considerable ingenuity in deriving quantitative estimates which could be supported by reasonable arguments and the results obtained were highly instructive. It was found that, although 45 per cent of the overall rise in non-agricultural employment by 1965 would be in industry and transport, in Brittany the percentage would be only 20 per cent of the increase in available non-agricultural manpower, and about 30 per cent in the other Western areas. In the Paris region, on the contrary, there would be no rise in numbers seeking work without internal migration. However, the Commission was led to conclude that there were good reasons for thinking that the growth of the Paris region would no longer be faster than the national average.

Finally, the Commission estimated the geographical distribution of the likely numbers of immigrants from abroad up to 1965, and was thus able to present a regional manpower balance sheet[1] which subsequently became the basic reference document for regional development policy.

3 *The Stages of the Syntheses*

Three stages can be distinguished:

a preliminary rapid aggregation leading to the major policy decisions;
the first synthesis proper;
the final synthesis.

(a) *The pre-synthesis.*[2] 'Before proceeding to the synthesis proper, the framework has to be fixed. The general outline of the Plan, notably the growth rate and the level of social investments, have to be fixed definitively.'[3] This task was carried out between February and April 1961. The main aggregates derived from the replies of the Commissions were compared with the initial projection (final demand, demand for manpower, balance of payments, internal financial aspects). Two major divergences from the initial forecasts were noted in employment and foreign trade.

The Commissions' forecasts of productivity tended to be higher than those used by the Plan and, as a result, the margin of security allowed for with a 5 per cent growth-rate was higher than expected. The rôle of margins of security is fundamental in making this sort of

[1] Before allowing for internal migration.
[2] It should be borne in mind in what follows that the Budget and Treasury Directorates of the Ministry of Finance were active participants in most of the discussions relating to the preparation of the synthesis (cf. Chapter XII).
[3] L. Blanc: *Les Techniques d'Elaboration des Plans de Développement Economique et Social,* SEEF, Roneotyped, January 1962.

projection for, although the forecast may be coherent and balanced for a linear growth-plan from the initial to the terminal year, in practice allowance has to be made for annual fluctuations which are inevitable. If the figures supplied by the Vertical Commissions were to be accepted, it appeared that it would be possible to aim at a rather higher growth-rate than the 5 per cent per annum fixed by the Government's directives. After consultations between the rapporteurs of the Vertical Commissions, the Equilibrium Working Party and the General Planning Commissariat, it was finally decided to recommend to the Government the adoption of a 5½ per cent growth-rate, a possibility already mentioned in the directives, and one which was in line with the opinion expressed by the Planning and Investment Section of the Economic and Social Council. It should be recalled that the growth-rate for agriculture—allowing for a big increase in exports—had also been raised following consultation with the Agricultural Commission. The Government accepted the new goal of 5½ per cent in May 1961, and informed the Vertical Commissions of its decision.

The estimates of foreign trade made by the Commissions appeared finally to the authorities to be excessively optimistic due to a high level of exports and a low level of imports, leaving an external trade surplus notably larger than the initial forecast. The General Economic and Financial Commission asked its Foreign Trade Working Party to assist the Equilibrium Working Party in examining the situation which had thus arisen. After discussions with the Vertical Commission for Transformation Industries—where the major divergence had occurred—it was decided to raise the import estimates and reduce the export estimates so as to leave a lower trade surplus. The branches where adjustments of some size were made were the motor-car industry and the production of agricultural machinery.

As for the Social Commissions, their investment totals exceeded the initial projections in several important respects, a result which follows normally from the preoccupation of the Commissions with needs and not with financial possibilities, and this despite the large increases already foreseen by the Government's directives. The final decisions on these questions were made by the Government during the spring of 1961. Account was taken both of the need to maintain overall balance between supply and demand and of the fact that, for some types of investment, it was unlikely that the spending administrations could organize efficiently such a rapid increase in credits. This applies notably to the Ministry of Education where there was already a gap between credits available and spent.

Whilst these decisions were being taken, the SEEF and the General

Planning Commissariat continued their work of harmonizing the replies of the Vertical Commissions and of helping them to complete correctly the statistical tables.

(b) *The First Synthesis.* By May 1961, the final decisions on the main objectives of the Plan had been taken and the Equilibrium Working Party was able to start work in drawing up the final synthesis. This meant that the estimates made by the Vertical Commissions had to be co-ordinated so that the detailed task of aggregating the result could begin. The summation took two forms: the physical balance and the financial balance.

A breakdown by sixty-five branches is used for the detailed verification of the production balance. The data collected from the Vertical Commissions on technical or structural changes are allowed for, and then the aggregation of the outlets for each branch gives the final structure of demand broken down according to major categories of expenditure. This being done, the analysis works back to the production levels for each branch needed to meet demand—taking account of consumption of intermediate products. In practice, as elsewhere in the methods used by the technical services, there is a continual process of checking and counterchecking as the adjustments called for are introduced in order to maintain the coherence of the overall picture.

The study of the financial aspects of the Plan was the special responsibility of the Equilibrium Working Party, particularly as the novelty of the exercise seems to have created some problems for the Vertical Commissions. This entailed reviewing the initial projections in the light of a more detailed search into public expenditure and the financial situation of the productive sector. The financial aspects are examined by groups, the nationalized sector and agriculture being separated from the rest.

The results of this work were co-ordinated by the Equilibrium Working Party—in consultation with the Manpower Commission—and, by the early days of June, a report was drafted, addressed to the General Economic and Financial Commission, which contained in fact a first sketch of the final Plan. This report of some eighty pages and another eighty pages of annexes, described the main sectors of the economy—households, Government, enterprises, external transaction.[1] The first chapter dealt with the balance of the economy in 1965 as it came out of the final synthesis viewed from the standpoint of the physical and financial balances. The con-

[1] *Projet de Rapport du Groupe de l'Equilibre de la Commission de l'Economie Générale et du Financement du Plan,* June 1961.

clusions of this part led the Working Party to envisage a series of policy measures—as it had received a mandate to do—which would make it possible to achieve balance in 1965. 'The extent of the growth objectives in some branches of production, the problems raised by the regulation of the various categories of home demand, the uncertainties surrounding the external balance, the problems of financing, the pressures which could make themselves felt concerning the burden of investment, wages and prices—all these factors carry the risk of losing control of development during the Fourth Plan. So the conditions and measures making it possible to achieve the balance planned for 1965 have to be examined with care.'[1]

In the second half of its report, the Working Party, therefore, reviewed a number of these specific conditions which can be summarized as follows:

> As regards production and demand, three factors stood out: the need to accept a growth of agricultural production beyond the possibilities of absorption of the home market, the ambitious housing goal and the big increase in public investment of a social character. The conclusions for policy from the likely volume of agricultural production were fairly clear. External markets had to be found but perhaps, in a broader perspective, the progressive contraction of the agricultural population would lessen the problem with time. The housing programme was seen to call for a reform of rent legislation and changes in the financing mechanisms. A higher level of public expenditure would not be achieved in satisfactory conditions unless there was a reform of administrative procedures used by the public departments for implementing investment plans;
>
> Employment would continue to raise a question of qualified personnel and a rapid development in training facilities was called for. In the second half of the Fourth Plan the arrival on the labour market of large age-groups made up of those born after the war made it necessary to have a fast growth-rate, but this called for an incomes policy which would have to be set up;
>
> Financing of investments would probably create a problem for the private sector of industry, especially if the external surplus turned out to be less than expected. It was likely that firms would have to make a wider use of share capital or borrowing. This in turn would demand some changes in the financial institutions. The problem of self-financing would have to be looked at, in addition,

[1] *Op. cit.*, p. 43.

from the points of view of the tariffs charged by the nationalized industries and the level of company taxation;

Foreign trade targets needed a competitive price level and this would be affected by the degree of success achieved as regards income policy and self-financing of investment. But structural changes also in the economy would be called for. Finally, as long as there was no co-ordination of development policies, at least among the Common Market countries, the objectives of the Fourth Plan for foreign trade would remain uncertain.

The reports of the Equilibrium Working Party, and of all the other Working Parties were submitted to the General Economic and Financial Commission which also received from the other Horizontal Commissions—in particular the Manpower Commission—and the Vertical Commissions the essence of their studies. The General Economic and Financial Commission then prepared a report which was ready by September 1961.[1] At this stage the final decisions of principle, and the main incoherences in the work of the Vertical Commissions, had been taken into account. The lengthy document of the Commission was divided into two parts: the conditions required to reach balanced growth along the lines defined by the objectives of the Plan, the means at the disposal of the authorities for achieving these objectives through financing of investments and fiscal policy. It is indicative of the general run of preoccupations behind the Fourth Plan that such heavy emphasis was placed upon maintaining economic balance and that problems pertaining to investment financing and income distribution should have received special treatment.

The main lines of the report of the General Economic and Financial Commission, although it omitted its technical annexes, did not differ sufficiently from the report of the Equilibrium Working Party, or the final version of the Plan which was submitted to Parliament, for it to be necessary to analyse it here.[2]

(c) *The Final Synthesis*. To all intents and purposes the Plan was now ready to be drafted as a policy document for the last round of consultations which we examine in Chapters VIII and X. There remained, however, a technical stage which had not been developed very far previously but which was needed with the Fourth Plan. It

[1] *Rapport de la Commission de l'Economie Générale et du Financement*, September 1961.

[2] The final version of the Plan, as it was published in the Official Gazette, is summarized in Chapter XI.

will facilitate the follow-up procedure which, as will be seen in Chapter XVI, is to be much more systematic from now on, in particular as regards the annual economic budgets. The object is to compile a statistical picture of the Plan which is as exhaustive and as coherent as possible, and which contains all the relevant background information on decisions taken. The work involved is considerable as the changes in the objectives of the Plan, which are introduced either as a consequence of the final consultations or of the vote by Parliament, have to be allowed for. It was not, in fact, completed until the autumn of 1962.[1]

[1] The work of the CEPREL, referred to in Chapter V, in checking the Third Plan against the facts, had shown how difficult this apparently straightforward task can be.

CHAPTER VIII

FINAL CONSULTATIONS

The main lines of the final version of the Fourth Plan were approved by the Government during the first half of October 1961. Before presenting the Plan to Parliament, at the end of November, two further consultations took place, the first with the High Planning Council which had played no rôle so far in the planning process, the second with the Economic and Social Council which was, therefore, consulted a second time and, contrary to previous occasions, before the date when the Plan was due to enter into application.

I. THE HIGH PLANNING COUNCIL

The Council met for three days in the middle of October 1961—its first two meetings were presided over by the Prime Minister, the last by General de Gaulle himself. Because of the very tight timetable to which the technical services had been working, it was not possible to submit a complete draft of the Plan to the High Planning Council, which received a document of some sixty pages entitled 'Introduction to the Fourth Plan'. This text, with some amendments, eventually became the Introduction to the Plan as it went to the Economic and Social Council and to Parliament.[1]

Consequently, the text was very much a policy document and, indeed, the High Planning Council is not a suitable place for a discussion of the technical aspects of the Plan. The meetings were confidential, and no communiqué was issued on the details of the discussions, but it appears that a limited number of questions occupied the major part of the Council's time. They were the 'sharing of the fruits of expansion', agricultural policy and the means of execution of the Plan.

Considering the first point, the authorities dwelt upon the difficulties of maintaining economic balance with a fast rate of growth and, although they did not envisage any concrete mechanisms for achieving this, it was their objective to provoke discussion of the problem. In the event, the debate in the High Planning Council seems to have cleared the way for an advance towards a solution at the technical level. The Council received a specific mandate to

[1] See the summary of the Plan in Chapter XI.

follow-up the question of an incomes policy and fixed a rendezvous in a year's time, that is, in the autumn of 1962. Meanwhile, the authorities tried to settle as far as possible the preliminary statistical problems necessary before any judgment could be made.[1] The undertaking that the lowest paid workers, earning the minimum basic wage, should get during the Fourth Plan a more rapid increase than the growth of GNP was written explicitly into the Plan, together with provision for improvements in the living conditions of old people.

The vexed question for agriculture was once more the claim both for a full acceptance of the output objectives of the Plan, with all this meant as regards finding outlets abroad, in the Common Market in particular, and for an improvement in the real living standards of farmers. As will be seen in the chapter devoted to agriculture (Chapter XV), the Government made the implementation of the common agricultural policy of the European Economic Community a *sine qua non* for agreement, early in 1962, to go over to the second stage of the Rome Treaty. As far as living standards were concerned, although the authorities resisted successfully, and continue to resist, making an inapplicable declaration in favour of equality between agricultural and non-agricultural incomes, a substantial increase in social investments in the countryside appears to have been secured by the farmers' representatives during the meeting of the High Planning Council.

The actual means of executing the Plan had not been listed very exhaustively in the initial text, but were inserted at the request of the Council.[2]

II. THE ECONOMIC AND SOCIAL COUNCIL

Three aspects of the Economic and Social Council's second examination of the Plan should be mentioned: the procedure adopted for organizing the debate, the final resolution, the distribution of the votes cast.

1 *Organization of the Debate*

The text of the Plan, after the changes introduced as a result of the discussions by the High Planning Council, was submitted to the Economic and Social Council by a letter from the Prime Minister dated November 7, 1961. Its examination was much more rapid than

[1] This work went on during the summer of 1962. The 1962 meeting of the Council is dealt with in Chapter XVII.
[2] See Chapter XI.

during the first consultation as the final vote was taken by the full assembly on November 18th; indeed, the Council complained that time had been so short.

The main work of preparing the draft decision was done by the Planning and Investment Section as for the previous consultation. The Section organized the consultation of all the other Sections of the Council—except the Conjuncture Section—through a set of questionnaires relating to the speciality of each one. Only a few days were available for this work. But the inconveniences of the short timetable were somewhat attenuated by the fact that a not inconsiderable number of the Counsellors had participated already in one capacity or another in preparing the Plan, for example, as members of Planning Commissions, or of the High Planning Council.

The text of the ESC's resolution was published in the Official Gazette together with, exceptionally, the ten replies received from the specialized Sections on the points in the Plan which concerned them.[1] The final debate by the full Council lasted three days; the Commissaire General attended it and answered questions. General de Gaulle was present at the last session.

2 *The Tenor of the Council's Resolution*

The tenor of the Council's resolution was favourable to the Plan. The Counsellors were pleased to point out that the growth-target and the rise in social investments in the final text conformed to the wishes of the Planning and Investment Section expressed during the first consultation. This opinion did not prevent the Council from scrutinizing the Plan carefully, and from introducing a series of criticisms or question marks.

A chief consideration was the social aspects of the Plan. Despite the intention announced in this document of promoting further the welfare of certain less-favoured groups of the population, the Council thought that something more precise was needed. It was suggested that the conclusions of the two Commissions on the problems of the family and of the aged, which had been set up by the Prime Minister and had just submitted their reports, should find a place in the Plan.[2] There was an urgent need to see that the lowest paid workers—those earning the basic legal wage[3]—should receive an immediate increase and for the future this wage should be linked not only to the price index but to the general growth of the economy. Moreover, the

[1] *Journal Officiel, Avis et Rapports du Conseil Economique et Social,* No. 26, December 12, 1961.
[2] See Chapter I, p. 41.
[3] Known as the SMIG—*Salaire Minimum Interprofessionnel Garanti.*

existing regional differences in the legal rates which only encouraged internal migration and were not really justified by differences in living costs, should be abolished. It is noteworthy that, in 1962, the Government complied with all of these requests as part of its policy for sharing 'the fruits of expansion'.

The Council also approved the principle of this policy, which we discuss at length in Part Four. It should be noted immediately that neither the Government nor the Council spoke simply of an incomes policy, which was seen as a part, but only a part, of the wider policy of sharing the fruits of expansion. The Council stressed that, besides questions relating to incomes, it was necessary to take into account such elements of living standards as education (scholarships, rural problems, equality of opportunity, etc.), working hours and social security. But a strong reminder was inserted that an incomes policy did not mean interfering with the freedom to negotiate wages and salaries and to conclude collective agreements. This could be taken at such an early stage in the debate on incomes as a bargaining counter which the trade unions and employers could 'interpret' later on.

The Council had some specific recommendations to make for implementing the Plan. The necessary link between the Plan and the budget was underlined and the idea was put forward that just as, since 1956, each budget has to be accompanied by an economic budget, so it should henceforth be accompanied by a text showing how the Plan was being achieved. Among the specific measures used to influence the private sector, credit mechanisms were singled out for attention. The suggestion was recorded that the scrutiny by the Plan of requests for long- and medium-term borrowing ought to cover the use being made by a firm of its self-financing powers. Also short-term credit priorities should be available to firms working to achieve planned targets. As regards fiscal policy, the Council considered that such a complex subject needed a special study, and this is now under way.

The sections of the resolution on agriculture bore the traces of rather difficult compromises. On this controversial issue, the opinion of the representatives of the agricultural group was recorded but the Council as a whole did not voice its disagreement with the Plan when it said that, from now on, improvement in living standards could only come from higher output and productivity, with less workers on the land, and greater assistance from the budget for specific investment purposes, and not from higher prices. Still it noted that the agriculturists' request for an immediate general increase of 5 per cent in producers' prices was not very large and could make it easier for the farmers and the Government to agree on agricultural policy in general.

On regional development, the Council was more restrained than Parliament.[1] The procedure for operational tranches, and a 'propulsive' public sector policy in the less advanced regions were approved. But the Council did not think that these innovations made the process of programme laws superfluous.[2]

Turning to foreign trade, the resolution remarked that this was likely to be the Achilles heel of the Plan due to the rather optimistic forecasts for imports and for exports (not only of agricultural products, but also of industrial goods). It will be recalled that these forecasts had already been scaled down by the Horizontal Planning Commissions, except for agricultural exports. The Council saw one way of limiting the risk of disappointments in this sector in an international co-ordination of development policies, a point to which we return in Part Four.

Finally, the Council accepted the evidence of the figures which showed that, however good a case could be made out for raising investments expenditure—particularly social investment—this could only be done by reducing other items, as the Plan as a whole appeared to be coherent. But a rider was added, according to which the Council felt that the acid test of the authorities' sincere desire to apply the Plan would be the way the objectives in the field of social investment were respected. Here also, the Council was of the opinion that programme laws would be a useful guarantee against the temptation to reduce budget credits below the objectives of the Plan.

In conclusion, the Council took a strong line on its rôle for the future in controlling the application of the Plan, and this with an eye on the High Planning Council which it obviously considered to be something of a usurper. 'Whatever the care given to drafting the Plan, it remains, particularly in present circumstances, a continuing creation whose objectives and, even more so, whose means of action will have to be adjusted periodically. Having been associated with the preparation of the Plan and, today, with its final drafting, the Council should be the body charged with following-up its execution. It should be informed periodically of its results and be consulted when changes or revisions are contemplated, as well as for the setting-up of four-year regional programmes. By its composition and structure the ESC is fully qualified to carry out this task.'[3]

[1] See Chapter X.
[2] The programme law procedure is discussed in Chapter XII.
[3] *Op. cit.*, p. 1097.

3 *The Council's Resolution*

The Council's resolution was carried by 127 votes for and 15 against, with 41 abstentions. Those voting in favour were two of the four trade union groups (CGT-FO and CFTC), the agricultural group, the nationalized industries, the artisans, the family associations, the co-operatives, the overseas representatives, miscellaneous activities and all the independent personalities except one who abstained. Only one organized group voted as a whole against the project—the CGT—with two members of the CGC—and one from the group of miscellaneous activities. The vote of the CGT merits some consideration. The attitude of the representative of this trade union federation towards the Plan was quite consistent with the majority tendency in the CGT over the years. (See Chapter XVIII.) Already during the meeting of the High Planning Council, the CGT representative had expressed himself to the Press in the following terms. 'There can be no question for the CGT of supporting such a Plan. People make a lot of song and dance about its social character. In fact, the promises of social investments are not only cruelly below needs but are accompanied by no financing guarantee. If, as its authors admit, the Plan contains a large number of uncertainties, it contains two certainties: firstly, the measures in favour of the monopolies to increase their power, to speed up their concentration and to provide them with new and substantial privileges, notably tax privileges; secondly, the Plan is a set of measures against the interests of the working class, it is openly directed against a reduction in working hours and announces, in the disguise of productivity and profitability, a new insensification of work.' (M. Krasuki, quoted in *Le Monde*, October 20, 1961.) Consequently, the attitude of the group in the vote on the ESC's resolution was quite logical.[1]

[1] However, it should be recalled that the CGT, although most of its leaders are members of the Communist Party, is not always as monolithic as this situation would lead one to conclude at first sight. We deal with the attitude of the trade unions to planning in Chapter XVIII. Meanwhile, it may be noted that, after the trade union split in 1948, some trade unions remained with the Confédération Générale du Travail even though their leaders are not members of the Communist Party. *A fortiori* the rank and file of the affiliated unions cannot be assimilated automatically to members of that party or to its sympathizers. Among the non-Communist members, the lead in a minority movement, inside the confederal bureau of the CGT, on economic and trade union problems (in particular the attitude towards economic planning and trade union unity) has been assumed for many years by M. Le Brun, a member of the bureau. The decision of the majority of the CGT group being in favour of voting against the ESC's resolution on the Fourth Plan, the position of M. Le Brun, who for years had been the leader of the CGT group in the ESC, was rendered extremely difficult, all the more as he

As for the abstentions, the major part consisted of the whole private enterprise group. This vote also calls for some explanation. It should be remembered that the Council was voting on the Council's resolution commenting on the Plan and not on the Plan itself. The original draft of the resolution by the Planning and Investment Section was amended in the full assembly in a number of minor respects, especially with reference to social policy. The decision of the employers' representatives to abstain was motivated essentially by this fact, so that their attitude cannot be interpreted as an act of hostility towards the Fourth Plan.

Looking back at the record of the Economic and Social Council's double participation in the consultation procedure for the Fourth Plan—early in 1960 and at the end of 1961—it would seem that the level of debate was quite high at the Section level. The proposals and criticisms made were, on the whole, well motivated, quite independently of the opinion which the authorities might be led to form of them. It is perhaps an indication of the value of this sort of consultation that so many suggestions were adopted by the Government, either in the text of the Fourth Plan or subsequently. The desire of the Council to see the growth-target set as high as possible was not without its importance in fixing the growth-rate of 5 per cent in the first instance, and taking the opportunity of increasing it to 5½ per cent. The same is true for social investments and social policy generally. The suggestions put forward in this connection were picked up again during 1962 as part of the French approach to an income policy which we discuss elsewhere. On the technical level, the scrutiny of the ESC did not perhaps teach the little band of technicians from the General Planning Commissariat or the SEEF anything they did not really know already about the statistical and analytical lacunae in their work, but the discussions inside the Planning and Investment Section in particular were not without their value in making clear the importance for policy of a vigorous attempt to overcome them. They provided a useful reinforcement for those members of the public departments who were anxious to develop the analytical and statistical bases of the Plan, both of which are desirable, but somewhat expensive, objectives.

had been vice-chairman of the Planning and Investment Section, and had approved, with amendments, its draft resolution. But, in conformity with the principle that members of groups in the ESC do not represent themselves but are delegated by their respective organizations, M. Le Brun decided to submit to the discipline of the vote, but announced during the debate that he had resigned from his post as leader of the CGT group in the ESC.

CHAPTER IX

THE VERTICAL PLANNING COMMISSIONS

We have already touched on one aspect of the work of these Commissions in connection with the various syntheses of the Plan (see Chapter VII), and the output targets for the sectors covered by each one are summarized in the last chapter of this Part (Chapter XI). But their contribution does not stop there. The Vertical Commissions were still the main channel of communication between the Government and the technicians of the Plan, on the one hand, and the representatives of the private sector, both employers and workers, on the other, during the preparation of the Fourth Plan. And they are likely to remain so, despite the big extension of consultation procedures now being envisaged. Hence the need to analyse in more detail the work they did.

There are other reasons why the Vertical Commissions should be singled out for attention. Part of the criticism levelled at the so-called technocratic aspects of the Plan, mainly by the trade unions, but by other groups also, is founded upon what happened, or did not happen, during the Commissions' preparatory work on the Plan. Now that these bodies are being called together annually to participate in carrying out the Plan, their rôle is greater than in the past. Finally, a closer analysis of the Commissions enables the outside observer to acquire the 'feel' of the planning procedure when looked at from a different viewpoint from the technical one which has been discussed at some length in the first two chapters of this Part.

Not all the Vertical Commissions by any means are responsible for directly productive sectors, and among those that are, some deal with nationalized industries, whereas others are concerned with private industries and services. The work of the Commissions therefore raises different problems as one moves from one type to another. These considerations point to a convenient division into three categories: private, nationalized and social. But as there are now twenty-two Commissions, it is necessary to be selective. In the private sector we shall discuss steel and the transformation industries. The nationalized sector is represented by the work of the Energy Commission. The social sector includes Housing, Education, Culture and Public Health.[1]

[1] The Commission for Urban Development is examined in Chapters III and XIII.

I. THE PRIVATE SECTOR

The steel industry is a key sector for the Plan as success in achieving its targets conditions the chances of many other steel-using sectors in reaching theirs. Although it remains in private hands, close collaboration with the Plan has been the rule since the very beginning of the planning experiment in France, and long before most branches which are covered today by the Commission for the Transformation Industries, which was set up during the Second Plan for the first time. This Commission is, nevertheless, the giant among the Vertical Commissions at the present time and its structure creates a number of problems for the Plan which are not the same as those met with in the steel industry.

1 *The Steel Commission*

The steel target under the Third Plan, from 1957 to 1961, was to raise capacity for crude steel production by 27 per cent, from 14.5 million tons to 18.5 million tons, and it was achieved. The target written into the Fourth Plan shows a faster rate of increase—32 per cent between 1961 and 1965—so that capacity in 1965 will be 24.5 million tons.[1] At this level, the capacity utilization rate will be over 90 per cent, the rate in 1961 having been 95 per cent, or rather higher than in a normal year.

To ensure this, the Fourth Plan states that the investment programme should 'be pursued very actively and should not be delayed, notably by financing difficulties'.[2] The same text adds that: 'Given the importance of the steel programme, financing problems will receive the full attention of the Government. In particular, if a slowing-down in economic activity caused a fall in self-financing possibilities, it would be necessary to see what measures were called for to preserve a balance between investment expenditure and available sources of funds.'[3] This does not go as far as the authors of the Steel Commission's report when they wrote: 'An increase in steel prices would be a decisive measure for reducing the foreseeable gap between expenditure and receipts, and the representatives of the profession insisted strongly [during the work of the Commission] on this point.'[4] But it hardly requires any reading between the lines of the Fourth Plan to

[1] The Steel Commission's report speaks of 24 million tons. Early in 1963, the industry's expansion programme was reviewed and it was agreed that the likely trend in demand justified a reduction of 1 million tons in the 1965 target.

[2] See Fourth Plan, p. 114.

[3] *Op. cit.*, p. 116.

[4] *Rapport Général de la Commission de Modernisation de la Sidérurgie*, 1962, p. 75.

conclude that the Government have no intention of treating the steel plan as a paper target.[1]

The Steel Commission's report dealt mainly with three topics: outlook for demand in 1965, the required level and structure of the investment programme, financing problems.

(a) *Demand outlook.* The terminal year of the Fourth Plan was used for projecting demand for steel. There was no attempt to project the intermediate years, but the possibility of an uneven growth of demand was taken care of by allowing for a margin of unused capacity of between 5 and 10 per cent, which is nevertheless a small percentage compared with experience in many countries. This means that the output target of 24.5 million tons corresponds to an effective demand for steel in an average year of about 22 million tons.

Demand estimates for the home and export markets were made separately. Home market prospects were studied by two different methods: the first by correlation with gross internal production, the second by direct inquiry, market by market. The result by the former method was markedly higher than by the latter. The extrapolation of the same relation between gross internal production and demand for steel which had held during the previous decade suggests that demand in 1965 would reach 19.7 million tons corresponding to a coefficient of elasticity of 1.35. When allowance was made for the slower rate of growth of some big consumers of steel in the future than in the past—that is the railways, coalfields and shipyards—the coefficient was reduced to 1.3, and total demand to 19.2 million tons of crude steel, equal to an annual increase of 7 per cent.

A cross-check was made by direct estimation of demand. Consumption by each consumer group in 1959 was projected forward to 1965, using the growth targets for each sector being studied by the other Planning Commissions. The railways and the coalfields supplied their own estimates directly. A number of technical changes were taken into account as far as they could be estimated, for example, the changing structure of the output of the electrical industry and the growing importance of sectors, such as electronics and motor-cars, whose demand for steel per unit of output is falling. In this way it was possible to draw up demand projections for the principal types of steel products. The Commission considered, too, the extra supply which would be called for if those Vertical Com-

[1] In fact, as is noted in Chapter XIV, steel prices were raised in August 1962, and it may be assumed that the talks between the authorities and the representatives of the steel industry which led up to this decision ranged over the whole field of the industry's development programme.

missions which gave two output targets—an average and a high one—all reached their highest estimates. The motor-car industry was a case in point. The total tonnage of crude steel required by this method was only 16.5 million in an average year, with an upper limit of 17.4 million.

Finally, it was decided to take 18.3 million tons as the estimate of home market requirements in 1965. This figure, which was nearer to the one given by correlation with the General Planning Commissariat's overall output target than to the results of the direct sector-by-sector inquiry, when added to the forecast of 3.6 million tons of net exports, gave the total of 22 million tons mentioned earlier.[1]

(b) *Investment programme.* The Commission sent a questionnaire to all the steel companies requesting details of their investment projects. It transpired that the total of the individual investment programmes corresponded to a crude steel capacity of 24.9 million tons in 1965, or a figure higher than the estimate of requirements. The discrepancy disappears in the Commission's opinion, if scrapping of out-of-date equipment included in the figures but which, in all probability, will not be capable of economic use in 1965, is allowed for. The detailed breakdown by products of output of steel given in the replies to the questionnaire were also compared with the Commission's own forecasts and the divergencies between them are commented upon in some detail in the final report. None of them was very substantial, however—the biggest was for cold strip production—and the Commission concluded that, if all the adjustments it recommended were made by the steel firms, their total investment bill would remain practically unchanged at 7.2 billion New Francs. But it was suggested that the irregular annual investment outlays likely between 1962 and 1965[2] could benefit from some smoothing so as to spread out the financing of the big items over the second half of the Plan.

This aspect of the Steel Commission's work is a good example of the Plan seen as an exercise in generalized market research. The projections made by the Commission, given the information at hand as to growth-rates and needs for steel, were certainly more complete and more reliable than anything a single steel firm, or the professional association of steel firms, could have produced. Whilst there was no compulsion on any of the steel firms to change their invest-

[1] The Steel Commission also estimated production and investment needs in the iron ore mines.

[2] Annual data were requested in this case.

ment and output plans as a consequence of the Commission's work, it is not unreasonable to imagine that the dictates of enlightened self-interest would incline them to do so. And, of course, the industry's perennial financing problem meant that the authorities were going to be in a position to look fairly frequently at the way things were turning out, for example the lower output target fixed in 1963.

(c) *Financing problems.* The sources of finance available to the French steel industry have changed considerably over the last fifteen years:

FINANCING OF GROSS INVESTMENT

(percentages)

	First Plan 1945-53	*Second Plan 1954-57*	*Third Plan 1958-61*
Self-finance	31	37	56
Equity capital	5	6	7
Debentures	3	19	26
Borrowing from public funds or specialized credit institutions	36	28	7
Medium-term bank credits	25	10	4
Total (percentages)	100	100	100
Total (million New Francs)	2,570	3,205	5,010

Source: Groupement de l'Industrie Sidérurgique

Besides the fall in the share of public funds and the rise in self-financing, the increased share of borrowing through the capital market is a striking feature. The steel industry has formed a group, called the Groupement de l'Industrie Sidérurgique which, for many years, has issued a collective debenture loan on the capital market, whose proceeds are distributed to the member firms. But debenture finance, which had its advantages in a period of inflation, despite the indexing system applied, proves costly when prices are more stable. The steel industry estimates that its present ratio of 50 per cent debt to turnover is a maximum and wishes to see it reduced to 45 per cent during the Fourth Plan; hence the importance attached to securing a larger margin for financing investments out of profits through a rise in prices for steel. An additional source of investment funds could be secured by the issue of equity capital, an idea the Fourth Plan supports.[1] The Commission enumerated a number of

[1] See Fourth Plan, p. 116.

other reforms of the fiscal system which, in its view, could be considered, either as eliminating existing anomalies, or as assisting the financing of investment, or both.

The chapter in the Fourth Plan dealing with the steel industry does not refer to these suggestions. But it is striking to compare them with the list of lines of investigation put forward by the Plan to improve the economic efficiency of the fiscal system in general, in its lengthy chapter on 'Fiscal Policy' where many of them do appear. In some cases, this coincidence is no doubt due to the fact that other Vertical Commissions made similar proposals. Also, as was seen in Chapters VI and VIII, the authorities themselves were very concerned from the beginning about the financing aspects of the Fourth Plan. Yet it would be surprising if the work of the Steel Commission had been without influence in this respect.

2 *The Commission for the Transformation Industries*

This Commission is probably the least homogeneous of all. Three branches, mechanical and electrical engineering and textiles, form well over three-quarters of the output of the sectors covered, but many more—leather goods, paper, plastics, toys and even dry cleaning—are also represented. There is no common denominator linking them as their production processes, raw materials and clients are all different. Nevertheless, the Commission deals with sectors constituting a vital part of the French economy. They employ 50 per cent of the industrial labour force and do one-fifth of investment in industry. Although many branches are widespread geographically, the modern ones are usually heavily concentrated around Paris; 75 per cent of employment in the motor-car industry and 60 per cent in the electrical industry are found in that region. But the possibility of changing somewhat this state of affairs is being studied actively in the framework of regional development policy. Attracting the electronics industry to Brittany, now that the decision to set up the public communications research centre there has been taken, is mentioned by the Fourth Plan in this connection. Since 1955, 90 per cent of the jobs created in the provinces are due to industries belonging to the Transformation Industries Commission.[1]

The diversity of the size of the firms is also very great. A large number are small, verging on the handicraft size,[2] notably in the textile and clothing sectors, whereas others are powerful public limited liability companies as in the motor-car industry. But overall, only 41 per cent of the labour force is employed in such companies,

[1] See Fourth Plan, pp. 67-72, and Chapter XI.

[2] However, handicrafts had their own Commission.

so that the small firms predominate. This situation has important consequences for the productivity and financing aspects of the Plan.

The structure and methods of work of the Vertical Commission for the Transformation Industries, the forecasts it made and its general policy recommendations will be examined in turn.

(a) *Structure and methods of work.* The Commission's structure is rather cumbersome, but this is inevitable no doubt given the size and diversity of the branches considered. The sixty-three full members were supplemented by about 1,000 other persons in the sixty working parties which were set up to examine the prospects of 240 distinct branches of activity. The size of the Commission has grown with each Plan. For the Second, when it was first created, there were only seventeen working parties. A division into two groups facilitates the work of the Commission. The first is for the mechanical and electrical industries, the second for textiles and all others not included elsewhere.

It may well be asked whether any further growth of the Commission is desirable, and many technicians would be inclined to reply in the negative, all the more so as, with the Fourth Plan, a number of new branches of industry were studied, whose activities need never be the object of medium-term forecasting at the national level. Uncertainties attaching to future trends in demand have not the same importance for heavy electrical equipment and for corsets, yet both are studied by the Commission. And, of course, they are not, in fact, treated in the same way in the planning process.

Yet the contribution of the Vertical Commissions not being limited to forecasting, does provide a justification for the present situation. The senior rapporteur to the Commission has expressed it as follows: 'In sum, what we invite the Commissions to do is to proceed to an examination of their conscience. From time to time, this leads to explosions of ill-temper, directed at the Government, but the exercise is really one of getting things off one's chest. Drawing up a plan is for the industrialist like going to see a psychiatrist. Once he has said all that is wrong, he tells himself that perhaps, after all, there are some things that are not as bad as all that. And so we manage to get out of these exchanges some extremely interesting suggestions which are then taken up by the various competent Commissions, such as the General Economic and Financial Commission.'[1] As with the Steel Commission, it is instructive to read the chapters of the Fourth Plan dealing with such questions as fiscal policy, credit policy and

[1] M. Chapel: *Le Plan et les Industries de Transformation, Commissariat Général du Plan,* January 1962.

professional training, bearing in mind the detailed report of the Commission for the Transformation Industries.

Furthermore, the information value of the studies done by the Commission and its Working Parties is considerable for the firms in each branch. The principal contact between the individual firms and the Plan is achieved by the professional associations, though. They bear the main burden of the task of getting their members interested in the Plan, and the frequent articles in the trade journals, with accounts of meetings and lectures about the Plan, indicate that most of them take this aspect of their work very seriously. They are also the major source of data of all kinds for the Commission. The rôle of such associations is fundamental for the whole concept of planning in France, which is founded not upon firms but upon branches of activity. For the industrialist, this arrangement has its advantages as the professional association acts as an intermediary between him and the authorities.[1]

(b) *The forecasts.* 'We shall frequently use the word "target" in this report, but there should be no misunderstanding as to its meaning. In the Fourth Plan, as in the Third, the "targets" are not obtained by adding up a set of "programmes" of production, exports and investments of individual firms. The figures given represent forecasts based upon a study of the home and foreign markets for each individual branch of industry, and upon a certain number of general hypotheses.'[2] 'Although the targets for production and foreign trade, which have finally been fixed for each branch, have the advantage of being coherent with each other and with the overall objectives [of the Plan], they must not be taken as intangible. . . . But, even if they had to be revised during the Fourth Plan, they would require, to be achieved, a continued and co-ordinated effort on the part of all the firms and, for that reason, they cannot be assimilated to mere forecasts.'[3] These two quotations summarize the philosophy which lies behind the work of Commissions like the one we are considering here.

[1] 'Clearly, direct contacts between the planning authorities and the private sector take place much more at the enterprise level when branches are highly concentrated and, on the contrary, much more at the professional association level when production is spread over a large number of units and direct contact with hundreds of thousands of small firms is ruled out.' M. de Calan, Secretary-General of the Cotton Textile Association, Conference organized by the *Groupe Français du Comité Européen pour le Progrès Economique et Social*, June 1962.

[2] *Rapport Général de la Commission des Industries de Transformation*, 1962, p. 15.

[3] See Fourth Plan, p. 121.

The insistence in the Plan on the value of coherent forecasts which, partly because they are consistent, are finally something more than mere forecasts, is a recent one. It was only with the Third Plan that the group of Transformation Industries was included in the Plan in a systematic manner, and, even then, it is doubtful whether the existing statistical knowledge was capable of supporting such an ambitious task. But progress is being made all the time and, partly as a result of the efforts of the professional organizations themselves, the data available for the Fourth Plan were infinitely more abundant and reliable than for the Third.[1] Thus the SEEF was able to give to the Commission the initial documentation we described in Chapter VI and this helped many working parties to get started along the right lines. Previously, each working party had to consult the others in the Transformation Industries Commission or elsewhere to see what its own demand prospects were. Hence a considerable waste of time at the beginning and a heavy task of mutual reconciliation of targets at the end. With the Fourth Plan, each took the SEEF's figures as the starting point for its initial forecasts. A second step was to send to each 'client' working party the results of the forecast with a request for comments. In this way, a current of exchange of information was established between suppliers and their clients. For consumer goods, the active participation of the CREDOC was an indispensable element in preparing the forecasts which were not secured directly.

Subsequently, as was noted earlier, the SEEF spent a great deal of time going over their replies to the questionnaires with the various working parties.[2] The insistence of the SEEF on coherent data was not always appreciated and some of them felt that 'they had less liberty in making their forecasts than for the previous Plan'.[3] But the exercise was a salutory one for all concerned, and was finally recognized as such.

Other problems arose where real questions of substance were at issue. Thus the SEEF, with the support of the General Planning Commissariat, had to make quite substantial adjustments in some of the estimates. A number of forecasts of investment needs were considered to be too low and higher figures were used for the general

[1] Cases are now rare indeed where, according to an example given by the general rapporteur of the Commission, one rapporteur of a working party filled in a whole page of forecasts on the basis of one figure, that of employment. 'It was probably wrong, but in any case it was perfectly coherent and, as there were no other statistics, nobody could refute it or give alternative data.' M. Chapel, *Le Plan et les Industries de Transformation, Commissariat Général du Plan,* January 1962.

[2] See Chapter VII.

[3] See *Rapport,* p. 12.

synthesis of the Plan and in the report of the Commission. Export data were often thought to be too optimistic, as was noted in Chapter VII. The motor-car industry is a case in point where, finally, two figures were given in the Vertical Commission's report, but the lower figure was used in the synthesis by the General Planning Commissariat for calculating overall production and the merchandise trade balance.[1]

Some statistical problems remain. In particular the different branches were able to give only very partial replies as to manpower needs by professional qualifications and regional distribution, which complicated the task of the Horizontal Manpower Commission.[2]

This being said, the forecasts finally decided upon and included in the Plan are shown in the table on page 175.

The production target is higher than during the Third Plan, but if allowance is made for the levelling-out in 1958 and 1959, it is about the same as from 1954 to 1957. As, during part of that period, there were marked inflationary trends, the target is quite an ambitious one. The foreign trade forecast is ambitious as well. The big increase in imports in 1960 and 1961, much greater than the rise in exports, is not expected to be repeated so that exports and imports should expand roughly in step from now on. Trade with other industrial countries will continue to grow faster than trade with the old French franc area countries. The biggest export effort will be called for from the electrical engineering sector.[3]

Productivity increases are expected to remain about the same as during the Third Plan as a whole, but, after taking into account the fall in productivity gains in 1958 and 1959 when output was not rising much, the rate forecast for the Fourth Plan turns out to be lower than during the mid-1950s. A reflection of this is the expectation of a higher ratio of investments in most branches to their turnover. Most of the working parties were inclined to estimate a lower level still of productivity gains during the Fourth Plan, but the General Planning Commissariat decided that their attitude was unduly influenced by the unfavourable experience of the years 1958 and 1959.

[1] 'Among the most uncertain of the basic hypotheses is first and foremost the value of foreign trade, the figure for exports even more than the one for imports.' *Rapport*, p. 8.

[2] See Chapter VII.

[3] This is the sector where the procedure of 'quasi contracts' is being used most actively. 'State encouragement to develop production of equipment goods will consist, as at present, on the one hand, of repayable financial assistance for research and the development of prototypes and, on the other, of financial aids during the production period.' M. Chapel: Radio Talk on the 'Transformation Industries and the Plan', January 1962.

TRANSFORMATION INDUSTRIES

Output Targets and Related Data

	(*percentages*) *Third Plan*	*Fourth Plan*
1. *Production*		
A	+23	+31
B	+18	+11
C	+21	+27
2. *Employment*		
A	+ 7	+10
B	− 2	+ 4
C	+ 3	+ 8
3. *Productivity*		
A	+17	+19
B	+21	+18
C	+20	+19
4. *Investments* (ratio to turnover)	1958 to 1961	1965
A	4.5	4.9
B	3.9	4.1
C	4.3	4.6
5. *Foreign Trade*	1959 to 1961 (annual compound rates)	1961 to 1965
Exports	+ 7	+ 8
Imports	+31	+ 8

A=Mechanical and Electrical industries
B=Textiles and others
C=Total

Source: Based upon data given in the *Rapport de la Commission des Industries de Transformation*, 1961

In order to achieve their targets, the Transformation industries will need to recruit over 200,000 additional workers, 150,000 of them in the mechanical and electrical engineering branches. About one-third of this demand will be for trained technical staff and employees; hence the importance attached by the Commission to a big expansion of all forms of professional training.

(c) *The recommendations*. These fall under three headings: financial problems; improvements in the structure of firms; manpower needs.

A general plea for lower taxes on company profits, and more special ones, put forward by the consumer durable goods branches, for lower indirect taxes and for cheaper petrol, were duly noted in the report but the Plan does not make any specific commitments on them.[1] But the authorities are taking the question of fiscal and financial policies very seriously as is illustrated by the importance given to such measures in the Plan. In reply to the Commission's query whether the special tax treatment of new shares should not be prolonged beyond 1963, its present limit, the Plan explains that, before then, a full-scale study of the incidence of direct taxation of company profits in the Common Market will be undertaken. In the credit field, a special committee was appointed in the summer of 1962, under the chairmanship of the Director-General of the Société Générale, one of the big nationalized banks, to examine the whole problem of the link between credit policy and the Plan.

The predominance of small-scale firms in the Transformation industries in France was noted earlier. With the prospect of increasing competition from overseas on the home market, and the need to expand exports of their products, this situation is considered to represent a considerable handicap. The Plan echoes the suggestions of the Commission when it declares that 'the authorities will assist in carrying out programmes for concentration and specialization of resources for research, study, production and distribution which are put forward by firms, either individually or collectively'.[2]

A structural problem of a different order arises in the motor-car industry. 'The opening of the Common Market has given the signal for a battle between the various European firms, including the subsidiaries of American companies, which runs the risk of leading to a state of excess capacity in the motor industry in Europe. This could be avoided by a better co-ordination of investments. The authorities will act to facilitate any moves in this direction in the future.'[3]

As for the need for more qualified manpower, the Commission noted that 'the existing shortage will get worse and will compromise the Plan's objectives, despite the increase in official training facilities, if the private sector does not raise its contribution to professional training schemes'.[4] This suggestion is recorded by the Fourth Plan

[1] It postpones the last for the time being. 'A reduction in the tax on petrol, which would in all probability stimulate demand for motor-cars, could be considered when the balance between the financial needs and resources of the public sector is more firmly established than it is at present.' Fourth Plan, p. 127.

[2] Fourth Plan, p. 121. The Commission also raised in this connection the problem of Common Market policy towards restrictive practices. See *Rapport*, p. 118.

[3] See Fourth Plan, p. 127.

[4] *Rapport*, p. 99.

in connection with the programme for professional training at all levels which it provides for.[1]

II. THE NATIONALIZED SECTOR

As was seen earlier, the nationalized sector in France is quite extensive. In the industrial field, the two main sectors are energy and transport and, of the two, energy is the most homogeneous. The very important sector of road transport remained outside the scope of the post-war nationalization measures whereas, in the energy field, although the activities of the international oil companies have to be taken into account, the range of the State's participations in the oil industry is considerable and coal and electricity are both publicly owned. Hence it seemed preferable to choose the examples in this section from the work of the Vertical Planning Commission for Energy.

For the Fourth Plan, the general energy picture in France was very different from the one which prevailed when the Third Plan was being drawn up. The Third Plan's targets were dominated by the idea of a pending energy shortage and stress was placed upon the urgent need to develop the energy resources of Metropolitan France through fixing high output targets for coal, hydro-electricity, atomic energy and natural gas.[2] But quite soon afterwards, there was a rapid change to a surplus position for some forms of energy, and some targets were revised downwards, notably coal. This time, the Energy Commission based all its work upon the assumption that there would be no return to the shortages of the 1950s, for the time being at any rate. 'This situation should furnish an opportunity for fresh reflection on the future conditions of supply and, in particular, on the comparative cost of the various forms of energy.'[3]

The way in which the Commission set about its task, the targets drawn up and the measures proposed in order to reach them are the main points dealt with in the Commission's report.

1 *Methods of Work*

Although there is also an Oil Commission, the Energy Commission is responsible for drawing up the overall energy balance of the country. This is by itself of some importance as it implies that energy

[1] Fourth Plan, p. 41.

[2] Similar measures were taken in the United Kingdom for coal and atomic energy, it will be recalled, although there was never any co-ordination between the targets fixed for the different sources of energy.

[3] *Rapport Général de la Commission de l'Energie*, 1961, p. 11.

problems are seen as a whole and not, as is sometimes the case in other countries, just when individual sectors of the energy industry call for corrective action.

The report presented by the Commission is a substantial document both in density and length.[1] The level of the analysis is very high, and the technical details of the work of the Commission are given in full. So it would be impossible to summarize it in a few paragraphs. Only the basic ideas behind the approach are reviewed here.

The parameters used for assessing future demand for energy up to 1965 were the trend in gross internal production,[2] the energy requirements of the steel industry and the index of transport activity. The value of studying at the same time future trends in output in all sectors of the economy according to a common growth objective is apparent at once. Without it, the Energy Commission would not have been able to use the overall growth target or consult the Planning Commissions for steel and transport. The end-year of the Fourth Plan (1965) appeared too near for it to be suitable for defining the main lines of a policy for energy. So the Commission decided to envisage prospects in 1975 as well, using the two growth-rates of 4 and 6 per cent annually supplied to it for this purpose by the General Planning Commissariat. The Commission considered that it was important to consider two growth-rates in this way, one high, the other modest, because of the need to envisage alternative solutions in the event of unforeseen developments occurring, and in order to allow for the likely difference between the growth of demand for each type of energy and the overall rate. This is particularly important for the coal industry.

The methodological framework adopted by the Energy Commission was that 'one can accept that the levels of production and foreign trade, of prices and manpower requirements, follow from the application of the principle that needs should be satisfied at least cost. But this simple statement hides a very great number of difficulties. One of these is that demand for energy depends upon price policy'.[3] The need to simplify, therefore, leads to the adoption of the hypothesis according to which *overall* demand for energy is not very dependent upon the price level, 'it being understood that, for competitive uses, one cannot ignore the influence of relative prices on the market shares of different fuels'.[4] Then 'if the overall demand for energy is given, as well

[1] It contains nearly 400 pages and is the longest of the Vertical Commission reports.

[2] That is, in GNP less Government services and certain other services.

[3] *Rapport, op. cit.*, p. 33.

[4] *Op. cit.*, p. 33.

as certain quality aspects, the economic problem consists of defining through time the lowest levels of expenditure making it possible to satisfy needs. . . . If a solution to the problem posed in these terms existed, it is evident that it would furnish the basis of a policy for energy . . . (but) it is so vast and complex that the corresponding "model" has not even been begun and, even if it had, and had been tested, most of its elements could not be supplied in quantitative form. Hence the need, provisionally no doubt, for important simplifications. These simplifications must naturally be guided by theory. As we are seeking an optimum solution for the whole of society, it must be one where, whatever the degree of economic liberalism in force, selling prices at the various stages equal marginal costs. Inversely then, if we know something about marginal costs at any stage of the energy chain—production, import, transport, consumption—we can consider certain selling prices not as unknown, but as known factors of the general theoretical problem. In this way, the approach to this problem becomes accessible and, at the limit, it can be divided up into various parts—for example, the study of production, of transport and of consumption'.[1]

2 *Energy Forecasts*

The forecasts of demand are given below:

CONSUMPTION OF PRIMARY SOURCES OF ENERGY

(millions of tons of coal equivalent)

	1959	*1960*	*1965*	*1975* 4 per cent growth-rate	*1975* 6 per cent growth-rate
Solid fuels	72.0	70.4	82.0	85- 67	101- 77
Oil products	35.7	39.1	58.4	109-125	131-152
Natural gas	2.4	4.5	9.2	22- 24	26- 28
Hydro-electricity	13.0	16.1	17.7	23- 24	23- 24
Nuclear energy	—	—	0.7	10- 11	13- 14
Total	123.1	130.1	168.0	250	250

Source: Rapport, op. cit., p. 35.

Although, with a 5.5 per cent overall growth-rate, demand for coal will continue to rise, at least until 1965, the Commission was of the opinion that production programmes, which are founded on a reduction in output, should not be changed, as it is necessary to keep the price of coal at a competitive level, and to avoid marketing problems

[1] *Op. cit.,* p. 34

after 1965. The French franc area is likely to produce as much crude oil in 1965 as it consumes, and this prospect raises the problem of finding outlets on the home and foreign markets. Output of natural gas from the Lacq deposit in Metropolitan France having reached its upper limit, the gap between demand and supply up to 1964 could be met by reducing consumption of gas by thermal power stations. After that date, ways would have to be found of transporting natural gas from overseas. Production of electricity will continue to expand rapidly, but stress will be placed more and more upon raising output from thermal power stations.

The investments corresponding to these forecasts are:

INVESTMENT EXPENDITURE
(*millions of New Francs, 1961 prices*)

	1959	*1960*	*1961*	*1965*
Coal (including cokeries at mines)	510	530	450	440
Oil (including research overseas)	2,670	2,460	2,700	2,900
Gas	1,020	660	530	1,250
Electricity	3,350	2,990	2,870	4,310
Total	7,550	6,640	6,550	8,900

Source: Rapport, op. cit., p. 110

These data show that investments in the coal industry will decline, and will rise at a slower rate in the oil industry, as compared with the second half of the 1950s. There will be an increase in investment for the production of gas but it will be sufficient to maintain the same rate of growth in expenditure in the electricity industry. These sectors being all under public ownership, with only some exceptions, the figures are quite firm targets which will be used each year to assess the annual investment needs of each industry (see Chapter XII).

(c) *Policy recommendations.* The recommendations of the Energy Commission, which are taken up by the Plan, are divided into two groups, those dealing with short-term questions and those of a longer-term character.

Stock policy plays a big part in the short-term policy recommendations. The Plan looks forward to improvements here, especially in the coal industry, so as to reduce the incidence of market variations on the level of employment in the mines. The thermal power stations at mines have a rôle to play, and long-term contracts for imported coal should not exceed in future the amounts which are unlikely to be influenced by short-term fluctuations.

These fluctuations affect the relative prices of the different forms of energy and impede the operation of a rational pricing policy. Whilst not proposing any concrete measures in this connection, beyond an improvement in stock policy, the Plan notes that as a last resort, quotas on all forms of energy imports cannot be excluded in the event of serious market disorders. A special committee has been created, which meets at the General Planning Commissariat to study all these, and other, short-term problems.

An important policy objective, from a longer-term point of view, is the definition of a national price system along the lines already mentioned. 'However, the freedom of choice of firms and other consumers is not without limits. It is recognized today that, in order to fulfil its rôle correctly, the market must operate within an appropriate institutional framework.'[1] Thus all forms of price discrimination are undesirable and the authorities have the duty to keep producers and consumers adequately informed, and to control and co-ordinate the programmes and strategies of each. 'The concrete forms of such a policy are varied. Producers of equipment can receive guidance, and suggestions for the improvement of production structures may be made. It may fall to the State to arbitrate between public and private firms concerned with energy questions.'[2]

Moreover, the behaviour of producers and consumers must be put into harmony with general government policy. There is no reason to think that spontaneous market trends would conform to the chief options of overall policy, for example in the field of regional development, and 'it is normal that stimulants or, even, obligations should be required occasionally'.[3]

These same considerations apply to international energy policy as well. The Fourth Plan underlines co-operation in research, in the transport of natural gas and in attitudes towards imports of oil from Eastern Europe. 'The solution to these problems calls for a co-ordinated energy policy in Europe and the Government attaches particular importance to this.'[4] But for the moment, the Government cannot give up measures which make it possible to attenuate the consequences of difficulties due to international trade, in particular guaranteeing the security of energy supplies.

III. THE SOCIAL SECTOR

As was seen earlier, the Fourth Plan envisages a big increase in 'collective' consumption. The forms such expenditure can take are

[1] Fourth Plan, p. 111.
[2] *Op. cit.*, p. 111.
[3] *Op. cit.*, *p.* 111.
[4] *Op. cit.*, p. 111.

diverse; they include housing, education and sporting equipment, cultural activities and public health. There were, in fact, Vertical Planning Commissions for each of the sectors. At several points, the specific programmes drawn up under each of these heads overlap with other aspects of policy under the Fourth Plan, for example with the policy of regional and urban development. Insofar as these topics are dealt with elsewhere (Chapter XIII), we shall not repeat them here.

The work of the Vertical Planning Commissions in the social field was different from that done by the Commissions whose reports were analysed in the first two sections of this chapter. The difference does not lie so much in the nature of the task of the social Commissions—like all the others, they were asked to define objectives and the ways and means of achieving them—but rather in the non-market character of most of the services supplied. The Commissions took needs, not likely solvable demand, as the point of departure for their analyses. This means that the final amount of such needs which can be satisfied during the Fourth Plan, after taking into account all the other calls upon available resources, is a result of policy decisions at government level. Hence the frequent arbitraments by the Commissaire General, despite which a number of objectives written into the individual reports of the Commissions remain higher than the commitments included in the text of the Fourth Plan.

1 *The Housing Commission*

The characteristics of the organization of housebuilding programmes in France have been described elsewhere (Chapter III). We shall be concerned here with the housing situation at the present time, with the forecasts for housebuilding, and with the general recommendations of the Vertical Commission for Housing.

(a) *The housing situation.* There has been a very considerable effort in the housing field in recent years. In 1952, 81,000 units were completed (29,000 of them under post-war reconstruction programmes) and, in 1961, the total had risen to 316,000. But other countries have done better—for example, France comes ninth on the list of European countries arranged according to the importance of their programmes per head of population. Also, a large percentage of houses are old, uncomfortable and poorly equipped, especially in rural areas.[1] There is, therefore, a problem of renewal.

Other problems, which often impede the expansion of housing

[1] The 1954 Census showed that 35 per cent of houses were over 100 years old, and 55 per cent over seventy years old.

programmes, are the increase in land values and the working of rent control legislation. A related aspect is the legal protection granted to certain types of tenants. We note the problem of high prices for building land when discussing the procedure of the ZUP and ZAD.[1] Rent control in France is based upon the 1948 Act, which fixed a ceiling on all rents for housing units built before that date with provisions, which have been changed from time to time since, for periodic increases. Tenants in accommodation built before 1948 are protected from expulsion, except after long legal procedures, as are their direct descendants living with them at the time of their death. On the other hand, all building since September 1, 1948, is in a free sector where rents are fixed by supply and demand, except for the category of housing called 'moderate-priced family houses'.[2]

As in other countries, where rent control and inflation have gone hand-in-hand, the working of the 1948 Act has reduced the mobility of tenants in pre-1948 houses, diminished the amount of expenditure devoted to the upkeep of such houses far below the desirable level, and created unjustified anomalies as between families living in old and new houses.[3]

(b) *Housebuilding targets.* The evaluations of the Commission were higher than the initial figures of the Plan and this situation gave rise to numerous criticisms. The targets in the Plan were revised upwards in 1962 in order to allow for the French nationals returning from Algeria.

The Commission took account of a number of factors in estimating future demand. They were: demographic trends, internal migration and immigration from overseas, the likely rise in consumer incomes and in expenditure on housing, the need to renew the existing stock of housing capital. Finally, the target proposed chose to stress the need to reduce the quantitative shortage to manageable proportions first of all, so that qualitative improvements, through a large-scale programme for demolition and renewal, will not receive priority during the Fourth Plan. The first estimates made by the Commission are given in the Table on page 184.

The Commission considered that the value increase implied by these targets, after allowing for a rise in the average size of housing units and for certain qualitative improvements, was over 30 per cent from 1959 to 1965. But the total of 1,420,000 from 1962 to 1965 was

[1] See Chapter XIII.

[2] Logements économiques et familiaux. About 12 per cent of urban housing units were in the free sector in 1960.

[3] The Commission estimates that in 20 per cent of existing houses, there are no expenditures on repairs at all.

taken as a minimum and the Commission expressed its preference for a target of 1,500,000. The number of cheaper, family houses should reach 215,000 for the period of the Plan.[1]

HOUSEBUILDING TARGETS

(Thousands)

	1959	*1962*	*1963*	*1964*	*1965*	*Total for the Fourth Plan*
Starts:						
Total	310	340	350	360	370	1,420
of which, State aided or financed	270	308	315	320	325	1,260
Completions	320	325	330	340	350	1,345

Source: Rapport de la Commission de l'Habitation, 1961, p. 83.

In fact, during 1962, the target was raised, in the light of the number of French nationals returning to France, and the Fourth Plan notes that: 'The target of 350,000 houses in 1965 could now be reached earlier than was foreseen.'[2] Special measures were taken in 1962 to execute this decision.

The forecasts of needs are likely to continue to be subject to further revisions. As regards cheap housing (the HLM),[3] a programme law was adopted by Parliament in June 1962 for the period 1962-65. This law fixed the amount of loans to the HLM associations at 10.9 billion New Francs for a programme of 390,000 units.

(c) *Measures proposed.*[4] The object of the measures proposed by the Housing Commission is, in the words of the Plan, 'to achieve, during the Fourth Plan, a greater degree of unity in the market for housing and to reduce, in that way, the inequalities which exist today between households with similar incomes, according to the rules in force governing the accommodation they occupy'.[5] Three broad

[1] The Commissaire Général informed the Commission that its opinion had been noted by the Government: 'The housebuilding programmes must move towards a position where 350,000 units will be completed and started in 1965. Although the annual figures enabling this have not yet been fixed, these programmes should make it possible, except in the Paris area, to absorb the most urgent demands by 1965 whilst taking account of the possible return of 100,000 families (to France) during the period of the Fourth Plan. Quoted by the Housing Commission, p. 84.

[2] See Fourth Plan, p. 74.

[3] See Chapter III.

[4] We leave aside here a number of measures relating to town-planning and the introduction of improved techniques in the building industry.

[5] Fourth Plan, p. 74.

groups of measures are envisaged. They concern: the personal contribution by families in order to house themselves adequately, reform of the rent control legislation, the contribution of landowners to the upkeep of their property.

It is suggested that a reasonable share of income which families should devote to housing is 10 per cent. But if an effort was made to reach this figure, it would be necessary to envisage setting-up, at the same time, a personalized form of State aid to certain categories of the population.[1] It would then become possible to have a bolder policy for decontrol of rents. The Commission considered that the average level of rents in pre-1948 buildings would have to rise by 80 to 90 per cent by 1965 so as to achieve a homogeneous market. The Plan did not accept explicitly all these points but announced that studies would be put in hand to see how a general system of personalized aid could be operated. As to rent control, whilst not going as far as the Commission, the Fourth Plan provides for a continuation of the present regular increases in controlled rents. A related problem here is to ensure that owners spend sufficient amounts on the upkeep of their property. The Housing Commission estimated that such expenditures ought to double by 1965. The Plan announces measures in this field but without giving details.

2 *The Commission for School, University and Sporting Equipment*

This Commission had already met on two previous occasions—for the Second and Third Plans. Its work on the Fourth Plan was conditioned by the context in which it was carried out. The Government had already given the green light in its directives when it announced a substantial rise in the State expenditure on education.[2] Also, everyone connected with education in France was aware that big problems were going to be met with during the 1960s, problems which were aggravated by certain shortcomings of policy in the past.

The total of investment expenditure on education during the Third Plan had fallen short, not only of the amount proposed by the Education Commission, but, for most of the period 1958-61, of the amounts proposed in the Plan itself. We shall see the general reasons why this should have been so in Chapter XII, and shall not mention them here. An attempt has been made, in 1960 and 1961, to make up for the lag by increasing budget credits but this policy was hampered by the inability of the Ministry of Education to organize immediately the use of these additional funds. So, by the

[1] That is replacing the system of 'aide à la pierre' by 'aides personnalisées', cf. Chapter III.

[2] See Appendix I, p. 374.

end of the Third Plan, 970 billion Old Francs had been contracted for but only 817 billion had actually been paid out. The Commission took account of these factors in drawing up its programme for the period 1962-65 and in estimating its financial cost.

(a) *The Commission's forecasts.* The scope of the work of the Commission covered all types of education—primary, secondary and higher—whether public or private. Its six working parties studied the following aspects of the Plan for education: forecasts of numbers of pupils and students, staffing needs, equipment of primary and secondary education, equipment of the universities, building procedures and techniques, administrative and financial questions.

Its forecasts were based upon two types of data. The Ministry of Education carried out an inquiry into future trends in numbers of pupils and students, needs for new buildings, problems of overcrowding, effects of raising the school-leaving age and so on. This inquiry was organized with the assistance of the local administrations as far as possible. The Education Commission did some forecasting of its own concerning the future size and distribution of the school and university population.

The numbers at school and in the universities were estimated at two future dates, 1965 and 1970, whereas previously only the end-year of each Plan had been considered. The years ahead will see a further increase coming on top of the one which has taken place in the 1950s. Since 1950, when the upturn of the birthrate during the war began to take effect, and under the influence of improved school attendance and a later school-leaving age, the school population has risen by about 50 per cent, one of the highest rates in the world. From now on, the numbers of pupils in primary education will increase more slowly and those in secondary education very much more rapidly. The demographic wave will reach the universities

SCHOOL AND UNIVERSITY POPULATION

(Public sector only)

(*thousands*)

	1960-61	*1966-67*	*1970-71*
Primary	4,100	3,927	3,695
Secondary	1,909*	2,660	2,942
University	211	440†	506

*1961-62
†1967-68

Source: Rapport Général de la Commission de l'Equipement scolaire, universitaire et Sportif, 1961.

during the second half of the 1960s, and the total of students is likely to be over 500,000 in 1970, compared with only 200,000 in 1960-61.

These global forecasts hide the notable changes which are expected in the relative importance of the different types of teaching at each stage. At the secondary level, stress is being placed upon the development of the 'cycle d'observation', which gives two years' schooling at the end of the primary school before pupils choose the type of secondary education they wish to follow, and upon all forms of technical and professional training which are to be expanded vigorously in line with the estimated future needs for qualified manpower. In the universities, science is expected to absorb the lion's share of the new entrants, and the scientific and technical faculties will represent nearly 45 per cent of the total in 1969, compared with just over one-third in 1960.

These forecasts determine the general frame of the Commission's estimates of staffing requirements. If the situation in the primary schools, which have borne the brunt of the increase in the birthrate up to now, is likely to become easier, it will grow more difficult at the secondary level where staffs will have to be doubled between 1960-61 and 1970-71. For higher education, it will be necessary to recruit, between 1960 and 1970, one and a half times the existing teaching staff and three and a half times the number of instructors.

(b) *Financial programme and related problems.* The total cost of the programmes proposed by the Commission would be 16.9 billion New Francs of which 14.6 billion would fall to the State, the remainder being borne by the local authorities.[1] The Commission also suggested a breakdown of the total for each year of the Plan so that the rhythm in carrying out the various programmes would coincide with needs, thus avoiding a repetition of the problem met with, at the end of the Third Plan, when the Ministry of Education was unable to spend all the credits available. The figure written into the Plan was lower than this, however (see table on page 188).

It is difficult to allow for the rise in prices during the period of the Third Plan, but it is nevertheless certain that the increase in credits is a very substantial one. The annual credit tranches are rising steadily, from 2 billion New Francs in 1961 to 2.3 in 1962 and 2.75 in 1963, so that the general trend is roughly in line with the programme set out in the Fourth Plan.

Other measures are proposed to facilitate the carrying-out of the

[1] This total includes the investments recommended by the Commission for Scientific and Technical Research, which, as is seen elsewhere (Chapter XI), represent twice the expenditure for the Third Plan.

INVESTMENT EXPENDITURE

	Millions of New Francs	
	Third Plan	*Fourth Plan*
Primary	2,560	3,045
Secondary	3,405	5,391
Higher	1,515	3,746
Sporting Equipment	405	1,240
Research (CNRS)	254	413
Others	81	180
	8,220	14,015

Source: Fourth Plan, p. 89.

investment programme. Increased standardization of buildings will only give its full results if administrative procedures are improved. The Plan approves the policy of giving the administrations concerned the possibility of concluding long-term contracts, and, for the 1963 budget, the Ministry of Finance authorized them to commit themselves, *vis-à-vis* contractors, three years ahead. A greater degree of decentralization in the work of the Ministry of Education in carrying out building programmes is proposed as well. During 1962, the Ministry implemented a number of these recommendations.

3 *The Cultural and Artistic Commission*

The creation of this Commission was a new departure of the Fourth Plan, and in agreement with its general intention of raising collective consumption expenditure. Already, in 1959, a Ministry of Cultural Affairs had been constituted with M. André Malraux as Minister. As a result, all the public departments dealing with cultural and artistic affairs, most of which were attached to the Ministry of Education, now come under the responsibility of this Ministry.

The new character of the task of the Commission did not enable it to go as far as its members would have wished in drawing up an inventory of needs, a calendar of priorities and estimates of costs. But a procedure has now been organized and the initial impetus given, so that it can be expected that work on all these questions will become increasingly systematic and complete.

The Commission described its task for the Fourth Plan as 'defining the method of study of such problems and pointing to the objectives to be reached rather than to the ways of achieving them. To that extent, it is not so much a "plan" that comes out of this report as the "plan of a plan"—a few foundations, stones and financial targets for the Fifth and Sixth Plans."[1]

[1] *Rapport Général de la Commission de l'Equipement culturel et du Patrimoine Artistique,* 1961, p. 7.

The general philosophy of the members of the Commission in fulfilling their mandate merits quoting at some length. 'It has been generally accepted in France, up to the present time, that culture was something that could be taken as given. State intervention, it is said, suffocates the creative spirit and infringes on the liberty of the amateur in the use of his leisure. If such intervention is now to be planned, will it have the effect of sterilizing culture? Can culture become the product of a market organized by the State for the benefit of producers and consumers? This attitude, which was understandable in the nineteenth century, is now outdated. It has been partly responsible for the gradual whittling away, through wars and crises, of the already modest credits granted to the cultural administrations, there being no available element of appreciation for fixing their share of total budget credits. The members of the Commission were unanimous, from their very first meeting, in their determination to react against this *laisser-aller*. Both its regular members, and the other persons who were invited to participate in its work, agreed that it was essential to lay down the guide lines for a fresh departure in public policy in this field so as to take account of the necessary sharing by all classes of society—the entire nation —in what used to be the privilege of a minority.[1]

According to the Commission, total public expenditure for cultural and artistic purposes had been 322 million New Francs for the Third Plan. It recommended, and the Plan accepted, a figure of 900 million for the Fourth Plan. This sum implies annual increases of over one-quarter from 1962 to 1965, if the starting point of the Fifth Plan is to be at an acceptable level. The proposed allocation of these funds shows that the Commission did not suggest increasing all credits indiscriminately. For example, the credits for historical monuments and official buildings, which had absorbed over 80 per cent of the 1961 budget allocations, represent less than the Third Plan total.

The various types of expenditure targets are divided into two groups—'traditional' and 'new' activities. Among the traditional activities is a programme for restoring historical monuments such as Versailles, Fontainebleau, Chambord, the Hôtel des Invalides and the Rheims Cathedral. Besides, a Museum of Popular Art and Customs is to be built in the Bois de Boulogne and a new Conservatoire de Musique constructed, together with six regional schools for teaching music, art and architecture. Other projects include building a new popular theatre for the Eastern suburbs of Paris and, in a longer-term perspective, a second popular national theatre and a

[1] *Rapport, op. cit.*, p. 5.

Museum of Twentieth-Century Arts. The Grand Palais, in Paris, is to become the home of a Museum of Science and Technology.

The big new venture announced by the Plan is the erection of twenty cultural centres by 1965. These will contain theatres, libraries of books and records, cinemas, and exhibition and lecture rooms. Work on two of these centres began in 1962 in Lyons, where M. Roger Planchon will be the Director, and in St Etienne, which is already the home of one of the most well-known provincial theatre companies. The cultural centres will be helped by a central body which will supply them with trained staff and with materials. If the experiment succeeds, it is intended to build other centres later on.

4 *The Public Health Commission*

Commissions of the same kind functioned for the Second and Third Plans, and the first part of the Commission's report for the Fourth Plan surveyed the results achieved in the past, before proceeding to propose expenditure goals for the period 1962-65. Finally, in common with the other Vertical Commissions, the Public Health Commission made a number of policy recommendations.

The programme for public health written into the Second Plan was carried out, but there were shortfalls in the Third because credits were insufficient during the early part of the Plan and, when they were raised in 1960 and 1961, difficulties arose in spending them quickly, as it was not easy to get the local authorities to accelerate their investment programmes.

Total expenditure during the Fourth Plan will be more than four times the amount spent in this sector during the Third. But this marked increase falls well below the Commission's initial proposals. These were divided into four categories: public health, social services, approved schools, medical and social research. For each category the Commission defined what it called the 'theoretical needs', which usually meant an extrapolation of the present situation in relation to demographic trends, with a quite substantial rise in expenditure in order to improve standards generally. An example will clarify the approach used. Of the total programme for hospital beds, which amounts to providing 29,000 extra beds between 1961 and 1965, 7,500 were estimated to cover the needs of a growing population, the rest being designed to improve the ratio of beds per head of population, which had declined slightly since 1953.

The ways these theoretical needs were calculated were as follows. The Ministry of Health issued a circular to all préfets and regional directors of health. The results were confronted with the Ministry's own estimates. For the social services for mothers and babies, young people and the aged, the chief basis of evaluation was a study done by the Ministry. Figures for approved schools were derived from the number of 'school years' required according to the annual total of cases examined by the children's courts. The essential factor behind the programme for medical and social research, in addition to the general encouragement given to plans for expenditure on research by the Government's directives, was the necessary expansion called for by the reform of medical studies.

Altogether, these four categories of needs would have cost 9.4 billion New Francs for the four years from 1962 to 1965. Although the Commission did not consider that this figure was excessive, it did realize that there was no chance of it being financed, and it therefore drew up a second, more modest, programme for 5 billion New Francs. In fact, during the process of fixing ceilings to various types of public expenditure in the Plan, which is discussed in Chapter XII, the General Planning Commissariat and the two Ministries concerned—Health and Justice (for the approved schools) —asked the Commission to go through its estimates again so as to get the total down to 3.7 billion New Francs. The Commission did this, although with considerable misgivings, which explains why it felt necessary to request a programme law for its sector.[1]

In the final section of its report, the Commission dealt with the measures which, in its view, were called for if the scheme was to give its full results. Looking back over the period of the Third Plan, it was fairly satisfied on this score as a great many suggestions had, in fact, been implemented, which is an interesting example of the value of this aspect of the Planning Commissions' work. This time, the main stress was on improvements in drawing up plans. Part of the difficulty was that insufficient research had gone into the problem of estimating needs, and the Ministry should receive an additional credit to finance this. When local administrations were not prepared to draw up the necessary programmes, it might be effective to use a system of differential subsidies from the budget to get developments under way in priority sectors, and this policy ought to accompany a reform of the existing subsidy rates. Finally, the evident and growing lag between urbanization and the provision of proper amenities, including public health, which was particularly great in the ZUP areas and the big housing estates, called for special credits and for a better integration of plans for urban development and for public health.

[1] *Rapport Général de la Commission de l'Equipement Sanitaire et Social*, 1961, p. 101.

CHAPTER X

PARLIAMENT AND THE PLAN

The ratification debate, during the summer of 1962, in the National Assembly and the Senate was only the second since the war on a four-year development Plan, the other Plans, except the Second, having been sanctioned by administrative order. Criticisms in the country of this state of affairs before the discussions in Parliament took place had been widespread, and no one was surprised when the Prime Minister announced, in his introductory speech on the first day of the debate, that Parliament would be more closely associated in future with the execution of the Plan and with the initial choice of key policy options for the Fifth Plan.[1] Despite this statement, which rather took the wind out of the sails of the Government's critics, a great deal of time was devoted to the theme of democracy and planning. In attempting to assess the real significance of the importance given to this aspect of the Plan, it is necessary to recall the general political atmosphere of the time, in particular the Socialist Party's systematic hostility towards Government policy for some months already, and the discontent of parliamentarians in many parties with the state of relations between the executive and the legislative branches of Government. Consequently, attitudes towards the Fourth Plan were highly coloured by political arrières-pensées on most benches.

The debates were long, in both Houses; in the National Assembly alone, 110 speakers took part during the seventeen sessions between May 22nd and June 22nd. But fewer party leaders intervened and the sessions were rather a backbenchers' holiday.

This probably explains why many speeches were so parochial in tone and content and why, if there were many speakers, there were fewer listeners; the spectacle of yawning empty benches contrasted with the insistence of members on the capital importance of close, and continued, consultation of Parliament on all aspects of the Plan. To be fair, though, the 1,500 pages or so of reports and analysis of the specialized commissions of the two Houses should be taken into account as well. They were, indeed, the most substantial part of Parliament's study of the Plan.

At the end of the discussions, the Fourth Plan was adopted by

[1] *Débats Parlementaires, Assemblée Nationale,* May 23, 1962, p. 1230.

comfortable majorities: by 410 votes against 98 in the National Assembly and by 173 against 66 in the Senate. Only two groups, the Socialists and the Communists, voted systematically against the Plan.

According to the Socialist Party's speaker in the winding-up debate in the National Assembly, the work of the General Planning Commissariat was not the object of the party's hostile vote. 'The responsibilities I am accusing in explaining our vote are political.'[1] The criticisms were numerous. 'The Plan starts from the wrong end, from the possibilities and wishes of the employers' representatives instead of being built upon a clear and unequivocal choice of the social objectives to be achieved. That is why it will crystallize social injustices. Finally, it will not mobilize all the means of action at the disposal of the State in an effective way.'[2] The Plan was insufficiently imperative and too liberal. The State ought to set up an Investment Bank to finance investment in the framework of the Plan, and self-financing out of profits should be controlled. Nationalization of private monopolies was required. The Government was not doing enough to introduce planning on a European scale. Price stability would not be achieved because 'to reconcile stability and expansion, either you have to have unemployment, as the Liberals want, or you have to plan seriously, which is the Socialist idea'.[3]

The impact of these criticisms is somewhat mitigated by the knowledge that putting into practice its views on economic planning has never been in the forefront of the preoccupations of the Socialist Party during the not inconsiderable periods when it has participated in Government coalitions since the war. It is also worthy of notice that the CGT-FO—the Socialist trade union confederation—voted in favour of the Fourth Plan at each of the two consultations with the Economic and Social Council.

The opposition of the Communist Party was more radical but, perhaps, less influenced by short-term political considerations. 'We cannot approve a Plan which is a plan in name only, as there can be no real planning in a régime whose very essence is hostile to it'; thus said the principal Communist Party speaker at the end of the debate in the Senate.[4]

The passage of the Fourth Plan through Parliament can best be looked at under three headings: the implications of Parliamentary sanction, the main subjects for criticism, the changes introduced into the Plan as a result of the debates.

[1] M. Leenhardt, *Débats,* June 21, 1962, p. 1920.
[2] M. Leenhardt, *Débats,* p. 1921.
[3] *Débats,* p. 1921.
[4] *Débats Parlementaires, Sénat,* July 13, 1962, p. 933.

I. THE MEANING OF PARLIAMENTARY SANCTION

The Fourth Plan, as it appears in the *Journal Officiel*,[1] is a lengthy document of 165 pages containing not far short of 250,000 words. But the law voted by Parliament has only three articles and fills half a page.[2] As it will be instructive, in the final section of this chapter, to examine it in some detail, the full text follows:[3]

'Article 1. The Fourth Plan, which is annexed to this law, has been approved as the framework for investment programmes during the period 1962-65 and as the guiding document for economic expansion and social progress. [As regards the second of these fields, its aims are: on the one hand, an improvement in the living standards of the least favoured categories of society, in particular, old people, heads of families, repatriates, working farmers, small artisans and low-paid workers, on the other, the speeding up of the economic and social progress of the underdeveloped regions.]

[Article 2. The Government will submit to Parliament, before sending its directives to the General Planning Commissariat, a draft law approving a report on the principal options for the harmonious development of the national economy, and in particular the options dealing with: economic growth, the division of output between investment and consumption, the general lines of social and regional development policy.]

Article 3. [In the report which accompanies the annual Finance Act, and which sets out the economic and financial balance of the economy for the year ahead, the Government will give details of the working out of the Plan and], in particular, the measures taken to implement it, the results obtained, the problems met with and any changes that may be called for.

[The Finance Act will also be accompanied by an annex setting out the total financial contribution in the budget which is proposed for carrying out the operational tranches decided by the Plan.]

[This document, which will have to be laid before Parliament by November 1st each year at the latest, will include notably a list of credits, programme authorizations and credit payments according to economic and social sectors, and a list of these credits according to programme regions.]

The present law will be applied as a law of the State.'

It will be seen that the Fourth Plan is not voted as a law with binding force upon the Government but is annexed to a law which

[1] *Journal Officiel, Lois et Décrets*, 94th year, August 6-7, 1962.

[2] *Op cit.*, p. 7810, Law No. 62-900.

[3] The sentences in square brackets were inserted during the debates. Their significance is discussed in the final section of this chapter.

refers to it. The point may appear an obvious one, when it is stated in this way, yet there is a real question of substance at issue here. If the whole of the Plan was to have legislative value and to be coercive, the Government would be placed in an impossible position. In the words of the Prime Minister, 'the Plan has no imperative value correctly speaking. It is not a budget document but a combination of objectives, options and goals which the Government sets out to implement or to reach, and it undertakes to do everything possible for that. But it is quite clear that the execution of the Plan can be upset; sometimes we may be ahead of, and sometimes behind, the Plan, as experience in the past proves. And this is the reason for the annual reports which will be sent to Parliament according to the terms of the draft law.'[1]

On the other hand, there are obvious advantages for Parliament if it can give its approval of the Plan in as binding a form as possible. If parliamentary practice in France allowed for one government majority as a general rule for each legislature—the overthrow of a Government leading to fresh elections, as is the British case—then the need for such precautions would diminish in all likelihood. But even in such an event, it is probable that some firm commitment of the Government would be sought by Parliament.[2]

Given the existence of these two documents—the draft law and the annex containing the Plan—the parliamentary game consists of trying to shift as many items as possible over from the latter to the former, a tactic which the Government attempts to resist, usually with a good measure of success. But the draft law can, nevertheless, be amended quite substantially. In the translation given above, the sentences between square brackets were all inserted during the passage of the Plan through Parliament. The implications of these amendments will become clear later on in this chapter when the changes introduced into both the draft law and the text of the Plan at the suggestion and request of Parliament are examined.

II. PARLIAMENTARY CRITICISM OF THE PLAN

The more sweeping criticisms of the Plan have been noted already in the attitudes of the Socialist and Communist Parties respectively. The specific issues raised during the debates may be grouped into four types: general considerations, social aspects, regional development and questions relating to individual sectors.

[1] *Débats, Sénat,* July 12, 1962, p. 927.

[2] The formula: 'One Government, one legislature, one Plan' appears attractive to many people in France today. Its implications and practical possibilities are studied later, in Chapter XVIII.

1 *General Considerations*

One aspect dominated all the others: the rôle of Parliament in the planning process, both at the preparatory stage and when the Plan is carried out. One theme was conspicuous by its absence, namely that the objectives of the Plan were excessive. 'It is a very striking fact that 110 members [of the National Assembly] were able to speak on our economic position without a single one expressing doubts whether our rate of expansion will continue over the years of the Plan. At a time when a number of countries in the world are looking for ways of securing economic growth, or restoring it, it is striking to see that no one questions the certainty of this fundamental result.'[1]

The small scope left for effective criticism of the Fourth Plan by Parliament was stressed by the General Rapporteur of the Commission of the National Assembly for Finance, Economics and Planning. 'The Plan represents a balance between national resources and expenditures. It is, furthermore, the expression of certain policy choices. We can discuss these and criticize certain insufficiencies, but we cannot call the objectives into question without running the risk of destroying the coherence of the Plan as a whole. In other words, our rôle as far as the Fourth Plan is concerned is inevitably a limited one.'[2]

The force of this argument was generally admitted by everyone, including the Government. Despite the intention of the authorities to follow a different procedure for the Fifth Plan, they were obliged to make much more precise commitments in this connection before the debate in Parliament was over, as we shall see in the next section.

However, the efforts of the Government to improve consultation procedures for the Fourth Plan were recognized by numerous parliamentarians, notably as regards the double consultation of the Economic and Social Council, the work of the High Planning Council and the improved representation of the trade unions in the Planning Commissions. Despite this, the fact remained that Parliament, although the Fourth Plan had been laid before it at the end of November 1961, that is one month preceding its entry into force, had not benefited from these efforts. The feeling of many members seemed to be due as much to the fear that a further extension of consultations would follow the same lines, to the continued detriment of Parliament, as to the wish to improve the efficacy of the planning procedure itself.

Turning to the execution of the Plan and its surveillance by the

[1] Minister of Finance in the National Assembly, *Débats,* June 21, 1962, p. 1912.

[2] *Débats,* May 22, 1962, p. 1236.

representative assemblies of the nation, members of both Houses had no difficulty in demonstrating the defects of existing arrangements. The logic of the suggestion put forward by the Finance, Economic and Planning Commission of the National Assembly on this point was difficult to refute. Pointing out that, just as the current economic prospects for the coming year were now given in the form of quantified forecasts annexed to the annual Finance Act, the Commission considered that the Government should also give sufficient data for Parliament to be able to make 'all useful comparisons between the objectives of the Plan, the progress made so far in achieving them, and the measures proposed in the budget to continue in the same direction'.[1]

2 *Social Aspects*

Noting that the Fourth Plan 'seeks a more desirable social balance between a relative plethora of individual goods and services and the obvious inadequacy of collective equipment',[2] the General Rapporteur admitted that this intention had been translated, by and large, in the Plan by an acceptable effort to put it into effect. This considered opinion was forgotten by many parliamentarians, the burden of whose interventions was to demand an even greater increase in budget credits for such purposes.

A sharp divergence between the opinion of the Finance, Economic and Planning Commission and other members of the National Assembly appeared also in connection with the Plan's forecasts of manpower requirements and working hours. Several speakers declared their disappointment that the Plan did not foresee a reduction before, at least, the second half of the period 1962-65.

Income policy and price stability were points which aroused some comment, although no extended discussion of the subject took place. The need for some mechanism ensuring that the objective for private consumption in the Plan was not exceeded, and that incomes were geared to productivity, was emphasized by most speakers who intervened on this matter. But whilst it was easy to criticize the prudent wording of the draft of the Fourth Plan on this subject, no very original suggestions were put forward to add to those enumerated by the Minister of Finance, who summarized the position in the following terms: 'We shall have to make the interested parties familiar with this problem by bringing them to recognize themselves what the situation is as regards the economic situation, income distribution and the equitable sharing of the fruits of expansion. Now this is not

[1] *Débats*, May 22, 1962, p. 1240.
[2] *Ibid.*, p. 1236.

a simple problem because not everybody talks the same language. The farmer's conception of what constitutes his income is not the same thing as the wage and salary earner's. We must get agreement on certain definitions and we must also agree on some instruments for measuring income which cannot be contested and, more important still, are not contested.'[1]

3 *Regional Development*

If the number of words spent on discussing regional development problems was counted, it would probably exceed those devoted to all other subjects put together. The enthusiasm of parliamentarians, of whatever political leaning, for more regional elements in the Plan, seemed to have no limits. In the process, the very considerable efforts proposed by the Fourth Plan tended to be overlooked. But the arguments put forward on numerous specific points smack often of special pleading, particularly when the geographical location of the constituencies of parliamentarians supporting them are compared with the regions which were the object of their solicitude. In acting in this way, members were no doubt fulfilling one of their legitimate functions, the defence of the interests of their electors, but one only.

The most constructive attempt to secure a revision of the Government's proposals was made by M. Pleven (who represents a constituency in Brittany) with the support of twenty-six other members of the National Assembly representing the less-developed regions of France. The group's proposal was for a programme law relating to all the regions to benefit from the Government's 'propulsive policy' for public investment expenditure, to be submitted to Parliament in 1963. In the view of its sponsors, without such a law 'we should have serious reasons to fear that budget arbitrements will continue, as in the past, to be to the detriment of those regions whose economic vitality needs to be reactivated by a large volume of public investment'.[2] It will be seen that the promotors of this idea received almost complete satisfaction during the debate.

4 *Specific Sectors*

The very large number of interventions on precise aspects of the objectives of the Plan for specific sectors are best regrouped under limited general themes: national defence, agriculture, transport and communications, housing.

National defence has been a sore point in discussions of government policy by Parliament for some years, and it was to be expected

[1] *Débats,* June 21, 1962, p. 1910.
[2] M. Pleven, *Débats,* June 21, 1962, p. 1915.

that the increase in expenditure of 13 per cent forecast in the Plan would be seized upon during the debates. But it was far from clear whether the policies suggested as alternatives would modify very much the total level of expenditure. Certain changes have been introduced, however, in the arrangements for incorporating defence considerations into the overall Plan. The liaison was not particularly close for the Fourth Plan, as was noted in Chapter VI, and in any case much less so than for other items of Government expenditure. But a joint Commission has been set up inside the General Planning Commissariat to study problems of harmonization between contracts for electronic equipment concluded by both civil and military spending departments. More generally, the Minister of Finance was led to remark that, personally, he thought 'it important to bring the study of the economic repercussions of the defence programme, and the examination of the social and economic aspects of planning, closer together for the Fifth Plan'.[1]

The agricultural objectives of the Fourth Plan seemed to many members of Parliament to be preoccupying and, at the same time, insufficient. Comments on the ambitious export targets for agricultural products were tinged with some scepticism as to whether even the decisions taken in Brussels early in 1962 on the common agricultural policy of the Treaty of Rome would be implemented with sufficient vigour for them to be achieved. But no one pointed out that a possible alternative policy would be to accelerate the decline in the agricultural population. The attitude of Communist speakers on this subject illustrates the difficulty of organizing a debate on the problems of agriculture, which would be relatively free from political, not to say electioneering, considerations. According to the principal Communist representative in the Senate's discussion, the Fourth Plan 'implies the disappearance over the years ahead of small- and medium-sized firms, of 270,000 family farms, of 50,000 small shopkeepers and an aggravation of the exploitation of the working class'.[2]

The rapporteur in the Senate for agricultural questions did not conceal his concern that, with the Rome Treaty, the French Government was 'going to find itself progressively divested of certain of its prerogatives'.[3] Moreover, although agricultural policy was to be laid down in the new Agricultural Act[4] the Plan did not appear to recognize this. There was no specific undertaking to reach parity in real income levels between agriculture and other branches, and farmers

[1] *Débats*, June 21, 1962, p. 1906.
[2] M. Namy, *Débats*, July 12, 1962, p. 933.
[3] *Débats*, July 9, 1962, p. 802.
[4] Discussed in Chapter XV.

were concerned when 'they read that the prices of their products were to remain stable at their present level'.[1] The rapporteur was supported warmly by M. Blondelle, the influential representative of the farmers, and member of the High Planning Council. On the whole, the debate remained rather inconclusive as it was apparent that the farming group counted much more on the vote of the new Agricultural Act than upon the text of the Plan for achieving its policy objectives. M. Blondelle suggested that the closer association between Parliament and the Plan as to the latter's implementation would have the advantage, at any rate, of making it possible to change the Plan. This prospect was sufficient to overcome his other misgivings and he would vote in favour of the Fourth Plan.

The transport policy of the Fourth Plan came in for rough handling. The criticisms were numerous, and were pressed home energetically. The efforts of their authors were rewarded by sundry concessions made by the Government. The proposed reform of the freight charges of the French Railways, so as to bring them more in line with marginal costs on each section of track, was a favourite subject for attack. The idea of this reform is to enable the railways to charge rather less on the main lines with heavy traffic, thus improving their competitive position *vis-à-vis* road transport. But for many members a counterpart of this policy would be an increase in fares on other, less used, lines and they were quick to point out that it would imply penalizing the less well-developed regions which, elsewhere in the Plan, were supposed to be the object of Government solicitude—an argument that did not lack a certain logic.

This was by no means all. Inland waterways seemed to exercise a special fascination. Starting from the grandiose project for linking the North Sea to the Mediterranean, which the Fourth Plan pushed out into subsequent years, whilst preparing the ground for it by proposing the improvement of part of the waterways concerned, the debate got decidedly out of hand and drew from the Minister of Finance the wry comment that, if all the suggestions put forward were implemented, by about 1980, France would begin to resemble Venice.

The question of the road programme came up for examination, especially the building of autoroutes which, many members thought, was insufficient. A similar opinion was expressed for the programme put forward for improving the telephone service.

Housing was a theme which could lead to divergent opinions, firstly as to the level of needs and secondly as to the extent to which it was possible to satisfy them without sacrificing something else. But,

[1] *Débats*, July 9, 1962, p. 802.

in the event, few people seemed to be willing to sacrifice anything else. An additional factor, for which the Fourth Plan had provided to a certain extent, was the housing problem which would be created by the arrival of many French citizens from North Africa.

III. CHANGES IN THE FINAL TEXT

The text of the Plan which was finally voted by both Houses did not differ in any fundamental respect from the initial project. There was no Fourth Plan A, as the Minister of Finance remarked. Indeed, if the first project was a coherent set of objectives, things could not have been otherwise. There were some additions and changes of importance, though, not only for the Fourth Plan but for future Plans as well. They concern in particular the specific commitments entered into by the Government for the follow-up procedure and the preparation of the Fifth Plan. Before discussing these two points, it is convenient to dispose of the more detailed changes and of the question of regional development policy.

1 *Changes in Specific Targets*

Detailed changes were introduced by new drafts proposed by the Government for sections of the initial project of the Fourth Plan. The agriculturists' grievances were met partially, but only in part, as regards social security and pensions for farmers, but credits for agricultural education were doubled.[1] The new situation created since January 1962 with the agreement, in Brussels, to begin applying the Treaty of Rome to agriculture, was dealt with by a drafting change in the Plan which, as will be seen in Chapter XV, was hardly to the liking of the farmers, but which it was difficult to avoid in the circumstances.

Several concessions were made in the field of transport. The most important in terms of actual expenditure was the undertaking to include, in the 1963 budget, a notably higher volume of credits for the autoroute programme than the target written into the Fourth Plan. It was promised that the reform of the charges of the French Railways would not be implemented before October 1, 1962, and meanwhile the General Planning Commissariat was invited to look at the question again, with particular reference to its likely repercussions on regional development policy.[2] The result of the debate on the North Sea-Mediterranean inland waterway project remained

[1] See Chapter XV.

[2] In March 1963, a further increase in the programme for autoroutes was decided. But opposition to changes in rail charges diluted the reform finally adopted.

indecisive, the Government agreeing only to speed up the technical prospection of the Rhine-Rhone liaison. Credits for developing and modernizing the telephone service would be raised beyond the target set out in the Plan.

At this point, the Minister of Finance summed up the position when he said that the draft of the Fourth Plan had allowed for a small margin of manoeuvre by leaving unallocated a certain sum of resources. But the total cost of the three changes made in the Plan to meet the wishes of Parliament, *viz.* agricultural education, autoroutes and the telephone service, had absorbed this margin and any further changes in resource allocation would imply upsetting the overall coherence of the Plan.[1]

2 *Regional Policy*

The effects of the discussions in Parliament under this head did not materialize as changes in the text of the Fourth Plan but as redrafts, with substantial additions, of the law to which the Plan was annexed. About half the amendments included in square brackets in the translation of this law which was given earlier, refer to regional development policy. The importance of an acceleration of the progress of the poorer regions was inserted explicitly in Article 1 but the references to regional development in Articles 2 and 3 were more significant still.

Without going back on the policy of operational tranches set out in the Fourth Plan, the Government accepted the request for a programme law for the less-developed regions. It will be laid before Parliament during 1963 and will refer to all public investments in the regions qualifying for the 'propulsive' policy of public investment described elsewhere.[2] The duration, and the exact terms, of this law have still to be determined. Meanwhile, the 1963 Finance Act will list the criteria to be used so that a definitive list of the areas concerned can be drawn up. Once the programme law has been approved, the operational tranche procedure will continue as before, except that each tranche will be, at one and the same time, part of the four-year Plan and of the programme law.[3]

Recognizing that this policy was only a first step towards a more ambitious one, of harmonious economic development in all regions, the Government took up a suggestion by the Finance, Economic and Planning Commission of the National Assembly which called for a development plan for the whole of the national territory. But the

[1] *Assemblée Nationale, Débats,* June 21, 1962, p. 1912.
[2] E.g. Chapter XIII.
[3] *Sénat, Débats,* July 12, 1962, p. 915.

issues involved raise considerations of a kind which are difficult to fit into a four-year Plan—they belong rather to the type of 'prospective' studies to which the Plan attaches so much importance.[1] It was decided that the new prospective study for 1985 to be undertaken by the General Planning Commissariat, and to which we return in Chapter XVI, will be designed to include regional aspects. The guide lines for a long-term regional development policy can thus be determined and future four-year Plans will draw their inspiration from them.[2]

3 *Follow-up Procedure*

Parliament obtained a very large measure of satisfaction in this respect also, as the new drafting of Article 3 of the law approving the Fourth Plan shows.

The position now is that the annual Finance Act will contain a report on the progress made in carrying out the Fourth Plan. Parliament will henceforth have both a conjuncture report, with estimates for the coming year, and a medium-term perspective giving the objectives of the four-year Plan, on the one hand, and the road left to travel before these are achieved, on the other. Both Houses will therefore be in a position to discuss the Plan each year in a broad economic context. Only time will tell what use will be made of this extension of their functions.

4 *Pre-consultation on the Plan*

It was noted earlier in this chapter that the Government announced, at the beginning of the ratification process on the Fourth Plan, that it would consult Parliament on the Fifth before the major options deciding its essential structure were taken.

Given the insistence on this point by all speakers in the debates, the Government had to go further and to state its intention in the new Article 2 of the law on the Fourth Plan. The solution proposed is that Parliament will vote a short draft law to which will be annexed a technical document setting out the terms of the choices available. The main headings of this annex will be those spelt out in Article 2. The importance of keeping the discussion on a very general level was emphasized by the Prime Minister when he informed the Senate that 'it will be a general draft law and not one which will have five lines to begin with and, from one amendment to another, will end by filling two volumes'. The technical problems raised for the Government and the General Planning Commissariat

[1] See Chapter VI.

[2] *Sénat, Débats,* July 12, 1962, p. 915.

by this sort of consultation are discussed later in Chapter XVI.

Meanwhile the last word on the subject may fittingly be left with the Minister of Finance. 'As far as I am aware, there is no example, in foreign countries, of a Parliament which is associated more closely with the preparation of the nation's long-term economic policy than ours will be from now on.'[1]

[1] *Sénat, Débats,* July 12, 1962, p. 918.

CHAPTER XI

THE FINAL VERSION OF THE FOURTH PLAN

The purpose of this chapter is to present a summary of the main characteristics of the Fourth Plan. Some overlapping with other chapters is inevitable but this is outweighed by the advantages of bringing together all the elements of the final document in a single chapter.

Reading through the Plan, it becomes clear that it is grouped around four subjects: the framework and general objectives, the main production goals, the problem of maintaining economic balance, the means of execution. This is not the order of presentation adopted by the Plan but it is the simplest one for a short survey.

I. FRAMEWORK AND GENERAL OBJECTIVES

France is fairly well placed at the beginning of the Fourth Plan as far as its economic situation is concerned. The previous decade was one of rapid growth, 4.5 per cent annually, and this rate is being exceeded today. However, the years ahead hold out a challenge due to the 'fervour of scientific and technical competition, the intensity of innovation, and the speed of change as much as to the opposition of ideologies in a world where distances are becoming negligible quantities'.[1] Besides these general influences to which all economies are open, France has to take account of three transformations which affect it particularly. They are: 'the demographic revolution and the arrival on the labour market, during the Fourth Plan, of young people',[2] the opening of the French economy as 'the decisive stage in the application of the Rome Treaty will coincide with the Fourth Plan', the changed relations between France and the French-speaking African countries which will have to be moulded to 'a new form of co-operation founded on the community of the zone, equal rights and the conciliation of interests'.[3]

In such a situation, what is the meaning of the Plan and what are its general objectives?

[1] Fourth Plan, p. 3.
[2] The relation between the active and inactive populations, which has been getting more unfavourable for a long time, will be stabilized during the Fourth Plan.
[3] *Op. cit.*, p. 3.

1 *The Meaning of the Plan*

The essence of the French system of planning in 'a régime where private initiative and public action exist together'[1] has lain traditionally in the reconciliation by the Plan of 'the imperative of development' and the 'cleaving to liberty'. Reaching the objectives of the Plan is not therefore the result of coercive obligations but of 'conviction and fervour founded on a civic sense, a correct appreciation of self-interest and the participation of all economic and social forces in the preparation and application of the Plan'.[2] This collective side of the Plan will be reinforced by the close collaboration of the Economic and Social Council and the meetings of the Planning Commissions, which will be annual in future.

The flexibility in the French planning system carries with it two contradictions. The first is the problem of planning in an open economy. 'The freedom of trade and payments between France and certain other countries can obviously lead to difficulties if it is not accompanied by a common policy having some of the aspects of a plan. France has, therefore, to strive to convince, by its example and by the philosophy of its own Plan, its partners of the value of such a Plan.[3]

A second contradiction arises from the opposition between the determinism of the Plan and 'the uncertainty of events and the freedom of behaviours'.[4] This allusion refers to the possibility of a recession in the other Common Market countries and to the evolution of the Algerian problem. Risks of this sort are very real ones and they could entail adjustments to the Plan or even its revision. But these adaptations will be easier to the extent that a distinction has been made between 'the long-term prospective which illuminates [the Plan], the quantitative forecasts which act as a reference framework, the priority targets inserted in that framework, the group of decisions that have to be taken immediately, and the sphere of the options reserved for the future'.[5]

2 *General Objectives*

(a) A first group of objectives relates to the direction of the Plan towards ends which are at one and the same time national and individual. The former can be defined as 'survival, progress, solidarity, dissemination. We must assure our own defence by modernizing our army and reducing its numerical importance, and contribute

[1] *Op. cit.*, p. 4.
[2] *Op. cit.*, p. 4.
[3] *Op. cit.*, p. 5.
[4] *Op. cit.*, p. 5.
[5] *Op. cit.*, p. 5.

sufficiently, from a material point of view, so that the French genius can participate fully in the great task of the century, which is to give to the least favoured categories and regions, whether it be the aged, the repatriates, low-paid wage earners or agriculturists, the concrete evidence of an indispensable solidarity and of national cohesion. Also we must follow up our assistance to the less developed areas, in particular to the French-speaking African States that have chosen to maintain special ties with France."[1]

The latter should lead to an improvement in living conditions through a reduction in the length, arduousness and risks of work, and to an increase in the consumption of both individual goods and services and the services rendered by collective investments, schools and hospitals for example.

Faced with a selection between these collective and individual ends, the Plan gives priority to the first. But this calls for a fast rate of growth and for a big productive effort. As France is experiencing a quantitative and qualitative shortage of manpower, any general reduction of working hours in the immediate future is excluded. Such a reduction would harm the prospects of expansion at a time when the Manpower Commission had to suggest the likely need for immigration of workers from abroad so as to 'give the French economy the maximum momentum which will ensure work for the growing numbers of young people, for the manpower freed by the modernization of agriculture and for the workers who may become available as a result of demobilization or repatriation'.[2] In this connection the Plan recalls that nearly 1 million jobs will have to be created between 1961 and 1965.

MANPOWER BALANCE

(thousands)

Increase in availabilities		*Increase in employment*	
Natural increase	180	Industry	290
Immigration	290	Other activities	640
Military service	190		
Agriculture	270		
Total	930	Total	930

Source: Fourth Plan, p. 5.

Among the national aims, regional policy is of special importance. The Plan conceives of this policy as ensuring a proper balance

[1] *Op. cit.*, p. 5.
[2] *Op. cit.*, p. 5.

between regions and as correcting the imbalances arising out of divergent trends in population, employment, incomes and growth-rates. Inter-regional migrations should be kept down to a 'reasonable' level.[1]

In regions where growth is taking place spontaneously and vigorously, regional policy should accompany expansion by providing the necessary infrastructure, schools and universities, and financial resources. In the less-favoured regions, it should exercise a stimulating effect thanks 'to more daring anticipatory actions and more substantial financial assistance'.[2] In areas where industry and population are too heavily concentrated already, public policy must 'associate itself with the positive aspects of growth and dissociate itself from its negative aspects'.[3]

The means at the disposal of the authorities for achieving this objective are varied. They include the geographical location of public investment expenditure, educational policy, communications, re-direction of agricultural production, pricing policy for energy and transport, selective stimuli to industry and setting up zones for priority measures. As to their application, the Plan refers to the mechanism of the operational tranches of the regional plans, which have already been described in Chapter XIII, and notes that a programme law will be presented to Parliament in 1963 for all regions covered by the 'propulsive policy' for public investment. 'The criteria used for the choice of regions to be the object of these two types of policy will be set out in the introduction to the 1963 Finance Act.'[4]

In the field of national and individual objectives, the Plan makes another choice when it prefers to a consumer society 'which in the long run turns towards futile satisfactions generating unrest', the need for a 'greater degree of recourse to the services of collective equipment'.[5] Of importance here will be the housing programme, with a target of at least 350,000 housing units a year by 1965, and the other social investments that are to rise by 50 per cent. 'The attainment of the whole of these programmes is an integral part of

[1] These kinds of imbalance are likely to concern three regions in particular. They are: Brittany, where the modernization of agriculture is proceeding parallel to the rapid growth in the population; the two départements Nord and Pas-de-Calais, whose traditional industries are stagnating and whose urban structure is obsolescent; the Massif Central, whose problems are somewhat similar to those of the Nord département and whose Southern regions could be called upon to receive persons repatriated from North Africa.

[2] *Op cit.*, p. 16.

[3] *Op. cit.*, p. 16.

[4] *Op. cit.*, p. 17.

[5] *Op. cit.*, p. 5.

the objectives of the Plan. But if it should happen that disappointments arose, either as regards the rate of growth, or the maintenance of economic balance, the Government would strive, in making the adjustments which would then become necessary, to safeguard the increase in this category of investments which only absorb 5 per cent of the expected rise in total resources. On the contrary, if the surplus of budget receipts over current State expenditures turned out to be larger than expected, some supplementary programmes could be envisaged.'[1] The entire fourth section of the Plan is devoted to these investments. It is noteworthy that this firm undertaking, for which there is no precedent, is in line with the wishes of the Economic and Social Council.

Among social investments, urban development receives special attention. The Plan considers that, from now on, it must be the 'obligatory complement' of housebuilding programmes, and a number of specific measures concerning it are spelt out in the Plan: modernization of old quarters of towns; re-establishing balance between work and home; changes in real estate legislation; programmes for the Paris region and some other big urban centres; programmes in rural areas.

As to education, the Plan has to take account of several facts, among them being the demographic wave 'which is now up to the secondary education level and will reach the universities by 1964', preparation for the new 'observation cycle' and for the increase in the school-leaving age, the expansion of higher education. The Plan refers, also, to the solution of the vital problem of 'permanent training', by which it means programmes for re-training at all ages, in order to avoid technical obsolescence or a lack of adequate skills, now that technical progress is changing requirements for skills so rapidly. On this last point, the recommendations of the Horizontal Manpower Commission have influenced Plan thinking and many of them are recorded in the final text.

It is expected that the need for engineers will be 18 per cent higher by 1965 and 50 per cent higher by 1975. In the tertiary sector, 10 per cent of the working population would require a degree of qualification in 1975 equal to eleven years' full-time education after the 'observation cycle'. To meet these requirements will call for a 50 per cent increase in the number of teachers by 1975 and a 30 per cent increase by 1965. A big school-building programme will have to accompany this rise in teaching staffs. An expansion of technical education is necessary and, at the present time, two professions should have priority in view of the imbalance between supply and

[1] *Op. cit.*, p. 12.

demand—draughtsmen and social workers. Professional formation through extended apprenticeship schemes and a development of the Ministry of Labour's Formation Centres for Adults do not come under the chapter on education in the Plan, but they are evidently an aspect of the same problem and they find their place here.

Expenditures on education proper, including sporting equipment, will entail programme authorizations for the Fourth Plan amounting to 12 billion NF.

As we noted in Chapter IX, cultural and artistic activities figure in the Fourth Plan for the first time. Credits to be allocated to historical monuments, museums, the arts and cultural activities in general amount to 900 million NF compared with 322 million in the previous four years. Public health and social equipment programmes are written into the Plan for a total of 3,700 million NF (1,200 million for the Third Plan).

(b) A second category of objectives in the Plan deals with the increase in production. The growth of gross internal production will be 24 per cent between 1961 and 1965, or 5.5 per cent annually, a rate only achieved in the past during brief periods when the external accounts were in serious imbalance. The target is, therefore, an ambitious one, even more so as it is to be achieved whilst respecting the fundamental balance of the economy.

The output targets for the chief sectors of activity are given in the Fifth Section of the Plan to which we now turn.

II. MAIN OUTPUT TARGETS

These are summarized in the table:

OUTPUT—1965

	(1961=100)
Agriculture	119
Energy	124
Metals	123
Chemicals	129
Transformation industries	123
Building, public works and other construction	132
Transport and communications	121
Others	127
Total	124

Source: Fourth Plan, p. 6.

N.B.—These indices are gross production figures and not value added.

1 *Agriculture*

This sector is undergoing a profound transformation which is, at one and the same time, a source of prosperity and of difficulties. The forecast is an expansionist one as the rate of growth, 4.5 per cent annually, is more rapid than during the Third Plan. The rise in productivity is more substantial still, but its effects on output will be somewhat attenuated by the reduction in the labour force. This expansion of production is a desirable objective in itself as it will contribute to the increase in exports and, in that way, raise the incomes of farmers much more surely than an increase in producers' prices would do. But there are dangers in so far as 'undesirable' products, like wheat and milk products which lead to surpluses, are produced in larger quantities alongside the 'desirable' ones.

Faced with this situation, the Fourth Plan 'gives first priority to measures tending to find new outlets, to adapt market and distribution circuits, to develop processing industries and competitiveness . . ., and to improve the living standards of farmers'.[1] The Plan also announces the ending of the previous system of target prices and stresses the need for a progressive adaptation to the Common Market.

2 *Energy*

Requirements are estimated to reach the equivalent of 168 million tons of coal in 1965. Any risk of an energy shortage seems to be eliminated and the key problem for the Plan 'concerns the impact of new sources of energy—oil and natural gas—on the traditional sources'. In this connection, 'the chosen objectives are to satisfy consumers' demand for energy at least cost without endangering the security of supplies and without imposing production cuts with too heavy social consequences'.[2]

Concretely, the output of coal will be reduced from 58 million tons in 1960 to 55 in 1965. 'This level will be protected against competition from other energy sources and against other risks of all kinds through measures dealing with stocks, prices, combined oil and coal burning equipment, and quantitative controls. . . . On the other hand, a vigorous campaign, which will have to be psychological and social as well as technical, economic and financial, will be necessary to ensure the re-adaptation of workers affected by the fall in coal production, without neglecting the re-activation of the localities concerned.'[3]

[1] *Op. cit.*, p. 6.
[2] *Op. cit., p.* 7.
[3] *Op. cit.*, p. 7.

Oil production in the French Franc Area will probably be between 35 and 50 million tons by the end of the Fourth Plan, and refinery building will continue at a rapid rate. Thermal electricity production will grow fast, but annual credits for hydro-electric plants will level off. The atomic energy programme will have to 'take care to explore a range of technical possibilities and to give a solid basis to the French atomic industry'.[1]

3 *Industry*[2]

The targets set for the main branches can be enumerated as follows. *Steel* output, at present 18 million tons, will be 24.5 million tons in 1965 thanks to the entry into service of two new rolling mills. Demand for *aluminium* will continue to increase rapidly, from 280,000 tons to 360,000, but after 1965 a problem will arise due to the exhaustion of cheap energy supplies in Metropolitan France. *Chemicals* are a branch in active development, particularly organic chemicals (plastic and artificial fibres) and a rise of 42 per cent in production can be forecast, which is, nevertheless, slower than for the Third Plan when it was 66 per cent. Problems in this sector are likely to concern the financing of investments, the concentration of production facilities, and the formation of scientific and technical personnel. The *transformation industries* which, as was seen in Chapter IX, cover a large and heterogeneous share of industrial output, will improve their production levels at a rapid rate in most branches but will have to contend with intense competition at home and on foreign markets. Given their presumed demand for man-power, the location of expanded production facilities will be of capital importance for the success of regional development policy. Outlook for production of capital goods is favourable and the trade balance surplus forecast by the Plan will depend in no small measure on them. The motor-car industry 'will be assisted by a reasonable effort to improve urban infrastructure and the road net-work'.[3] Textiles will probably face strong competition from abroad. The overall production indices, and the targets for the different branches are shown opposite.

4 *Transport*

Transport needs are expected to grow rather more slowly than production of goods and services, except for air transport, as a conse-

[1] *Op. cit.*, p .7.
[2] Total employment in the handicrafts sector is expected to be stable but stress is laid on improving arrangements for professional training.
[3] *Op. cit.*, p. 7.

OUTPUT TARGETS, 1961-65

	(1961=100)
Agriculture and forests	119
Food-processing industries	116
Solid mineral fuels	96
Gas	127
Electricity, water and others	152
Oil products and natural gas	123
Construction materials	125
Glass	126
Iron ore and steel products	123
Non-ferrous metals	130
Primary metals	122
Mechanical machines and equipment	135
Electrical machines and equipment	152
Motor-cars and cycles	132
Shipbuilding, aircraft and arsenal	100
Chemicals	133
Textiles	111
Clothing	121
Leather	111
Wood products industry	120
Paper and paper-making products	125
Printing	125
Miscellaneous industries	143
Building and public works	132
Transport	120
Telecommunications	130
Services	127
Total	124

Source: Fourth Plan, p. 34.

quence of the stable level of traffic in mineral fuels. Taking 1959 as a base year, goods traffic will be about one-third higher in 1965. Passenger traffic on the public transport system will be only 15 per cent greater, but private transport—mainly motor-cars—will rise by 60 per cent. Air traffic, expressed in numbers of passenger-kilometres in 1965, will be twice that in 1959, and transport of goods by air will no doubt expand even faster.

The French railways are expected to invest 5,950 million NF, including general overhead costs. By the end of the Fourth Plan, the electrification programme will be practically completed on the main lines with a high traffic density and the diesel traction programme will continue. Modernization of rolling stock and investments to improve productivity are provided for. A reform of rail charges will be applied progressively and 'will represent a big step in the direction of true prices which will contribute to putting competition between road and rail on a healthy footing'.[1]

Of the programme for building 1,835 kilometres of autoroutes by 1975, 50 per cent will be put in hand during the Fourth Plan in order to relieve congestion in urban centres, and 25 per cent for liaison routes. A plan for spending 1,450 million NF on the improvement of sea ports will be carried out, priority being given to the larger ports, and internal waterways will receive 830 million NF, of which 700 million NF will come from Government funds. The chief projects will be for the Seine, the North Canal and the widening of the Canal Dunkirk-Valenciennes. The much-debated question of the scheme for a navigable waterway linking the North Sea and the Mediterranean is discussed in Chapter X but no firm commitment is made. Sea shipping will not face very favourable demand conditions during the Fourth Plan and will invest less than during the Third.

As a general comment on these investment programmes, the Plan says: 'If it seems possible latter on to increase the amount of credits for investment purposes, the transport sector, among others, will benefit. In that case, the requests for credits already presented in the specialized reports (of the Transport Planning Commission) will guide the choices to be made.'[2]

5 *Post Office and Telecommunications*

A 40 per cent expansion in investment expenditure is forecast, compared with the Third Plan. The broadcasting system will be improved and a second television programme will be provided.

6 *Building and Public Works*

This is a key sector in view of the general rise in investment expenditure and the stress being given to housing and infrastructure projects. Its products represent about one-half of total gross fixed capital formation. The Plan notes that progress is being made in introducing mechanized production methods, and points to the quite rapid increase in productivity of 5 per cent annually per man hour which has been achieved in recent years. It goes on to state that, if this rate is to be maintained, 'a continued and concerted action by customers in the public and private sectors and the building firms themselves, helped by the public departments' is called for. 'The relatively homogeneous character of the branches of the industry justifies studying them as a whole and not separately, or in an

[1] *Op. cit.*, p. 18.
[2] *Op. cit.*, p. 140.

incomplete manner; this was the object in creating a Planning Commission for Building and Public Works for the Fourth Plan.'[1]

The following estimates are given of the volume of work for the industry during the period 1962-65:

	Annual average rate of increase
Building	6.4
of which: New housing	4.2
Repairs	7.5
Public works	7.3
Total	6.6

Source: Fourth Plan, p. 133.

The rapid rate of increase in repair work is in line with the policy, proposed by the Housing Commission, of tying the rise in rents to a larger volume of expenditure on upkeep of houses.

The expected improvement in productivity should make it possible to keep demand for extra manpower down to 110,000 between 1959 and 1965.

7 *Tourism and Internal Trade*

Tourism is a valuable source of foreign exchange, and its income elasticity in France is high. The investment objectives of the Third Plan were not reached and the Fourth stresses the expansion and modernization of hotel facilities and other types of accommodation. To achieve this, the credits granted by the Crédit Hôtelier will be increased to 15 million NF in 1962-63 and to 20 million in 1964-65, and investment expenditure for the equipment of seaside resorts and winter sport stations will be raised.

The Planning Commission for Tourism had recommended a change in the tax régime applied to investments in hotels and restaurants so as to avoid the incidence of double taxation as a result of the working of the turnover tax. A decree, published in August 1962, gave effect to this suggestion.

As regards *internal trade,* provision would have to be made for a rise of 23 per cent in consumers' expenditures by 1965. The sector would also have to adapt itself 'to the abundance now achieved in agricultural production, to the mass production of industrial goods, to the growth of the urban population and to the consequences of freer foreign trading conditions'.[2] Retail trade is going through a

[1] *Op. cit.*, p. 133.
[2] *Op. cit.*, p. 9.

period of rapid change with newer methods of sale—self-service, buyer groups, grands magasins, super-markets and chain stores—competing with the traditional small shop.

Investments are expected to reach 3 billion NF in 1965, compared with about 2 billion in 1961. The number of selling points will continue to decline, by several tens of thousands, at the same time as employment rises by about 100,000.

In recent years, considerable breaches have been made in the system of retail price maintenance by the cut-price ventures of a few energetic individuals such as M. Leclerc. The authorities have on the whole supported this movement, for example through reinforcement of the rules concerning refusal to trade, which procedure was used against M. Leclerc at one time. Echoes of this policy are found in the Plan. 'The authorities will endeavour to bring about equitable competitive conditions, in particular through a neutral fiscal system[1] and by eliminating restrictive practices which are contrary to the public interest. They will amend the rules governing commercial property. . . . A special commission for commerce will be set up, charged with giving objective advice to the Government on the costs and operation of commercial and distribution circuits.'[2]

The problem of meat prices is to be tackled by renewing and concentrating the existing system of slaughter-houses. For other perishable foodstuffs, twenty-six public markets are being built, or will be, during the Fourth Plan.

This summary covers the main points dealt with in the Fourth Plan in relation to production. Of course, even the text of the Plan is not a complete exposition of the intentions of the Government as it gives the main principles and measures only. Behind each paragraph of the text voted by Parliament, there is usually a study by a Planning Commission—either a Horizontal or a Vertical one.[3] The statistical data are also only a selection of the key figures, the full compilation not being published for the moment although, as was mentioned in Chapter VII, this work has been done much more consistently for the Fourth Plan than in the past.

8 *Overseas Départements and Territories*

It remains to say a few words about the relations of the Plan with the development programmes of other countries in the French Franc Area. The position can best be described by saying that the pro-

[1] At present highly concentrated forms of commerce are taxed more heavily than others.
[2] *Op. cit.*, p. 9.
[3] As was noted in Chapter I.

grammes, or plans, where they exist in these areas outside Metropolitan France, are related to, but are not part of, the Fourth Plan. This was true of the Constantine Plan for Algeria before the country became independent even though the General Planning Commissariat had taken an important part in drafting it.

The Fourth Plan looks forward to a current balance of payments surplus for Metropolitan France during the period 1962-65, which will permit the export of capital to the Area. The foreign trade projections were done separately from those for trade with foreign countries. This implied, among other things, making an assumption about likely growth-rates in the rest of the French Franc Area and the trend in its exportable surpluses. But, given the complete transformation which has recently taken place in the political status of the ex-French territorities in Africa, it was practically impossible to go further than that. This does not mean that the General Planning Commissariat is not helping these countries to draw up development plans; it is doing so actively. There is no doubt that the Fifth Plan will deal with this question much more explicitly than the Fourth. For the moment, however, the overseas chapter of the Plan refers only to the small areas which are still Overseas Départements or Overseas Territories.

The Overseas Départements (Guadeloupe, Guyane, Martinique and Réunion) already had a programme law for the period 1962 and 1963 and the Fourth Plan prolongs its investment schemes. 'The local populations were more closely associated with their drafting than in the past, through the work of local commissions.'[1] The economic situation is dominated by the rapid rise in population. So far since the war, a solution has been sought through raising production, but as the staple exports of the Départements are agricultural, and principally cane sugar which competes with the French sugar-beet industry, other solutions have to be found as well. The Fourth Plan comes down strongly in favour of a systematic policy of emigration to Metropolitan France and promises measures to facilitate it. Not much hope is held out of expanding cane sugar production and the wish is expressed that it will be possible to diversify production by introducing new crops. Finally, the Plan earmarks a credit of 46 billion NF for investment between 1962 and 1965.

The Overseas Territories (Comores, Nouvelle Calédonie, French Polynesia, Côte française des Somalis, St Pierre et Miquelon, Franco-British Condominium of the New Hebrides) also had a programme law which the Fourth Plan adopts and extends to 1965.

[1] *Op. cit.*, p. 17.

III. ECONOMIC BALANCE

The problems raised by maintaining economic balance, both externally and inside France, were dealt with by the Plan in its introduction and in the two first chapters of the second Part, the first being devoted to a survey of the results of the Third Plan. The main policy conclusions from this analysis were brought together under the heading: 'Distributing the Fruits of Expansion'.

1 *External Balance*

The background to the present situation is the very rapid increase in foreign trade which has been taking place since 1959 following the devaluation and the deflationary policy implemented at the end of 1958, the abolition of most quantitative restrictions on imports, tariff reductions, the transformation of the French Franc Area, and the intensification of aid programmes to less-developed countries. The Plan sets out to analyse France's external relations for the period up to 1965 in the light of these new factors and it draws a number of conclusions which it calls 'urgent'. The analysis was made from two points of view: by considering Metropolitan France's external balance on goods and services in 1965 in a national accounting framework, by studying the balance of payments of the French Franc Area as a whole in 1965.

The first approach is summarized in the table below:

EXTERNAL BALANCE ON GOODS AND SERVICES

(Billions of New Francs) 1961 prices

	1961			*1965*		
	Foreign Countries	*French Franc Area*	*Total*	*Foreign Countries*	*French Franc Area*	*Total*
Exports	27.6	11.5	39.0	34.8	12.3	47.1
Imports	25.0	7.5	32.4	31.2	8.7	39.9
Balance	2.6	4.0	6.6	3.6	3.6	7.2

Source: Fourth Plan, p. 9.

The hazardous nature of projections of foreign trade trends is well known and the special factors enumerated in the previous paragraph make it even more so. The Plan notes that the areas of uncertainty are in trade with foreign countries. On the whole, industry and the Vertical Planning Commissions were optimistic in their forecast; the increase in imports was generally low and, in exports, it was very high. The General Planning Commissariat had adjusted some of these figures to a more realistic level. But it had worked on the hypothesis that the agricultural clauses of the Rome Treaty would be applied 'in their letter and spirit'; if this proved not to be the case, 'the external surplus in 1965 would be much lower'.[1] We have seen in Chapter VI how the estimates of foreign trade were made.

With the balance of payments approach, the exchanges of the French Franc Area with foreign countries were taken as a whole. This implied incorporating capital transactions in the balance, together with some services excluded in the national accounts approach. The biggest margin of uncertainty here was in the balance of the transactions of the rest of the Franc Area with foreign countries, where it had been reckoned that a current deficit of 300 million dollars (US) would be matched by an equivalent amount of net capital receipts.

CURRENT BALANCE OF PAYMENTS OF THE FRANC AREA

(Millions of US *$)*

1961 prices

	Receipts		*Expenditures*		*Balance*	
	1960	*1965*	*1960*	*1965*	*1960*	*1965*
Merchandise trade	4,460	6,300	4,420	5,800	+ 40	+500
Invisibles	2,100	2,610	1,520	2,300	+580	+310

Source: Fourth Plan, p. 10.

The current account surplus in this projection would take into account net capital outgoings, such as repayment of public debt, net direct investments abroad, aid to less-developed countries, and participating in international monetary co-operation.

The fragile nature of some of the estimates should be allowed for when considering the favourable picture they give. 'This should not lead to a reduction of the growth target, which has been fixed so as to achieve social progress and full employment, any more than to a return to restrictive (trade) policies. . . . But it does imply that a certain number of recommendations which are among the most urgent in the entire Plan have to be implemented.'[2]

'In the absence of an agreement between States for a policy of development we must have an export strategy which will protect us from untoward events in international competition. A prime condition for the success of this strategy is the maintenance of price competitiveness, and, in particular, securing price reductions in progressive sectors which will attenuate the consequences of some increases difficult to avoid. Any insufficiencies in the search for innovations,

[1] *Op. cit.*, p. 9.
[2] *Op. cit.*, p. 10.

any slackening in our productivity effort and any distribution of its fruits which neglected the interests of consumers, would favour the reappearance of an external imbalance and, as a result, restrictive measures to reduce growth would be called for, with a consequent waste of previous efforts. Nothing is more important than getting a general understanding of the logic of these developments.'[1]

2 *Internal Balance*

The key factor here is to keep price stability. The choice of a high rate of growth for the Fourth Plan makes this balance both more difficult to achieve and yet more necessary than ever. To preserve balance, certain conditions will have to be fulfilled. Income increases must not exceed, on an average, the rise in productivity. Public receipts and expenditures must expand together and this means that great prudence is called for in introducing tax reductions. The balance between savings and investments must be respected. 'But, in the final analysis, the maintenance of a sustainable rate of growth will depend upon our aptitude to develop, in an harmonious manner, the various categories of final demand. This is another way of stressing the importance of the ways in which the fruits of expansion are distributed.'[2]

3 *The Fruits of Expansion*

The expected fruits of expansion, that is to say total available resources, are shown in the table opposite together with their proposed distribution.

The share of investments in total demand will rise over the period of the Fourth Plan from 20 to 22 per cent. The increase in productive investment expenditure will be rather more rapid than in production (28 per cent compared with 24 per cent). The growth of 'social' investments is 25 per cent for housing and 50 per cent for other types of social equipment. This progression of investment expenditure is required to achieve the objectives of the Fourth Plan and to ensure that expansion can continue after that at a high rate. Thanks to the investment programme in housing, the quantitative aspect of the housing problem should be solved by 1965 and attention can then concentrate more on qualitative considerations. The beneficial effects for the mobility of labour will be appreciable.

The target for private consumption is 23 per cent above the 1961 level in 1965, or one point less than the rise in total output. This is the, still modest, sacrifice which is called for in order to expand in-

[1] *Op. cit.*, p. 10.
[2] *Op. cit.*, p. 11.

THE FINAL VERSION OF THE FOURTH PLAN

(*Billions of New Francs*) *1961 prices*

	1961	*1965*	*Increase* (+) *Decrease* (−)
I. *Resources:*			
Gross internal production	271	336	+65
Plus imports	+ 33	+ 40	+ 7
Minus exports	− 39	− 47	− 8
= Available resources	265	329	+64
II. *Expenditures*			
Household consumption	192	235	+43
Consumption of the public departments	14	17	+ 3
Directly productive investments	36	46	+10
Social investments	19.5	26	+ 6.5
of which:			
Housing	12	15	+ 3
Other	7.5	11	+ 3.5
Stocks	4	6	+ 1.5
= Available resources	265	329	+64

Source: Fourth Plan, p. 11.

vestments, especially in the social field. But private consumption will nevertheless absorb over two-thirds of the additional resources available; hence, securing an 'harmonious development of consumption expenditure is one of the major problems of the Fourth Plan'.[1] The Third Plan had already made a number of general recommendations but 'it is necessary today to go further and to begin an analysis of income distribution'.[2]

Whilst it is not denied that the large rise in private consumption makes selective measures in favour of certain categories, such as the aged or the least-paid workers, indispensable, 'actions of this kind must go hand in hand with a policy for all incomes, both direct and indirect, and for tax payments and saving, so that the target fixed for private consumption is not exceeded'.[2] This situation should lead to elaborating a 'national incomes policy'. 'But because of the social and psychological habits prevailing in the country, and which find a particularly vehement expression in the legislation on collective bargaining, no new measures in this field have been written into the

[1] *Op. cit.*, p. 14.
[2] *Op. cit.*, p. 14.

Fourth Plan. Free wage bargaining which will remain the general rule, will be informed by studies, done in the framework of the national accounts, and put forward for open debate.'[1]

Although the State has no direct powers as regards wages and salaries in the private sector, the situation is not the same with social transfer payments. The uncertainties as to the results of a harmonization of social policies in the Common Market countries make impossible the adoption of a rigid programme, but the Fourth Plan will set up a procedure similar to the one to be used for direct incomes, so that decisions can be taken on an annual basis. Some measures are envisaged immediately, such as the 10 per cent rise in family allowances in 1962, and improved transfers in favour of the aged. One longer-term commitment concerns the workers, now few in number it is true, who are still paid at the legal minimum wage. 'One of the firmest objectives of the Fourth Plan is to see to it that these workers receive in 1965, in one way or another, and without repercussions on other wages, a remuneration notably higher than the one they would receive if the basic wage continued to be calculated as at present.'[2]

IV. EXECUTING THE PLAN

The Third Part of the text of the Plan is devoted to this subject. It is divided into four chapters: scientific and technical research, productivity, financial mechanisms and investments, fiscal policy.

1 *Scientific and Technical Research*

The Fourth Plan echoes the report of the Commission of that name when it states that: 'in the same way as the inventive spirit of its research workers and the capacity of its laboratories constitute for the private firm the guarantees of its future, so the future of a nation is being increasingly determined by the energy it shows in opening-up new paths to knowledge which are the source of its influence in the world and the indispensable condition for the renewal of its techniques'.[3] Noting that the French contribution to science was especially important formerly, before research took on the systematic character it has today, the Fourth Plan goes on to lay down two main directions for policy; firstly, to give a new impetus to fundamental research, secondly to pay more attention than in the past to the needs of technical research. It is no accident that this chapter of the Fourth

[1] *Op. cit.*, p. 14.
[2] *Op. cit.*, p. 15.
[3] *Op. cit.*, p. 55.

Plan comes at the beginning of the section headed 'Means of Action'.

The concern of the planning authorities with scientific and technical research is easily understandable as it appears that France is lagging behind some other industrial countries. Although no strict relationship exists between amounts spent on research and the results obtained, nevertheless, in the absence of any better indicator, such comparisons do give an idea of the situation.

According to the Scientific and Technical Research Commission, expenditure per head on research in France is about half that in the United Kingdom and less than half that in the United States and the Soviet Union. This is due, in part, to the small scale of much of French industry and to the low level of public interest in problems of this kind. But even the amount of State expenditure on research is said to be only half that in the United Kingdom.

The decision to raise the amount of funds, both public and private, devoted to research figured already in the Government's directives issued to the Planning Commissions in the spring of 1960.[1] The investment credits for the public sector written into the Fourth Plan attain 1.5 billion New Francs, or about twice the amount spent during the Third Plan.[2] Current expenditure, notably salaries, will have to be increased by about one-fifth to support this investment programme.[3]

The distribution of the total is as follows (in millions of New Francs):[4]

Ministry of Education (CNRS,* Universities, Technical Education)	735
Agriculture	158
National Institute of Hygiene	75
Telecommunications	80
Industry	78
Technical assistance	38
Other	36
Non-allocated funds	290
Total	1,490

* Centre National de la Recherche Scientifique.

1 See Appendix I, p. 374.
2 This figure excludes credits for military research, 450 million New Francs in 1960, for which no estimates are given in the Fourth Plan, and the credits for the Atomic Energy Commission.
3 About 700 million NF in 1960.
4 *Op. cit.*, p. 59.

The Scientific and Technical Research Commission[1] itself had presented its estimates of needs in the different sectors according to two hypotheses. One was described as a first priority tranche. It corresponded to the figures included in the Plan and given in the table on page 223. A second list of credits of less urgency was also supplied for a total of 500 million New Francs, but these were not retained by the Plan.

2 *Productivity*

Productivity has risen substantially in France since the war because, with a working population and a number of hours worked which remained practically constant, total output increased by over two-thirds between 1949 and 1960. But the ambitious target set by the Fourth Plan makes it necessary to continue these efforts.

The Plan assigns three major objectives to the policy for increasing productivity: to improve the ways of exact measurement of productivity, to introduce modern methods of organization and control, to facilitate the optimum use of progress being achieved by science.

Several specific measures are proposed dealing with research into productivity, training of personnel, information and publicity, social problems and automation.

3 *Financing of Investments*

The preoccupations expressed in this chapter go back to the analytical work done by the Equilibrium Working Party of the General Economic and Financial Commission which was referred to in Chapters VI and VII. 'Maintaining overall balance is a necessary, but not a sufficient, condition for the Plan to be achieved. It is not sufficient for the total volume of savings to equal investments, or for the level of fiscal receipts to be satisfactory, compared with expenditures. Savings have also to be put at the disposal of those who invest in conditions which are adapted to their needs. In other words, the ways in which an economic and financial policy is applied are just as important as its general principles.'[2]

The balance of saving and investment in 1965 can be estimated as follows:

[1] There is a close link between the governmental organization of research and the Plan in so far as the Planning Commission for Scientific and Technical Research was, to all intents and purposes, the permanent Consultative Committee for Scientific and Technical Research. This Committee advises an Inter-Ministerial Committee created in 1958 to co-ordinate all matters pertaining to research. Its secretarial work is carried out by a permanent official called the Delegate General for Scientific and Technical Research who was also the rapporteur for the Planning Commission.

[2] *Op. cit.*, p. 63.

SAVINGS AND INVESTMENTS IN 1965

Resources	Billions of NF	Index (1961 = 100)	*Uses*	Billions of NF	Index (1961 = 100)
Savings by firms	39.5	135	Investment by firms*	56.4	134
Savings by households	29.6	137	Investment by households	9.5	105
Surplus of the public departments	7.6	100	Investment by public departments	10.5	150
			Balance of foreign transactions	+0.3	
Total	76.7	131	Total	76.7	131

* Including stocks.
Source: Fourth Plan, p. 35.

A substantial rise in savings by households is expected, much faster than in their incomes (+37 per cent compared with +23 per cent). Although it is probable that enterprises will be able to rely less than in the past upon self-financing, due to growing competition from abroad, a rate of increase equal to that of investment expenditure has been assumed. The surplus of current receipts and expenditures of the public departments is therefore fixed at between 7.5 and 8 billion New Francs. An independent estimate of the likely trend in the public finances, allowing for the objectives of the Plan among other things, confirmed that this was a reasonable figure. Projections of public sector investments and loans show that the corresponding budget deficit to be borne by the Treasury in 1965 would be about the same as today, that is 700 million New Francs. But the balance described above requires an increase in the transfer of savings from households to firms.

At the present time, gross fixed capital formation is financed from the following sources:

FINANCE OF GFCF IN 1960

	Billions of NF	*Per cent*
Public Funds	12.5	25.2
Specialized credit institution, banks, insurance companies	5.7	11.4
Capital market	6.0	12.0
Medium-term credit	6.2	12.5
Other sources (mainly self-financing)	19.3	38.9
Total	49.7	100.0

Source: Fourth Plan, p. 63.

Reviewing these sources, the Plan concludes that the critical ones for the future are the capital market and the banking and specialized credit sector.

'Self-financing, including depreciation allowances, must continue to cover the largest share of gross investment, but the Government has scarcely to intervene here. Our fiscal legislation, since the introduction of degressive amortization rules, is now as favourable as in any other country as regards the stimulus to invest. As most prices have been freed, self-financing by firms, except in some important sectors which are not numerous, will depend upon competition.'[1]

But 'private firms are going to need more funds in the future (from other sources). If these demands are to be met without an upward pressure on prices, the savings and financial mechanisms will have to be adapted to them. There are several points where our existing procedures could be perfected or are in want of adaptation to new, and changed, conditions.'[2]

After having stressed the rising trend, over the years, in recourse to the capital market, the Plan notes that there is an imbalance between the market for shares and the one for debentures, as investors prefer the former. This must be corrected. It is desirable for companies to ask shareholders to pay a larger premium when new issues are made than at present. To encourage firms to make capital issues, the exemption from the profits tax of up to a 5 per cent annual dividend on new capital, which was to expire at the end of 1961, has been prolonged for two years. Small family firms, who hesitate to issue new shares because they fear they will lose control of their businesses, should inquire into the possibility of an issue of preference shares, which are still too rare in France. 'If one considers the frequent absenteeism among small and medium shareholders at annual general meetings, this (break with the equality of rights of all shareholders) appears less shocking.'[3] Whenever the authorities have to give an opinion on an issue of debentures, or the granting of medium-term credit, 'they will be able to recommend a larger contribution to investment from an increase in the issued capital of the company, and could even make their agreement subject to this'.[4]

Turning to the debenture market, the Plan concludes that the cost of long-term credit in France is comparable to practice in other countries, in particular since the reduction of nearly 2 per cent in interest rates which has been achieved since 1958. But the market

[1] *Op. cit.*, p. 63.
[2] *Op. cit.*, p. 64.
[3] *Op. cit.*, p. 65.
[4] *Op. cit.*, p. 65.

is unable to absorb all the potential debenture issues and, for that reason, they continue to be subject to prior authorization by the Treasury. Usually the delay for a prospective borrower is six months. In some cases permission is refused.

Of the total of debentures issued in 1959—266 billion New Francs —120 billion were taken up by the Caisse des Dépôts et Consignations and the insurance companies. Most of the remainder, or about half the total, probably went into private hands. This percentage needs to be raised, however. The upward trend which can be expected as a result of the high savings rate likely to be met with over the next few years will help, but will not be sufficient. Consequently, means are needed of attracting other savers, especially those who prefer shares for the time being, on to the market for debentures. Convertible debentures could be used for doing this, if the period before conversion was longer than the present average of two years. Preference shares, which have some of the characteristics of debentures, could be employed more widely, too. As the reputation of the borrower is important for the success of a loan issue, the authorities will try to leave the market to well-known firms, or groups of firms, and will direct other would-be borrowers to alternative forms of long-term credit.

The banks, the specialized credit institutions and the insurance companies financed about 15 per cent of total investment in 1959, part of it through issues of their own debentures on the capital market. Cheaper than debentures, and requiring practically no provisions for repayment, the deposits available to these institutions—savings banks deposits, deposit bank accounts, etc.—are a valuable addition to investment finance.

The Plan considers that the banking arrangements for medium- and longer-term credit in France are satisfactory on the whole as to cost and availability, and notes that no very widespread criticisms of them were made by the Planning Commissions. But some improvement is needed in the degree of understanding, by the banks, of their clients' problems. Long-term credit facilities for small firms could also be improved if the Regional Development Societies were reinforced, financially and technically, and studied more varied methods of helping firms in their region than simply taking up issues of debentures.

Whatever the success of these measures, demand for investment funds will probably remain greater than supply. 'In this connection, mechanisms exist for giving priority to the financing of the fixed capital necessary to achieve the objectives of the Plan through control of credit and capital issues. In the likely event of a relative shortage of capital, these mechanisms will continue to be used to implement the Fourth Plan.'[1]

4 *Fiscal Policy*

There are three main considerations which will have to be borne in mind during the Fourth Plan as far as fiscal policy is concerned. 'The first is fundamental; it means finding measures which encourage economic growth, particularly by eliminating the present brake on progress resulting from some aspects of existing fiscal arrangements. The two others have, as their objective, to place the country in as favourable a situation as possible *vis-à-vis* its major competitors, taking into account existing international agreements, and to simplify certain tax rules whose complexity is detrimental both to clarity and equity between taxpayers and to productivity.'[2]

These reflexions brought the authors of the Plan to approve the principle of a 'neutral tax system' which would not discriminate between the various legal forms of economic activity. The legalistic tradition which still inspires French tax law makes this a difficult task, but progress has already been accomplished, especially with the institution of a turnover tax. But this type of 'neutral' fiscal policy does not exclude the active use of taxes to implement selective measures.

The Plan takes the neutral policy first and devotes three full pages of closely printed text to the subject.[3] An important problem, but one which is too complex to summarize here, is to iron out any discrepancies which arise in the tax treatment of parent companies and their subsidiaries, principally as regards double taxation. The Plan enumerates several reforms to achieve this. Given the need for firms to appeal more frequently, and on a larger scale, to savings through the capital market, reforms are suggested to facilitate new issues. The exemption from profits tax up to 5 per cent of dividends paid on new capital is being prolonged until 1963, as already noted, by which time the entire problem will have been looked again at from the point of view of the harmonization of tax systems in the Common Market. Some measures will assist professional groups, or firms, which make collective issues of debentures on the capital market, or will improve the functioning of investment companies. A reduction of the stamp tax for many transactions is also envisaged. Indirect taxes produce 54 per cent of the tax revenues of the State. Since the

[1] *Op. cit.*, p. 67.

[2] *Op. cit.*, p. 67.

[3] As was mentioned earlier, tax questions are under intensive study at the moment.

introduction of the turnover tax, the most flagrant discrimination against new investments has been corrected and the present system is satisfactory on the whole. But it is desirable to extend the tax to all sectors, including those at present exempt from indirect taxes, so as to create a single, unified scheme.

Going beyond these considerations, inspired by a concern with the neutrality of the tax system, the Plan enumerates the various tax concessions which the authorities are empowered to grant, either to branches of activity, or to individual firms.[1] '... The fiscal weapon is amongst the most important selective means the authorities possess ... it will be used in narrowly limited cases to facilitate the achievement of the most difficult objectives of the Fourth Plan. ... Some of these measures are semi-automatic, the approval of the authorities being designed merely to eliminate requests having no economic value; others are real "fiscal controls" when a specific privilege is granted to a firm as a counterpart of an investment programme of particular interest.'[2] Research, and the introduction of a new product, are examples where this procedure could be applied.

The Plan notes that 'the investment policy of the private sector is the object of permanent dialogues within the framework of the Plan, which enable the numerous available forms of government action to be put to use'.[3] But 'a more difficult case remains where the problem is not one of encouraging, modifying or discouraging an activity which exists already, but of creating in a branch which is not sufficiently developed, an initiative which would not appear spontaneously'.[4] After stressing the importance of very careful studies of such situations before deciding on direct action, the Plan considers nevertheless that cases can occur where 'the Government will apply the most appropriate measures (to remedy the situation) by addressing itself to the firms in the branch, by provoking the entry into the branch of a newcomer from a neighbouring branch, or finally by taking up a majority or minority share, either temporarily or on a permanent basis, in the capital of a newly constituted firm'.[5]

[1] These measures are listed at the end of Chapter XIV.
[2] *Op. cit.*, p. 71.
[3] *Op. cit.*, p. 16.
[4] *Op. cit.*, p. 16.
[5] *Op. cit.*, p. 16. See also p. 348.

PART THREE

IMPLEMENTING THE PLAN

The French authorities dispose of a considerable armoury for ensuring the implementation of the Plan. We discuss these measures in this Part. The means at the disposal of the State appear to be particularly extensive as regards the activities of the public sector itself, and we deal with them first (Chapter XII). A special case, which is rather astride the public and private sectors, concerns regional development policy, so important in the Fourth Plan (Chapter XIII). The private sector is in a rather different position but it cannot be dealt with as a whole. A distinction which appears immediately is that between non-agricultural and agricultural activities, and we devote separate chapters to them (Chapters XIV and XV). There remain a number of more general considerations which are at the heart of the lively debates going on in France at the present time on the nature and scope of planning. It has seemed preferable, for expositional purposes, to touch on these only lightly in this Part, and to deal with them in a systematic manner in Part Four, when the reader has had an opportunity of seeing what are the practical institutional, legislative and administrative arrangements in force for implementing the Plan.

CHAPTER XII

IMPLEMENTING THE PLAN IN THE PUBLIC SECTOR

It is essentially in relation to the public sector that the obligatory character of the Plan appears. As was seen earlier in Chapter III the central Government has a greater degree of responsibility for social investment and for infrastructure than in many countries where local governments have a larger say in the spending of money on such objects. Again, the Ministry of Industry and the Ministry of Transport have important powers of tutelage *vis-à-vis* the nationalized industries. Consequently, the problem which is most likely to arise here is that the credits actually made available, usually on an annual basis through the budget, will fall short of what the four-year Plan foresaw and, even more so, of what the spending units would wish to disburse. It does happen, though, that the amount of credits available is not the limiting factor. The problems being met with by the Ministry of Education at the present time in speeding-up the school building programme are a case in point.

It is important to recall, in this connection, that the General Planning Commissariat is not the body which ensures the implementation of the programmes for the public sector written into the Plan. Such a responsibility would be in contradiction with its rôle. Inside the administration the authorization of programmes in the public sector, in the sense that they can be said to be authorized by the vote of the Plan,[1] is only a first step, but a vital one, towards their implementation. For them to be achieved, however, other Government bodies as well as Parliament itself have a capital rôle to play—namely in granting the specific authorization to contract expenditures and in providing the necessary finance. These are the key issues for the public sector,[2] and the major rôle here falls to the Ministry of Finance. Three areas merit examination in this respect: the budget proper, the local authorities, the nationalized industries.

The following table gives a breakdown of public investment expenditures under these three headings. The total represented over one-third of overall fixed capital formation in 1961, and the same

[1] See on this subject, Chapter XI.

[2] Other aspects of the Plan are achieved through measures such as the location of public investment and the decentralization of public administrations (see Chapter XIII on regional development policy).

relation held for the share of the nationalized industries in the productive investments. In addition, it should be noted that nearly 90 per cent of housebuilding is financed in part with public funds.

FIXED CAPITAL FORMATION IN THE PUBLIC SECTOR

(*Billion* NF *current prices*)

	1959	*1960*	*1961*
Central administrations	1.3	1.3	1.7
Local authorities	3.6	4.0	4.5
Other public administrations	0.7	0.7	0.6
Nationalized industries	11.1	11.3	11.8
Total	16.7	17.3	18.6
Housing (by firms)*	2.8	3.0	3.4
Housing (by households)*	8.6	8.9	9.2
Total	11.4	11.9	12.6
Total fixed capital formation	46.3	49.9	55.1

* Mainly public.

Source: Rapport sur les comptes de la Nation de l'année 1961, Imprimerie Nationale, 1962.

I. THE GENERAL BUDGET[1]

The administrations which bear the main responsibility for drawing-up the budget are the Budget Directorate and, secondly, the Treasury Directorate of the Ministry of Finance, as was seen in Chapter III, where the distinctly closer collaboration between these two directorates and the Plan in the drafting and implementing of the Fourth Plan was noted as well as the reasons for it. We shall consider briefly this collaboration at the drafting stage of the Fourth Plan, i.e. during 1960 and 1961 for the most part, and subsequently with reference to the annual budgets for 1962 and 1963—the first two years of the Fourth Plan—before discussing the problems for traditional budgetary practice raised by the need to ensure regular execution of medium-term objectives, and the way attempts are made to solve these problems.

(1) Collaboration of the Budget and Treasury Directorates, but in particular the former, with the planning process at the drafting stage took two forms. The first concerned the work of the Horizontal General Economic and Financial Commission and especially its Working Party, the Equilibrium Group. The second involved par-

[1] See p. 235, footnote 1.

ticipation in the work of the Vertical Planning Commissions. The Budget and Treasury Directorates are represented on all these Commissions.

For work at the Horizontal Commission level, the Budget Directorate built up, with the collaboration of the SEEF, a set of budget accounts for 1965, the end-year of the Fourth Plan, on the basis of the projections being made in the Plan for such items as social services, housing, defence expenditure, and so on. Other estimates were made for the level of public consumption of goods and services and, separately, for salary and wage costs of the civil service. It was the first exercise of this kind carried out in a systematic manner. At the same time, in view of the efforts being made to integrate the financial aspects of the Plan into the 'real' aspects, the Treasury Directorate participated in the work of the Equilibrium Group on the conditions necessary for financial balance during the Fourth Plan.

When one examines the Vertical Planning Commissions dealing with public expenditure, it appears that a much greater degree of agreement than for the Third Plan was achieved between the Budget Directorate, the Ministries and other bodies interested as spending units, and the General Planning Commissariat. It will be recalled that, up to the Third Plan, the problem did not really arise as the only objectives of the Plan which were quantified seriously concerned productive sectors of the economy, except housing. The fact that insufficient co-ordination had taken place between the spending units and the Budget Directorate in the preparatory work on the Third Plan could only lead to disappointments when the annual process of drawing up the budget began. The best indication that there has been a radical change in this respect for the Fourth Plan is given by the practice followed with the 1962 budget.[1]

Until 1961, the various spending administrations did not play a

[1] We omit here any consideration of the annexed budgets. This procedure is adopted mainly for government activities which consist of the production and sale of goods and services. There are nine of these annexed budgets (Savings Banks, Government Printing Office, Légion d'Honneur, Order of the Liberation, Mint, Post Office, Agricultural Social Security, Petrol, Arsenal). The only one whose investments are important for the Plan is the Post Office. In addition to the annexed budgets, there are a number of Special Treasury Accounts. In the early post-war years, these flourished and became so many hidden budgets which never came before Parliament at all. Today the situation has been brought under control. Most of the special accounts are concerned with investment through grants to, or direct expenditure by, government agencies, notably the Road Fund, the National Water Supply Fund and the National Forestry Fund. One account is of capital importance for the Plan. It is the Economic and Social Development Fund which we discussed in Chapter III and to which we return in the final section of this chapter in relation to the nationalized industries.

very active rôle in the preliminary phase of budget preparations which occupies the first half of the year until some time during July, by when the credit ceilings of the main categories of expenditure have been decided upon.[1] Hence it could indeed appear to them that they were being invited to play a game where all the cards were carefully stacked against them when, in the second half of the year, they sent in their detailed credit requests and discussed them with the Budget Directorate. At best, they could hope to be left to make their own choice of what items of expenditure to sacrifice.

In 1961, in order to improve this state of affairs, the Ministry of Finance requested provisional estimates from the spending administrations as early as March. Their purpose was not to go into details but rather to outline the policy each intended to follow. In this way it was possible for discussions to take place between each public department and the Budget Directorate on what should be preserved and what should be sacrificed before the credit ceilings of major categories were fixed in July 1961. This system seems to have been a marked improvement on previous years, and the 1962 budget could be regarded as an attempt to adhere to the lines laid down by the Fourth Plan.

This procedure was carried further for the preparation of the 1963 budget.[2] Current expenditures were kept at their 1962 level except for education and scientific research where the Fourth Plan foresees big increases. Expenditures on grants and subsidies (for example, agriculture, aid to repatriated persons from Algeria) went through the traditional process of discussion. For all capital items where the Fourth Plan had set quantitative objectives, the budget allocations were based upon achieving them as planned; for the others allocations were kept at the same level as in 1962 whenever possible. The principle now seems to be clearly established in the habits of the administrations, which is more important than being enshrined in a legal text, that the Plan is the proper norm against which the budget, as well as economic policy in general, should be judged.

'For the first time, as far as I am aware, the Plan, which was traditionally accepted by the Minister of Finance as a general guide to policy, now takes on a much more precise meaning for him. The Minister of Finance adopts the objectives of the Plan and his policy must be defined in such a way that it becomes the methodical and liberal instrument for reaching them.'[3]

[1] See Chapter III for a description of this process.

[2] We are indebted to M. Pallez for these details. Cf., *op cit.*, Chapter VII.

[3] The Minister of Finance, M. Giscard d'Estaing, opening speech in the debate by the National Assembly on the Fourth Plan. *Débats Parlementaires,* Wednesday, May 23, 1962, p. 1234.

A representative of the General Planning Commissariat attends the budget discussion between the Budget Directorate and the spending administration. In the past this was a factor favouring an attempt to keep the budget allocations in line with the Plan even when this was not entirely possible, for the reasons already given. The representative of the General Planning Commissariat was likely to add weight to the arguments of the spending administrations where they could refer to objectives which had been written into the Plan. The obstacles in their way, however, were such that they were usually tempted to join the ranks of the claimants for programme laws as an extra guarantee. It appears that, to some extent, the improved understanding between all parts of the Government administration as to the meaning and importance of planned targets has reduced this sort of pressure coming from the spending administrations, although it is a procedure which still has many advocates in Parliament and in the public. But, before dealing with this subject, it is necessary to understand the basic process for authorizing expenditure for investment purposes through the budget which is used in France. We concern ourselves with the general budget which includes any direct investment undertaken by the administration or grants for investment purposes, notably to local authorities.[1]

(2) In France, a fundamental *principle of budget law* is an annual budget. So it has been necessary to find ways of attenuating the difficulties met with by spending administrations in executing investment projects which take several years to complete. Two concepts are relevant here, the programme authorization and the payment credit. An important decree issued in 1959 on budget procedure states in its Article 12 that: 'Financial provisions for capital expenditure or loans . . . can include programme authorizations and payment credits. The programme authorization is the upper limit to the investment expenditure each Ministry is authorized by law to undertake. It remains in force without any fixed time period until it is cancelled. It can be revised if needs be to take account of technical or price changes. Payment credits constitute the upper limit to expenditure which can be paid, or authorized for payment, during the year in the framework of the corresponding programme authorization.'

Thus the payment credits have an annual character whereas the programme authorizations have a longer duration, but both have the same legal value as both are approved with the budget. The pro-

[1] These allocations are found under three budget chapters, as they are called: Chapter V, investment undertaken directly by the State; Chapter VI, grants for investment purposes; Chapter VII, war damage.

gramme authorization is consummated by the annual payment credits. An example will clarify the distinction. If it is supposed that the total cost of an investment project, say a bridge, is 10 million NF and the duration of the work three years, a programme authorization for 10 million NF will be voted and then, assuming no changes in the initial estimate of the total cost, three annual payment credits for, say, 3, 5 and 2 million NF will be included in the successive budgets. Naturally, programme authorizations included in the budget each year are not counted for purposes of measuring the level of public expenditure, only the payment credits. Besides, a programme authorization can be amended if necessary by not making available the corresponding credit payments, although this would be rare in practice, given the expense incurred when contracts have been signed. To reduce expenditure it is rather the level of programme authorizations which is compressed, but this only produces its effects with a delay.

The system of programme authorizations has been criticized because the operations for which it is used are not actually all 'individualized' as they should be theoretically. They do not refer to complete units, or self-contained sub-units, of a project (such as a stretch of autoroute), but are used by the spending administrations (an example which has been given is the Ministry of Education) to finance annual tranches of a large number of such units, whereas a strict compliance with the principle of 'individualization' would mean concentrating credits on fewer projects at once. Thus the programme authorization system does not always give the results it is intended to give, of greater continuity in investment expenditure and, hence, better pre-planning and lower tendering prices from contractors. The alternatives appear to be, either to abandon the rule of annuality for the budget, and to vote payment credits for the whole cost of investment projects—a solution which is not near to winning acceptance and which would raise serious problems for budget policy, in the framework of overall economic policy—or to increase substantially, in one or two successive budgets, the amounts of programme authorizations so that the principle of 'individualization' can really be applied by all spending administrations. For the moment, a beginning on this second course is discernible in the 1963 budget where programme authorizations have been raised somewhat.

The procedure of programme laws[1] has been grafted on to these

[1] A somewhat similar procedure existed before that called the programme decrees taken in 1955. These decrees dealt with sectors such as atomic energy, electricity, telecommunications and led to the opening of programme author-

traditional arrangements. The 1959 decree states in Article 1: 'Plans approved by Parliament which define long-term objectives cannot lead to undertakings committing the State save within the limits fixed by programme authorizations . . . (which) can be grouped in programme laws.' Article 2 adds that: 'Programme laws cannot be used to commit the State *vis-à-vis* third persons except within the limits of programme organizations contained in the Finance Act (i.e. the budget) of the year.' Consequently, from the outset, the limited scope of the programme law was stressed; unless it is translated into concrete decisions in a series of programme authorizations, it is without executive value and amounts to no more than a declaration of intentions. This does not prevent the procedure of the programme law from enjoying considerable popularity for several reasons. In many cases, ignorance of the real nature of the programme law is at the bottom of demands for its application to specific issues. This is particularly so when local interests are at stake and when it is tempting for parliamentarians in the area to support claims for a programme law despite its non-imperative nature. Perhaps such views are not as mistaken as a strict interpretation of the texts would lead one to conclude. There is no doubt that a programme law once voted provides a reference for future action which can be easily invoked and which can be used as a stick to beat a recalcitrant government.

The taste for programme laws had also spread after 1955 to government departments themselves, each wishing to have one for its pet schemes. Such an attitude is easily understandable as the existence of a programme law can always be an argument in the annual discussion with the Ministry of Finance on budget allocations. But the inconvenience of the generalization of the procedure is obvious. Not only is the margin of freedom of action of the Government unduly restricted, but the juxtaposition of programme laws gives no guarantee that they correspond to planning periods and to balanced objectives.

The text of the Fourth Plan refers explicitly to the need for a reform of the programme law procedure. 'As to the financing (of investments) out of public monies, the method of programme laws calls for reconsideration. These laws, which should ensure a supplement of continuity in public expenditure for investment purposes,

izations, which gave the power to commit expenditure, for several years in advance, usually three years. The idea was that it would be easier to achieve the Second Plan by committing the budget in advance. But the need, in 1957, to cut public expenditure showed that such a procedure could be too inflexible. As a result, the looser procedure of the programme laws was introduced.

are still not properly adapted to this aim. Thus, if the numerous programme laws which exist constitute moral obligations, which it is difficult not to respect, for the State to spend money, they do not authorize the spending departments to conclude long-term contracts with suppliers. But these contracts, which can represent a means of achieving the modernization and reorganization of the industries in question, were the most evident advantage which could be expected from such long-term commitments.'[1] Consequently, two types of measures are envisaged to correct this situation: procedures which will enable spending authorities to conclude contracts over a period of several years with suppliers and to obtain in exchange price reductions (prices would be revised later on if it appeared that budget allocations were insufficient); a reduction in the number of programme laws so as to limit them to those sectors where the conclusion of long-term contracts has advantages.

So it can be expected that from now on there will be a serious effort to refuse the renewal of programme laws which expire and to prevent the vote by Parliament of new ones.[2] The promise of a programme law in 1963 for the Western regions, described in Chapter XIII, is rather a special case in this respect.

II. LOCAL UNITS OF GOVERNMENT

These are of two kinds—the 'département' and the 'commune'. We saw in Chapter IV on regional development policy, how the structure of local government is subject to strain at the present time, and the solutions being adopted in order to improve the local unit's position as an active link in the formulation and application of economic policy at the regional level. It so happens that it is precisely in the field of regional development that the local units of Government have a large measure of freedom from central control, due either to the types of activity involved (town planning) or to the organizational procedures adopted (Sociétés d'Economie Mixte). Even here, however, the financial weakness of local government authorities puts them under the control of the central Government, that is in the last analysis, of the Ministry of Finance.

[1] See Fourth Plan, p. 64.

[2] At the end of 1961 the following laws were in operation: General economic equipment (mainly roads), 1959; Health and sanitation, 1959; School and University building, 1959; Agricultural investments, 1960; Overseas departments, 1960; Military installations, 1960; Sahara installations, 1961; Technical and scientific research, 1961; Overseas territories, 1961; Sporting equipment, 1961. In 1962 the following programme laws were voted (to June 1962): housing, agricultural education.

This situation is in line with the trend in local governments' finances in most countries of course, but, in addition, there is in France a strong centralizing tendency which goes back a long way in French history. The existence of a State representative—the préfet—in the départements with wide powers of control and sanction is eloquent of this. Central control of expenditures of local authorities is also secured by the system of public accountants responsible to the Minister of Finance. As regards the revenues of the two major local taxes—a tax on property and land and a turnover tax—the freedom of the local authorities to alter their rates is restricted in the second case. Finally, the current expenditure accounts of the local government units must be voted in balance and the préfet, to whom the budget must be submitted, can refuse it if it is not and insist on extra receipts being found from tax revenue.

On the capital side, the freedom of the local authorities is also subject to fairly strict limits imposed by the Ministry of Finance besides those entailed by the nature of the capital market itself. Thus the issue by local authorities of long-term bonds on the capital market calls for prior Treasury authorization—this being given in preference to the bond issues of the specialized credit institutions such as the Crédit Foncier or the Crédit National as these specialized institutions have built up their clienteles so that only big local authorities (for example, the Ville de Paris) can hope to compete with them. At the short-term end, the possibilities of borrowing are limited by the underdeveloped state of the French money market both for French and foreign capital.

All this means that local authorities are forced back to public bodies for their funds, which observation does not imply, of course, that they thereby receive less, or on less favourable terms than they would be likely to get under a more liberal system, but merely that the central Government has extensive powers of control.

Most local authority borrowing is done from the Caisse des Dépôts et Consignations,[1] the Crédit Foncier and the Crédit Agricole. This system does not imply a close scrutiny by the Ministry of Finance, or the Economic and Social Development Fund, of all loan applications. In some cases, the Caisse des Dépôts et Consignations will assist groups of local authorities to place issues of bonds directly with the insurance companies, many of whom are public bodies also. Another instrument which the Ministry of Finance possesses is that

[1] The Director General of the Caisse is the Chairman of the Planning Commission for Urban Development and of Group 1b of the Economic and Social Development Fund (cf. Chapter III).

no loan from a public credit organization can be secured by a local authority unless it obtains simultaneously the inscription in a Ministry budget of a subsidy, even a symbolic one, to help towards financing the same project. And subsidies from the State budget to help the local authorities to carry out all the obligations imposed upon them by the central Government give the Ministry of Finance a powerful weapon for controlling local authority expenditures.

As was mentioned earlier, the most interesting developments taking place in this field relate to regional policy where the Fourth Plan, and the measures being taken to implement it, are changing the nature of the problem of French local government. This policy is likely to weaken the present centralized system of control.

III. THE NATIONALIZED INDUSTRIES

The impact of the Plan on the nationalized industries is felt at two points: firstly, when the output objectives are fixed and, secondly, when their financing is considered. The difference from the private sector is, of course, marked. The public character of these industries means that they can be obliged to conform to a Plan if needs be. Again, as the nationalized firms are usually in heavy industries but, unlike private firms, have no recourse to equity capital financing, nor very large self-financing possibilities, they depend upon public funds for investment purposes, and this situation gives the State an opportunity to influence their operations.

But it would be erroneous to see the relations between the Plan and the nationalized sector in a too authoritarian light. Such a simplification hides a complex situation and omits to distinguish between the process by which targets are set, and the degree of certainty that they will be carried out as planned. As to the first point, there is no question of an outside authority, say the General Planning Commissariat, fixing output targets unilaterally; these are adjusted to the overall growth-rate of the economy, just as those of the private industries are.[1] As to the second, it is true that there is every reason to expect—other things being equal, notably the general output and demand forecasts of the medium-term plan—that targets in these basic sectors stand a good chance of being achieved. And arrangements exist for discussing each year the investment programmes with the authorities which ensure that any undesirable divergences are corrected. The most striking fact which emerges

[1] In principle that is for, of course, a private firm is not assigned a precise target, even an indicative one, whereas each nationalized industry is at the end of the drafting phase of the Plan.

from this system is the way the nationalized sector has been encouraged to take a bolder view of its growth prospects.

These procedures can best be illustrated in the case of Electricité de France by asking the two questions raised earlier—how are output targets fixed and how are they financed?

1 *Fixing Output Targets*[1]

Electricité de France (EDF) is a giant among giants for it carries out the biggest annual investment programme of all the nationalized industries (about 3 billion NF), which represents 5½ per cent of total gross fixed capital formation in the economy whilst its contribution to value added in GNP is about 1 per cent. At the same time, its ratio of investment to value added is extremely high (over 60 per cent) compared with other basic sectors (20 per cent for the railways, coal mines and steel industry, and 40 per cent for the gas industry). The importance of rational decision-making in this sector for the economic health of the economy in general is therefore easy to grasp.

The application of econometric techniques to the problem of drafting development plans in the electricity industry was a pioneer effort whose example has stimulated other industries to improve their own methods. Thus the linear planning programme of EDF was started in 1955.[2] It is all the more interesting to see what contribution the planning mechanism makes to the development plan of an industry of this kind.

The principal variable used by the EDF to estimate future demand is the GNP—or the French variant of GNP called Gross Internal Production which excludes all government administrative services. Its rate of growth is fixed by the Plan. A problem arises for the time covered, as the EDF requires a perspective of at least ten years and, in some cases, twice as much. The General Planning Commissariat's prospective work provides a link here, but at present only a range of rates is given to EDF in this way of between 4 and 6 per cent annually. This obliges EDF to adopt a probability calculation as it has to maintain adequate safety margins. Of course, the EDF could make its own calculations of the growth of GNP but, even if the rate was as high as the one chosen by the General Planning Commissariat, the greater margin of insecurity surrounding such an estimate would make it difficult to accept if it happened to be a high figure; there is likely,

[1] We have drawn upon a note prepared for the General Planning Commissariat by M. Boiteux, Director at EDF, for some of the material used in these paragraphs.

[2] This work is described by one of its principal authors, M. Massé, in his book: *Le Choix des Investissements,* already referred to, especially in Chapter IV.

that is, to be a downward bias in all such individual projections. M. Boiteux gives a concrete example of this process for the choice of the output target for 1965. In the autumn of 1960 some specialists reckoned that the empirically verified law of a doubling of consumption of electricity every ten years did not demand more than an output of 100 billion kWh in 1965. But subsequently it was found in the light of the preparatory work on the Fourth Plan, that the general prospects of the Plan called for an output of 109 billion kWh in 1965. Compared with the actual level at that time (about 70 billion kWh), adopting the Fourth Plan's target was equivalent to boosting the rise in output of EDF by over one-quarter.

The influence of the Plan appears also when means of production are being chosen. EDF's linear planning programme implies that an overall analysis by major categories of equipment is first made, and then the concrete choice is determined by studying each possible type of equipment in isolation at the margin. But this type of calculation requires additional information, the main one being the rate of interest. This is fixed by the General Planning Commissariat at 7 per cent at present for all theoretical calculations. The interest rate level has a considerable influence upon investment choice, especially as between thermal and hydro-electric plants. Again, the participation of EDF in the work of the Planning Commission for Energy, with a liaison with the Liquid Fuels Commission, makes available to it data on the likely price and cost trends of other types of fuel which can also act as a factor reducing uncertainty as to the future. Finally, the prospects for the trend in real wages according to the Plan are not without interest for the investment programme of EDF.

2 *Financing Investments*[1]

It is here that the Ministry of Finance enters the picture through the mechanism of the Economic and Social Development Fund and its Committee No. 4. The dependence of EDF on the ESDF is very heavy as it supplies over 55 per cent of the total cost of gross investment whereas self-financing provides less than 15 per cent, the rest coming mainly from issues of debentures on the capital market. Loans from the ESDF are for thirty years, with an initial period of three years' grace and at a rate of 4½ per cent. Over the years, EDF has practised an ingenious policy of public debenture issues with various sorts of premia and indexation formulae. These are no longer possible since 1959, and the most recent formula is 5 per cent plus a premium which

[1] Cf. the article by H. d'Ormesson, Director of the Legal and Financial Services of EDF, in the *Revue Française de l'Energie*, November-December 1961.

makes the average cost to EDF 6.7 per cent, or notably higher than the rate paid on ESDF loans. The Treasury Directorate of the Ministry of Finance has to authorize the annual loan issues of the EDF as well as their terms. This results from the annual discussions which take place in Committee No. 4 of the ESDF on the programme for the coming year.

The Committee examines each year the overall financial position and prospects of EDF and its proposed equipment programme, not just the second in isolation. After this examination, a letter is sent to the EDF by the Minister of Industry, indicating which equipment projects it is authorized to proceed with. In fact, of course, insofar as the four-year programme of EDF has been thoroughly discussed in the Planning Commission for Energy, there is no *a priori* reason to expect that the ESDF would not be led to recommend the Minister to approve an annual programme in line with the four-year Plan.[1] On the other hand, an increase in the programme compared with the Plan would call for a whole series of discussions and could not be envisaged by the EDF on its own initiative, *nor* could a decrease either. Apart from this, the financial means of achieving the agreed target—a certain total of investment expenditure of a certain structure—do give rise to debate in Committee No. 4, and, before that, during contacts with the Ministry of Industry and the Ministry of Finance. Given the wide powers of the Ministry of Finance as regards prices, wages and salaries (see Chapter III), the financial policy of EDF is strongly influenced by official views. The general policy of the ESDF in making credits available was stated in the Fourth Plan: 'The ESDF assumes equipment costs which cannot be covered by other means. In other words, its activity depends upon the limits of the efficiency of the traditional source of finance.'[2] As we have seen, the success of EDF in securing a clientele on the capital market has been considerable but despite this, its financial position can hardly be conceived of without the continued support of the ESDF.

By July each year, the examination by Committee No. 4 is completed, and the total volume of investment authorized for the following year is decided upon.[3] The precise details of its financing will be filled in later in the autumn. It is of interest to note that at the final session of the ESDF in July 1962, which was presided over by the Minister of Finance, the Minister stated that the 1963 pro-

[1] Nevertheless, EDF has benefited up to now from pluri-annual programme laws for its investments, the current one being for the period 1962-63.
[2] Fourth Plan, p. 64.
[3] This is part of the process of fixing budget expenditures by 'grandes masses' described for the budget proper in the first section of this chapter.

grammes just fixed for the nationalized industries were consistent with the objectives of the Fourth Plan.[1]

The relations of other nationalized industries with the ESDF can be indicated only briefly. Air France does practically no self-financing and relies heavily on the ESDF as well as on medium-term credit (which EDF ceased to use a few years ago). On the contrary, the French railways rarely use the resources of the ESDF but have regular recourse to the capital market.[2] So there is no uniformity in the financial situations of the various industries.

[1] *Le Monde*, July 28, 1962.

[2] The railways receive, too, certain subsidies and grants from the State through the budget. See also an article by S. Wickham: 'Development of French Railways under the French Four-Year Plans', *Bulletin of the Oxford University Institute of Statistics*, February 1962.

CHAPTER XIII

REGIONAL AND URBAN DEVELOPMENT: EXECUTING THE PLAN

The French planning authorities' approach to regional and urban planning was described in an earlier chapter (Chapter IV). The specific objectives laid down in the Fourth Plan have also been reviewed (Chapter XI). A question which remains is to see what means are used for ensuring that Plans are carried out.

This is a field where, in the nature of things, the rôle of the State is predominant. The distinction made in the Fourth Plan between a 'complementary policy' and a 'propulsive policy'[1] as regards public investment illustrates this. It envisages two regional situations. In the first, the region's growth prospects are considered adequate without special measures to stimulate them further. In the second, without an external stimulus, growth would be inadequate compared either with the national growth target or with the resources of the region. Public policy is being directed especially towards the second type of region.

However, the rôle of the State is not exclusive; if it was, it is doubtful whether the objectives of the Plan could succeed. The State has also to act as a catalyst for private initiatives by creating conditions favourable for them. A preoccupation of the General Planning Commissariat is to avoid stimulating private activities in such artificial conditions that, without an indefinite continuance of State aid, they will never be able to stand on their own feet and it is hoped that the programme of prospective studies now under way will help to clarify the decisions taken.

There are three aspects to the problems of implementing regional policy: investment undertaken directly by the State, assistance by the State to local authorities, attitudes towards private enterprise.[2]

I. DIRECT STATE INVESTMENT

The central Government and the nationalized industries together

[1] See Fourth Plan, p. 45.

[2] A very complete collection of legal texts dealing with regional development was published by the *Moniteur des travaux publics et du bâtiment* in July 1962.

undertake directly each year over one-third of total fixed capital formation. As the choice of the location of these investments is by no means predetermined by technical, administrative or other considerations, a considerable margin of latitude remains which can be put to good effect in promoting regional growth.

In recent years, there have been many examples of a deliberate choice of location in the light of the needs of a particular region or town. The nationalized industries have been especially active in this respect. The thermal power stations built by the nationalized coal and electricity authorities have taken account of the situation of the various coalfields, notably to the South of the Massif Central. The project for the construction of a tidal power-station on the estuary of the Rance in Brittany, after some years of hesitation, is being speeded up in the framework of the general plan for the development of that area. The natural gas produced at Lacq—in the South-West—by the Société Nationale des Pétroles d'Aquitaine (where the State is a majority shareholder) would probably have been brought directly to the Paris region by pipeline if the rôle of cheap energy in the development of the South-West had not been taken into consideration.

It is difficult to measure the overall importance of these, and similar, decisions as, in many cases, they never become known. But it is certain that the vast ramifications of public sector activities in France—which go far beyond the nationalized industries proper to include nearly 500 industrial and commercial undertakings where the State is a majority or minority shareholder—give the authorities wide potential powers for action in this field.[1]

The procedure of operational tranches described in Chapter IV is the *modus operandi* being used to implement regional development policy as regards public sector investment. Moreover, as was noted in Chapter X, the Government has pledged itself to Parliament to go further than this and to submit, during 1963, a draft programme law on regional development. It would not appear practicable for the moment to make the programme law apply to all the regions of France although, as was seen earlier, each has, or will have soon, its own development plan. On the contrary, the most urgent problem for regional policy is the disparity in development which exists between what can be called the 'Western regions' and the rest of France. So the programme law will concentrate on these areas, that is, it will follow the basic distinction in the Fourth Plan, which has just been referred to, between regions where the State will apply a propulsive policy and those where State investment will accompany

[1] See Chapter III.

the development of the region.[1] The procedures set up for the implementation of the Fourth Plan through the operational tranches and the work of the Interdepartmental Committees will continue as before, with the difference that the operational tranches for the Western regions will be, at one and the same time, tranches of the Fourth Plan and of the programme law. Eventually, the guide lines for a more comprehensive regional development policy will be fixed by the 'prospective' study of the French economy in 1985 now being undertaken by the General Planning Commissariat.

The novelty of these arrangements, and the fact that they cut across so many existing administrative structures, make it doubtful whether the operational tranches procedure will become fully effective before the Fifth Plan.

II. ASSISTANCE TO LOCAL AUTHORITIES

The intention of the Government to promote regional and urban planning by stimulating the local authorities themselves rather than by substituting itself for them, was noted in an earlier chapter.[2] Such a policy has to solve two types of problem: firstly, assisting financially the local units of Government and, secondly, giving them the powers they need to put such aid to good use.

1 *The Financial Problem*

The financial problem has always existed insofar as the local units of Government dispose of insufficient resources to do all that their own representatives and the central Government require of them. The stress being put in the Fourth Plan on 'collective consumption' projects implies inevitably a very considerable increase in their investment expenditures—of about two-thirds between 1961 and 1965 for urban areas alone, according to the Commission for Urban Equipment. This prospect makes an extensive reform of local authority finances inevitable.

The ways in which the local government units finance their investments at the present time illustrate this. In 1961, total investment expenditures, in urban communes, were 3,465 million NF, of which 57 per cent, or 1,980 million NF, were taken over by the State in one form or another. Of the remaining 43 per cent, or 1,485 million NF, only a few million came from a surplus of receipts over current expenditures so that practically all of it was financed by borrowing.

[1] The precise criteria to be used in defining the regions to be included in the programme law will be given in the 1963 Finance Act.
[2] See Chapter IV.

According to the Vertical Planning Commission on Urban Equipment, their total capital expenditures will be 5,700 million NF in 1965, of which sum only 3,235 million NF will be paid by the State leaving 2,470 million NF to be found from other sources. As it is unlikely to be possible to finance all of this from borrowing—given the likely resources of the Caisse des Dépôts et Consignations—the Commission felt that something like one-third of the local authorities' share of the total will have to be met from their own resources in that year. This conclusion led the Commission to make a number of suggestions for developing the receipts of the local authorities, notably through an increase in the tariffs charged for the services they provide against payment, and an increase in their tax income. Such a reform would require legislation, though, and, so far, no measures have been adopted to deal with this thorny subject where local, and parliamentary, passions run high.

At present, local units of Government procure the funds for investments they need over and above their own current budget surpluses from three sources. Normal budget subsidies are written each year into the Finance Act under the relevant Ministry.[1] The basic rate is 30 per cent of total cost but the maximum rate is not always reached. Examples are the Ministry of the Interior for roads, drainage, water and housing in urban centres where the average participation rate is 16 per cent, and the Ministries of Education and Health whose participation can reach 80 per cent of total cost. Exceptional subsidies are given by the Ministry of Finance after a favourable decision by Committees 2a or 2b of the Economic and Social Development Fund. The General Planning Commissariat is represented on each of these committees and also undertakes the work of secretariat for them. Until now, these subsidies have been neither frequent nor large, but, as will be seen later concerning the Zones for Urbanization in Priority (ZUP), they will be called upon to increase over the years ahead. Borrowing remains as the final resource. Most large towns have issued debentures at some time or another on the capital market. But such issues have remained sporadic and the mass of borrowing is done from public bodies, in particular from the Caisse des Dépôts et Consignations, the Crédit Foncier, and from the Fonds National d'Aménagement du Territoire. The first two of these specialized credit organizations have been described in Chapter III; the FNAT requires some explanation.

It was created in 1950 with a capital of 500 million Old Francs, increased to 1 billion the following year. Its sponsors were the

[1] But French local authorities do not receive block (i.e. unconditional) grants as is the case in the United Kingdom.

Ministries of Finance, Construction and the Interior. The object of the FNAT was to help finance the equipment necessary to prepare provincial areas to receive new industries and their personnel. Since the early years, the functions of the FNAT have been broadened and its financial possibilities varied. It operates in three ways: by granting credits (in principle for two years only, but renewable and at low interest rates—generally 2½ per cent), by direct intervention either on its own account, or in participation with a local authority, to finance regional or urban development projects, by giving interest subsidies to reduce the actual cost of borrowing to local authorities.

Although the FNAT is an organization which should have a useful rôle to play in achieving the objectives of the national Plan, its success in doing so does not seem to have been considerable and, until now, its funds have been granted with too little concern for the type of operations being financed and their relation to the objectives of the Plan. The Fourth Plan looks to a better co-ordination of local initiatives in the framework of comprehensive regional development plans to improve the situation in future.[1]

2 *The Powers of the Local Authorities*

The powers of the local authorities were woefully inadequate for the new task of implementing a policy of regional development and, despite the progress made in recent years in this respect, a great deal still remains to be done, particularly in view of the large increase projected in social investments. This implies granting certain additional legal powers to local authorities.

The biggest obstacle is the real estate problem. To appreciate how it presents itself, it is necessary to examine the procedure called Zones for Urbanization in Priority (ZUP)[2] and, subsidiarily, that of the Zones for Delayed Development (ZAD).[3] We shall then turn to the instrument which is often linked with the use of ZUP, the Sociétés Mixtes d'Equipement whose activities are co-ordinated by the Société Centrale d'Equipement du Territoire (SCET).

The object of the ZUP, of which there are fourteen at present covering 3,800 hectares, is to avoid a disorderly development—either industrial or residential—of towns. The Zones are defined by the Ministry of Construction and consist of areas where it becomes obligatory in the case of housing, for example, to build groups of at least 100 houses or flats whose construction elsewhere in the town would be costly or undesirable. The existence of the ZUP concentrates

[1] *Op. cit.*, p. 50.
[2] *Zone à Urbaniser en priorité.*
[3] *Zone d'aménagement différé.*

housebuilding activity in a given sector, all the more so as the mayor is empowered to refuse a building licence elsewhere. The creation of the ZUP gives the local authorities a right of pre-emption for the purchase of any ground put up for sale in the Zone within a period of four years. This measure is designed to limit the rise in price which accompanies any big housing project. Also the local authorities can have recourse to expropriation procedures once the ZUP has been created. An additional technique designed to counteract the rise in prices in areas reserved for future development is the ZAD. The local authorities in these areas can purchase land at a price corresponding to its value one year before the Zone was created.[1]

The ZUP confers certain financial advantages on the local authority for the area, notably the right to apply to the FNAT for short-term finance with two renewals (which means, in practice, credit for six years) and the possibility of receiving an exceptional subsidy from the Ministry of Finance through the Economic and Social Development Fund's Committees 2a and 2b. An example of the use of the ZUP is given by the town of Toulouse, in the South-West of France. A new town, Toulouse 2, is projected in the Mirail district which benefits from the ZUP status. After a vote by the local council in the summer of 1962, the council will purchase the entire area and buildings in the ZUP, including existing buildings, if necessary by using the special expropriation procedure.

It does not appear, however, that these measures have solved the problem of the rise in land-values, which has been considerable in recent years, and which handicaps local authorities in executing a plan for urban development. The Act of Parliament just mentioned is too recent for it to have had much effect as yet. Meanwhile, as the Commission for Urban Equipment pointed out, it would be a mistake to attribute high prices for land to 'speculation' without seeing that demand for building land had been rising for years and will go on doing so as supply is less and less able to meet it. The measures proposed by the Commission to deal with the problem are various: fixing of prices in cases of expropriation by an independent judge, improved application of the rule that prior guarantee by the Ministry is required for any housebuilding financed with the help of loans from the Crédit Foncier (one-third of the total), publicity for all real estate transactions so as to make the market more 'transparent'. Other measures envisaged are the creation of land reserves in advance by the local authorities, relaxation of some of the rules protecting sitting tenants, and the setting-up of a Government real

[1] The law relating to the ZUP and ZAD procedures was published in the *Journal Officiel* on July 27, 1962.

estate service to advise all local authorities and other public bodies on these matters.

The task of defining and carrying out development programmes is, nevertheless, one which is beyond the means of many local authorities, in particular if they are small. This is a problem similar to the one met with in the case of regional development. To overcome this difficulty a specialized body called the 'Société d'économie mixte' has been created. Since 1955, communes and départements have been authorized to participate in such societies whose object is 'the drafting or the carrying-out of projects of public interest or the operation of public services'. The most common type is the 'Société d'économie mixte d'équipement'.

In practice, the scope of these societies differs greatly. Some operate in a regional framework, such as the Société d'Equipement du Bassin Lorrain, the Société d'Aménagement et d'Equipement de la Bretagne, the Société d'Equipement de la Basse-Normandie. About thirty are departmental (mainly in the départements of the Nord, Rhône, Loire and Haute Garonne). Some large towns have used this procedure (Bordeaux, Marseilles). Sometimes a society has been created in a town for a limited purpose such as slum clearance (Gap, Nice, Le Mans), or for the transformation of the Maine-Montparnasse district in Paris. In all, there are about seventy such societies in existence.

Fifty per cent of their capital at least belongs to local authorities (départements and communes). Specialized public financial institutions—the Caisse des Dépôts et Consignations, the Caisse de Crédit Agricole, the Crédit Foncier—or private banks supply from 30 to 40 per cent, the rest coming from various departmental organizations (Chambers of Commerce or Chambers of Agriculture).

The type of activity which can be organized in this way is also very varied. In addition to town planning operations, the Sociétés d'Economie Mixte are concerned with markets for agricultural products (Rungis, La Villette—in Paris—and twenty-six others), and with building motorways (the autoroute Esterel—Côte d'Azur). The oldest example of a Société d'Economie Mixte is the Compagnie Nationale du Rhône created in the 1920s. Since the war, other similar societies have been formed to carry out major regional improvement projects (Bas-Rhône—Languedoc, Coteaux de Gascogne, Landes de Gascogne, Canal de Provence, etc.).

An original feature of this system is the existence, since 1955, of the Société Centrale pour l'Equipement du Territoire (SCET). A joint creation of the Caisse des Dépôts et Consignations, the Crédit National, the Crédit Foncier, the Bank of France and other public bodies, the SCET is supposed 'to assist local authorities, or bodies set up with their help (i.e. the Sociétés d'Economie Mixte), in the development or improvement of regions or industrial, agricultural and residential areas'. The Deputy Commissaire General is a member of the Board of the SCET, which reinforces the intention to link its activities to the implementation of the regional development policy defined in the national Plan. At the technical assistance level, the SCET's specialists can be called in to elaborate a detailed programme, as well as to follow through all the stages of its execution (economic, technical, administrative, financial). The participation of the SCET is specified in a contract drawn up with the local authority or Société d'Economie Mixte. A recent innovation is the project decided on in 1962 of building a dozen factories to be rented to private firms in Brittany along the lines of the British trading estates.

III. POLICY TOWARDS THE PRIVATE SECTOR

This takes two forms, negative and positive. On the negative side, there exists a series of measures designed to discourage private firms from expanding, or setting themselves up, in the Paris region. Positive encouragement is given to those who establish themselves in the provinces in particular areas.

1 *The Negative Aspect*

Three policy instruments are available: building controls, the procedure known as the 'prior approval' for building in Paris, the tax on building in that area.

Building licences are applicable in other regions as well as Paris. For example, it was noted earlier that the mayor of a commune can refuse a permit outside of a ZUP. But in Paris it is a form of control that has proved inadequate and has had to be reinforced.

An administrative order created the procedure of prior approval in 1955. Under this order, all plans for the creation or expansion of industrial and commercial buildings above a certain limit in the Paris region require prior approval by the Ministry of Construction. A possible loophole was closed a few months later when the prior approval was required, in addition, for buildings used for research, study and experimentation. This ruling applied to buildings employing more than fifty persons or occupying a surface of more than 500 square metres. At the same time, in order to try to restrict the growth of public administrations in the same area, a committee was established, attached to the Prime Minister's Office, to draw up a plan for their decentralization and progressive transfer to the provinces. The continued pressure on available accommodation in Paris led to a further tightening up of controls in 1958, when the procedure of prior approval was extended to the case of the expansion of industry in already-existing buildings. At the same time, the work of the committee on the decentralization of public administrations was transferred to the General Planning Commissariat. Finally, new construction, other than housing, authorized is subject to a special tax of 200 NF per square metre, whereas a premium of the same amount is paid when industrial or office buildings are demolished or vacated in favour of green spaces, houses, schools or parking sites. This type of encouragement forms part of a series of measures of much wider application.

2 *Positive Measures*

As a rule, these are all authorized after approval by Committee 1b of the Economic and Social Development Fund. The chairman is the Director-General of the Caisse des Dépôts et Consignations, and the General Planning Commissariat is represented on the Committee. Three types[1] of stimuli are particularly worthy of notice: subsidies, loans and interest subsidies, fiscal exonerations.

(a) *Subsidies.* Two types of subsidy are used: the special equipment premium and subsidies related to the labour force employed.

Equipment premia were first instituted in 1955. Since then the system has been modified twice, in 1960 and in 1961, so as to integrate the granting of subsidies with the overall policy of regional development. Until 1960, there were three premia: a variable one of up to 20 per cent of investment expenditure in a certain number of regions, fixed ones of 15 or 20 per cent in eight critical regions (defined in 1959), those used in unemployment areas (defined in 1959 also). In 1960, the eight critical regions were reduced to four and called zones for priority development (Nantes, Bordeaux, Limoges, Montpellier) where firms received a fixed premium.[2] A general system was created alongside these zones where there was unemployment or the threat of unemployment or over-population of rural origin. Special arrangements were made for Brittany where payments could not be less than 10 per cent. This decision marked the beginning of a concerted

[1] In certain cases also, loans contracted by private firms can be guaranteed. This procedure is dealt with in Chapter XIV.

[2] These four urban centres of the West and South-West suffer from the lack of dynamism of their old-established industries and are not attracting new ones at a rate which would enable them to become growth-points stimulating the development of the areas in which they are situated.

attack on the problem of the underdeveloped regions, and on that of Brittany in particular.

A key element for evaluating the premia is the labour force involved. The 20 per cent grant in respect of investment expenditure is subject to a limit fixed by the number of new jobs created. The basic rate is 7,500 NF per worker. This restriction has been relaxed somewhat since the vote of the law on agricultural orientation in 1960.[1] This law foresees the setting-up of small industrial units in special zones (Zones d'action rurale) where the equipment premium can be paid even if the investments made do not create twenty new jobs. In 1961, the following areas were classified as special zones: the two départements, Lozère and Morbihan, with populations of 80,000 and 527,000 respectively, and thirty-two cantons in the départements of Finistère (Brittany), Côtes du Nord, Ille et Vilaine and Loire-Atlantique. In 1961, the maximum rate for the calculation of the equipment premium was raised from 7,500 NF to 10,000 NF for new establishments or the complete reconversion of existing ones, and from 5,000 NF to 7,500 NF in cases of extension or partial reconversion. The 1960 régime applied to Brittany was extended to the départements of the Manche, Mayenne, Loire-Atlantique and Vendée. The amounts actually paid under these schemes have been as follows:

(thousand NF)	*1955*	*1956*	*1957*	*1958*	*1959*	*1960*	*1961*
	nil	8,000	5,400	5,719	45,856	88,394	53,005

Source: 1961 annual report of ESDF, p. 185.

Employment premia are paid, either as subsidies for re-training manpower, or as grants for changes of residence. Disbursements up to 1961 are given below:

(thousand NF)	*1959*	*1960*	*1961*
Re-training	2,314	2,649	6,688
Change of residence	593	452	1,226

Source: ESDF, *op. cit.*, p. 187.

(b) *Loans*. The Economic and Social Development Fund can make loans to private firms from Treasury funds. But their amount is falling rapidly, as the data indicate, in view of Committee 1b's policy of directing demands to the specialized financial organizations or to the Regional Development Societies where possible.

(thousand NF)	*1955*	*1956*	*1957*	*1958*	*1959*	*1960*	*1961*
	16,000	34,000	46,100	37,700	20,605	49,042	21,045

Source: ESDF, *op. cit.*, p. 185.

[1] See Chapter XV.

Subsidies for interest payments can also be granted by the Fund. The same criteria of geographical location and employment creation are applied as in the case of loans. Since 1960, not only industrial concerns qualify but commerce and service industries also.

The following data, which show the number of requests received by the Committee 1b under these schemes, and the number of refusals and acceptances, illustrate the rising trend in recent years in these types of activity:

	1957	*1958*	*1959*	*1960*	*1961*
Requests received	300	183	269	297	356
Requests refused	153	75	83	79	97
Requests accepted	127	107	152	229	259

Source: ESDF, *op. cit.*, p. 184.

Mention was made in an earlier paragraph of the Regional Development Societies. These represent an important link in the institutional framework designed to implement the carrying-out of regional development policy, particularly the mobilization of private initiatives. The decree allowing their creation was published in 1955. They were to be limited liability companies with a minimum subscribed capital of 2,500,000 NF (now 5 million NF). Their object is to act as poles of attraction to centralize the savings of the region and to make these available to industry and trade which, otherwise, would be unable to secure the funds they need. In practice, the major shareholders have been the Parisian banques d'affaires and public financial organizations; local interests have been in a minority. This result is not altogether surprising as, in the poorer regions which the Societies are designed to help, the level of savings is low and they are not readily available for this sort of investment.

Two sorts of privileges are granted by the State to these regional banques d'affaires in respect of their activities: they are exempt from the corporation tax and from the tax on distributed profits; they can receive a guarantee from the Ministry of Finance, after consultation with the Economic and Social Development Fund, for the payment of a minimum dividend. In exchange, the State has the right to supervise their activities.

The Societies for Regional Development operate essentially through taking up shares in private firms, the limit being 35 per cent of the capital of a firm financed, or 25 per cent of the capital of the Society. Since 1956, they are also allowed to make loans to the firms in which they are shareholders, such loans coming either from the Society's own capital or from the funds raised by the issue of debentures guaranteed by the State. The second form is the one most frequently used. The procedure is for the Societies to group together to make an issue of debentures. Furthermore, a regional Development Society can give its own guarantee to a loan contracted by a firm in which it holds shares. Since 1960, the restriction according to which loans could only be made to firms where the Society was a minority shareholder has been lifted.

There were fifteen such Societies at the end of 1961, with a combined own capital of 71.5 million NF of which they had used 38 million since 1955. But they had raised, and re-lent, during the same period, 303.8 million NF through group issues of debentures. The relatively modest level of these sums should be assessed, however, taking account of the fact that the Societies for Regional Development have assisted only small and average-size firms with a regional basis. In this perspective, their rôle has been a useful one in filling a gap no other banking units were equipped to fill. They have succeeded in collecting a certain volume of local savings which were unlikely otherwise to have been available for local industry. The Fourth Plan looks forward to an extension of their activities but considers that the existing Societies are too dispersed, and that it would be preferable to see some of them merge with others or create common subsidiaries with increased technical resources for assisting local enterprise in its efforts to expand and diversify production.

3 *Fiscal Exemptions*

The two major exemptions from which private firms can benefit are: a reduction from 13.2 to 1.4 per cent in the transfer tax when firms regroup their activities, reconvert them or create new ones, and when they are located in zones where unemployment is chronic or serious; a reduction of 50 per cent (since 1961) in the payment of the patent (tax) on transfers, creations or extensions of firms, and complete exemption when the firm receives a special equipment premium in respect of the same operations. These exemptions are approved by Committee 1b of the Economic and Social Development Fund.

Despite the great deal of ingenuity which has gone into formulating and applying a policy for regional balance, as the measures described in this chapter show, the main task for a coherent regional development policy still lies ahead. The figures available on decentralization operations, although they are not always easy to interpret, indicate that the results achieved have been rather modest up to now. Between 1955 and 1960, 561 requests to install industrial firms in the Paris region were refused but 1,914, or 80 per cent of the total, were accepted. In 1960, 43 industrial establishments employing more than 200 workers were set up in the Paris region, but only 24 disappeared due to decentralization or other causes. The hopes entertained a few years ago that it would be possible to put a stop practically to the growth of the Paris region have been disappointed, and the Fourth Plan expects, more modestly, that such a result can only be achieved after a number of years. At present net immigration into the region is probably about 150,000 persons annually. Overall data on the effects of the decentralization policy are as follows:

Year	*No. of enterprises*	*Floor surface in the region of arrival ('000 sq. metres)* Use of already existing space	New construction (final)	*Employment (final)*
1956	103	290	300	27,950
1957	140	280	384	19,120
1958	85	196	225	15,225
1959	140	254	569	27,585
1960	185	367	466	23,700
1961 (11 months)	271	297	763	36,924
Total	924	1,684	2,797	150,504

Source: Reply by the Préfet of the Seine quoted in the *Moniteur des Travaux Publics et du Bâtiment*, March 17, 1962.

These data refer only to decentralization operations and do not give a picture of the whole regional development programme, of course.

But before concluding that the policy of decentralization has failed, it should be recalled that the whole policy of regional development, of which decentralization of the Paris region is a part, is of very recent date; indeed, it really got under way only in the 1960s. There are clear signs today that the policy of development in the West and South-West of France is yielding its fruits. Inherently, there is no reason, such as lack of natural resources, poor geographical location, or inadequate labour force, why most of these regions should not be able to prosper once the initial stimulus has been given. In a few years' time, the Paris region may begin to lose its attractive force whilst that of the provinces increases. In any event the planning authorities have no intention of relaxing their efforts. Regional development is not an emergency programme but a permanent and, in the long run, perhaps one of the most notable features of the Plan.

An example of what can be done concludes appropriately this chapter. Brittany was, until recently, a forgotten region characterized by a fast-growing population, by old and few industries in decline, and by increasing pressure of population on available jobs.[1] In the last two years the situation has been transformed. The Citroen car firm was persuaded not to choose the Paris region for the extension of its plant but to go to Rennes. Administrative decentralization has been secured by the decision to set up the National Centre for Telecommunications Studies at Lannion. A large private electrical firm, the Compagnie Générale de TSF, has built a factory at the western end of the peninsula, which will provide jobs for 2,500 workers in 1963, and two other electrical firms announced in 1962 their intention of setting up factories there.

[1] In the inter-censal period 1954-62, the natural increase of the population was 120,000 but as 85,000 persons left the region, the total population rose by only 35,000 in the same period.

CHAPTER XIV

IMPLEMENTING THE PLAN IN THE PRIVATE NON-AGRICULTURAL SECTOR

This is, from many points of view, the crux of the planning problem. Just what reasons are there which would lead one to suppose that the private productive sector does carry out the Plan? The question needs further definition before it becomes meaningful. If, for example, it means: 'What leads one to suppose the firm X or Y carries out the Plan?' then the reply is usually that nothing does because there is no plan for firm X or Y in any strict sense of the term. 'The French Plan is a plan by branches, sometimes highly aggregated, and not a plan by firms or products.'[1] What the Plan does contain, as we saw in Chapter XI, is a number of objectives of production and investment by main sectors with some indication of the trend in output in the others. Even the full statistical data behind the Plan do not go down to the firm level except in special cases where fairly large-scale investment projects are involved, for example the building of a steel mill.

Such a reply may appear to be merely dodging a key question, but it is really a very important consideration which influences the choice of policy instruments used to carry out the Plan. These are bound to remain largely indirect and to rely upon incentives much more than upon authoritative methods, even when a particular firm solicits the assistance of the State, as there is rarely an individualized quantitative target which can be used as a yardstick to judge the efficacy of an individual firm's contribution to the Plan but only the overall goal assigned to the branch. The key goals are usually defined in terms of real investment although there are instances in limited, but strategic, sectors in the capital goods industries where the main stress is placed upon the need to raise production of a particular type of equipment.

An opposite method of approach to the question why the Plan should be implemented, is to envisage the planning process as a pre-concerted exercise between all the production units who then apply the 'plan' as it results from the mutual conciliation of their output and demand objectives. At the limit, that is at a point where analysis always yields nonsense answers compared with reality, there would

[1] P. Massé: 'Colloquium on Democratic Planning', reprinted in the *Cahiers de la République*, July 1962.

be no problem of carrying out the Plan. It would carry out itself.

There seems to be good reason to think that what takes place in fact is situated somewhere between these two extremes, the exact position varying moreover from branch to branch. Thus, the target for the steel industry is not only one which, in the nature of the forecasting procedure, is more likely to be achieved than most, it is also one which the French authorities are likely to follow-up closely and to 'do something about' if it appears that it is not being achieved. On the other hand, no one in the General Planning Commissariat knows how many shirts, or perhaps even how many radio sets, ought to be produced in 1965.

A distinction is sometimes made between two types of planning called respectively 'imperative' and 'indicative'. The general characteristic of French planning seems to place it in the latter category, whilst planning on the Eastern European model belongs to the former. Such a distinction is of increasingly doubtful value, not least because of the changes underway in Communist planning. In France, the insistence of some people on the indicative character of the Plan, whilst it usually has a very real sociological or political foundation, seems to obscure rather than to clarify the facts at issue. The French planning process is something complex. From certain points of view, when the implementation of the Plan by the nationalized industries is considered, for example, one is tempted to conclude that the Plan is pretty much an obligation. Yet in many industrial sectors it appears more appropriate to see in the Plan an attempt at a 'generalized market research'.[1] If a common qualification is sought for, it is probably best found in the suggestion that French planning is 'active'.[2] That this is so in the public sector and in regional planning, the previous chapters have shown. In the paragraphs which follow, we discuss the means used by, or at the disposal of, the authorities to implement the Plan in the private non-agricultural sector, and we reserve further discussion of the broader aspects of the planning process in relation to the private sector for Part Four of this book. We examine in turn: public sector purchasing policy, price control, credit and finance, fiscal incentives, policies towards particular activities.

I. PUBLIC SECTOR PURCHASING POLICY

The public sector as a whole is by far the largest purchaser of goods and services in the economy. A single nationalized industry—Elec-

[1] P. Massé, Lecture at the National Economic Institute, Dublin, April 1962.
[2] P. Massé, *op. cit.*, *Cahiers de la République*, p. 455.

tricité de France—is the biggest industrial investor in France. The influence the public sector could exercise on its suppliers is, therefore, enormous. If this influence is used consciously in order to facilitate, or to provoke, adjustments in the behaviour of suppliers along the lines of the Plan, it can be a powerful instrument in achieving it. The electronics industry, for example, sells 70 to 80 per cent of its production to the public sector. For heavy electrical equipment, mining equipment, public works and even textiles, the figure is from 10 to 15 per cent. We have already noted elsewhere that the budget procedure for passing contracts by public administrations is being amended to permit them to offer more stable markets to their suppliers, and this with a view to being able to secure a counterpart not only in lower prices but also in a greater degree of conformity with Plan objectives. These objectives are not only, or even mainly, output or investment targets but, much more frequently, encouragement towards standardization, research, specialization and market research. However, for such a policy to be effective, it is necessary for the public administrations to act in unison along comparable lines. There is an official body called the Central Market Commission which is actively studying this problem now at the suggestion of the General Planning Commissariat. But, according to one qualified observer, 'considerable progress remains to be achieved as, due to a lack of appreciation of the importance of this lever for guiding the economy, it is too often improperly used or operates in a reverse direction to the preoccupations of the central administration of the economy'.[1]

II. PRICE CONTROL

Price control, once such an important weapon in the armoury of French policy instruments, although it was rarely used in a way compatible with the objectives of the Plan, is very much a withering asset today.[2] On the other hand, appreciation of the havoc wrought by indiscriminate use of price control, and of the economic function of the price mechanism as a policy instrument, has gained ground both conceptually and in practice. 'Setting up price controls and price ceilings were perhaps necessary evils to prevent still greater disorders. But they were a cure that attacked the consequences and not the causes of monetary depreciation. They were able to slow

[1] M. Brac de la Perrière: *L'exécution du Plan. Commissariat Général du Plan*, 1961, p. 13.
[2] The big bonfire of price controls occurred in 1961 when several hundred controls were abolished. See the *Bulletin Officiel des Prix*, March 31, 1961.

down the latter but were not able to vanquish it. Moreover, their persistent use had grave repercussions on the lives of millions of French people.'[1]

At the present time, agricultural prices apart,[2] the only basic products still subject to price control are steel, aluminium and cement. Of course, the tariffs and prices of the nationalized industries have to be agreed with the tutelary Ministry and thus enter the general planning process.[3] In the nationalized sector, very interesting experiments with marginal pricing have been carried out, and are at the basis of the present tariff system of Electricité de France[4] and of the projected reform of the tariffs of the French railways, but this reform has been difficult to apply in a uniform manner due to the exceptions it has been necessary to introduce in favour of the less-developed areas.

Price policy has to accommodate itself to conditions in the real world, not the least of these being the problem of financing investment, as the availability of funds from a firm's own resources is in inverse proportion to the price at which goods are sold.[5] The balance between price increases and provision of finance from other sources than profits is explicitly considered when the investment plans of the nationalized industries are examined.[6] The main private sector where the same is true is steel. The possibility for the French authorities to exercise a *de facto* control over steel prices despite the rules of the European Coal and Steel Community, is an important factor in the continuing dialogue between the authorities and the steel industry on the Plan. Thus, in 1960, an increase of 4¾ per cent was accepted following a more general agreement on the investment programme of the steel industry and again, in 1962, after several

[1] P. Massé: 'La Pensée Moderne et l'Action Economique', *Le Bulletin*, April-May 1961.

[2] See Chapter XV.

[3] See Chapter III.

[4] See M. Boiteux: 'La Politique tarifaire de l'Electricité de France', in *Le Bulletin d'Information des Services Publics Communaux et Départementaux*, June 1961.

[5] See, for example, P. Massé: 'La Logique et l'Action': two lectures at the School for Higher Commercial Studies, Paris, January 1962. 'In econometric models where costs and receipts are brought to their actual value by the influence of a rate of interest, the idea is adjacent according to which all investments are, or can be, financed by borrowing. But, due to the existence of a risk element and other factors of uncertainty as regards the future, no firm accepts a 100 per cent ratio of indebtedness. It is generally admitted that financing is one-third, in roughly equal shares, from equity capital, borrowing and self-finance. The financial balance of the Plan is, therefore, more complex than it appears in the model.' P. 9.

[6] See Chapter XII.

months of discussion, a further rise of about 4½ per cent took place in the same conditions. In this way, the surveillance of the carrying-out of the Plan in the steel industry is closer than for most private sectors where less direct policy measures have to be relied upon.[1]

III. CREDIT AND FINANCE

It is useful to recall the means by which private firms in France procure funds, as they are rather different from the ones used in the United Kingdom. This is notably so in the case of recourse to the capital market which is much smaller due to a variety of factors of which the most important appears to be the small size of many firms and the persistence of the tradition that control must not be let out of the family (see table).

EXTERNAL SOURCES OF FINANCE FOR PRIVATE ENTERPRISES

(*Billion* NF)

	1957	*1958*	*1959*	*1960*
Stocks and Shares	2.58	1.96	3.16	2.37
Debentures	0.64	0.92	1.81	1.88
Total capital market*	3.11	2.73	4.79	3.90
Net long-term borrowing ...	0.71	0.38	0.34	0.81
Net medium-term borrowing ...	0.97	1.08	0.29	1.17
Grand Total	4.79	4.19	5.42	5.97
As a percentage of total gross private investment (excluding agriculture and dwellings)	34%	29%	39%	36%

*Net of repayments excluded from first two lines.
Sources: National Accounts and annual reports of ESDF.

Access to medium-term credit and long-term capital is a major means used by the authorities to influence the activities of the private sector. In addition to this power of selection, the authorities possess a number of means of stimulating activity along lines which are in harmony with the objectives of the Plan.

1 *Selection*

As regards selection, access to both the capital market and to medium-term credit are controlled. All issues of debentures in excess

[1] See *Le Monde*, August 5 and 6, 1962.

of 1 million NF require prior Treasury approval of the amount and the conditions of the loan. The Treasury consults the General Planning Commissariat before entering the name of the firm, or group of firms, on the waiting list. And new issues of shares must also be notified to the Treasury. The Treasury and the Commissariat have encouraged firms in the same branch to group together to issue debentures, and this policy has succeeded in giving a popularity to these issues which an individual firm would have been unable to secure. From 4 per cent only of all debentures issued in 1956, these issues rose to 12 per cent in 1960. The steel industry has put out a loan each year for the last ten years and the electrical equipment, automobile, shipbuilding, oil and mechanical industries have all made issues of this kind. An important consequence of Treasury control of access to the capital market is that the General Planning Commissariat is led to discuss with the majority of large firms each year their general financing programmes. But these annual discussions do not relate specifically to medium-term intentions and are not to be confused with the work of the Planning Commissions in drafting the medium-term Plan.

The reforms at the end of 1958 included the ending of the method of indexation of debentures which had become very popular during the years of inflation. It must be admitted that the wide range of indexation formulae had led to considerable confusion as to the real value of the anti-inflationary guarantee being given, the more so as many loans set out to offer a capital gain linked to the prosperity of the branch. In this way, curious hybrid securities had been created which would probably have brought the debenture market into disrepute in the long run. Although this decision does not seem to have been followed by a decline in demand for debentures, the problem of the lack of balance between demand for debentures, on the one hand, and shares, on the other, remains as investors tend to prefer shares whereas firms prefer debenture finance. Since 1957, the State can grant an exemption from profits tax on dividends paid on new shares up to a limit of 5 per cent of the cash contribution. About half the present increases in capital enjoy this concession.

The authorities are aware of the need by French industry to increase its recourse to the capital market during the Fourth Plan. The new measures proposed include a larger use of convertible debentures and preference shares, and a rise in the offer price when new shares are issued. The Plan suggests that these possibilities should be taken into consideration in granting Treasury permission to issue new shares.[1] At the same time, the fact that the Treasury has not had

[1] See Fourth Plan, p. 64.

urgent financing needs recently has made it possible to discourage savers from subscribing to Treasury bills—which in France run for up to five years—through widening the gap between returns on such paper and the yield on debentures. In all these financial measures, the influence of the conclusions of the General Economic and Financial Commission[1] on the financial conditions and problems likely to be met with in carrying through the Fourth Plan is apparent.

Selection of prospective borrowers is more important and widespread in the matter of access to medium-term credit which is a chief source of investment finance.[2] The key organization here is the Crédit National which stands ready to discount medium-term paper on the condition that it carries four signatures and that its agreement in principle has been solicited in advance.[3] By an arrangement with the General Planning Commissariat, the Crédit National submits for advice the files of all requests for loans exceeding 1 million New Francs for medium-term (five years) and 2.5 million New Francs for long-term (over five years). The General Planning Commissariat, in consultation, if necessary, with the Ministry of Finance and the Ministry of Industry, takes account, in formulating its opinion, of the investment plans of the prospective borrower and other aspects of his activity such as exports. Such requests can also be presented by branches of foreign firms. This kind of 'intervention', which remains extremely discreet, nevertheless gives the planning authorities an opportunity to orientate decisions being taken by private firms along the lines of the policy laid down in the Plan. It can influence not only the level of output, exports or investments, but equally the choice of a type of production (promoting, for example, one not yet produced in France), or can show the advantages of a certain specialization of production.

2 *Stimulation*

Stimulation consists mainly of reductions in the cost of interest payments, of facilitating access to the capital market and of arrangements to limit the impact of fiscal measures on certain legal forms of business.

Two types of justification for interest subsidies can be advanced—the type of activity of the firm and its geographical situation. It is rare to see the Treasury intervene directly by assisting credit establishments who make loans. More usually, firms benefit directly from interest grants. Examples of this are steel and shipbuilding. Since

[1] See Chapter VII.
[2] See Chapter III.
[3] See Chapter III.

1955, this procedure is used to facilitate regional development, concentration and specialization of firms, and decentralization. As was seen in Chapter XIII, approval of the Minister of Finance is required after consultation of the ESDF. Interest subsidies are used less and less today since the level of interest rates has fallen.

As to access to the capital market, ever since 1946, the Treasury has been empowered to give its guarantee to issues when the borrowing firms contribute to achieving the objectives of the Plan, particularly as regards conversion and reconversion. The major use made of this procedure at the present time is in regional development policy.[1] Such a guarantee encourages bodies like the insurance companies, whose statutes restrict them to taking up certain types of loans, to subscribe.

Regional Development Societies[2] can also benefit from a State guarantee of payment of a minimum dividend (in principle, 5 per cent for twelve years). The first companies to be granted this privilege were in oil research, however.

IV. FISCAL INCENTIVES

The complexities of company taxation in the French fiscal system—due to a spirit of excessive legalism which had progressively lost touch with economic needs—have been frequently attacked in the post-war period for their undesirable effects in penalizing investment and in keeping archaic business structures in existence. But the main reform, which saw the replacement, in 1954, of the old indirect tax 'in cascade' by the present tax on value added, eliminated the double taxation of investment implicit in the previous system. The institution of this tax also saw a correction of the previous system which continued to consider concentrated units of production and distribution as if they were in fact separate.

There is, therefore, no massive reform of the fiscal régime as applied to private firms in view at present, nor does the need for it appear evident. Progress must be more prosaic and detailed. There remains, of course, the problem of fiscal evasion. Finally, all these problems now have to be seen in the light of the Common Market and the eventual harmonization of fiscal policy it will imply. However, the Fourth Plan does suggest certain changes, essentially concerning investments.

Depreciation allowances for tax purposes, until the law adopted at the end of 1959, were calculated obligatorily on a linear basis.

[1] See Chapter XIII.
[2] *Ibid.*

Since then, this is only optional for certain equipment goods acquired after December 31, 1959, so that a firm can, if it wishes, choose a non-linear system. Before 1959 also, there were provisions for granting accelerated depreciation in favour of selected firms, or types of material and equipment. Thus there was, since 1954, a reduction of 10 per cent of the cost price for purchases used to modernize plants; eligible products figured on a list drawn up by the General Planning Commissariat (handling equipment, anti-air pollution devices, safety and research equipment, etc.). In some other cases, for equipment acquired after December 31, 1950, the first year's depreciation could be doubled. Research buildings were eligible for a 50 per cent exceptional depreciation allowance. Steel and mining are granted accelerated amortisation. All these provisions disappeared as from January 1, 1960, with the vote of the 1959 law on taxation, except in respect of goods produced or purchased before that date. As for the old accelerated depreciation system, where it was applicable, firms have a period of five years during which they can choose between it and the new degressive depreciation calculation.

The advantages of the degressive system are sufficiently well-known to dispense with any extended treatment of the subject here. The objective is to increase the amount of the deduction in the early years and to carry over, as a result, the payment of the tax. It is a tax-free loan for the firm in question. The system now in force is not to be universal. It does not apply to used or to new equipment with a life of less than three years, and only goods acquired since January 1, 1960, are eligible.

Reducing the impact of taxation on investment expenditure is secured in other ways also. The revaluation of balance sheets, now obligatory, allows depreciation to be calculated on the basis of the new accounting value of the firm's fixed capital. But the main reform in this field—the 1954 reform of the tax on value added—has already been referred to. The Fourth Plan suggests that the 1954 legislation should be extended to all capital goods now excluded, such as non-industrial buildings, vehicles other than internal handling equipment and furnishings of salesrooms.

These measures are of a general, non-discriminatory character as they apply to all firms alike, or at least to all firms in the same branch of activity. The Fourth Plan enumerates also eight types of fiscal exemptions which can be granted to individual firms by the Ministry of Finance in 'a strictly limited number of cases' against specific undertakings by the recipients, notably in relation to their investment programmes. These agreements have been christened 'fiscal contracts'.[1]

V. POLICY TOWARDS PARTICULAR ACTIVITIES

Three examples of such assistance are instructive. They concern industrial decentralization, industrial conversion and scientific and technical research.

Industrial decentralization is the object of a series of measures already mentioned in this and other chapters (especially equipment premia and low-interest loans).[2] When a firm founds an industrial establishment in the provinces, it can claim a reduction in transfer duties from 13.2 per cent to 1.4 per cent, and in the patent tax of 50 to 100 per cent during five years. Financial aid from the State is also available for meeting social problems raised by the decentralization operation. The local authorities in the receiving area assume part of the cost of equipment. The general policy of a firm in the field of decentralization is an element which is likely to be taken into account at various times when, for example, permission to make an issue of shares or debentures on the capital market is sought, or when a request for credit is received by the Crédit National.

Industrial conversion has been assisted so far by the ESDF in a modest way (25 million NF in 1960) and mainly for small- and medium-sized firms. Bigger problems are now on the agenda. They concern the coalfields in the Massif Central, some sections of the armament industry and shipbuilding. Consequently, a new procedure is being organized with the creation of the Company for Industrial Development and Conversion[3] in 1960, which has the support of some of the big financial institutions (Crédit National, Caisse des Marchés de l'Etat, Crédit Hôtelier).

In addition to the financial assistance which is available there are several fiscal exemptions. These are decided by a Tax Committee

[1] See Fourth Plan, p. 71. They are: exemption from transfer duties on building required for industrial regrouping, conversion and regional development; seven years' exemption from profits tax on dividends paid on new shares; taxation of assets brought in in exchange for shares; transfer, to firms joined in a common enterprise, of their individual rights to fiscal deductions; deduction from profits of contributions to approved groups engaged in industrial regroupment and conversion; deduction of patent (tax) dues in regional development schemes; assimilation to the general ruling on parent companies and subsidiaries in cases where participations are below 20 per cent; tax exemptions for approved companies set up by small- and medium-sized firms to facilitate adaptation to the Common Market.

[2] See Chapters IV and XIII.

[3] *Société pour la Conversion et le Développement Industriel.*

which meets at the General Planning Commissariat but which acts by delegation from the ESDF. It can grant exemptions whose general objective is to eliminate the incidence of taxation on mergers between companies and on the setting-up of subsidiaries. This last point is stressed by the Fourth Plan.

As regards scientific and technical research, a wide range of measures are used. These are: loans at 5½ per cent for eight to twelve years or outright grants; tax exemption, such as immediate depreciation of a sum equal to 50 per cent of shares paid-up in a research company set up by a group of firms; possibilities for deducting from profits up to 0.02 per cent of turnover and the subsidies paid to approved bodies, total exemption from taxes on transfers and donations to approved scientific organizations.

CHAPTER XV

AGRICULTURE

Agriculture would be a key sector in the Plan in any case given its weight in total output and employment. But the problems facing it at the present time complicate notably the task of the planning authorities. In all countries where attempts have been made to plan agriculture in an authoritative way, the results have been highly disappointing. There has never been any attempt to follow such a policy in France but, nevertheless, the nature of the agricultural problem is so different from those which arise in industry that even a flexible planning mechanism must adapt its methods. Furthermore, agriculture is at the beginning of a new era with the opening of the Common Market, as the whole concept of the scope of, and rôle reserved for, a purely national plan is being called into question. The example of agriculture is therefore of wider significance insofar as it is likely to be repeated, with variations, in other sectors over the next few years.

The problems of French agriculture can be looked at from two points of view—economic and social.

Economically, the structures of production are not adapted to modern conditions. The pattern of land holdings is often an obstacle to a rational use and depreciation of modern equipment, and to an optimum use of manpower. Nearly 60 per cent of holdings represent less than 10 hectares each but form only 16 per cent of the total area under cultivation, whereas 5 per cent of farms occupy 30 per cent of the total. Moreover, a large number are split up into several small parcels of land, often some distance from each other. There are 2.3 million farm units but 76 million parcels of land, or an average of 30 per farm.[1]

Hectares	*Number of Farms*	*Area*
1 –10	56%	16%
10–50	39%	54%
+50	55%	30%

Source: Fourth Plan, p. 96.

In general, the large farms are found in the Paris region and the North and they have a high level of productivity. In the Centre and

[1] *Rapport Général de la Commission de l'Agriculture*, p. 53.

South-West, where farms are small, yields tend to be lower also. Since the end of the war, agriculture has nevertheless reached a stage where the annual rate of increase of production, allowing for annual fluctuations, is between 4 and 5 per cent as a result of the spread of modern methods of production, in particular of mechanization, and despite the continued fall in the active population on the land. On the other hand, the growth of home demand is not buoyant as income elasticity is low[1] so that, even when the rise in consumers' incomes is rapid, as it is expected to be during the Fourth Plan, demand for agricultural products will expand less fast. There are also serious marketing problems due to the changes taking place in consumer demand—more meat and high quality products such as fruit and vegetables are being consumed and less cereals—so that some products are already in surplus and require expensive schemes for stocking and exporting them. More generally, 'supply and demand are not well adapted in time or in space, in quantity or in quality, and commercial circuits for agricultural and food products are too cumbersome on the home market and ill adapted to a policy of exporting'.[2] It is significant that, although French agricultural prices at the production level are the lowest in the Common Market, at the retail level they are the highest. The producer, therefore, finds that the prices he receives are not sufficiently remunerative whilst food prices are too high for the consumer.

But the major problem facing French agriculture is the prospect of growing surpluses of some products, especially cereals, and the urgent need to find outlets for them abroad. The increase in production by 1965, compared with 1959, is put at 30 per cent and home demand will not rise by more than 21 per cent. So the decision to accept the growth of production described as 'ineluctable' by the Fourth Plan,[3] led logically to fixing high export targets, of 80 per cent more than the level in 1961 by 1965 whilst exports to countries outside the French Franc Area are to double. The estimates used by the foreign trade working party of the General Economic and Finance Commission for its balance of payments synthesis were lower however; a global increase of 64 per cent, and 80 per cent more for exports to non-French Franc Area countries. The authors of the Fourth Plan comment that: 'a vigorous effort to develop (agricultural) exports is a condition for the success of the Plan'.[4] In these circumstances, the insistence of the French authorities on the strict

[1] The income elasticity of demand for food is 0.8.
[2] Fourth Plan, p. 95.
[3] *Ibid.*, p. 97.
[4] *Ibid.*, p. 97.

application of the common agricultural policy of the European Economic Community, and their reluctance to envisage any changes in that policy which might endanger French export prospects, are understandable. In any case, the Fourth Plan suggests that international schemes for disposal of agricultural surpluses to developing countries could represent a second line of defence against the piling up of unsaleable surpluses. The products where markets abroad are needed most urgently are cereals, meat and dairy products.

The social grievances of the farmers are numerous. It has become a common theme that the farmer's income has risen much less than the incomes of the rest of society in recent years so that his efforts to raise productivity have gone unrewarded. Hence the persistence of the claim for 'parity with other groups'. Besides, the often painful conditions of work in agriculture, combined with poor housing amenities, and a social security system, including pensions, which is less advantageous than for non-agricultural workers, lead to increasing criticism, and favour a movement out of agriculture to other occupations—at present about 80,000 persons annually. This exodus carries with it certain undesirable features. The young workers are the first to leave so that the average age of the active population in agriculture is rising. Also the disorganized way in which they abandon the land, due to inadequate provision for re-training and job finding, implies that this valuable addition to the non-agricultural labour force is not used to the best effect. In some regions, the decline in the agricultural population has now reached a critical point, which endangers any attempt to achieve balanced economic growth, whereas elsewhere, in Brittany in particular, the problem is one of an excess of population without jobs.

Finally, it should not be forgotten that the French agricultural population represents a large political force. It is not one which systematically rallies to any one party and this helps to explain the solicitude of all political groups for the farmers' grievances.[1] Recently, the farmers have had recourse to 'direct action' in order to obtain a hearing from the Government.

For all these reasons, French agriculture has been the object in the last few years of a number of policy measures by successive Governments. But these have not, to date, given all the results expected of them.

In examining the measures taken we shall have to go beyond the framework of the Plan. The most important (the 1960 and 1962 Laws referred to below) have been prepared separately from the Plan although it takes account of them. In an international context,

[1] Cf. the debates in Parliament on the Fourth Plan in Chapter X.

as noted earlier, the national Plan has to reckon with the pluri-national agricultural policy being drafted by the Common Market. This means that the system of guaranteed prices, which was the keystone of agricultural policy as it emerged from the early post-war years, has to be given up with the Fourth Plan.

Agricultural policy during the first three Plans may be summarized as follows. The First Plan did not deal very much with agriculture despite the Planning Commission set up to study agricultural problems—agricultural machinery, vegetable production, animal production, rural infrastructure. The main emphasis was on agricultural machinery which was a 'key sector'. With the Second Plan, there was an attempt, through the two Commissions for agricultural production and rural equipment, to see the problems of agriculture as a whole, and more importance was given to technical improvements in production methods. These seem to have borne fruit as the curve of agricultural production began to rise steadily during the second half of the 1950s, so that the objective of the Third Plan, an increase of 20 per cent, was achieved. It was the Third Plan also that saw the beginning of a systematic price policy for agriculture.

During the first year of the Fourth Plan, a law called the Agricultural Orientation Act was passed, which is likely to remain the basic document of French agricultural policy for a long time to come. Its major provisions are referred to in the text of the Fourth Plan although, in point of time, the Plan was voted before the Agricultural Act. The final text, which was approved by Parliament in August 1962, did not correspond in all points to the draft supported by the Minister of Agriculture, M. Pisani, as the latter contained sixty-four articles whereas the former has only twenty-three. The law has a varied origin. Not all of its provisions are new by any means. Some of them were included in a first Agricultural Orientation Act voted in 1960 but which was never applied.[1] Some questions have been on the agenda of the agricultural community's claims for years and were brought forward by the Vertical Agricultural Planning Commission among others.[2]

[1] The 1962 law only acquires operative force as the decrees applying its various clauses are issued.

[2] The Commission had 70 members of whom 43 were representaives of the farming community. In addition, the 17 working groups set up by the Commission brought in over 200 other persons, most of them agriculturists. In the past, the demagogic character of the Agricultural Commission had tended to be quite marked. For the Fourth Plan, this was less so although there remains a difference in tone between the draft of the Commission's report and the text of the Plan. Criticisms of the Fourth Plan and the way it was drawn up,

The policy measures which are summarized in the Fourth Plan are given in detail in the 1962 Agricultural Act. They fall into four groups: market organization; improvement of agricultural structures; education and related topics; regional development.

I. MARKET ORGANIZATION

There are two fundamental ideas behind the measures to improve market organization. The first is expressed by the Fourth Plan as follows: 'In an agricultural economy which remains free . . . efforts to increase the economic power of producers on markets for their products will often be more decisive than a nominal increase in prices which frequently brings only an illusion of satisfaction.'[1] The second refers to the organization of a price support policy for agricultural products.

1 *Producer Groups*

The idea of the 1962 Agricultural Orientation Act is to give producers the legal right to combine to achieve certain objectives. That this should be considered a novelty in France, where co-operation in agriculture has a long tradition, is explained by the, potentially, more far-reaching nature of the producer groups which are envisaged by the Act. The Minister repeatedly announced that what he called disparagingly the 'small-scale pals co-operatives' do not qualify, but only really effective and substantial groups. These will have to be approved by the Ministry of Agriculture. They can be co-operatives or other types of associations such as the flexible

are not lacking. Thus M. Blondelle, Chairman of the powerful Assemblée Permanente des Présidents de Chambres d'Agriculture (APPCA) and a member of the High Planning Council, declared in December 1961 that the drafting of the report of the Vertical Agricultural Planning Commission had not been done in a democratic way, that the general report was written before the working groups had finished their studies, and that he considered a revision of the Fourth Plan was necessary (quoted in *Le Monde*, December 1, 1961). Similar criticisms were made by the Fédération Nationale des Syndicats d'Exploitants Agricoles—the major representative body in French agriculture, whose policy reflects the ideas of the older, more traditional, elements of the profession—which added that the 'Fourth Plan is the Government's plan'. The attitude of the Centre National des Jeunes Agriculteurs—the militant group in the FNSEA—was hardly more conciliatory. But it should be noted that the Fourth Plan did make concessions to the ideas of the CNJA, which is represented in particular in the poorer agricultural regions such as the West and South-West, as regards the reform of agricultural structures. A lively account of the peasant demonstrations in recent years and the reasons for them, written from a left-wing viewpoint, is given by S. Maillet: *Les Paysans contre le Passé*, Editions du Seuil, 1962.

[1] Fourth Plan, p. 96.

organizations called SICA (Sociétés d'Intérêt Collectif Agricole), created in 1960. But the rule is that they must be specialized in a particular product designated by the common agricultural policy of the Treaty of Rome—general co-operatives are therefore excluded—and they must operate on a sufficiently large scale. When recognized, the groups will have priority in the allocation of State aid.

Further stages are envisaged. The groups will be able to associate with similar ones on a regional, or national, basis to form Economic Agricultural Committees whose task will be to draw up common rules for production and marketing. Eventually, a Committee will be able to request the Ministry of Agriculture to authorize holding a ballot of all producers and, following a favourable two-thirds majority, or a vote representing half the value of production, the rules of the Committee can be made binding upon all producers.[1] For pork and poultry, two products which can be the object of Economic Agricultural Committees, the 1962 Act stipulates that, during the seven years of the transitional period of the common agricultural policy, no producers on an industrial scale can operate without authorization. This measure is designed to protect small-scale producers and represents a concession to the small farming interests.

2 *Price Support*

The chief reform in this field was approved in 1960 with the creation of a central Fund for the direction and regulation of agricultural markets (FORMA).[2] Before that date there were a number of 'Primary Funds' for specified products—meat, milk, oil-bearing plants and wine. There was also a first attempt in 1955 to organize a central Fund but this did not live up to expectations. Although the FORMA has now superseded these specialized bodies, the problems they met with are a good indication of the sort of difficulties which will continue to arise. Two markets—meat and milk—are particularly instructive in this respect.

(a) The special *Fund for meat* was created in September 1953 and functioned until 1960. It was managed by the Ministry of Agriculture and was financed by a fraction of the tax on meat plus some subsidies through the Budget, and by borrowing. The object of the Fund was two-fold—to stabilize meat prices and to encourage exports. The second mission went very much by default, however. The instrument for carrying out the decisions of the Fund was a

[1] This system is similar to the one some producers of vegetables in Brittany tried to set up in 1961.

[2] *Fonds d'Orientation et de Régularisation des Marchés Agricoles.*

Company set up by subscriptions of producers, traders and industrialists in the food industry and called the Société Inter-professionnelle du Bétail et de la Viande (SIBEV). The Company was 'to carry out, or have carried out, all freezing and stocking operations decided by the Government with a view to stabilizing the meat market, as well as to carry out, or to have carried out, all export or import operations on Government account or financed by the Government'.

The SIBEV intervened to buy meat when prices fell below the floor price fixed by the authorities, and froze and stocked it. The problem was to dispose of these stocks. The home market could not absorb them and practically all of them were sold abroad at a loss. Although the SIBEV was able to keep prices from falling catastrophically on several occasions, it was not able to solve the question of unremunerative prices for producers despite high prices for consumers. This raises the subject of distribution circuits in France which has bedevilled the meat market in particular since the war.

In brief, the meat market is organized in the following way. Two circuits exist by which meat reaches the consumer from the producer—the live and the dead circuit. The live circuit is the traditional one for cattle sent to Paris. The cattle merchant in the provinces, having bought cattle from the producer, sends them to the Villette market in Paris where a 'commissionaire' sells them on his own account to a wholesale butcher who undertakes the slaughtering and sells to the retail butcher. But some meat is not sold to the wholesaler at the place of slaughter but elsewhere—the Central Paris Market for example. This is the dead circuit and it is supplied from various sources such as provincial butchers who slaugher surplus cattle for which there is no sale, and a few large regional slaughter houses. Whatever the circuit followed, the characteristics of the system are that Paris prices predominate on all markets and that the profit margins of the numerous intermediaries are very high.[1]

The *milk marketing organization* resembled the meat market in some respects. A special Fund was set up in 1954 for milk and milk products under the responsibility of the Ministry of Agriculture, and financed by a 6 per cent share in the meat tax. Its operative agency was 'Interlait', a Company created to stabilize prices through stocking and processing, and to facilitate exports. The latter task was not carried out with more success than for meat. It should be

[1] There have been numerous spectacular campaigns since the war to break this system, and in particular the hold of the big merchants on the meat market. The last was launched in 1961 by the Secretary of State for Internal Trade and fizzled out after a few months.

noted, when evaluating the work of Interlait, that, as 40 per cent of milk is for human and animal consumption, the stabilization of prices can only concern the remaining 60 per cent as fresh milk cannot be stocked; only the retail price can be fixed. Also, at the time, there was a special system for fixing the price of milk under the Laborbe Law (1957) which is discussed later.

Interlait had the same status as the SIBEV. Its possibilities for action were two-fold. It purchased butter, skimmed milk powder, and some types of cheeses when prices fell below the average of the ceiling and floor prices fixed by the authorities, then resold them at home, when prices rose above that average, or abroad. It guaranteed the private sector, willing to stock products, that there would be no financial loss incurred. This method was less expensive but did nothing to correct other than seasonal fluctuations.

The benefit of the activities of Interlait for the farmers was rather variable. Although actual prices followed pretty closely legal prices, an INSEE enquiry in 1960 showed that from 30 to 45 per cent of farmers were paid less than the legal price. In sum, the producers who benefited from the scheme were those selling to big creameries and firms producing milk powder, who were in competition with each other and in contact with Interlait.

The general Fund—*Fonds de Garantie Mutuelle et d'Orientation de la Production Agricole*—set up in 1955 had similar objectives to the special Funds.[1] As the latter did not cease to operate, this Fund was limited to products representing only 30 per cent of the incomes of farmers. Its functioning was very inflexible due to a tight system of control over its activities. Moreover, its financial resources remained exiguous and the new body was unable to live up to expectations. During the first two years, its activities were limited to operations of a seasonal character for hops, dessert grapes, mushrooms, etc. But nothing was done in the important sector of fruits and vegetables, and there was no real policy for exports.

Consequently despite all these efforts during the years 1953-60, no basic reform of distribution circuits, and no real export policy were achieved.

(b) *The* FORMA was created in two stages, against a background of agricultural surpluses and with a desire to unify policy towards them. The 1960 Supplementary budget, and a decree taken in July of the same year substituted, as from January 1, 1960, for the Fonds de Garantie Mutuelle and the special Funds for meat and milk products, an annexed budget called FORMA. It was to be managed by

[1] Another important one was the *Office National Inter-professionnel des Céréales.*

the Ministry of Agriculture with the assistance of a Committee, and to be under the joint control of the Ministry of Agriculture and the Ministry of Finance. As from July 1961, this annexed budget was replaced by a new style FORMA, a public office with civil responsibility and financial autonomy. As compared with the first version, the new body has considerable liberty of action.

The FORMA is administered by a Director and a Board comprising a chairman and twenty members (five from the Ministry of Finance, five from the Ministry of Agriculture and ten representatives of the farmers). Its task is a double one. It will serve as a mechanism for regulating markets, and its interventions will be designed to facilitate desirable long-term adjustments.[1] Nearly 90 per cent of FORMA's budget comes from the State and, in 1962, the budget allocation reached NF 1,500 million. FORMA also benefits from profits from exporting and importing and has a share in the profits of the Companies charged with interventions on the different markets—two sources of revenue which are hardly likely to be very buoyant, however.

In 1961, two markets—meat and milk— absorbed 94 per cent of its expenditure. Export subsidies were large for frozen and tinned meat as the SIBEV had increased its purchases of meat that year. They were heavy for milk products, fruit and vegetables as well. It is probable that the cost of FORMA will rise further in the future.

The extent to which it does so will depend very largely upon the success of French export policy. The FORMA is expected to be very active here and, since 1961, it has subsidized the Centre National du Commerce Exterieur which is carrying out market surveys abroad, and initiating publicity and other campaigns to sell French agricultural products.

But the action of FORMA, and its subsidiary bodies, in supporting prices differs radically from the price policy followed since the Third Plan, which was designed not only to direct production along desirable channels but to improve agriculturists' incomes—and for many farmers the second function was more important than the first.

From 1957 to 1960, *price policy* followed the lines laid down by the Decree of September 1957, which was inspired by the philosophy of the Third Plan that production objectives could be achieved mainly by 'a coherent system of target prices', to be reached pro-

[1] Two products—cereals and sugar beet—continue to have special Funds. These organizations limit supplies through a quantum for production, or a restriction on areas cultivated, and producers participate in the cost of disposing of surpluses. Subsidies from the State for cereals reached 655 million New Francs in 1962.

gressively by 1961. So the previous policy of fixing prices product by product and at different times of the year, which had proved to have the disadvantage of being based on the least profitable farm, and of encouraging the production of goods whose sale was already difficult, was abandoned.

The object of the new system was to favour beef and fodder production and to reduce average cereal prices so as to be able to maintain exports and to encourage the use of cereals as feed for animals. So 'target prices' were fixed without limit of quantity for barley and maize, and with a production quota for wheat and sugar beet. Base prices were established for beef, pork and eggs and were to serve for setting maximum and minimum prices. All these prices were indexed. They had to be revised each year before October 15th in the light of trends in three price indices—industrial products used in agriculture, retail prices excluding food, agricultural wages (or the minimum legal agricultural wage as no agreed statistics of agricultural wages were available). The target prices were not applied immediately but were to be reached by the end of the Third Plan.

To accomplish this the Government had to fix an annual 'indicative price' before October 15th each year, whose purpose was to make it possible to move progressively from prices as they were before the reform to the target prices. These indicative prices were not actual prices but were used to calculate the annual 'campaign price' which took account of the size of crops, availabilities and market prospects and, therefore, of the level of farmers' incomes.[1] This third price was the key one for the farmer as regards the price he actually received for his products.

This new system was welcomed on the whole by the farming community as it offered a guarantee against inflation or a rise in agricultural production costs. But it was abolished by a decree in January 1959 as part of the reforms made late in 1958, a move which inspired many protests from farmers. The principle of target prices remained, though, and the same decree fixed new ones for 1961 which were in fact the old ones of the 1957 Act, increased by the working of the indexation system for the 1957-58 season, plus 6 per cent on an average to compensate for the disappearance of indexation. Unrest in the countryside made it necessary, in March 1960, to go back to partial indexing, however. This applied to wheat, barley, maize, sugar beet, wine, milk, beef, pork and eggs, and used four indices—the basic minimum agricultural wage, the cost of industrial products purchased by agriculturists, other manufactured

[1] The milk price was left outside this system and was governed by a special Act—the Laborbe Law, 1957.

products and feed cakes. Whereas the 1957 system was a full indexation, the system adopted in 1960 took account of the relative importance of the goods and services in the index so that, for example, cereal prices were only indexed at 55 per cent and milk at 70 per cent. But it was stated that the Government would in fact consider the trend in farm incomes compared with the trend in other categories of income when prices were fixed.

Quite soon afterwards, the problem of the common agricultural policy of the European Economic Community was envisaged in the 1960 Agricultural Orientation Act. 'Before October 15, 1961, the Government shall fix by decree, and for a period of four years, new target prices proceeding by stages towards the alignment of production prices in application of the common agricultural policy. If this policy has not been begun sufficiently by July 1, 1961, the Government will propose a draft law laying down the conditions for the establishment of the next target prices. In any case, notwithstanding contrary dispositions and whilst awaiting the application of the policy quoted in Article 2 which will guarantee the viability of the farm, the agricultural prices fixed by the Government as from July 1, 1960, will have to be set at a level taking full account of the costs and remuneration of labour and capital in agriculture. These prices will be set in such a way as to ensure that agriculturists receive a purchasing power at least equal to that of 1958.'

The main ideas which emerge from this text are that the target price system was to be kept but that indexation in any automatic sense was to go, and that price policy was to be seen in the framework of the agricultural policy of the European Economic Community. As the latter had not begun to operate by July 1, 1961, the Government submitted a draft law to Parliament in accordance with the provisions of Article 31 of the Orientation Act with a view to fixing agricultural prices. But this text was thrown out by Parliament in October 1961, so that no decision on target prices for the period 1961-65 was taken by October 15, 1961.

We thus reach 1962, a year marked by the important decisions taken in Brussels in January on the common agricultural policy. This situation explains why the French Government gave up the idea of fixing either target or indicative prices, and decided to go on directly to campaign prices, which have the advantage of being valid for only one year, for each product according to the legal timetake (April for milk, before July 1st for cereals, before the end of the summer for sugar beet and so on). A letter of rectification to the Fourth Plan in May 1962 then being discussed by Parliament, stated: '. . . the system of target price, which was well adapted to the circumstances of the Third Plan, no longer finds a place in the policy of the European Economic Community. Although it would not be wise to give up all attempts at direction (of production) through prices, in the present phase of final elaboration of the common agricultural policy, it would be impossible in any case to fix target prices for 1965'. This decision implies that the policy of raising farm incomes through price increases, which remains a chief claim of the agriculturists, goes by the board also. Hence the stress being placed in the Fourth Plan upon other ways of improving living standards on the land.

The Fourth Plan's only specific reference to long-term price policy, as a means of guiding production along desirable channels, concerns meat for which an increase of 10 per cent, compared with 1961, in producers' prices is envisaged, beginning with a 2.5 per cent rise in 1962. But as was seen earlier, raising production prices is a complex problem which is linked to the improvement of market structures generally. The section of the Plan dealing with internal trade sketches in the lines for a policy towards the meat market, such as building a new chain of modern large-scale slaugher houses to which the producers will have direct access so as to eliminate the abuses of the present system.[1] Only time will show whether this policy will be any more effective than previous efforts.

II. IMPROVED AGRICULTURAL STRUCTURES

As was noted earlier, the small size and fragmented character of many farms make it difficult for them to adopt modern methods of production. There is, therefore, a problem of creating large and more homogeneous farm units without destroying the family character of French farming.

Respect for the rights of property has been a constant factor in French agriculture for a long time, which explains to some extent the persistence of a conservative spirit on the land which has often checked the revolutionary ardour of the town dwellers since the nineteenth century. By a paradoxical twist of history, however, the younger elements in the farming community, represented notably in the CNJA, are much less concerned today about preserving property rights than with the problem of securing access to the land for young farmers. Feeling on this point is running high.[2]

[1] Fourth Plan. p. 137.

[2] One of its expressions is the 'visits' paid to wealthy town-dwellers who happen to possess two or more farms. Thus the actor Jean Gabin and the Minister of Finance, M. Giscard d'Estaing, were both the object of peasant demonstrations in 1962.

An important contribution towards finding a solution to this problem was the granting in certain conditions under the 1962 Agricultural Orientation Act of pre-emption powers to the *Sociétés d'Aménagement foncier et d'Etablissement Rural* (SAFER) created by the 1960 Agricultural Act. Another measure concerns the encouragement to older agriculturists to give up active farming in favour of younger men. Also the traditional programme of 'remembrement', or grouping of scattered land parcels, is being speeded up. We now turn to each of these measures as they appear in the Fourth Plan and in the 1962 Agricultural Act.

There are some fifteen SAFER in existence and they cover about three-quarters of the country. They usually correspond to the administrative areas marked out in the regional development programmes. They are non-profit-making bodies and benefit from fiscal exemptions for their activities in buying and selling land. They can also receive subsidies from the State which appoints a Government commissioner to be attached to them permanently. Their object is two-fold: to discourage further splitting-up of holdings, and to prevent large-scale units falling into the hands of wealthy farmers, who already own one farm, or of non-agriculturists. The SAFER are supposed to construct homogeneous holdings and to see that they are sold, on reasonable terms, to farmers who will exploit them directly. The difficulties of the SAFER in purchasing land in order to fulfil their mission were the cause of a big struggle both in the Government and in Parliament when the 1962 Agricultural Act was passed. Finally, the Act did give the SAFER a qualified right of pre-emption when land comes on to the market, but only after specific authorization by the préfet of the département who will consult a departmental commission before taking his decision.[1] A procedure is also foreseen which will check an excessive rise in land values when a SAFER intervenes on the market.

A parallel measure to the activities of the SAFER is the encouragement to older farmers to give up direct exploitation of their land. Until recently, the fact that old-age pension arrangements in agriculture were less advantageous than in other sectors of activity, led older persons to remain on the land even when they could no longer exploit their holdings efficiently. This situation has now been corrected and, under the 1962 Agricultural Act, supplementary pensions can be paid to older farmers who consent to give up their land, for example in the framework of a regroupment carried out by a SAFER.

[1] The decree applying this clause of the 1962 Agricultural Act was published in October 1962 together with a number of other decrees relating to the same Act.

This is one of the objects of the new *Fonds d'Action Sociale pour l'Aménagement des Structures Agricoles* (FASASA) financed by the State budget. It is reckoned that some 2 million hectares of land could be put under more economic and intensive cultivation in this way.

The FASASA will also be able to assist financially farmers who consent to move from regions where land is scarce—that is the West and the North—to regions where it is under-cultivated, principally in the South and South-West, and to provide for the re-training of young workers who leave agriculture so as to avoid their moving into unskilled industrial employment.

Lastly, the policy of regrouping scattered landholdings by exchange and purchase, which has been going on slowly since the war, is to be speeded-up as the Agricultural Planning Commission estimated that, at the present rate of progress, the programme would take 30 years to complete. It is likely that the new measures being applied through the action of the SAFER and the FASASA will make a bigger contribution to the solution of the problem of scattered landholdings than the traditional 'remembrement'.

III. EDUCATION AND RELATED TOPICS

This is a field where, despite good intentions, progress has been slow. The increasingly commercial character of French agriculture, combined with a greater degree of dependence upon overseas markets makes it necessary for the traditional semi-subsistance farming to adopt modern methods or disappear. Yields in France are still low compared with other European countries; wheat yields are 2.3 tons per hectare in France against 3.6, 3.5 and 2.8 in the Netherlands, Belgium and Germany respectively, and the annual yields of milk cows are in similar proportions.

The Fourth Plan recognizes the scope for improving yields. Funds for agricultural research are being tripled compared with their level during the Third Plan.[1] Also the application of new methods to various regions is to be studied more systematically in future so that the necessary adaptations to local conditions can be made.

The biggest effort concerns rural education. Already, in 1962, a law had laid down the principles for policy in the field, viz preparing young farmers to become real heads of modern enterprises and forming a corps of agricultural engineers and technicians. The amount of credits written into the Fourth Plan under this heading was 456 million New Francs, but a programme law for agricultural

[1] Fourth Plan, p. 103.

education was proposed by the Government in July 1962, and voted by Parliament, for an amount practically double this sum (800 million New Francs). This four-year programme is seen as part of a ten-year programme for higher and technical education in agriculture.

When the credits for agriculture written into the Fourth Plan are added up, taking account of subsequent increases, as in the case of education, the total looks impressive, at least compared with the Third Plan (5.8 billion New Francs instead of 2.9 billion).[1] The detailed figures are as follows:

PROGRAMME AUTHORIZATIONS

(millions of current New Francs)

	Third Plan	*Fourth Plan*
Individual equipment	236	356
Education, research and related programmes	210	1,024
Infrastructure	1,549	2,693
Major regional programmes	360	526
Re-afforestation	44	96
Stocking, processing and distribution	456	1,133
Other	11	16
Total	2,867	5,844

Source: Fourth Plan, p. 103.

These figures concern only direct budget allocations. If funds distributed by the Economic and Social Development Fund, the Caisse des Dépôts et Consignations, the Caisse Nationale de Crédit Agricole and the Fonds Forestier National are included, the total is not far short of 11.5 billion New Francs, compared with 6.4 million New Francs during the Third Plan.

IV. REGIONAL DEVELOPMENT

A regional policy for agriculture forms part of the overall regional policy described in Chapter XIII. The Fourth Plan notes that the funds from public sources enumerated in the preceding table will be spent in priority in those agricultural regions where development is lagging behind the rest of the country. They will, therefore,

[1] This substantial increase did not prevent the representatives of the FNSEA from pointing out, firstly, that the figure of 2.9 billion New Francs actually spent for the Third Plan was lower than the target and, secondly, that the Fourth Plan's objectives of 5.8 billion New Francs is well below the figure the Agricultural Commission wished to propose.

be included in the operational tranches for those regions, that is, essentially the Western areas of the country. The programme law on regional development to be drafted in 1963 will, no doubt, extend the area of the existing priority regions for agricultural development, called zones spéciales d'action rurale, which were set up in 1960. These zones cover at present all of Brittany, the north of the Massif Central, the regions of the Causses and the Cévennes to the south of the Massif Central. The action of the SAFER and the FASASA will be particularly marked in these areas also. Finally, the big regional development projects under way at present in the Bas-Rhône-Languedoc, Gascony, Corsica, and the Western Marshes and Eastern fallow lands will be continued and intensified.

PART FOUR

TOWARDS THE FIFTH PLAN

The Plan is a continuing creation, each phase of whose development raises new problems and offers new possibilities for action. We have discussed the phase of intense activity which accompanied the preparation of the Fourth Plan. In so doing, we noted how often the Plan innovated as to the objectives, and means of achieving them, compared with previous practice. But we saw also that, frequently, the Fourth Plan constituted only a preliminary approach in the application of new ideas which continue to make their way by permeating current thinking on economic and social policy. At the present time, the first results of this collective effort of reflection on the meaning and possibilities of action offered by the Plan are crystallizing around the preparation of the Fifth Plan which is now in an active phase.

How far will the achievement of the objectives it is hoped to set for it call for adaptation and changes at the technical level in the preparation of the Plan? Two problems come to mind in this respect; the methodology of planning and the adequacy of statistical knowledge for the new tasks allotted to the planners. We discuss these aspects of work in progress in Chapter XVI.

A preoccupation with the Fifth Plan, when the Fourth has still three-quarters of its life to run, may look like a proof of temerity. But the Plan is too firmly anchored in the institutional habits of the country for it to run any great risks of disappearing. This is not to say that the Fourth Plan will not have to face some serious tests. Events such as a general slowing down in the rate of growth of the main European economies, of an important decline in activity in the United States in addition to that country's already slow growth rate, or of imbalance in the international payments system would impose changes in French economic policy, just as they would in the policy of other countries. But there is a *prima facie* case for considering that the existence of the Plan would facilitate such adjustments rather than the contrary. The decisive problems for the Fourth Plan lie elsewhere. They can be grouped under the two headings 'income policy' and 'the open economy' which are discussed in Chapter XVII. The degree of success in achieving them will condition to a large extent the scope and nature of the Fifth Plan.

It would be surprising, and rather disquieting, if the present stage of French planning enjoyed the unanimous support and approval of all groups. Surprising, because the divergent interests of those groups exist in French society as they do elsewhere, and the Plan, although it is a powerful instrument for controlling these divergencies so that they do not disrupt society, and for channelling them towards constructive aims, is not a magic formula for effacing them. Disquieting, because the absence of criticism of the Plan would be the sign of a lack of interest, rather than a consensus as to its objectives. Fortunately such is not the case, and the Plan is actively fulfilling its rôle as a catalyst for thinking on the ends of economic activity and their relations with the other aims of society by provoking the dialogue between the Plan and opinion which is the subject of Chapter XVIII.

CHAPTER XVI

WORK IN PROGRESS

It was seen in the preceding chapters that the calls being made upon the General Planning Commissariat, and the other technical bodies with which it works, have grown in number and in complexity with the Fourth Plan. To enumerate a few of them, in 1963 the Parliament has to discuss a programme law for the development of the poorer regions of France, and, in the spring of the following year at the latest, the first experiment in pre-consultation on the broad objectives of policy for the Fifth Plan is to take place. Meanwhile, implementing the Plan now entails detailed annual reports to Parliament, and half-yearly reviews by the High Planning Council and the Economic and Social Council. In addition, the High Planning Council will continue with its work on income policy for which the planning authorities have to supply the documentation.

Some of these tasks are so recent that the General Planning Commissariat will really be setting out on unchartered seas with no experience, either in France or abroad, to act as a guide and a fresh methodological approach seems required to deal with them. Again, all these calls being made upon the planners are themselves making new needs felt, which were previously less urgent. This is notably the case for statistical knowledge. The progress of 'information' in the widest sense and that of applied methodology go hand in hand. 'Information is after all an economic good like any other and its production is related to the pressure of demand. The principal merit, from this point of view, of a formal model will be to bring out into the open the need for, and usefulness of, a "plan" for collecting information.'[1]

In this chapter, we shall look at these two aspects of the current work-programme of the French planning authorities, beginning with the problems of methodology, before considering the work under way in the statistical field. But it should be borne in mind, as the quotation in the previous paragraph illustrates, that they are in fact two sides of the same coin.

[1] P. Massé: 'Suggestions préliminaires pour un essai de programmation mathématique', *Commissariat Général du Plan*, October 1960, p. 4.

I. METHODOLOGY

Parallel with the work on the Fourth Plan, a methodological debate was proceeding among the members of the small band of technicians grouped around the Commissaire General, on the planning methods to be adopted for the future once the Fourth Plan was completed.[1] The virtues and shortcomings of the techniques used by the SEEF, and described in Chapters VI and VII, were weighed in the light of the new demands being made on the planners. The Fifth Plan, it had been promised, would be based upon a policy debate in Parliament *before* the Government issued its directives to the Planning Commissions. The closer links that can be hoped for between short-term and medium-term economic policy from now on, and the much more elaborate arrangements for the 'follow-up' of the medium-term Plan had brought into the open the problem of harmonizing the methods used for short-term forecasting and for the medium-term Plan. This consideration led naturally to another: whether the medium-term Plan itself should not be made more flexible, either by organizing a thorough stock-taking midway through each Plan or, a more radical solution, by going over to a process of continuous, or revolving, planning. That these, previously theoretical, problems should have come to a head when they did in the form of operational decisions to be implemented in practical work was due in part to the planners' awareness that the advent of large-scale electronic computers had widened considerably the scope for methodological experiment.

Fundamental to the whole debate is the question of the method of approach. Until now, French planning has been of the discretionary, iterative kind described earlier and a decision to go over to a formalized computable model would represent a sharp break with the past. It is discussed here first. The practical applications which derive from such a step may be grouped under three headings: the initial choice of policy objectives: the link between the short and medium-term aspects of the Plan; the place of longer-term prospective studies.

1 *Discretionary or Formalized Planning?*[2]

There is at bottom no analytical opposition to the adoption of a formalized planning technique; the objections and reticencies a

[1] For example, the note just quoted: P. Massé: 'Suggestions préliminaires', etc., and an article by the SEEF: 'Les modèles et l'action économique', in *Etudes de Comptabilité Nationale,* April 1960.

[2] This terminology is used in a communication by M. Massé read to the International Economic Association in Vienna in September 1962. We have

formal mathematical approach encounters are rather of a practical and operational nature. The use of a general decision model is usually seen as an ultimate objective, but one which it is not possible to achieve immediately.

A major obstacle, namely the extremely arduous and time-consuming nature of the resolution of any but the simplest models, has been lifted since the electronic computer has become available, and its use for linear programming at the enterprise level has become a commonplace. A second difficulty still remains, i.e. the incomplete and imprecise, not to say unreliable, nature of the basic statistical information on which the relationships of the model rely. But here also, progress is fairly rapid and, as the quotation given in the introduction to this chapter suggests, the effort of setting up the model can itself be a powerful instrument stimulating the collection of information. A more fundamental problem relates to the uncertainty factor itself which should, ideally, be treated in a formal way although, in practice, this is difficult to achieve, and renders the calculations involved more complex. Again, linked to the uncertainty element in formal planning, the much greater difficulty in quantifying certain relationships compared with others is a permanent temptation to neglect some of the former, or to assume that they can be described with a sufficient degree of approximation through the latter, more easily measurable factors, for example, the predominance of net investment in many simple growth models, all the other conditions of progress (technical and organizational) being grouped in a residual, and ill-defined, single factor. Here also, progress is possible and the existence of the problem should be a stimulus to further research rather than a justification for maintaining the status quo.

The drawbacks of discretionary planning are the opposite to those attached to a more formal approach. The time-consuming character of the process is very marked and is a heavy drag when, in addition to a single variant, the desired result is a range of possible solutions to be submitted for discussion and choice at the 'political' level before a final variant is developed as the full-blown Plan. Besides, discretionary planning, with its constant reference

borrowed heavily from this paper in drafting the paragraphs which follow. A useful check list of the relative advantages and disadvantages of the two methods discussed here is given in the final section of Prof. Bénard's contribution to *Europe's Future in Figures*, edited by R. C. Geary, cf. *Production et Dépenses Intérieures de la France en 1970*, pp. 104-6. Prof. Bénard's views are particularly valuable as he was for some years an active collaborator of the SEEF.

back to the 'real world', ensures ideally, although by no means invariably, that the planners do not drift too far away from facts, and where they appear to be in danger of doing so, corrective action can be taken. But it is precisely in making these adjustments that the discretion of the planners is constantly called into play. The end product of the 'personal' contribution of the technician may be very considerable but, nevertheless, impossible to evaluate, even by the technician himself. Formalized planning, on the other hand, separates in an unambiguous manner the arbitrary aspects of the model from the working out of the formal relationships. Moreover, if it diverges from reality, it does so in an unmistakable fashion due to the patent absurdity of the solution reached.

Clearly, no final decision on such a complex issue could be taken until a great deal of experience in the actual handling of problems by the methods of formalized planning had been acquired, even more so as French planners are not playing mock battles but are called upon to tackle live issues of public policy.[1] But a capital decision of principle has now been taken. It is that, for the future, the traditional discretionary or iterative methods will be accompanied by an attempt at formalization. The implications of this will be examined in the following paragraphs. A word of caution to the reader is in order before doing so, however. The questions raised are policy issues which relate to future events where, although in some cases the views of the General Planning Commissariat have been expressed in detail, in others the precise solutions which will be adopted depend upon discussions which are still going on inside the public departments, and also upon the results of researches which have not yet been completed. The description given below is not therefore one which necessarily corresponds to final decisions taken at the official level.

2 *Initial Choice of Options*

The pioneering attempt at pre-consultation on major options in the Plan made at the end of 1959 and early in 1960 has been described in Chapter VII. The lessons of the experiment have been drawn for the next, and more ambitious, step which will involve not only the Economic and Social Planning Council but Parliament as well.

The problem at issue is in essence a simple one, but its implica-

[1] 'The scope of the problems raised is such that we shall certainly not solve them all in a short time. But we are only at the beginning of a long series of Plans and the key thing is to make some decisive progress with the elaboration of each one.' P. Massé, 'Suggestions préliminaires . . .', p. 24.

tions are decidedly less so. The justification for a choice which is made in the Plan cannot rest solely upon its economic rationality unless it is enshrined in a general framework which has been fixed as democratically as possible. In other words, the optimum in the Plan is the result of political decisions as well as of the optimization of technical factors, and indeed there is no other way in which the term optimum used in this sense can be said to have any meaning. As R. Frisch has put it: 'To carry such techniques of analysis (i.e. formal decision models) over into the field of optimum choice of economic policy working at the national level is the crucial problem of the Western democracies today,'[1] a view from which no one in the General Planning Commissariat would dissent. The stakes are not then mean ones. How can a satisfactory solution be found?

One way is to profit from past experience. The verdict of the Commissaire General on the significance of the consultation with the Economic and Social Council is: 'There was agreement each time a clear-cut option could be presented between two alternative objectives. . . . The conclusions were less persuasive, and were only followed in part, when the choice lay between a concrete objective of obvious value such as a faster rate of growth, and an abstract advantage, difficult to perceive in its content and implications, such as the degree of security of the fundamental balances (in particular the external balance).'[2] It is fair comment to add that, if Parliament had been consulted on the Fourth Plan in the same conditions as the Economic and Social Council, it is unlikely that the result would have been any more satisfactory.

But, in this type of exercise, as in many other fields, the answers one receives are in no small measure a reflection of the questions which are put or of the way in which they are put. And this is the main avenue of progress which is being explored at the present time. Recourse to a formalized model holds out the possibility of making a significant improvement in the formulation of the issues involved which the discretionary type of model building does not. It ensures that the whole implications of policy measures are seen, and when they are, that they can be explained in an unambiguous manner. Moreover, the need to present a range of significant, and feasible, choices for debate by a representative assembly is one which would be too unwieldy and time-consuming for any but a programmed model approach. The intention of the General Planning Commis-

[1] R. Frisch: 'Preface to the Oslo channel model, a survey of types of economic forecasting and programming', in *Europe's Future in Figures, op. cit.*, p. 257.

[2] P. Massé: lecture at the Economic Institute in Dublin, April 1962.

sariat is to use a formal general model for this purpose; but in view of the novelty of the attempt, the two methods—formalized and discretionary—are to be combined.

Thus a central model will be built up along the same lines as for the Fourth Plan, using, that is, discretionary methods together with a number of formalized variants which differ from the central model but remain fairly close to it. The closeness of the two types of model is considered to offer a safeguard against errors for the first attempt at formalized planning. 'The presentation of these variants increases the interest of formalization. As a consequence, all the assumptions have to be made explicit and placed at the beginning of the process, thereby reducing the risks of misunderstanding to a minimum and facilitating reasonable discussion on an equal footing with outsiders to the technical planning procedures. Besides, time and money will be saved by using machines for all work of a repetitive nature.'[1] The formalized approach must distinguish clearly between three groups of variables; those which are to be the object of choice by representative assemblies or groups (X), those which require optimization at the technical level (Y) and exogenous variables as regards the political and technical authorities of the country concerned (Z). The group of variables under X can be taken as representing the collective demand curve. It may include, in differing proportions, choices between work or leisure, private or collective consumption, internal migration, professional or regional migrations and so on. The technical variables, Y, are of a different kind. They cover factors such as the volume of imports for given levels of production, the export volume necessary to produce a desired external payments surplus, capital requirements by branch and manpower inputs. The exogenous variables, Z, refer to the basic uncertainties of the future or to those variables which are controlled by decision centres outside the national frontiers, for example the rates of growth of foreign markets and the institutional arrangements governing world trade and payments.

In the process of defining an optimum solution, one of the X group of variables has itself to be maximized technically, that is with respect to the group of Y variables, for a given set of other X type variables. The X variable selected for maximization will be final consumption. In this way a number of technically optimized variants can be built up consisting of assortments of X for each maximized level and structure of consumption. For the first attempt at formalized planning, and as a safeguard against errors, a common characteristic of all the variants will be that they are 'in the neigh-

[1] P. Massé, *op. cit.*, Vienna, September 1962, p. 7.

bourhood' of the central, discretionary model. This restriction would seem also to correspond to the scope of choice in the real world where any sharp change of trend is unlikely for institutional and political reasons.

There remains the problem of the treatment of variables of the third type, Z. One method would be to assign a degree of probability to each variant but appreciation of the significance of different probability co-efficients is not one which lends itself easily to a general debate of the kind envisaged for the Fifth Plan. A solution is to be sought in the presentation of coherent variables each of which has an equal chance of success. In other words, each variant will respect the fundamental balances (savings and investment, imports and exports, demand for a supply of manpower) to the same extent.

The originality and difficulty of carrying over into practice the programme just outlined are evident, as is the importance of the political issues at stake. 'The General Planning Commissariat's mission is unequivocal. It is to strive to present variants which will be, at one and the same time, clear and yet precise, simple and yet significant, so that the nation, through the meditation of its representatives, can make known its preferences. On our part, we shall make all efforts to bring our task to a successful conclusion. However, although it was desirable to announce the principle of action, it would be premature to freeze here and now the forms of a procedure to which, as one of your reports says, "use will give its practical form". We shall have to reflect carefully on all this. For example, there is no question of bringing forward by two years the final debate which we are having today with all its precision and detail. We must find an original approach for an examination and discussion of the general outline of the Plan, and it may be that such a task will not be an easy one.'[1]

3 *Short- and Medium-term Plans*

We have already seen in earlier chapters that, although for a long time there was little co-ordination between the short-term economic situation and the medium-term Plan, with the Fourth Plan the need for such a liaison is fully recognized inside the Government departments. And arrangements for a more intensive follow-up procedure by Parliament, and other representative bodies, have been made. These considerations lead naturally to seeking the most convenient method, at the technical level, for achieving this object.

[1] M. Massé, the Commissaire Général, in the ratification debate on the Fourth Plan in the Senate, *Débats,* July 3, 1962, p. 666.

The methodological problems we have just been discussing are relevant here also.

Up to the present, the preparation of the annual 'economic' budget, which is annexed each year to the budget documents and, before that, is examined in detail by the National Accounts Commission, has been done using methods which we have called discretionary as opposed to formalized ones.[1] This procedure is open to the same objections as its use for medium-term planning and, of course, offers the same advantages. But the decision to explore the possibilities of formalized planning for the four-year Plan cannot stop there; indeed it would be illogical for it to do so as the need for a rapid means of testing alternative policy measures is even greater with short-run projections than in longer-term work. Thus the advantages of a formalized approach appear to be overwhelming. If, and when—and the date is unlikely to be far off—this occurs, repercussions on the medium-term Plan itself will be likely.

As from now the position is that Parliament will discuss the four-year Plan as a whole every two years—once when it approves a 'guide-line' document, and once when it votes the final text of the Plan. Besides, each year Parliament will debate a progress report on the four-year Plan so that, every two years, there will be two Parliamentary examinations of the Plan. If the half-yearly consultation procedures with the High Planning Council and the Economic and Social Council are also taken into account, the total makes a very heavy work load indeed for the General Planning Commissariat and it may soon become urgent to find ways of lightening it. Moreover, a strong case can be made out for flexibility in projecting medium-term targets at the present time when changes in techniques of production and in economic and social, not to mention political, factors tend to occur both rapidly and in ways which are increasingly difficult to predict. These two types of considerations have provided French planners with matter for reflection for some time now.[2]

The adoption of the method of the Intermediate Plan, used in

[1] See J. Mayer: 'La Préparation des Budgets Economiques', *Etudes de Comptabilité Nationale,* July 1961.

[2] 'The Plan which is drafted on the basis of the outline chosen (by the representative Assemblies) is unique but it is not rigid. Annual adjustments give it the required flexibility. Moreover, the importance of the risks and unknown factors has suggested providing for a systematic use of the procedure called the Intermediate Plan, that is a revision after two years until such time as the lightening of work methods makes it possible to go over eventually to the concept of a revolving Plan.' P. Massé, colloquium on 'Democratic Planning', in the *Cahiers de la République,* June 1962.

1960, as a permanent procedure would be the simplest solution at present.[1] But it has its disadvantages. The revision of a four-year Plan after two years means that the time horizon remaining, two years, is not sufficiently different from the construction of an annual 'economic' budget and the rest of the follow-up arrangement now made, for it to be a very useful exercise. Also it would add to the already lengthy consultation procedures, particularly at the Parliamentary level. Hence the advantage of a 'revolving' Plan.

The idea behind this suggestion is that the time horizon for the medium-term Plan is always the same number of years ahead. Thus, with a four-year Plan, set up initially for the period from 1962 to 1965, at the end of 1962 a new set of objectives for 1966 would be worked out, and so on each year. The annual revisions consider, on the one hand, achievements to date and decisions already taken or in the course of being implemented and, on the other, new information which has come to light in the meantime. This procedure has its adepts elsewhere than in France. The Soviet Union has applied it since 1959, when the decision to move over to seven-year planning periods was taken.[2] It is what Ragnor Frisch has called 'moving' or 'sequential' planning.[3] Clearly, it is a process which calls for a formalized model as, by other methods, it would be impracticable. It offers the advantage of linking in an organic fashion the two aspects of planning—the short-term and the medium-term—and enables the necessary degree of flexibility to be introduced. At the same time, it overcomes one of the obstacles to the Intermediate Plan as a regular procedure; that the time horizon for such a Plan is too short.

The most serious objection to the principle of the revolving Plan is that it is difficult to explain to the non-initiated to whom the whole proceedings can appear very much like a pure mystification by the authorities trying to evade their responsibilities. The value of the Plan as a symbol is very great and its approval by Parliament, for example, should be an event surrounded by a certain ceremony and solemnity which it would be difficult to give to a document whose targets were constantly being extended and revised.

Progress towards the point where this question will have to be decided one way or another will take some years, although con-

[1] For the Intermediate Plan, see Introduction, p. 32.

[2] J. G. Sorokin: Optimum Organization of the National Economy, etc., International Economic Association, Vienna, September 1962.

[3] R. Frisch: 'Preface to the Oslo channel model', in *Europe's Future in Figures, op. cit.*, p. 278.

siderations of the kind enumerated in this section are already being debated among the technicians and other groups interested in planning. A possible line of compromise so as to preserve the advantages of fixed and revolving objectives may well appear of its own accord if the pre-consultation procedures on the main guidelines for medium-term action are successfully developed, for it is at this stage that the really fundamental decisions are taken, and it is they, and not the detailed approval of a voluminous and detailed Plan, which should call forth the interest of Parliament and of public opinion in general. In such a case, there is no reason why the adoption of a revolving Plan should not modify the system of four-year Plans itself in favour of a rather longer time horizon. Considerations of this kind were behind the decision taken in the autumn of 1962 to change over to a five-year period for the Fifth Plan which will cover the years 1966-70.

4 *Prospective Planning*

The debate on the time horizon of the medium-term Plan may be influenced also by the development of prospective studies. In future, the former will be incorporated much more systematically than in the past in the framework of a longer-term perspective.

We have already discussed the rôle of prospective studies in French planning in Chapter VI and shall not return to the subject here. What is relevant for the problems which have been examined so far in this chapter is the current work programme of the General Planning Commissariat in this field.

It was seen earlier that the passage of the Fourth Plan through Parliament was the opportunity for lively debate on its regional policy aspects, and that the Government undertook to submit, during 1963, a draft law for regional development. It will be recalled furthermore that, until the Fourth Plan, regional development had been very much a marginal activity in the Plan. If it is now to become more than that, a new, and promising, field for research is opened up. So far, regional considerations have not been easy to deal with theoretically, quite apart from the usual paucity of regionalized statistical data, and regional optima have been determined largely by the commonsense of planners under the stimulus of prodding by representatives of regional interests. Prospective studies offer an opportunity for basing regional analyses more firmly in the context of the outlook for the growth of the national economy and, by the same token, of giving depth to plans at the national level. 'Thus the opposition which had sometimes appeared to exist between the Plan and regional development is overcome and the unity of view required for unity of action is re-established at a higher level.'[1]

The General Planning Commissariat is at present engaged on a study of this kind with 1985 as the terminal year. The object is 'to derive from the mass of data available those which are "carriers of the future". . . . The first is the growing precision and delicacy of our production techniques, and the fact that expansion is based more and more on highly worked-up products and increasingly perfected machines, with the result that materials weigh less. In this manner the disadvantages of distant locations are reduced for a whole range of light industries. . . . The second is the larger extent to which, foreign trade being freer, we shall be working-up imported raw materials. In the longer term we shall very likely witness the growth of industries at ports, a phenomenon illustrated already by the growth of refineries, petro-chemicals production and the steel plant at Dunkirk. . . . The third is the process of urbanization which is going on before our eyes.'[2]

It may appear that these different methodological changes incur the risk of changing the character of French planning, of dehumanizing it as it becomes the domaine of econometricians and electronic computers with the average businessman and trade unionist being relegated to a secondary rôle. The danger exists but it has been perceived so that it is likely to be guarded against. Insofar as the new methods allow the political and other representative assemblies to express an opinion on the major options for future economic policy, it can indeed be maintained that progress will have been all the other way. It is at the stage of detailed elaboration that such criticisms would be valid if the rôle of the Planning Commissions was diminished. But it is not the intention of the Plan to supersede the Planning Commissions. Although the scope of their work is not to be extended to other branches and some lightening of their methods is to be achieved, in particular as annual meetings of each Commission are now taking place, the adoption of a revolving Plan would be likely to lead to a more continuous contact between the Commissions and the technicians of the Plan than at present. But even without this, the functions of the Commissions are by no means lessened by the use of a formal model. The model builders will need these bodies, for example, in order to adjust the technical co-efficients and other structural relations in the model to likely future conditions; the exclusive use of past coefficients being one of the pitfalls awaiting experiments in formalized planning due to the

[1] M. Massé, debate in the Senate, July 3, 1962, p. 665.
[2] *Ibid.*, p. 666.

perpetual changes in techniques of production.[1] And, of course, the wider implications of the task of the Commissions as we have discussed it already would not be diminished in any way either. The convergence of interest groups they achieve, the coherence of development projections, the throwing-up of suggestions for policy changes, in brief all the hundred and one aspects of the dialogue between the Plan and the private sector which are reached through the work of the Commissions remain.

II. STATISTICS

'*A priori* statistics, where one tries to collect the maximum amount of data in all directions without having a predetermined plan for their use, meets with much more scepticism and indifference than a programme for gathering information which is linked to a definite task to be accomplished.'[2] Since 1961, the Statistics Working Party of the Horizontal General Economic and Financial Commission has been working on the preparation of a plan for improving statistical data with a view to the drafting of the Fifth and subsequent Plans, and to the execution of the Fourth Plan. The Working Party has drawn up the general framework for a statistics programme during the years 1962-65 and has also drafted so far two annual tranches of this programme, for 1962 and 1963. The programmes are firmly linked to the needs of the Plan and are destined to fill some of the gaps in statistical knowledge met with during the drafting of the Fourth Plan, such as savings, and to provide for the new demands which will arise for the Fifth Plan, for example, regional data. In the paragraphs which follow we shall indicate the principal lines of study at present under way. We shall not refer to the problem of income statistics here: thanks to the need to define an incomes policy, a special effort in this field has been made, which is so closely linked to the success of the policy as a whole that the subject is best left over for the next chapter.

It is significant in this connection to note how frequently statistical programmes are the consequence of requests formulated by the Planning Commissions for the Fourth Plan. Thus the groups who

[1] 'Thus any temptation to use, say, a 1954 table of input-output coefficients (for projecting growth in the United Kingdom up to 1970) on the grounds that it is the best and most recent available must be firmly resisted. . . . It is particularly in this context that we stress the need for co-operation between economic statisticians and technologists in industry.' R. Stone and J. A. C. Brown, in *Europe's Future in Figures*, op. cit., p. 309.

[2] P. Massé, 'Suggestions préliminaires . . .', *op. cit.*, p. 4.

will be called upon to supply data are associated with the programme for their utilization.

The bulk of the work will fall to the INSEE, with the assistance of the CREDOC for the more specialized studies on consumption. The INED will be called upon to study the results of the 1962 population census in collaboration with the INSEE. Other bodies such as the Social Security Administration and the University Statistical Bureau will also be invited to collaborate.

The scope of the statistical programme planned and being implemented appears from the following headings: consumers' expenditure, employment, education and professional training, production, trade and investments, tourism, health statistics, external trade and payments, regional data.

1 *Consumers' Expenditure*

The importance of a sound statistical foundation for forecasts of consumers' expenditure in the Plan is self-evident as the structure of demand depends to such a great extent upon the income elasticities used. In this field, direct and continued surveys are irreplaceable but they are expensive to operate.

During a full year, from the end of 1962 to the end of 1963, a continued survey of family budgets is planned with a sample of 20,000 families. It will follow the first sample, on a smaller scale, studied in 1956, by the CREDOC which will assist the INSEE in its new work. Three specialized surveys will be also undertaken on textiles, household furniture and other equipment, and on holidays. The choice of these three categories was determined by the suggestions put forward respectively by the Planning Commission for Transformation Industries and the Tourism Commission.

The Housing Commission asked for a survey of expenditures on family accommodation. Some 17,000 families will be asked to supply data on the costs of housing and to give their opinion as to their present accommodation and wishes for its improvement. The results will have to be ready for the Housing Commission's work on the Fifth Plan which will begin in the summer of 1964.

2 *Employment*

The problems encountered by the Horizontal Manpower Commission in drawing up projections on employment by sectors of activity, types of professional qualification and regional distribution for the Fourth Plan were noted in Chapter VII. This experience is to guide the programme of work for the Fifth Plan.

At present only the quinquennial population census gives full data on employment by sectors of activity and inter-censal estimates have been rather crude. It is intended to remedy this situation by a more systematic use of existing data such as returns for the payment of the payroll tax and the information collected by the Social Security Administration, and a new bi-annual inquiry composed of 50,000 family units is to be instituted in 1963. The bottleneck at the present time is the shortage of qualified personnel and this makes it necessary to be satisfied with a relatively small sample. In order to improve knowledge of short-term conditions on the labour market, the quality of the quarterly inquiries of the Ministry of Labour is to be enhanced.

The call for data on professional qualifications and their evolution comes not only from the Manpower Commission but also from the Education Commission which needs them for its estimates of requirements for school and professional training. The 1962 population census will furnish new information as will the 1963 industrial census. But the whole problem of the creation of new job specifications in the private sector, the link between professional qualification levels and employment, and the methodology of forecasting will entail a special research unit whose establishment is planned for the near future.

3 *Education and Professional Training*

In addition to the studies just enumerated, two others are projected dealing, firstly, with the relations between the type of training received, the level of qualification reached and the type of employment and secondly, with the reasons for the choice of a career or profession. This work should be complemented by a thorough and permanent study of all types of educational facilities in the country.

4 *Production, Trade and Investments*

A big effort is to be accomplished in this field in 1963. In conjunction with the Planning Commission for Agriculture, a programme for 1962-65 was drawn up for agricultural statistics. The full scheme comprises three main lines of inquiry: the structure of production units as to location, size and manpower; agricultural production, notably for a limited number of products such as meat, milk, cereals, fruit, with a view to improving forecasts of output trends; means of production including equipment, wage labour and remunerations. The intention is that a tranche of this programme should be put into operation each year, usually on a limited scale initially and on a national scale later on.

An industrial census of production is taking place in 1963, and is the first of its kind to be made in France. Besides, a special effort will be made to improve the indices of industrial production. There will be annual surveys in some sectors without data, such as the leather industry; in other cases, for example, mechanical industries and clothing and furniture, the existing surveys will become monthly.

The annual investment inquiry undertaken by the Ministry of Industry will be extended to cover certain sectors excluded until now, and the Ministry of Agriculture will do the same in the food processing branches. Elsewhere, the size of the samples used at present will be increased. The twin objectives are to obtain data in two forms, by sectors of activity and by regions. The forward-looking investment inquiry of the INSEE will also be reinforced.

The building and construction sector will be the object of a special effort to improve the quality and scope of the existing annual inquiry as well as the short-term indications of the level of activity and costs and prices.

The first complete census of the transport sector will be carried out in 1963.

The commercial sector is in a phase of rapid growth and transformation as consumers' real incomes rise and the percentage of the population living in towns increases. The INSEE has assisted in the establishment of a new Bureau for Commercial Statistics whose initial work-programme includes revising and bringing up to date, so as to organize a general census of the distribution sector, the INSEE card index of commercial establishments. Other activities concern the collection of data on investment activity, and the study of new forms of distribution circuits.

5 *Tourism*

Various bodies ranging from the Planning Commission on Tourism to the External Relations Directorate of the Ministry of Finance, have come to feel the need for improved statistics on tourism. It is proposed to link the inquiries to the work to be done on family budgets, notably the inquiry with 8,000 samples into holiday expenditure already mentioned. Studies of business travel and of expenditure by foreigners in France (reason for visits, their length, cost and so on) will also be undertaken. The first two of these inquiries will be completed by 1964, the third will extend over three years (1962-64).

In relation to the need for increased investment in hotel renovation and new building, noted by the Tourism Commission for the

Fourth Plan, sample inquiries are projected into hotel and other accommodation for tourists, turnover and working costs in hotels and restaurants, annual migrations at holiday periods, etc.

6 *Health Statistics*
It was noted in Chapter IX that the Public Health Commission was severely handicapped in its work for the Fourth Plan by the lack of any systematic framework for drafting a comprehensive and well-balanced programme for investment in its sector. The statistical programme proposed for 1963 sets out to remedy this state of affairs. Thus a small team of research workers, collaborating with the CREDOC, is now examining the problems raised by the definition of an optimum capacity and structure of hospitals, numbers of beds required, and personnel needs. Other work will include hospital and health services for infants and old people.

7 *External Trade and Payments*
The object of this work is threefold. The present price indices of exports and imports are defective and it is intended to initiate work in 1963 to improve knowledge of actual prices. The balance of payments on capital account with the rest of the French Franc Area presents statistical problems due to the complete freedom of transfer into and out of Metropolitan France. With the changed structure of the area now that practically all the former overseas territories have become independent, it is necessary to possess more accurate data. Finally, an attempt is to be made to evaluate systematically the amount of French capital invested abroad in different forms.

8 *Regional Problems*
A great many of the inquiries already enumerated will be designed to throw up data of interest for regional policy. But the systematic approach to regional development problems being adopted from now on will call for more than this. There is an immediate need for data to draft the annual operational tranches of the regional plans. In the longer run, a thorough study of regional structures will be called for as the 1985 prospective study proceeds.

The regional offices of the INSEE will have a key rôle to play here. It is intended to concentrate use of the existing resources in qualified personnel in those regions which fall within the framework of the 1963 programme law for regional development. The major gaps to be filled are considered to be of breaking down national statistics by regions, notably production data, of collecting statistics of manpower availabilities at the local or regional level, and the construction of regional input-output tables leading, finally, to regional accounts which correspond to the existing national accounts. A research team at the INSEE is working on this last point at present.

Looking over this very extensive statistical programme, one is forced to the conclusion that a considerable step forward in knowledge of economic and social phenomena will be accomplished over the next few years. It will support the similar progress which is being prepared in the methodology of the Plan. Certainly, up to now, the quality and quantity of statistical knowledge in France have been something of a handicap for a correct elaboration of economic policy, although this situation can be exaggerated. The absence, until 1963, of an industrial census of production is a rather spectacular example which may mislead the outside observer. The tight control of the French economy during the war and in the early post-war period entailed a very notable collection of data. And, over the years, the Planning Commissions, in conjunction with the professional associations, have done a large amount of statistical work.

Until recently, a severe obstacle in the way of improvements in statistical knowledge was the traditional suspicion of the average businessman and citizen towards any requests for figures. This attitude is related in turn to fiscal evasion. But there have been changes. The Planning Commissions find less resistance than previously when they ask for data, and large-scale modern enterprises no longer feel the same desire for secrecy as the traditional small firms. Reactions by consumers to inquiries into their spending habits are more favourable than a few years earlier. But a big item still on the agenda—which we shall have to turn to in the next chapter—concerns the analysis of income distribution.

CHAPTER XVII

NEW PROBLEMS IN IMPLEMENTING THE PLAN

Until the end of 1958, the rapid and, on the whole, sustained growth of the French economy was decidedly inward-looking. As was seen in the general introduction, exports were never a leading demand sector, apart from freak periods as during the Korean crisis, and imports were heavily controlled most of the time through quantitative restrictions, whilst tariffs were fairly high.

That this should have been so was not the result of a law of nature. It is true that the French industrialist had not had much experience of a prolonged export effort since the war, but, if he had not been handicapped by an uncompetitive exchange rate, particularly from 1952 to 1958, there is no reason to believe that French exports would not have done better than they did. Their rise since the end of 1958 when French prices became competitive once more supports this conclusion. The industrial base of French industry had been strengthened and diversified during the 1950s and, with the opening of the Common Market on January 1, 1959, looming up, an additional spur to modernization and prospecting of foreign markets was given.[1] But the new international context in which the French economy had to operate after 1958, with currency convertibility, the almost complete abolition of quantitative controls on imports, and sharp and progressive tariff reductions imposed new limits on the liberty of manoeuvre left to the authorities in framing economic policy. The medium-term Plan had no option but to project a sharp rise in exports to meet the inevitable increase in imports. At the same time, the corollary of such a policy was that an upward movement of prices could not be allowed to create balance of payments problems once again.

In other words, the two problems of internal prices and external balance are linked too closely for it to be realistic to consider the second independently of the first. It is not surprising, therefore, that the twin questions of income policy and the open economy should figure prominently among the new tasks in implementing the Fourth Plan.

[1] It can be argued that the so-called 'liberal' policy adopted at the end of 1958 when most quotas were abolished and tariffs were reduced represented, on the contrary, the severest jolt administered to private business by Government in years.

I. INCOME POLICY

French policy in this regard was conditioned until recently by special circumstances which made it less urgent to find a solution to the problem of adjusting the rise in nominal incomes to increases in productivity. There is rather less evidence than in most developed countries that the wage push was a big item in post-war price rises in France.[1] This can be explained in part by the lack of unity, and the small numerical importance, of the trade union movement.[2] Also the small-scale nature of many business units does not give much scope for branch-wise collective bargains to push up wage and salary levels generally. In particular, the last big inflation from 1956 to 1958 was a fairly clear-cut example of excess demand pulling up wages.

Nevertheless, successive French Governments have attempted to restrain in various ways the rise in incomes. Price controls have been used to hold down the cost of living index to which the basic minimum wage, and hence many other wage rates, were linked. The tight control exercised over remunerations in the whole of the public sector—including the nationalized industries—allowed the authorities to resist wage demands for some time. The results of these measures were no more, and no less, successful than elsewhere where they have been tried. Real prices rose as price controls were eroded and the official price indices fell into disrepute. The lag between wages and salaries in the public sector and those in the private sector was a continual source of friction and has left a difficult heritage for Government policy today.

The most radical solution was the one applied at the end of 1958 as part of the economic programme adopted in December of that year. It included the abolition of indexation systems tied to the cost of living and the freezing of remunerations in the public sector. In the private sector, the trade unions were unable to maintain real consumption levels for many wage and salary workers, yet no large-scale industrial unrest followed, due no doubt to the unsettled political climate at that time. The farmers had no alternative either but to accept the end of guaranteed target prices, though the decision still rankles with them.

In 1959, and again in 1961, the Government resorted to exhortatory methods. The Prime Minister sent a letter to the President of

[1] Cf. *The Problem of Rising Prices.* A Report of a Group of Independent Experts, OEEC, 1961, p. 46.

[2] The three major confederations together group less than 2 million members, about half of them being with the CGT, out of a total of nearly 13 million wage and salary earners.

the Conseil National du Patronal Français (the French Employers' Confederation) in November 1959 asking for moderation in granting wage increases and in making price changes. In March 1961, a second letter was more precise in asking for a limit of 4 per cent—the assumed annual rise in productivity—for increases in wages. The National Accounts Commission, whose chairman is the Minister of Finance, suggested that an 8 per cent rise in wages in 1962 was the maximum compatible with price stability, the rate being higher than in the previous year due to the existence of spare capacity in many sectors.

Meanwhile the Fourth Plan, which was completed at the end of 1961, gave particular prominence to the problem of income policy, as we saw in an earlier chapter, and set out to define a new approach to it.

The strategy proposed by the Government became progressively clearer between the first meeting of the High Planning Council, in October 1961, and the Parliamentary debates in the summer of 1962. It can be summarized in three points which we deal with below before turning to an analysis of the main currents of opinion in the country on the question of a policy for incomes. Firstly, the authorities attempted, in the Fourth Plan and in subsequent ministerial decisions, to define the scope of such a policy and to give satisfaction to those groups which had manifestly not shared in the rise in living standards in the last few years. A second stage, which in point of time was implemented parallel to the first, set out to reach some agreement with all interested parties on the facts of income changes over recent years. Finally, the High Planning Council was chosen as the body where eventual discussions on incomes would converge.

1 *Defining the Scope of a Policy for Incomes*

Until the Fourth Plan, the Plans had made only passing references to incomes and prices and there had been no consistent attempt to situate the growth of private consumption squarely in the perspective of the overall growth of the economy.

The tone of the future debate on incomes was given by the link established in the Fourth Plan between the growth of individual and collective consumption. The Plan holds out the prospect of a rise in private consumption of 23 per cent by 1965, or 5.3 per cent a year at a compound rate which, taking account of population changes, means some 4½ per cent per head. But an interesting innovation was to situate the debate on real incomes in a wider context than in the earlier discussions which had been restricted to questions of prices, and wages and salaries.

Firstly, there was the small, even symbolic, reduction of one point in the growth of private consumption to 23 per cent by 1965 (1961 = 100) compared with the rise of 24 per cent in total production, so as to make room for the very substantial rise in investment in collective services of 50 per cent.[1] Secondly, the Plan made several specific commitments as to improvements in the living standards of certain less-favoured groups (workers earning the minimum legal wage, the aged, large families). But the chief question, which conditions all the rest in the last analysis—the adjustment of the rise in nominal incomes of the majority of the population to the rise in output in such a way that overall price stability would not be endangered—was left open.

The text of the Plan stated that:

'The very considerable increase forecast in private consumption makes it morally and politically necessary to adopt certain selective measures benefiting the least favoured sections of the population.

'It is, nevertheless, indispensable for the success of the Plan itself that measures of this kind should be linked to the evolution of incomes, whether direct or indirect, of tax payments and of private earnings so that the target fixed for the growth of private consumption is reached, but not exceeded.

'This requirement of the Plan should lead in future to laying down and applying progressively a national incomes policy, in particular for agricultural incomes and for salaries and wages, which make up more than 60 per cent of the national income. In the public sector, policy in this field depends directly upon Government action, but the situation is different in the private sectors. However, some Western countries do apply an incomes policy, such as Holland, whose dependence on overseas trade renders it particularly sensitive to price instability. Due to our growing participation in international trade and payments, the same causes will tend to produce the same effects in France. But, in view of existing psychological habits, which find their strongest expression in the legislation on collective bargaining, no new departure in this field has been written into the Fourth Plan. Free discussions, which will remain the general rule, will nevertheless be informed by studies undertaken in the framework of the national economy and submitted for comment and study. The Government counts on an improvement in information, on a wider appreciation of the logic of the situation and on the feeling for the importance of what is at

[1] Cf. Speech by the Commissaire Général in Appendix II, p. 384.

stake, to establish the elements for an income policy from the working out of the facts of economic life itself. The bodies whose responsibility it is to follow up the execution of the Plan will have an important rôle to play in elaborating this policy."[1]

During the drafting of the Plan, however, the problem had been thoroughly aired. This was the case, in particular during the two debates in the Economic and Social Council and the first meeting of the High Planning Council as well as during the work of the General Economic and Financial Commission and its working party, the Equilibrium Group, where trade unionists, agriculturists and employers were all represented. From 1961 onwards, the problem became a subject for public debate generally as we shall try to show in the final section of this chapter.

But, from the beginning, Government policy has been extremely prudent and has tried to carry opinion along with it rather than announcing the imminence of spectacular initiatives which would, in all probability, have failed in their object and have endangered future progress.

This prudence was justified for a number of reasons. Between 1957 and 1960, as we saw in the Introduction, living standards had marked time for many wage and salary earners, though by no means all of them, and some groups saw their real incomes diminished. A further point remaining as a legacy from the past was the lag which had developed between the levels of remuneration in the public sector compared with those in the private sector. Clearly if the exercise was to be a serious attempt to study, and to implement, a policy of sharing the fruits of expansion, it would be asking a lot of the trade unions to suggest wiping the slate clean as from 1962 and letting bygones be bygones. The complexity of the issues involved did not stop there. As previous chapters have shown, the agricultural population was also profoundly discontented with the end-1958 measures and their consequence (the ending of price indexation) just as they were with the new policy of the Plan as regards increases in real living standards in the countryside. In the opinion of the farmers, their claim for income parity with other groups was still on the agenda and should also be taken into account.

During 1962, certain measures were announced by the Government to implement its undertakings towards the less-favoured groups of the population. Old-age pensions were raised and the Ministry of Labour and Social Security has promised that the second stage

[1] *Op. cit.*, p. 14.

of the progressive increase in these pensions, which was proposed in 1961 by the Special Commission on the Problem of Old Age, will be implemented in 1963. Family allowances were raised by 4.5 per cent at the end of 1962 and will be increased by 4 per cent in July 1963. The lowest paid workers, those earning the minimum legal wage, were promised by the Plan a larger increase in their living standards than the national average. The Government has confirmed that it accepts the principle that the minimum wage should be linked to the rate of growth of the economy and not solely to the price level, and an increase in this wage of 4.5 per cent, of which only 1.7 per cent was called for by the rise in prices, was granted in 1962. Regional disparities in the wage were also reduced and this will have a favourable effect on family allowances paid in the provinces as they are attached in part to the minimum wage.

These decisions can be seen as an attempt, by the authorities, to round-off the awkward angles of the inheritance from the past, to extend the scope of the definition of an incomes policy and to give the trade unions an earnest of their intentions for the future. But the kernel of the problem remains, for although all these measures were clearly desirable in themselves, their effect is to add to available purchasing power.

2 *The Statistical Problem*

It has been recognized from the beginning that the relative paucity of systematic data on income distribution in France would be an obstacle in the way of reaching an agreement in income policy. The existing situation where the Government, the trade unions and the farmers, to mention only the most important groups, each brandished their own figures was hardly conducive to clear thinking on the subject. Hence the mission given to the Commissaire General, during the summer of 1962, to undertake a study of the statistical and conceptual aspects of the question. But before we consider this work, it will be useful to mention the longer-term programme under way in this field and which was left over from the discussion in the preceding chapter of the long-term programme for improving statistical knowledge.

In the view of the official services, this programme should have two objectives: the first designed to improve statistical measurement of the total of incomes distributed, the second being concerned more particularly with income distribution as such.

(a) *The longer-term programme.* The two main sources used at present to measure the total volume of wages and salaries are a quarterly inquiry by the Ministry of Labour and the fiscal returns for payment of the wage tax. The Ministry of Labour's inquiry gives hourly wage rates but hourly earnings, which are much more significant for following the course of incomes, are only known twice yearly. Information as to the remuneration of other categories than wage earners becomes available once a year. It is hoped to improve both the coverage and reliability of these data as a result of the work programme put in hand for 1962 and 1963.

The question of the wage tax returns is almost the contrary one to that raised by the Ministry of Labour inquiries. The mass of data received by the fiscal authorities is enormous. Up to now, it has been sampled in the proportion of 1:30 but this is to be raised to 1:10. Besides, employers will probably be asked to give data separately for each establishment rather than sending in consolidated returns. This will assist in building up regional income data.

Agricultural wages are known only very imperfectly and, although their numerical importance is fairly small—there are less than a million workers in this group—improvements are planned here as well.

If the question of incomes is looked at from the receiving end, that is from the point of view of the individual wage and salary earner, there are two potential sources of data which have been but little used up to now but which will be exploited more intensively in future. The first is direct inquiries from a family sample. The programme for the study of consumption mentioned in the previous chapter will be of help here. The second, fiscal statistics from income tax returns, raises the difficulty of tax evasion but this is much less widespread among wage and salary earners than other groups, especially traders.

The lacunae in data on other, non-wage and salary incomes, are greater still, particularly as concerns the artisans and the liberal professions.

(b) But these projects belong to the future for the most part. Meanwhile, it was urgent *in 1962* to make a start with the initial fact-finding stage of the elaboration of an incomes policy. To this end, a committee was set up by the Prime Minister in the summer of 1962 with the Commissaire General as Chairman, and was given the task of preparing an inventory of all available data on incomes. All the major groups—employers, agriculturists, trade unionists—participated in the work of this Committee whose report was presented to the National Accounts Commission in September and to the High Planning Council in October 1962. It would be fastidious to go over the results in detail. In essence, the conclusions were simple. There was a general agreement that the data available were adequate on the whole for following annual relative changes in remunerations although their absolute variations, particularly in constant prices, were not sufficiently certain or detailed to be very useful as operative concepts. Once the overall categories used in the national accounts were broken down into sub-groups, it became apparent that the evidence for judging the evolution of the incomes of homogeneous social groups was flimsy indeed; 'wages and salaries' constitute a heading which is too heterogeneous to be useable and the same is true for profits.

However, certain trends in recent years seem now to be established with a fair degree of precision. Firstly, the lowest paid workers, those earning the minimum legal wage, have been the least favoured and their real incomes have probably not increased very significantly since 1956. But it should be recalled that this group is diminishing regularly in size as the level of wages rises and concerns probably not more than 300,000 workers outside of agriculture. The interest of the trade unions in securing an increase in the minimum legal wage is to be explained in part by the link between that wage and family allowances. In the past, this was not the case as changes in the minimum wage were often used to raise other wages as well. For the rest of the workers and employees of the private sector, salaries of highly qualified or semi-skilled workers have risen notably faster than those of unskilled or semi-skilled workers, a phenomenon which has been noted in other countries also, especially in the United Kingdom. But there are marked differences between large families and single workers as the real purchasing power of family allowances—which are a substantial part of family incomes in France—has fallen. Another conclusion which appears inescapable, although the figures used differ, is that wages and salaries in the civil service and the nationalized industries have not risen as fast as those in the private sector. The trade unions themselves estimate that the gap since 1956 has now reached 11 per cent. But judgments based upon average data should be interpreted with care. There has been recently an undoubted effort to improve the position of civil servants, not least through widening the scale of salaries which had become artificially compressed during the years of inflation. In the nationalized sector, each category of salaries and wages needs looking at separately as the position varies from one grade, and from one age group, to another.

3 *The Work of the High Planning Council*

It became increasingly clear during the summer of 1962 that it would be premature to expect any major move forward towards the definition of a policy for incomes during the October meeting of the High Planning Council. The lacunae in the statistical data revealed by the work of the special committee mentioned above, were too great. Also, for economic policy and general government policy can rarely be discussed in isolation, the political situation in France in the autumn of 1962 was not propitious; there was only a caretaker Government in office at that time.

The atmosphere of the meeting of the Council was not unfavourable, though. There was a general recognition of the efforts made by the Government towards implementing the commitments written into the Fourth Plan and concerning the less favoured groups. But the Council contented itself with noting the statistical difficulties in the way of a more comprehensive policy and passed the ball back to the authorities. Subsequently, the Government concentrated its efforts upon the most critical sector—the claims of the workers in the nationalized industries and the civil servants. In the autumn of 1962, all employees in the nationalized sector and all civil servants were granted a rise of 4.5 per cent as from January 1, 1963, with payment of a premium during the last quarter of 1962. This percentage corresponded to the estimated annual average increase in national productivity. In addition, negotiations on the setting-up of an annual review procedure for remunerations in the whole of the public sector began.

But the vexed question of comparative wage and salary levels in the public and private sectors came to a head again in the spring of 1963 with a strike in the coal mines which led to renewed agitation in other branches. The additional increases averaged about 8 per cent and were therefore substantial. The key question which remains, following this settlement, beyond the immediate problems of its repercussions on costs and prices generally, and on the budget balance in particular, is whether it will facilitate a long-term agreement on ways of maintaining a proper relationship between the growth of incomes and the growth of natural productivity. And it will be some time before a judgment on this point becomes possible.

Meanwhile, it is clear that the working-out of the Fourth Plan encountered in 1963 its first severe test as the out-turn during the first year of the Plan (1962), and the tentative forecasts which can be made for 1963, show. Gross internal production rose by 6.3 per cent in volume in 1962, or by nearly 1 per cent more than the planned target. And a further rise of between 5.5 and 6 per cent is likely in 1963. This situation would be a cause for satisfaction if it were not for the fact that private consumption rose even faster—by about 6.5 per cent. It is true that investment also increased by more than the planned target, by 7.5 per cent compared with 7 per cent. But it is likely that the weakening of private investment expenditures noted late in 1962 will lead to a lower percentage rise in 1963. To that extent, there is room for another faster rise in private consumption in 1963; but such divergent trends would be a danger if they persisted. There were signs of pressure on prices during 1962—for the year as a whole retail prices rose by nearly 5 per cent due only in part to the effects of bad weather on food prices. The impact of these trends on the foreign trade balance with countries outside the French Franc Area was a growth of imports of nearly 14 per cent compared with an increase in exports of less than 9 per cent. The credit restrictions announced in March 1963 will no doubt moderate the growth of imports during 1963 and, in any case, the balance of payments was still in surplus during the early months of the year. But the sizeable fall in the foreign trade balance between 1961 and 1963 is a warning which is not to be taken lightly.

4 *The Fruits of Expansion*

It should not really surprise anyone that the elaboration of an incomes policy in the framework of the Plan should turn out to be a long and delicate task once it has been decided to go beyond the measures in force in practically all countries—except perhaps Holland and Sweden—and which rarely get beyond the stage of expedients. A question which remains open is how far it is possible to go in this field without a radical change in the existing balance of political forces and without modifying the character of French planning. This is not to say, however, that workable compromises are not possible. Class, and group, antagonisms exist in France as elsewhere and the Plan does not exorcize them by a magic wave of the wand. But the French are nothing if not realists. Moreover, if the success of the Plan is compromised, the responsible leader knows that those whom he represents have something to lose. 'For a 5 per cent increase a year in real wages, I am ready to sign on the dotted line right away.'[1] We now turn to some of the most representative of the suggestions which have been put forward recently in the field. A word of caution is in order, though. Their authors do not make

[1] A trade union member, quoted by M. Darricaux, Confederal Secretary of the CFTC—The Christian Trade Union Confederation—at a round table discussion in Paris on 'The Plan and Opinion' in May 1962.

them in isolation, but usually as part of a general reform of the planning system. We consider this issue in the next chapter; meanwhile the references below to an incomes policy should be seen in this wider context.

Two principal lines of thought run through the various proposals. The first is a global approach favouring the conclusion, at the national level, of agreements on the increases in real incomes which would be compatible with maintaining the general balance of the Plan and, at the same time, sufficiently acceptable to all concerned to offer some reasonable hope of being respected. The second, although it does not exclude the first, concentrates on the branch of economic activity, or even the individual firm, as the point of convergence for a policy for incomes.

(a) *Agreements at the national level.* The negotiation of agreements on wages and salaries at the national level between the trade union organizations and the employers' representatives is supported by the CFTC. These negotiations would respect the main lines of the Plan but the participation of the State is viewed with some suspicion—a sentiment which the use by the Government of its power to control the level of remunerations in the public sector for many years goes a long way to explain.[1] The annual examination of the results of the Plan would set the guide lines for such a policy to be implemented by bi-partite discussions between employers and workers. This procedure would have the advantage of preventing excessive disparities in the growth of incomes by sectors; branches with a rapid rate of increase of productivity would agree to reduce their prices in return for a lower rate of increase in wages than their specific productivity rates would justify. Moreover, regional disparities, unrelated to economic conditions, could be evened out by agreement.[2] The CFTC's programme would call for a notable change in the structure of French trade unions and in the procedures for collective bargaining. Although, since 1950, discussions on wages and salaries have been left for workers and employers to organize freely, in practice not many nation-wide agreements have been concluded; the division of the trade union movement does not facilitate them, and many employers still feel a certain repugnance when it is a question of admitting the trade unions as negotiators and representatives of the workers inside the factory. Indeed the difference between the present situation at the

[1] Cf. M. Descamps, reported in the *Le Monde,* August 5 and 6, 1962.
[2] See 30th Confederal Congress of the CFTC, June 1959, and the report to the 31st Congress, June 1961: 'Pour une politique des Salaires'.

national level, where the trade unions have their place on all the consultative bodies, and that on the factory floor where the personnel delegate, who must be elected by law, is considered by many employers to be the proper channel for communication with management rather than the trade union, is somewhat incongruous.[1] Besides, the weak numerical importance of the trade unions—whose paying members represent less than one in five of wage and salary earners in the combined public and private sectors—and their ideological divisions into three main groups, do not make it easy for their leaders either to make constructive suggestions or to ensure they are carried out. This situation has led some observers to propose legislation similar to the Wagner Act of 1935 in the United States in order to confer official, and binding, recognition on the trade unions.[2]

For some writers, sympathetic to the tendency represented by the CFTC, the tripartite discussion—State, employers, workers—at the national level is an acceptable formula. Thus two extremes for permissible increases in incomes would be fixed each year. The maximum would be determined by the economic outlook and the need to maintain economic balance. It would include all incomes and would apply to all collective bargains which would become obligatory in each branch. The minimum increase would concern the guaranteed wage and would be based upon the average increase in wages and the price level.[3] In September 1962 the first collective agreement was signed in France which specifically took account of the objectives of the Plan. It covers some 400,000 workers in the textile industry and foresees annual confrontations on wage and salary questions in the light of the execution of the Plan and its prospects for the year ahead. It was signed by all the unions except the CGT.[4]

The attitude of the CFT-FO (the Socialist trade union confederation) has been constructive in the sense that its representatives have

[1] An agreement early in 1962 between the commercial vehicle producer, Berliet et Cie, and its trade union representatives was hailed as a significant innovation in this respect. The agreement specified that: 'The management recognizes the trade union representatives as a means of expression and representation by the workers, without this provision modifying the functions given by the law to the personnel delegates and the staff committee.'

[2] See a report of the Club Jean Moulin in the *Cahiers de la République,* January-February 1962, p. 63.

[3] R. Jacques: 'Pour une approche syndicale du Plan', *Esprit,* July-August 1961.

[4] It would be premature to expect the CGT to make any constructive proposals in this field for the time being. But this does not mean necessarily that it will not follow tacitly such agreements, or others, if they are generally

participated at all levels in the preparation of the Plan and the Confederation has drafted an 'Economic and Social Plan' which sets out its position on planning in general.[1] One of its Confederal Secretaries went on record during the Union's Congress in November 1961 as saying: 'There are scarcely any Governments who can propose an increase of 24 per cent in the national income in four years. The presence of the confederation's representatives in the official bodies dealing with the Plan has made it possible to defend the interests of its members.'[2] This participation by the leaders was attacked by a minority group as being too enthusiastic. But the motives of the critics appear to have been largely determined by political considerations and, in particular, by their hostility to the Fifth Republic in general. The existence of the High Planning Council was welcomed by the leadership as offering the possibility of organizing annual 'economic and social round table conferences' where, among other things, problems of wages and salaries could be discussed. More recently, the attitude of the Confederation has hardened, possibly as a consequence of the strong opposition to the Fourth Plan by the Socialist Party in the ratification debate in the National Assembly and the Senate.[3]

A number of ideas for implementing an incomes policy have been put forward by a prominent member of the UNR (Union pour la Nouvelle République), the majority party in the National Assembly, Mr Chalandon, a banker by profession.[4] Mr Chalandon notes that there is a contradiction between achieving a Plan for rapid growth and full employment, and the existence of freedom for incomes to follow the laws of supply and demand. The difficulties associated with a policy which sets out to determine increases in incomes in accordance with productivity gains by branches, or firms, are insurmountable if only because of the mass of small firms which

accepted by the other trade unions. Certain non-Communist members of the CGT have actively participated in the debates on democratic planning to which we turn in the next chapter and have made no secret of their acceptance of a certain discipline as regards wages and salaries if some arrangements were made for other categories of incomes and if other changes in the Plan are envisaged.

[1] See 'Plan économique et social. Force Ouvrière', presented the 7th Congress, November 1961.

[2] M. Babau, 7th Congress, November 1961.

[3] Cf. Chapter X, it will be recalled that the Socialists and the Communists were the only two political parties to vote against the Fourth Plan. The CGT-FO had approved it in both of the debates in the Economic and Social Council.

[4] Cf. in particular his articles in *La Vie Française*, May 26, 1961, and *Le Monde*, May 30 and 31, 1962.

would have to be excluded from such an arrangement. 'The only reasonable solution is . . . to fix a ceiling and a floor for wages when the Plan is drafted, and to revise both of them at regular intervals.'[1] But if rises in wages and salaries in firms with a high increase in productivity are kept below that rate, then profits benefit. The existence of monopolistic tendencies in industry holds out little hope of seeing selling prices fall. So 'discipline for wages calls for a discipline for profits'.[2] A solution would be to allocate the part of profits arising out of the working of an incomes policy to a special Fund whose management would be confided to the professional association of the branch. The firm would pay interest on the money set aside in this way but would retain full freedom to use it in the business so that its expansion would not be hampered. The Fund could be used progressively to supplement pensions for retired workers or to raise the incomes of less favoured groups. In this way, the workers would secure a share, and an interest, in the prosperity of the firm. An active price policy by the Government would be required also. This would not exclude direct control of prices, but it would be preferable to stimulate competition where it is lacking and to reduce tariffs so as to bring pressure to bear on recalcitrant employers.

In this scheme, the upper and lower limits to wage and salary increases would be fixed by discussion and agreement between the representatives of the State, the employers and the workers. The elements taken into account in fixing these limits at regular intervals would be the current economic situation, the objectives of the Plan and the changes in other factors entering into living standards. Such a policy would call for a radical transformation in the habits of trade unionists and employers. 'For the unions, it implies reversing a long tradition of combat, thanks to which they have improved the living standards of those whose interests they defend . . . , for the employers (it means) giving up progressively exclusive possession of certain information which has always seemed to them to be their most sacred right.'[3]

The majority of the members of the UNR party do not seem to be disposed to go along with M. Chalandon in his proposals. The predominant tendency in the party is that represented by Mr Debré, who was Prime Minister from 1958 to 1962, and whose ideas are reflected much more in the philosophy and strategy set out in the text of the Fourth Plan and which we have already analysed.

[1] *Le Monde*, May 31, 1962.
[2] *Ibid.*
[3] *Ibid.*

In all these discussions, the employers' representatives have observed a prudent silence. We shall have to consider their general attitude to the Plan in the next chapter, but it may be noted here that, so far, they have agreed to participate in the meetings of the High Planning Council and the President of the French Employers' Federation has extended a carefully phrased welcome to the idea that the Council's regular meetings should be a forum for a discussion of incomes. 'To ensure that social progress continues to be achieved as steadily as possible and that the inevitable recessions which are associated with inflation are avoided, it will be a good thing to organize every six months, instead of every four years, a fair appreciation of the opportunities opened up by economic growth and to explain them to the country.'[1]

(b) *Agreement at the Level of the Firm*

The distinction made earlier between the two levels at which an incomes policy could be applied is a useful expositional device but it should not obscure the fact that the two approaches are often put forward jointly and are not, therefore, mutually exclusive. M. Chalandon's proposals, which were analysed in the preceding paragraph, illustrate this.

Complementary arrangements which would at one and the same time secure the objectives of an income policy and notably reinforce the weapons at the disposal of the authorities for achieving the output objectives of the Plan have been inspired by the example of the fiscal quasi-contracts discussed in Chapters XI and XIV.[2]

The scope for an extension of the quasi-contract scheme is offered by the fairly heavy concentration of employment in a few large businesses despite the large numbers of small firms in French industry.[3] If, so the argument runs, the wages policy of these firms can be controlled, the others will be unable to refuse to follow their example.

The quasi-contracts concluded between the State and each firm would cover all the existing objectives of the Plan—investment, types of production, exports, plant location and so on—and would also have a social content. These objectives would not have to be specified in exact quantitative terms. As we saw earlier, the Plan operates at

[1] M. Villiers, *Bulletin du Patronat Français*, November 1961. The High Planning Council will meet twice a year as from 1963.

[2] An echo of these proposals, of civil service and trade union origin, can be found in an article by G. Mathieu in *Le Monde*, September 14, 1962.

[3] *Statistiques et Etudes Financières*, March 1961. (Only 4,302 firms pay over 52 per cent of wages in the private sector.)

the branch, not the firm, level.[1] But annual conversations between the General Planning Commissariat or the Technical directorates of the Ministries and each firm would reveal clearly whether the objectives assigned to the branch were being respected or not. The firm would be obliged to maintain its increases in wages and salaries within two limits; the upper one would comprise a weighted average of the level of productivity in the branch and of the general increase in national productivity for the economy as a whole, but special cases could be allowed for and the precise formula would need to be worked out in practice. The lower limit would take as a guide-line the growth in overall productivity. Collective bargaining between the employers and the trade union representatives would be obligatory but would take place within these limits. In exchange, the State would offer a number of special advantages including those already in existence but, in addition, the nationalized banking sector would be called upon to give priority to such firms in allocating credits.

The practical applications of all these suggestions cannot be expected for some time. In approaching the matter of income distribution, the French Plan is taking up one of the thorniest problems for economic policy. But a start has been made. In this summary, however, we have already broached the question of making changes in the Planning mechanism itself, which forms the subject of the next chapter.

II. THE OPEN ECONOMY

The Plan will have to take account increasingly from now on of the new international context created by the entry into force of the Treaty of Rome.[2] It is the hope and intention of all those in France who attach value to the planning experiment that the influence shall not be all one way but opinions differ as to the degree to which it will be desirable, or possible, to maintain the essential elements of the Plan. An ex-Prime Minister, M. Pflimlin, has declared that

[1] Cf. Chapter XIV.

[2] The problem acquires some perspective when it is recalled that the Dutch Plan, for example, has to accommodate itself to a total volume of imports and exports of goods and services which is slightly higher than the volume of Gross National Product. In the United Kingdom, the corresponding figure is less than 50 per cent, whereas in France it is only one-third, although it has been rising rapidly in recent years. It should be added, however, that comparisons of this kind illustrate only one aspect of the questions which arise in connection with economic integration.

'we shall either have to give up real planning, or consider planning at the European level.'[1] This view differs notably from the more pragmatic solutions suggested in the text of the Fourth Plan itself. Also it should be borne in mind that opinions differ in France as to the proper approach to the problems of integration. Thus the ideas put forward by the supporters of 'supranational' European solutions in the planning field have not failed to provoke a riposte from those who incline towards the concept of 'Europe of States' of which General de Gaulle has spoken.

To the Anglo-Saxon observer, these debates may appear rather unreal and hardly the business of practical policy making. Such a view may well be excessively short-sighted. Again, the prospect of a weakening of national planning efforts as international economic integration gathers speed, is perhaps welcome to those who are hostile to planning in any case. But it may yet be necessary to have recourse to a coherent and conscious effort to guide the development of the European economy, which is what planning is about, in order to affront the multiple stresses and strains which will arise from the new style open economy now being built in Western Europe. But before looking at the state of the debate in France on this aspect of international integration policy, it is preferable to review the relations between the Plan and the traditional problem of international trade.

1 *The Traditional Problem*

The Fourth Plan is a good example of the difficulties met with in fitting international economic relations into a national development Plan. Although the thought of the Common Market was never far from the minds of those responsible for the Fourth Plan, as previous chapters have sought to show, the solutions adopted follow traditional lines, with the exception of agriculture. This proposition can be illustrated by looking in turn at the procedure used for making projections, the strategy in the Plan for foreign trade and the question of maintaining economic balance.

(a) In making *projections of foreign trade*, an obvious, yet fundamental, fact is that, whereas imports can be assumed to bear some, not too unstable, relation to the growth of internal demand, which in turn can be projected with a certain degree of confidence, the same is not the case for exports. Their value depends upon a number of unknown variables such as the rate of growth of foreign markets, relative movements in competitive positions and changes in taste, which can only be estimated very approximately. We saw in

[1] *Entreprise*, July 14, 1962.

an earlier chapter[1] what solutions were adopted by the planning technicians to deal with these matters.

An additional handicap the technicians laboured under in all their work on foreign trade for the Fourth Plan, and which affected estimates of imports as much as those of exports, was the unknown impact of the devaluation and trade liberalization measures decided at the end of 1958. Such a sharp break in trend is notoriously difficult to allow for. Data before 1958 were not a valid guide as French prices had not been competitive for some years and, as a result, imports had had to be controlled. The sharp divergencies in some instances between the forecasts made by the SEEF and the estimates of the Vertical Planning Commissions must be attributed in part to this situation. The Fifth Plan should not suffer from the same disadvantage and, with a few years of more stable trading conditions behind them, the experts will have a more solid basis upon which to build. The statistical programme referred to in Chapter XVI should also contribute to improving projections in future.

In the last analysis, though, it would probably be illusory to expect too much from this very necessary progress in factual knowledge and from a more sophisticated use of it. French foreign trade may not go through the same violent transformation as in the recent past, but other changes are continuing in tariff policy—both inside and outside the Common Market, itself now an area whose frontiers are uncertain—and in the relations between France and her ex-colonial territories.

(b) These hard facts of life can be palliated to a certain extent by an appropriate *strategy for foreign trade.*

One element in such a strategy is making provision for adequate safety margins. Of course, existing international arrangements for providing short-term credits when countries experience temporary balance of payment difficulties, provide a safety net against some unexpected event upsetting the balance of the external accounts. But although such arrangements can, and should, make it possible for a country to avoid taking restrictive action in the face of unfavourable trends of this type, it is necessary to envisage something more definite in the Plan itself. In the Fourth Plan, the estimates of exports, apart from those for agricultural products, were generally rather below what the producers themselves expected, just as the import data were rather higher. Also it is likely that the balance of payments projections of the Fourth Plan were designed to leave a current account surplus over and above the one required to give

[1] Cf. Chapter VII.

assistance to underdeveloped areas and to cover repayment of debt. And, of course, France's foreign exchange reserves had to be built up again.

A further element of a strategy for foreign trade is the application of measures designed to strengthen the structure of the national production potential. The Fourth Plan noted the high foreign currency cost of fixed capital investment in plant and equipment in France which it attributed to the insufficient development of certain branches of the French capital goods industry.[1] The procedure known as quasi-contracts which we examined in Chapter XIV is designed for use in this field in an attempt to encourage the production in France of a wider range of capital equipment. This does not exhaust the measures taken or envisaged by the Plan to improve foreign trade, but we need not repeat what was said earlier as regards tourism, maritime transport and agriculture.

Both of these solutions—providing for safety margins and attempting to strengthen the national production potential by selective measures—raise problems for the future. The first amounts to fixing national growth targets at a level which underestimates real growth possibilities. Moreover, if a number of major countries set out to achieve balance of payments surpluses a potentially dangerous deflationary influence would be introduced into the world economy. The second depends upon the possibility of using selective policies which may prove not to be compatible with a process of harmonizing economic policy as international economic integration proceeds.

(c) As to maintaining *external balance,* the major considerations are avoiding a return to inflationary conditions and ensuring, in particular, the growth of incomes and productivity. We have discussed the present stage of policy on incomes in the first part of this chapter and shall not return to it here.

2 *The New Style Open Economy*

The Treaty of Rome foresees a progressive, but rapid, abolition of tariffs between member countries and the setting-up of a common external tariff. Freedom of movement for capital and manpower will be practically complete. At the same time, a number of common rules and institutions come into operation for the whole area of the Community.[2]

The essential feature of this programme, from the point of view

[1] A sector whose growth-rate during the 1950s was slower than in the rest of industry. Cf. Introduction, p. 26.

[2] The details of the working of the Common Market have been spelt out in several publications. The most complete is by J. F. Deniau: *The Common Market,* Third Edition, Barrie and Lockliff, 1962.

which concerns us here, is that the various national economies will become wide open in relation to each other with practically no possibility for resort to traditional weapons of economic policy, such as a devaluation and/or the use of quantitative controls on imports, in the case of external imbalance. The Rome Treaty foresees co-operation among its members as regards short-term fluctuations, including the granting of temporary financial assistance. In the main, though, it is hoped that continued co-operation and 'good neighbourliness' in general will iron out unwelcome disparities between the economic situations in the member countries. As to the longer term, agriculture is in a special category as there is to be a common agricultural policy which, in the nature of things, cannot help taking account of longer-term considerations. For the rest, though, there are no provisions at present for anything which resembles a co-ordination of development policies, just as there is nothing in the Rome Treaty against such a policy being instituted. The question as to whether there should be such provisions is very much in the air in the Common Market headquarters as well as in the capitals of the individual member countries at the present time. M. Marjolin, Vice-Chairman of the Common Market executive, has referred to it in the following terms: 'Beyond differences in the methods and degrees of refinement of forecasts, all national [planning] efforts have in common the attempt to understand the problems facing us. I have no hesitation in saying that a similar attempt is no less necessary for the Common Market as a whole then it is for the individual firm.'[1] Since then events have moved fast and, in October 1962, the Common Market Commission made specific proposals for a co-ordination of development programmes among the six Member countries.

What is the scope of the problem to be dealt with and what lines of approach to a solution are being proposed in France?

(a) *Scope of the Problem*

It can be seen at different levels: the national, the sectorial and the regional. Together they raise the whole question of the degree to which differentiation in national policies is desirable or will be possible.

At the national level, the matter can be put in its simplest terms by imagining a national economy inside an integrated pluri-national economic space, with the rules of the Common Market in full

[1] Speech to the Congress of the French *Confédération Nationale de la Mutualité, de la Co-opération et du Crédit Agricoles*, reported in *Le Monde*, May 27 and 28, 1962.

operation. Clearly the rate of growth of the national economy in question is related to the rate of growth of its environment. In other words, the maximum likely growth of exports, which depends, other things being equal, upon the rate of growth of foreign markets, governs the permissible growth of imports which, in turn, is related to the rate of growth of internal demand. Although there is nothing startlingly new in this state of affairs, dependence upon the growth of foreign markets when economic frontiers are practically non-existent becomes much closer than in the past, all the more so if trade is heavily concentrated inside the Common Market, as is the case for France, 45 per cent of whose foreign trade is with that area.[1] It is highly unlikely that marked divergencies in growth-rates inside the Common Market can continue for long, at least in the main countries, without balance of payments difficulties arising.

At the sector level, not all branches of activity are influenced to the same extent by economic integration. But it should be recalled that it is not sufficient to define 'sensitive' sectors solely with reference to the existing scale of foreign trade in their products or services. With freedom of movement for factors of production also, i.e. capital and labour, and the liberty granted to nationals of any country in the Common Market to establish themselves anywhere in the area, few forms of activity will be exempt from the repercussions of economic integration.

In the immediate future, nevertheless, some branches will probably be more affected than others. Agriculture is an obvious example where it is difficult to bring about any notable change either in the volume of production or its structure in a short space of time. Moreover, the sociological, not to mention the political, aspects of agricultural problems are arduous to solve, and indeed have not been solved in a satisfactory manner by any of the chief developed countries where expedients have been the rule since the war. Other activities in the basic sectors of the economy—transport, energy and heavy industry such as steel—where production techniques call for the investment of large sums of capital which 'freeze' the structure of productive capacity for long periods, also give rise to numerous difficulties. Competition in these branches is at present much more the result of administrative decisions—public or private—then of free play of market forces. The optimum use of resources, when it is achieved, is consciously organized at the national level and this situation can hardly be expected to change in a pluri-national space.

[1] We ignore possible compensatory effects such as the attraction for direct and portfolio investment from other countries offered by the fast-growing country.

In the consumer goods industries, the trend away from direct control for most activities in favour of decentralized decision-making in the framework of the market meets a wide measure of agreement from planners. But one industry at least raises problems, the production of motor-cars. By its technical structures, it belongs to the group of heavy industries and is subject to the same constraints, though its market conditions are more volatile.

The results of the intensive competition which now reigns on the European market for motor-cars may be lower prices or better value for money which would benefit consumers. They are certain to be increased concentration and a sharp reduction in the number of competing firms in an industry where it is doubtful whether any further significant economies of large-scale production can be reaped. If the only consequence of the present trend was the creation of mammoth undertakings, each capable of earning profits at a very low rate of capacity utilization, it would be difficult to conclude that scarce resources for investment were being used to the best advantage.

The regional problem is to some extent similar. At the present time, the economic geography of Western Europe shows an increasing concentration of industrial production in certain zones—the Ruhr, the Paris region, the valley of the Po, the Midlands and the Home Counties. The efforts required, not to reverse this process, but merely to prevent the relative and, often, the absolute decline of the population of other regions are already considerable. Moreover, each Government, inside its own frontiers, is more and more committed to an active policy of regional development. There is at least a strong likelihood that the process of international economic integration will stimulate even further the trend to geographical concentration of production and population in the areas where it is already the highest. This would be the case if, for example, a competitive race were to develop between Member countries to persuade industries to establish themselves on their respective territories.

(b) *Solutions Proposed*

It would be premature indeed to suggest that any fully satisfactory answers to the questions just enumerated have been found. There is not even any general acceptance in all Member countries of the Common Market for the thesis that its working-out is likely to give rise to problems of this kind. The subject is 'in the air'—the programme put forward in the autumn of 1962 by the Common Market Commission attests this—but for the moment, in France—perhaps because a well-established planning mechanism exists there, the debate has begun to assume importance as a key issue of public policy.

The general proposition that the existence of the Common Market calls for a spread of some sort of planning techniques which, given the relatively long history behind the French experiment, could well start by the adoption of methods similar to those used in France, wins wide approval. We noted that, during the ratification debate in Parliament on the Fourth Plan, all the political parties, except the Communist Party whose position is rather a special case, supported some kind of a European plan. But, as it is coming to be realized, there are dangers in such an attitude. To invoke the solution of international planning can become a universal panacea which dispenses those who propose it from acting themselves. Fortunately, this attitude is not a common one and an increasing number of persons are conscious of the fact that the time for general declarations of principle is past and the moment for specific solutions to practical problems has arrived.

The main tendencies of present thinking on these matters can be grouped under the following headings: a national policy of safeguards, the generalization of indicative growth policies, the elaboration of active planning techniques. Of course, progress need not be limited to one only of these lines of approach.

A policy of safeguards is one the Fourth Plan adopted and which the Fifth Plan will no doubt have to follow. Prudent hypotheses as to growth prospects abroad will be combined with provision for a comfortable external surplus 'in case' any untoward events occur. But such devices, apart from the fact that the need for them diminishes the value of the experiment in international integration itself and runs the risk of creating another type of international imbalance, can hardly be considered sufficient to cope with the problems that are being met.

A different line of approach is to encourage the adoption by all the main trading partners, at least by those in the Common Market, of policies for rapid and sustained economic growth. At this level of analysis, methods employed to achieve this are of minor importance. It is the result—a reasonable certainty of securing a high growth-rate in the other Member countries—that counts. There are sufficient signs that this is happening today to justify a certain optimism on this score. In 1960, there were national planning offices in only two Western European countries—France and the Netherlands. In 1962, there were six of them.[1] The existence of national planning efforts, unless they are to be entirely vain, which is improbable, should

[1] France, Netherlands, Belgium, United Kingdom, Italy, Spain.

itself do something to ensure that growth is more rapid in future in countries where previously it was slow, for example in the United Kingdom. From there, it is only a step to envisaging that these national bodies will have some contact with each other—as indeed they have already—and that exchanges of information on targets, problems and methods will develop.[1]

Insofar as high growth targets are adopted by each country, the eventual appearance of a dilemma for any one country faced with a choice between achieving its own optimum growth-rate and not respecting the provisions of the Treaty of Rome, would be rendered more remote. But this situation, although it offers great advantages, does not constitute a fully satisfactory answer to the question: what is to become of the more active, purposive aspects of national planning?

The means used to implement the French Plans are—the public sector apart—largely indirect; they incite rather than they coerce. They imply, nevertheless, a wide use of fiscal and monetary policies to encourage certain types of activity, or particular firms. The system of quasi-contracts, of access to credit through the capital market or the Credit National and other specialized credit institutions, the measures to discourage firms from setting themselves up, or extending their activities, in the Paris region, the encouragements given to firms going to the less-developed regions, all these are examples of the active and selective use of policy measures to achieve the Plan. Will it be possible to maintain them in an integrated European economy, not to mention the proposals put forward for differentiating much more than at present economic policy in relation to the Plan, which we touched on in connection with income policy and to which we return to in the next chapter?

An advocate of integration and supranationality, M. Pflimlin—who has already been quoted—sees the eventual elaboration of a common development policy as taking place in three stages. 'Firstly, there would be a drafting stage which would be confided to the official organs of the Community. Then would follow a common decision by Member Governments, on the basis of proposals made by the Community, as to the direction to be given to the European economy. The third stage would be the application of the policy, and here each Government would be free to choose the means of implementation it preferred.'[2] The question which this outline leaves

[1] 'The tendency is for certain Western countries to set up Planning Commissariats or Planning Councils which could become the correspondents of the French General Planning Commissariat.' P. Massé, talk at the Economic Institute, Dublin, April 1962, p. 25.

[2] Interview in *Entreprise*, July 14, 1962.

unanswered is whether the third stage would be possible. Elsewhere in the same article, M. Pflimlin expresses his preference for an empirical approach which would avoid sterile debates on ideology as 'after all, we cannot exclude the hypothesis that, inside the Community, one country will have a Socialist Government and another a Liberal one'.

Other commentators have felt the need to point out the possibility of a conflict between the aims, and methods used to achieve them, of a single country, and the functioning of the Common Market. 'There is no contradiction between national planning and participation in an international grouping which adopts a planned policy. . . . On the other hand, it is difficult to conceive of the integration of a national Plan with a Common Market based upon strictly liberal principles and an absence of public policy interventions, the economy being left to the working-out of market laws only. In such a case, economic progress would tend to be located in those countries—and, inside each country, in those regions—whose development is already further advanced than elsewhere.'[1] A similar opinion has been expressed by the Club Jean Moulin: 'If it turned out that the forces, whether public or private, which are hostile to any European planning have the last word and are strong enough to stop any concerted European approach to structural and short-term economic problems, then France would have to choose between calling into question the Rome Treaty and giving up any effective planning of her own economic development.'[2]

Grafted on to this debate is a further consideration as to the form which an internationally planned policy would take. M. Pflimlin, in the text quoted earlier, favoured a 'supranational' type of solution where the initiative would be with the organs of the Community. This approach is the one which the European Coal and Steel Community has attempted to apply, with little success. The Common Market, as it has functioned so far, has followed the opposite policy according to which the Member States retain full initiative. The agreement on the common agricultural policy in January 1962, as

[1] P. Mendès-France: *La République Moderne*, Gallimard, 1962, p. 133.

[2] 'La Planification Démocratique', by the Club Jean Moulin in the *Cahiers de la République*, January-February 1962, p. 68. The Club Jean Moulin—named after a French leader and martyr of the Resistance Movement—is a confidential grouping of co-opted members whose action resembles that of the Fabian Society. It publishes in the name of the Club studies on questions of current policy—political, economic and social. Its members include senior civil servants, university teachers, trade unionists, members of the liberal professions, representatives of private business and members of the armed forces.

regards the respective rôles played in those negotiations by the Member Governments and the organs of the Community, illustrates this. Consequently, it has been objected by those who reject a supranational solution that the responsibility for initiative in the field of a European development policy must remain where it is now, that is, with national Governments. A trade union leader, and the Vice-Chairman of the Planning and Investment Section of the Economic and Social Council has insisted on the fact that: 'None of the technical and political conditions required for democratic planning exist, or can be created at present at the level of the Europe of the Six.'[1]

We shall describe the policies suggested by the advocates of 'democratic planning' in the next chapter. Meanwhile, the French authorities are pursuing their policy as concerns integration along the two lines—national and sectorial—which were announced in the text of the Fourth Plan: 'The Government considers that, in expressing the hope that a co-ordination of investments, the procedure for which could be inspired by the French example, can begin inside the Common Market, they are adopting a positive attitude. This preoccupation could be applied as a first step in those sectors where the risks of over-investment are the most evident.'[2]

[1] P. Le Brun: 'Planification Démocratique, Direction moderne et Marché Commun.', *Le Monde*, August 17, 1962.
[2] *Op. cit.*, p. 36.

CHAPTER XVIII

THE PLAN AND OPINION

Opposition to the concept of planning itself is rare today in France. If such critics exist, they are seldom vocal. The target for criticism is rather particular aspects of the Plan. Still it would be incorrect to conclude that the Plan has achieved a general consensus which overcomes the divergencies between group interests in contemporary French society. The Plan, as it exists now, is the result of a certain balance of social forces and there are limits to its possible transmutation without a decisive shift in that balance. But its frontiers are neither immutable nor sharply defined. They can be, and have been, modified by the foresight and initiative, sometimes of a single man, sometimes of a small group of like minds. Moreover, the interests which the various groups in society represent are not all articulate in the same degree nor are they always clear themselves on the objectives they are seeking or the means of achieving them. Thus new solutions can appear, and be accepted, which seem unexpected to an outside observer only to the extent that the state of flux in opinion which characterizes all modern societies, and the general search for appropriate institutional forms to cope with new and unusual problems, have been underestimated.

The main line of cleavage in France at the present time is the one which separates the advocates of the 'concerted economy' (l'économie concertée) from those whose preferences go towards 'democratic planning'. There are free-shooters at the frontier who it is sometimes difficult to classify under one or the other of these labels, but the distinction is, nevertheless, pretty firmly marked. Because the debate on the Plan is dominated by this issue, it should be examined first before considering the concrete proposals for amending the Plan which can be grouped under the three headings—approval, drafting, and application.

I. CONCERTED ECONOMY OR DEMOCRATIC PLANNING?

(1) The idea of *concerted economy* has the longer history behind it. A rather fastidious search for legitimation has tracked down a somewhat similar use of the term in a draft of the First Plan itself so that, according to one version of the concerted economy, France was, like

Monsieur Jourdain, practising concertation for years without knowing it. But, more recently, the expression has been given a much wider and more precise implication by some writers.[1]

'It is a régime where the representatives of the State (or the local units of government) and those of firms (whatever their status [employers or workers]) meet together, in an organized fashion, to exchange information, to confront their forecasts and to take decisions or to draft recommendations for the Government.'[2] The advantages of, and need for, such arrangements derive from a number of factors. Firstly, there is the increasing difficulty for the individual firm to adapt itself with sufficient speed to rapid changes in techniques of production and in markets without a supplement of external information. Secondly, there is no longer any clear-cut division between the State and the productive sector; the State is also a producer of goods and services and its financial relationships with the private sector are more and more complex. Thirdly, as opposed to those who continue to think that the less the State knows, the better it will be for everyone, the lucidity of Governments is the best guarantee of the real liberty of those they govern. 'The civil servant who is ill-informed, and therefore hesitant, is necessarily inquisitorial, suspicious and fiddling . . . a public administration which is well informed knows what it wants and how to get it. It can make its intentions or wishes precise well in advance and it can then leave to the people it administers a great deal of initiative and responsibility in meeting them.'[3] Finally, the best way of 'depolitizing' exchanges of information, forecasts and projects between Governments and firms is to ensure that the technical aspect dominates the tactical 'so that these exchanges become as impervious to shifts in the political climate as possible'.[4]

The value of the Plan as a framework for systematic comparisons of different viewpoints is now fully accepted on the employers' side in France. But even those employers who have supported consistently the planning experiment view with some misgiving the notable increase in the consultation procedures at all levels which is now taking place. A fair expression of their opinion would probably be to say that they consider that the 'big step forward' which has been taken with the Fourth Plan has brought the planning experi-

[1] In particular by M. Bloch-Lainé, Director General of the Caisse des Dépôts et Consignations (c.f. Chapter III) and by M. Chalandon whose ideas on income policy were noted in the previous chapter.

[2] Fr Bloch-Lainé: *A la recherche d'une économie concertée*, Editions de l'Epargne, 1959, p. 5.

[3] *Ibid.*, p. 9.

[4] *Ibid.*, p. 10.

ment to the limit, for the time being, of what is desirable and practicable. In any case, as a leading French industrialist put it to the writers, there would be a mortal danger for the whole planning mechanism if the Plan were to become 'a place for show-downs'.

Other variations on the theme of the concerted economy go well beyond the practice of the Plan today, however. For M. Chalandon, it implies 'formulating a doctrine which attempts to go beyond the contradiction between capitalism and Communism'.[1] But for an ex-Minister of Industry, the immediate and concrete utility of the concept remains that it entails a permanent dialogue between the Government, the employers and the workers. 'I consider that the simple virtue of such a circulation of ideas would make it possible to improve a great many things. But I did not say it would simplify them.'[2] This being so, it is not surprising that those who wish to introduce changes in the planning system have sought out an alternative expression to describe their attempts to re-define the problem. 'The idea of the concerted economy flourishes mostly on the right; the idea of democratic planning flourishes mostly on the left. The former, it is said, pleases the intelligent Conservative; the latter the non-extremist reformers.'[3] But there is more than a difference of fashion between the two concepts. As is usual in these things, those who are seeking to transform the system are more vocal than those who view with some disquiet the changes which have already taken place. Our account, in the rest of this chapter, of the various ideas which have been expressed should be read with this point in mind.

(2) *Democratic planning* has been the theme of a great deal of study in the last two years. At the end of 1961, the most substantial analysis yet to appear in French of the possible futures open to the Plan was published by the Club Jean Moulin.[4] It was followed in March 1962 by a Colloquium organized in Paris by a group of trade unionists (all

[1] A. Chalandon: Une 3ème voie, l'économie concertée, *Jeune Patron,* December 1960.

[2] J.-M. Jeanneney—Espoirs et difficultés d'une économie concertée, *Jeune Patron,* January 1961. M. Jeanneney, Professor of Economics at the University of Paris, was Minister of Industry from 1958 to 1962 before becoming French Ambassador to Algeria.

[3] Fr. Bloch-Lainé: Economie Concertée et planification démocratique. *Cahiers de la République,* July 1962, p. 573.

[4] Cf. 'La Planification Démocratique', *Cahiers de la République,* December 1961, and January/February 1962. A background note on the Club Jean Moulin is given in a footnote to page 332 in Chapter XVII.

the three confederations being represented), politicians (from the MRP—Catholic Party—the Socialists and the PSU—a Socialist minority group of which M. Mendès-France is a member), representatives of the CNJA—the minority group in the farmers' union—the Jeunes Patrons—a minority group in the French employers' federation—and several university teachers.[1]

'Planning can be considered to be democratic when the two following series of conditions have been fulfilled:

> 'The active participation of the citizens, by their representatives, in the drafting, execution and control of the Plans. This means not only that there must be broad agreement between citizens as to the ends of each Plan, but a general consensus on the finality of economic activity. Without that agreement and participation, it is difficult to see how the needed discipline of the Plan can be imposed.
>
> 'The direction of production so as to satisfy in priority the basic social needs: education, health, old age, housing, town planning, equality of opportunity for all, a harmonization of incomes as between social groups.'[2]

This broad programme, although it would have been accepted by and large by all those who actively support the movement for democratic planning, allows for many nuances as to its exact content. Thus, for some people, democracy in planning is a way of giving new life to political democracy itself. 'Democratic planning can offer the political parties the opportunity of renewing themselves and of showing their usefulness in a particularly striking way.'[3] For others the decentralization of the Plan, through its programmes for regional development, with adequate participation of local interests, is seen as a means of creating the grass roots of democracy and of reacting against a too highly centralized administrative system.[4]

But there are clearly dangers in attributing to a name all the virtues which one wishes to see incarnated in society without envisaging the practical content of a programme destined to achieve it. This is a trap of which the majority of the participants in the debates on

[1] A summary of part of the debates was published in the *Cahiers de la République*, June 1962.
[2] Report of Commission No. 2 to the Colloquium on Democratic Planning, March 1962.
[3] M. Gazier—ex-Minister and Member of the Socialist Party. *Cahiers de la République*, June 1962, p. 496.
[4] Club Jean Moulin: *L'Etat et le Citoyen*, Editions du Seuil, 1961, Chapter IV, 'La Décentralisation, rêve d'intellectuels ou nécessité pour la démocratie?'

democratic planning were aware and they have succeeded, on the whole, in avoiding it.

II. APPROVING THE PLAN

Well before the final draft of the Fourth Plan was ready at the end of 1961, the problem of how to associate Parliament more satisfactorily with the planning mechanism had been thoroughly aired and, as we saw in Chapter X, the Parliamentary onslaught on the Plan in this respect was rather a shadow fight as the Government had already undertaken to introduce radical changes in the procedure to be used for the Fifth Plan.

This was a theme which could rally unanimous support among the political parties, whatever their tendency, and indeed appeared to many an opportunity to redress in the eyes of public opinion their rather battered reputation of recent years. It was difficult to conceal a certain embarrassment, though, in many attacks on the undemocratic character of the Plan in view of the notable lack of interest of the parties in the past for planning matters.[1] The principle of adequate consultation of Parliament having been accepted, what remains is nevertheless the essence of the problem, that is how to put it into practice.

We have already discussed in Chapter XVI the work being done at the present time by the General Planning Commissariat on this question. Besides, a number of other proposals have been put forward. The main one is summarized in the formula: 'one Government, one Legislature, one Plan'. Another concerns the rôle of a new-style Economic and Social Council.

The case for linking more closely the fate of the Plan to the fate of the Ministry has been put most clearly by Professor Duverger. 'The Plan is not only an economic programme. Whether we like it or not, it is the programme for action by the nation, the framework for its life, and the rhythm of the Plan should be the rhythm of the life of the nation as a whole. If we want democratic planning, the nation must be able to appoint at one and the same time the people who are going to complete the drafting of the Plan and are going to apply it during most of its duration. And in the end, judging the results of the Plan, the nation is going to repeat the same process by means of fresh elections, and to send Parliament and the Government

[1] Political parties as divergent in their programmes as the Centre National des Indépendants, the Radicals, the MRP (Catholics) and Socialists were unanimous in calling for more consultation of Parliament on all aspects of the Plan but, in particular, on the initial policy choices.

back for another period of the same length.'[1] The importance of this aspect of the question for a French audience is easily understandable. An ex-Planning Commissaire General, M. Hirsch, had put the question in a striking way when he declared that, in thirteen years of office, he had had to deal with twenty-six Governments.[2] His plea for more stability in political life was echoed by M. Mendès-France and by the majority of those present at the Colloquium.[3]

Less unanimity was achieved, however, as to the institutional changes required to give effect to the programme for democratic planning. A solution which appeared seductive to some delegates was a reform of the Senate and its amalgamation with the Economic and Social Council to form an 'economic and social' second chamber. It received the support of several delegates—not least M. Mendès-France[4] and Prof. Duverger. The arguments favourable to the reforms were based upon the increasing complexity and range of the activities of the State in the economic field and the difficulty for Parliament to control effectively the work of the Government. Its advocates considered that the dangers of corporatism in such a system could be guarded against, notably by ensuring that the representation in a new-style Economic and Social Council corresponded to the real economic importance of the different sectors and was revised periodically to take account of changes in the relative weight of each group. Also it was proposed that the representation of the interests of consumers should be provided for specifically. Some observers, though, found this distinction between the respective rôles of a 'political' and 'economic' assembly difficult to put into practice.[5]

On the whole this part of the debates was the least fruitful in comparison with discussions of the problems relating to the drafting and application of the Plan. In the end, many participants appeared to share M. Mendès-France's view that too much importance had been given to problems of institutions by many speakers whereas the essence of the problem of improving the planning mechanism lay elsewhere.

[1] Colloquium, *op. cit.*, p. 483.

[2] *Ibid.*, p. 480.

[3] Cf. also P. Mendès-France: 'Each National Assembly will adopt, at the proposal of the Government and a year after its election, a Plan whose execution it will follow up and supervise during the duration of the legislature. . . . Thus the life of Parliament, the Government and of the Plan will coincide.' *La République Moderne*, Gallimard, 1962, p. 88.

[4] See also: *La République Moderne, op. cit.*, Chapter V, 'Représentation Politique et Représentation Economique'.

[5] Colloquium, *op. cit.*, Interventions by M. Leenhardt and M. Hamon, p. 488-9.

III. DRAFTING THE PLAN

The procedures used here have also been the object of public debate. The views expressed can be grouped under three headings: the work of the Planning Commissions, the rôle of the trade unions, the effects of the system of Planning Commissions on competition and business efficiency.

1 *The Planning Commissions*

The conditions in which the Fourth Plan was drafted by the Planning Commissions have been the source of sharp criticism by the trade unions. This rather paradoxical result—for they were invited to participate in their work on a scale never achieved by any of the previous Plans—was due in no small measure to the surprise and frustration felt by many trade unionists when put in contact with Commissions and their Working Groups. The experience, the first surprise being overcome, has been a salutory one and has led many trade unionists to reflect on planning matters in relation to the rôle which they could, and should, play in it.[1]

'The trade unionists expected that the subjects discussed would be employment, wages and protection of workers, whereas, in fact, the main points in the debates were production, markets and investments.'[2] Hence an initial obstacle. A second, and one which was less in the nature of things, concerned the type of data put before the Commissions, notably as regards costs of production and investment plans. 'We soon noticed that the employers often took refuge behind the need for business secrets by saying: You cannot put that question about our forecasts of production, or sales, or foreign trade because they are confidential and we cannot give them to you because our competitor is sitting there next to you in this room and he will learn them as well. We can only give global figures but we cannot enter into details.'[3]

The attitude of many trade unionists proceeded in part, no doubt, from a misunderstanding of the nature of the work done by the Planning Commissions. For many of them, the 'adjustment' of targets to render them coherent with the overall scheme ought to have implied the exercise of a power of arbitration to impose decisions on private firms, whereas, as we say earlier,[4] such is not the practice of French planning outside the public sector.

[1] Cf. E. Descamps: Secretary General of the CFTC, *Socialisme et Planification, Les Cahiers du Centre d'Etudes Socialistes*, 1962.
[2] G. Ducaroy: *Planification, Socialisme et Démocratie, Perspectives Socialistes*, February 1961, p. 5.
[3] E. Descamps, *op. cit.*, p. 9.
[4] Cf. Chapters VII and IX.

It is interesting in this connection to compare two versions of the same incident during the work of the Vertical Commission for the Transformation Industries, the first by a businessman and Chairman of the Commission, the second by a trade unionist (CFTC) member.

'The Plan implies no obligation and yet it is followed pretty well in a certain atmosphere of liberty which respects private initiative and which, as a result, probably gives the maximum of efficiency to the planning mechanism. But, of course, there are not only bright spots in the picture and I should add that the temptation is great, and we very often meet with it, either from the technocrats or our trade union friends, to make a Plan which is much more rigid. A trade union member of the Commission reproached us bitterly for not having made a serious Plan for the motor-car industry because we had not fixed, for each firm, the models and quantities of each it should produce each year, etc.'[1]

'What is the point in having a forecast of investment needs of X billion francs for the motor-car industry, without at least discussing the distribution by categories of motor-cars, without knowing whether these investments will make it possible to produce a balanced range of models, adapted to likely market outlets, or whether on the contrary they will be used to produce identical, competitive models which will lead to over-capacity.'[2]

This incident illustrates a fundamental divergence between two approaches to the Plan. The first considers that the system must remain on the general, overall level in so far as it studies the whole of the economic life of the country, and that it should not isolate parts of it as would be the case if certain industries were singled out for particular attention. Referring to British experience, a member of the Conseil National du Patronat Français declared: 'There is no question of an organization similar to the Iron and Steel Board which is a body having special links with a particular industry. We consider that the character of our relations with a planning organization limited to a single branch would be quite different. We should have much more serious motives for distrust of a limited Plan than of a Plan for the whole economy, designed to inform us (the employers) and all the other responsible bodies in the country.'[3]

[1] F. de Clinchamps, 'Le Rôle de l'Entreprise privée dans la préparation du Plan', Paper read to a meeting of the CEDES, June 1962.
[2] Colloquium, *Cahiers de la République*, June 1962, p. 477.
[3] M. P. Huvelin, 'Ce que les Chefs d'Entreprises pensent du Plan', Paper read to a meeting of the CEDES, June 1962.

The second seeks on the contrary to accentuate the obligatory character of the Plan in order to achieve certain objectives which would not result from the marginal adjustments implied at present by the Plan in the private sector. For the advocates of this thesis, it is necessary to increase the data at the disposal of the Plan as to the industrial plans of private firms. It has been suggested that all large firms should be obliged to draw up a plan for their activities and to communicate it to the Commissions, perhaps using the professional organization in their branch for this purpose so that data could be centralized by them in the first instance and then sent on anonymously to the Plan.[1] It will be recalled that an analogous reporting procedure is used by the European Coal and Steel Community for investment projects exceeding a certain figure.

A further proposal would make it obligatory for the Commissaire General to consult the Planning and Investment Section of the Economic Social Council each time important arbitrements had to be rendered during the drafting phase of the Plan.[2] When the nature of the 'co-ordination' and 'arbitration' which accompanies the work of the Commissions is considered, however, this idea hardly seems practicable.[3] It would probably cause the whole process to grind to a stop.

2 *The Rôle of the Trade Unions*

A greater degree of participation of trade unionists in the planning mechanism will call for adjustments in attitudes and habits of mind on the trade unions' as well as the employers' sides. As was noted in the previous chapter, the French trade union still has great difficulty in getting itself recognized inside the factory as a representative force. Perhaps in part because of this, 'in France, traditionally, the trade unions only consider themselves to be organs for contesting and claiming. . . . But the question which is raised today is whether that action should not be enlarged and supplemented, and whether there should not be a transformation resulting from current economic trends and the nature of democratic planning itself.'[4] There are signs that this may be happening now.

But, to play a more active rôle, the trade unions have to face the handicaps due to their comparative poverty (there are only some 2,000,000 paying members in France, about half of them with the CGT) and to the lack of preparation of their members for their new

[1] Cf. Club Jean Moulin, *La Planification Démocratique, op. cit.*, p. 39.
[2] Colloquium, Report of Commission No. 1.
[3] See Chapter VII.
[4] M. Mendès-France, Colloquium, *op. cit.*, p. 509.

tasks.[1] Suggestions have been put forward for paid leave from work for further education, for pooling of research facilities between the three confederations and for the supply of data to the trade unionists by the official services to supplement their own resources.[2]

The existing disparity between the numbers of the employers' delegates and those provided by the trade unions is explained very largely by the factors just enumerated. But the question remains whether the object should be to try to reach parity. We noted earlier in this chapter the opinion of the French employers on the need to keep polemics out of the Planning Commissions, whereas the call for parity smacks of precisely that. The matter is not a simple one. It has perhaps been expressed most concisely by M. Bloch-Lainé: 'The attack by the trade unions and the Left-wing parties was not indifferent to the civil servants concerned with the Plan. They asked themselves, with that intellectual honesty which characterizes them, if the investment programmes in the Plan would have been different, had the discussions been different. More precisely, would the four-year programmes for the steel industry, or chemicals, have been changed if the representatives of the workers' organizations, who were theoretically present at the meetings of the Planning Commissions, had been capable of discussing more than they did what the representatives of the professional associations of these two large industries got their leaders to agree to? Personally, I do not believe they would. But I also believe that it is of the highest importance that such a suspicion should be impossible.'[3]

The intentions of the General Planning Commissariat in this field are two-fold. On the one hand, and in conformity with the conviction of the technicians that there is a limit to useful information gathering just as there is a limit to useful planning, the work of some of the Planning Commissions is to be lightened and the detailed studies done by some Working Parties discontinued. The annual meetings of the Planning Commissions from now on will facilitate this. On the other, rather than to seek to increase the number of trade unionists at any cost, it is intended to facilitate the accession of their representatives to posts of Chairman or Rapporteur of certain Planning

[1] The efforts made by the CFTC in this respect during the Fourth Plan preparatory period are described in E. Descamps' *op. cit.* The CFTC sent over two-thirds of the total numbers; the contributions of the CGT and the CGT-FO were much less substantial.

[2] Some of these suggestions are being studied now by the General Planning Commissariat.

[3] Fr Bloch-Lainé: *Cconomie Concertée et Démocratie, op. cit.*, p. 578.

Commissions.[1] Nevertheless, the opportunities for doing this appear to be limited, for some time to come, to Commissions other than those dealing with the private sector.

3 *The Plan and Competition*

A further aspect of the work of the Planning Commissions which has been commented upon by observers outside of France should also be mentioned. It has been suggested that the procedure of the Commissions favours restrictive practices and market sharing and that the rate of advance of each firm is adjusted down to the pace of the average level of performance so that progressive firms are muzzled.[2] But fears of this kind are based largely upon a misconception of the work of the Commissions, when they do not express a certain *parti pris* towards planning in general.

For example, even if the objection raised by an employers' representative to the request by a trade unionist for more details of his firm's output plans, which he quoted on page 340 above, contained an element of special pleading, it is not to be discounted entirely and would seem to indicate a state of mind rather hostile to a pooling of information, which market sharing would imply, than the contrary. Moreover, the presence of civil servants and a few trade unionists in the Commission would not appear conducive to such methods. Private business does not lack more discreet opportunities for reaching agreements on market sharing.[3]

Furthermore, there is no indication that anti-restrictive practice legislation in France is less effective than in other European countries,[4] although it has been suggested that the introduction of anti-trust legislation, on the American model, could be a useful additional arm against abuse of monopolistic power. A possible source of misunderstanding on this point is provided by the comments in the Fourth Plan, quoted in Chapter X, on the need for a further rationalization of production structures in French industry. It should be recalled, though, that not only the giants of French industry—in steel, chemicals and, except for Renault, motor-cars—are smaller than many of their European, and extra-European, com-

[1] Cf. P .Massé: Note addressed to the Colloquium on Democratic Planning and reproduced in the *Cahiers de la République, op. cit.*, p. 459.

[2] Cf., for example, T. Wilson in *Planning: a Business Economists' Conference*, Eyre & Spottiswoode, 1962, p. 37.

[3] Is it necessary to recall once more Adam Smith's verdict on this subject? 'People of the same trade seldom meet together, even for merriment and diversion, but the conversation ends in a conspiracy against the public, or in some contrivance to raise prices.' A Smith: *Inquiry into the Nature and Causes of the Wealth of Nations,* 14th Edition, 1826, p. 128-9.

[4] Cf. P.E.P., *Cartel Policy and the Common Market,* 1962, pp. 220-4.

petitors, but more important still, that many branches of French industry, not least in the capital goods sector, are still made up of a large number of small and medium-sized firms.

Also it would be less than frank not to recognize the spur given in all Western European countries to the rationalization of production structures, and to the constitution of networks of international agreements between firms in the same branch of activity, by the opening of the Common Market. The problem of restrictive practices belongs to a growing extent to the field of international economic policy.[1]

The second issue raised by the criticisms of the eventual restrictive character of the work done by the Planning Commissions is founded upon a misconception as to what this work really consists of. Thus we have tried to show in earlier chapters that the global targets for each branch are not allocated to individual firms, and that the latter are in no way bound to respect any limits on their activities. Moreover, there is no instance of a firm being penalized for 'doing too well'. If it belongs to a branch which is thought to be underdeveloped and which has been set an ambitious growth target, it will be received by the planning authorities with open arms. It is the firm which drags its feet that is likely to get a cold welcome.

In the same way, the fear that progressive firms are kept back by the less-efficient ones, should be seen against the background of the way in which the production 'targets' are fixed. As we saw earlier, the initial target levels are put to the Commissions by the General Planning Commissariat and they are coherent with an overall growth target which is practically bound to be ambitious. If a Commission wished to adopt a lower target, it would have to convince the planners that their initial estimate was unreasonable. Those who have been intimately connected with the planning process on the technical side are unanimous in their opinion that, in the early years, it was the technicians who had to fight to overcome the reticences of many branches of private industry when they contemplated the ambitious growth targets proposed to them.[2] More recently, there have been other examples, such as agriculture and steel, where the planners have joined forces, in the Planning Commissions, with the most dynamic elements in each branch against the less enterprising firms.[3]

[1] See also P. Massé in *Economic Planning in France*, P.E.P., London, 1961.

[2] Cf., for example, E. Hirsch, Colloquium, *op. cit.*, p. 465.

[3] It can be argued, of course, that whereas the planning process favours a high level of investment and capacity utilization, more effective competition between firms calls for a higher margin of spare capacity. However, it is not certain that this second solution achieves a high rate of investment also.

IV. APPLYING THE PLAN

We have noted in earlier chapters the changes which have been introduced, or have come about, with the Fourth Plan as regards applying the Plan.[1] Today, the Plan is subject to a follow-up procedure infinitely more thorough than at any time in the past if one considers the various bodies which are called upon to give their opinion once, and sometimes twice, a year on its execution. Thus, Parliament, the High Planning Council, and the Economic and Social Council all discuss regularly the working-out of the Plan and the Planning Commissions meet each year as well. At the same time, there is a greater cohesion than ever before between the Government departments *vis-à-vis* the objectives of the Plan, in particular between the Ministry of Finance and the other Ministries. As to carrying out the required policy of the Plan, the procedure for operational tranches and decentralized consultations with local interests open up a wide field for future action. In relation to the private sector, the practice of quasi-contracts and the discussions under way with a view to improving the liaison between the credit system and the Plan are signs of the times. It remains, nevertheless, that the Plan contains only a small amount of constraints for the private firm.

Despite, or perhaps because of, these changes, critics of each of these features of the Plan are not lacking. The old debate on the appropriate administrative structures for implementing the Plan has flared up again. The rôle of public ownership is also a theme which merits attention, not so much because of the importance critics of the Plan attach to it but as an illustration of attitudes to the, by now, rather jejeune debate on the imperative or indicative aspects of the Plan. We discuss these two issues first in the following paragraphs before reviewing the proposals of a general nature which have been made for modifying the methods used to apply the Plan.

1 *Administrative Structures*

For one of the rapporteurs to the Colloquium on democratic planning, a concentration of the economic powers of the Government is called for 'to speed up the decisions required to set the Plan in motion and to avoid, when decisions on minor issues are taken, different public departments acting in contradictory manner'.[2] There is a need 'to end the dictatorship' of the Ministry of Finance and this task could be given to a Deputy Prime Minister who would

[1] We shall not return here to the questions of a policy for incomes or the open economy which were discussed in the preceding chapter.

[2] *Colloque pour une Planification Démocratique,* Commission No. 1.

head a group of three or four ministers responsible for economic affairs and would form an inter-ministerial committee with a permanent secretariat. The Planning Commissariat would be attached to this super-minister. This general outline has also been approved by other observers, in particular by M. Mendès-France.[1] The opposite view was expressed energetically by an ex-Commissaire General, M. Hirsch: 'Let us take the example of the Ministry of Finance which is the object of much opprobium. I consider it to be quite unreal because power is always found where the money is and whatever you do, whatever administrative structures are set up, this cannot be avoided. What is required is to convert the Ministry of Finance and show it that the Plan is a good thing. And I must say that, to a very large extent, the success of the Plan is due to the conversion of the Ministry of Finance, a conversion which is very profound, in the same way as we have succeeded in changing radically the outlook of the French businessman.'[2]

The regional aspect of the Fourth Plan has also given rise to many suggestions for the creation of regional assemblies which would participate in drawing up, and in controlling, the execution of the regional development plans.

The intention of the authorities is to use the interdepartmental conferences created for each region.[3] Some suggestions have been put forward which would reinforce the representation of local interests. The most frequent is for the establishment of a network of regional Economic and Social Councils following the pattern of the existing central body of that name and linked to it.[4] But, although this idea enjoys wide acceptance in principle, certain divergences appear when the scope of the powers to be given to these regional Councils are discussed.

'A parallel control of the public administration must be organized at every level. It is indispensable that the preparation of the Plan, its surveillance and execution should be carried out at the regional level. . . . Democratic planning is not possible except to the extent that local and regional life are revivified in our country by giving its representatives real possibilities.[5]

For Prof. Duverger, however, there is a danger in this for: 'If

[1] *La République Moderne, op. cit.*, p. 125.
[2] Colloquium, p. 465.
[3] Cf. Chapter IV.
[4] The report of the Commission No. 2 at the Colloquium on Democratic Planning and Fr Bloch-Lainé: 'Réflexions sur le partage du pouvoir économique', *Promotions*, No. 61, 1962.
[5] Prof. A. Philip, ex-Minister and member of the Socialist Party, Colloquium, *op. cit.*, p. 470.

decisions on regional planning are taken by local committees resembling regional economic councils, I fear that the end result will be regional corporatism which would be a mistake because it would amount to giving the power of decision to the producers and not to the consumers.[1] Other speakers also felt the need to limit the effective degree of decentralization. Thus, for M. Hirsch, there are some decisions that have to be made at the national level although this need not prevent a decentralization of problems of purely local interest.

2 *Nationalizations*

The existing scope of the nationalized sector in France is very extensive, although the main sectors are in heavy industry and transport.[2] Since the early post-war years, when the big wave of nationalization measures took place, the question of further nationalizations has not been a theme for party politics. The Socialist Party, it is true, maintains the principle in its programme but, at election time, it has never been even a minor issue in the campaigns of the Party. The chief reason for this situation is, no doubt, the fact that no majority exists in the country, or seems likely to exist in the near future, favourable to fresh nationalization measures. But the subject did reappear in discussions on the Fourth Plan, and in rather an unexpected manner.

In October 1961, the Prime Minister, M. Debré, announced that 'at the same time as the Fourth Plan is ratified, the Government will ask you to vote certain legislative dispositions . . . in particular a text authorizing the State to substitute itself for private companies when the objectives set out in the Plan, in sectors which are essential for economic expansion and for the Plan's social programme, are not being achieved by private enterprise'.[3] The riposte of the principal organs of business opinion was immediate.[4]

The drafting of the text of the Fourth Plan no doubt reflects this incident as the principle mentioned by the Prime Minister is surrounded by heavy qualifications. 'There remains the more difficult case of creating . . . in an insufficiently developed branch of activity an initiative which does not manifest itself spontaneously . . . the Government will be able to apply the most appropriate measures (to achieve this), either by soliciting the co-operation of the firms in the

[1] *Op. cit.*, p. 470.
[2] Cf. Chapter III.
[3] Quoted in the *Journal des Finances*, October 13, 1961.
[4] Cf. in particular *L'Usine Nouvelle*, October 5, 1961, and the *Journal des Finances*, October 13, 1961.

branch in question, or by provoking the entry into the branch of an already existing firm coming from a neighbouring activity . . . or, finally, by the State taking up a majority or minority holding, on a temporary or permanent basis, in a new company to be set up."[1] It can be concluded that the third possibility mentioned above is unlikely to be used and, in any case, not until the measures opened up by the quasi-contract formula have been exhausted. This incident reveals in a short form the existence of limits to changes in the present system of implementing the Plan in France.

This is not to say that recourse to nationalization has been abandoned by the French Left as a useful policy instrument. But it is striking to note the extent to which the debate is now based upon practical, rather than ideological, considerations and the general recognition that other types of policy measures can often be more effective in implementing the Plan. The rapporteurs to the Colloquium on democratic planning suggested that 'nationalization is necessary for all large private oligopolies where it is clear that they are pursuing political ends'.[2] The authors of the study of the Club Jean Moulin, which has already been quoted, are more explicit. For them, there are three possibilities open to the State under the heading of nationalization: taking up participations in private companies which exist already, taking over certain activities (in particular, housebuilding, where costs are excessively high, and the automobile industry, where experience has shown that the State-owned firm—Renault—is obliged to act as if it was a private company), and setting up new public undertakings (for example, in some of the less-developed regions where the cost of a policy of encouragement to private initiative would be prohibitive).[3]

But the Club Jean Moulin, and many other observers, consider that it is necessary, before envisaging an extension of the public sector, to seek to make a more effective use of what exists already. Three examples are often quoted in this respect, the banking sector, insurance, and the oil companies.

We saw in Chapter III that the four big nation-wide deposit banks were transferred to public ownership immediately after the war. It is a common theme with critics, not only of the Plan, but of the way the nationalization experiment has worked out, that these banks are in no way called upon to collaborate in implementing a selective

[1] *Op. cit.*, p. 16.

[2] Report of Commission No. 1.

[3] Cf. La Planification Démocratique, *Cahiers de la République*, January 1962, p. 67. Similar views were put forward by the CFTC at its 30th Congress in June 1959.

credit policy. 'It is a commonplace for a limited number of specialists but a fact which is still not perceived clearly by public opinion, that the nationalization of credit has failed in its object . . . the persistence of competition between banks has proved to be incompatible with a selective credit policy related to the objectives of the Plan, without benefiting the banks' clients, because competition is hardly ever based upon the quality or cost of the services rendered.'[1]

This observation leads to a call not so much for the further nationalization of banks but for the effective nationalization of credit.[2] This policy plays a big rôle in all schemes for amending the present procedures used in applying the Plan. It may be noted, however, that the rôle of the banques d'affaires in financing industry is perhaps more important than that of the nationalized banks.

The insurance companies are often criticized for the very similar reasons that their investment policy is only marginally influenced by the State, and more rarely still when it comes to directing savings to channels thought to be desirable from the point of view of the Plan. For example, these companies have been very reluctant to build up portfolios of private industrial debentures, a fact which becomes increasingly important now that firms have to appeal more frequently to savings on the capital market.

As to the oil companies, which have their own Planning Commission, as we saw in Chapter IX, instead of being grouped with the energy sector, it is often claimed that their international character, even in the case of Compagnie Française des Pétroles where the State holds 35 per cent of the capital, renders the companies recalcitrant to national planning imperatives.[3]

In the last analysis, the Club Jean Moulin concludes that 'control of the budget purse strings, direct control of the nationalized sector, the presence of the State in practically all large private companies thanks to the subsidiaries of the nationalized industries, to the mixed companies (sociétés d'économie mixte, part private, part public[4]) to the share portfolios managed by the nationalized banks, and to the blank voting rights collected by the nationalized banks for the share-

[1] Club Jean Moulin, *op. cit.*, p. 63.

[2] M. Mendès-France: 'When one hears in meetings and conferences motions in favour of the nationalization of credit, it can mean only one thing, that the State has not used so far the powerful weapons it possesses.' *La République Moderne, op. cit.*, p. 164.

[3] In the course of 1960-61, the Ministry of Industry took the initiative in establishing a new distribution company—the Union Générale des Pétroles—in connection with the importation of Saharan oil, a task which, at first sight, the Compagnie Française des Pétroles was equipped to carry out.

[4] See Chapter IV.

holders' meetings—all these instruments of persuasion or dissuasion added together would be so powerful that it would probably be sufficient for the State to show its strength for it to be unnecessary to use it'.[1]

3 *Overall Reforms*

Proposals for 'making a better use of the powers the State already possesses' are usually incorporated into more comprehensive schemes for reform. In this respect, there is a fair measure of agreement among reformers in favour of indirect controls and decentralized decision-making which is indeed among the most striking features of thinking on planning matters in France today. 'It does not appear to be necessary, to achieve these ends (of democratic planning), to have frequent recourse to direct controls, in particular of raw materials, prices and employment, for their use has been too often disappointing and psychologically difficult. It is preferable to establish normal conditions of functioning so as to be able to foresee more exactly the effects of the stimulants used.[2]

The authors of the study by the Club Jean Moulin raised a similar question when they asked: 'must the Plan become more detailed and imperative than it is already for private firms just as for the public and semi-public sectors? Or must it, on the contrary, deal differently with public and private undertakings, and fix imperative objectives for the former whilst being content with indicative objectives for the latter?' To which they replied: 'the problem seems to us to be badly put, for the first solution concludes, wrongly, that all economic activities lend themselves to planning to the same extent, whilst the second makes use only of a legalistic (is the firm publicly or privately owned?) and tactical (as the public sector is the only one where the State is the acknowledged master, let us give up the idea of planning the private sector) criterium'.[3]

This judgment led them to suggest a three-fold division of economic sectors: non-profit-making activities and those whose eventual profitability is still a long way off in time (that is, activities where by definition, private enterprise is excluded); directly productive activities calling for long-range decisions where private business is already subject to the power of arbitration of the State in the framework of

[1] *L'Etat et le Citoyen, Editions du Seuill*, p. 49.

[2] Report of the Commission No. 2 to the Colloquium on Democratic Planning. It is interesting to contrast this opinion with that expressed by a British Labour M.P. after a visit to France who regretted that the system of building licences in force was too limited. Cf. B. Castle, *New Statesman and Nation*, September 29, 1961.

[3] La Planification Démocratique, *Cahiers de la République*, January 1962, p. 59.

the Plan (steel and chemicals are already in this group and motor-cars and captial goods could be added to them); activities which it would be impossible to plan because demand is too volatile, or where planning is not needed as the firms are sufficiently numerous to ensure competition. The study concluded that the real issues for securing the execution of the Plan arise as regards the second of these groups.[1]

The main instruments of control envisaged deal with the direction of investments and their financing. An obstacle in the way of a more selective and active credit policy (in addition to the reasons which explain the continued autonomous character of the nationalized banking sector, and which are of a political, even sociological, nature) lies in the fact that the Plan is not a plan for firms but for branches.[2] This means that there are no precise objectives for each firm which could be given to the banks and which would guide them in their credit granting. In other words, the Plan remains largely an exercise in macro-economics whereas the banker needs micro-economic criteria which are operative concerts for him.[3] No satisfactory solution to this problem has been found but it has been suggested that the Planning Commissions could be invited to draw up norms for each sector.[4] A variant of this idea was noted in the preceding chapter

[1] This general approach is similar in spirit to the views expressed by two trade union leaders.

'Planning must be decidedly imperative in what one can call the basic sectors—public investments, town planning and credit—and must then leave more and more liberty as we get closer to products put at the disposal of individuals.' G. Levard, President of the CFTC, quoted by M. Mendès-France, *op. cit.*, p. 157.

'From an economic and technical point of view, democratic planning should remain largely indirect, indicative, incitative and be based upon the maximum of auto-determination, in the framework of markets which would be orientated in an acceptable manner, not only as concerns wages, with the greatest number of economic agents, taking care not to incline towards a narrow, fussy and technocratic dirigisme which would be a threat for democracy. But how then can it be effective and not merely in conformity with the interests of the dominant groups? By making the Plan imperative and obligatory for the whole public sector . . . by making the nationalization of credit a reality so as to ensure overall control of the use of the country's savings, including business savings. Finally, by making more systematic the use of selective measures as regards fiscal and credit policies.' P. Le Brun, Confederal Secretary of the CGT, Colloquium, *op. cit.*, p. 464.

[2] Cf. Chapter XIV.

[3] This is a familiar problem in many countries when governments attempt to instruct banks to encourage particular types of activity, e.g. exporting.

[4] By the Club Jean Moulin, *La Planification Démocratique, op. cit.*, p. 64. The same idea was put forward by some members of the Economic and Social Council also during the debates on the Plan. See also P. Mendès-France: *La République Moderne, op. cit.*, p. 167.

as regards the application of a policy for incomes through the procedure of the quasi-contracts: a firm having reached agreement with the authorities on its major objectives—output, investment, wage and salary margins, and so on—would be given special treatment by the State banks.[1]

A more drastic reform, often proposed by Socialist speakers, for example during the ratification debate on the Fourth Plan[2]—envisages setting up a State Investment Bank which would amalgamate and replace existing bodies such as the Economic and Social Development Fund.[3]

Another thorny problem arises in respect of business savings out of profits. We saw in Chapter XVII that some observers favour a control of self-financing by private firms as part of a policy for incomes.[4] One of the rapporteurs to the Colloquium on Democratic Planning suggested allocating 'planned margins' of self-financing to each branch of activity. The State would intervene to ensure that they were respected; a surplus over and above the margin would be syphoned off by taxation and a short-fall would open up negotiations with the authorities to find means of correcting the situation. The application of such a policy raises, of course, conceptual problems of immense difficulty and it is doubtful whether such a scheme could be applied in practice.

Other observers have been aware of these obstacles and their recommendations are less draconian. For the Club Jean Moulin, it is preferable to combat excessive profit margins by stimulating competition if it is insufficient, or by favouring the constitution of consumer groups to balance the market power of large-scale enterprises.[5] Again, the Club's opinion is that it would be unnecessary to control

[1] Cf. Chapter XVII, p. 322.

[2] Cf. Chapter X, p. 193.

[3] In the opinion of M. Hirsch, ex-Commissaire General, a State Investment Bank is not called for: '. . . it was suggested by the General Planning Commissariat already in 1948 and accepted by the Ministry of Finance at the time. Then the project was blocked. What did we do? Seeing we could not progress along that line, we had to find other mechanisms which, from a rational point of view, looked shocking but which were very effective in practice. We succeeded in securing the very close co-operation of certain banks, the Crédit National in particular, so that now all loans of some importance are given after a favourable opinion by the General Planning Commissariat. We must avoid rejecting what exists and just adding fresh superstructures.' Colloquium, p. 466.

[4] Cf. the proposals made by M. Chalandon, quoted in Chapter XVII, p. 321.

[5] An idea analogous to that of 'countervailing power' which has been put forward to Professor J. K. Galbraith, in the United States, in his book with the same title.

self-financing margins if the General Planning Commissariat, as the Club suggests, was informed of all the medium-term investment plans, and their financing possibilities, of the large private firms.[1] At present, the financial services of the Commissariat do have the opportunity to discuss with the majority of the big private firms their investment and financing plans on an annual basis but not for the medium term. The communication of this data would imply a marked change in the methods of the Plan used up to now, in particular if it was given to the Planning Commissions.

It would be vain to attempt to draw any conclusions from the varied points of view we have noted in this chapter. A remark of a general character is in order, though. The Plan is a powerful catalyst. It provokes thinking about the major problems—economic and social, even political—which present themselves. In so doing, it is certainly the enemy, both of routine and of a short-sighted view which would prefer to let sleeping dogs lie. Its contribution to raising the general level of discussions of problems of public policy cannot be denied. So far, however, a clearer appreciation of the issues involved in planning a modern market economy remains limited to relatively small groups of employers, trade unionists and civil servants. The next stage, which all these groups favour, is to carry this educational process a stage further to embrace public opinion as a whole.[2]

[1] See earlier in this chapter, p. 342.

[2] Various aspects of this educational process have been noted in the course of this book and the bibliography given at the end attests a growing interest in planning matters in many sections of opinion. The members of the General Planning Commissariat themselves have been tireless in writing and lecturing in an attempt to popularize knowledge of the Plan. A recent initiative is the production of an attractively designed booklet on the Fourth Plan of which 170,000 copies have been distributed free to all representative bodies.

PART FIVE

'I think that we live in a time which has few historical parallels, that there are practical problems of human institutions, their obsolescence and their inadequacy, problems of the mind and spirit which, if not more difficult than ever before, are different and difficult.' *J. Robert Oppenheimer*

'Planning is a way of taking decisions but it does not presuppose their content.'
Club Jean Moulin

CHAPTER XIX

GENERAL CONCLUSIONS

The more one reflects upon the multiple aspects of the French Plan the less satisfactory attempts to squeeze them into a simple formula, such as 'flexible' or 'indicative', as opposed to 'imperative', become. Moreover, the question to which they seek to provide a reply —what is the Plan?—should be seen in the light of the ends which the Plan sets out to achieve, for the Plan is essentially a way of solving problems with no finality in itself. If this is recognized, it follows that the French Plan is, first and foremost, an attempt by Frenchmen to find solutions for problems they meet with. But it remains that, as inhabitants of developed industrial societies in the Western tradition, we are all in the same boat, and, to change the metaphor, we shall no doubt sink or swim together. The specific experience of France, which we have been studying throughout this book, can hardly fail to evoke parallels with other national experiences.

I. WHAT IS THE PLAN FOR?

It will be as well to clarify, first of all, a question which often springs to the mind of the outside observer, and which the present writers have also put to themselves. If there was no Plan, what difference would it make? We have gradually come round to the view that this is not, on the whole, a very helpful means of approach. It depends too much upon an impossible reconstruction of 'things as they might have been' as France's whole post-war development has been coloured to a, varying, extent by the Plan. Moreover, it is usually put by the observer with his own preoccupations in mind. The most obvious example of this is the difference the Plan makes to the rate of growth, and understandably so in view of the fact that this is still the overriding justification for, and ambition of, planning efforts in most countries. A fast rate of economic growth is still the dominant preoccupation of the French Plan. But to centre the analysis on growth is to risk missing some of the most significant contemporary trends in the whole experiment.

It is very largely because of the achievement of the planning experiment since 1946 that securing a rapid rate of growth is not the arduous problem for France today that it is, for very different reasons, for the United States or the United Kingdom. The economy is growing rapidly and has been for years, the external accounts are in balance, there are no very serious obstacles in sight as to the supply of factors of production or any likelihood of a saturation of demand for goods and services, on the home market at least. This privileged situation could have afforded the opportunity for the planners to rest on their laurels and to choose a quiet life. Instead, it was decided to go on to what can be called a 'plan for consumption' in contrast to the earlier Plans which were 'plans for production'. Just what this change implies is only gradually becoming apparent, but clearly it is something different from, and more difficult than, what was attempted by the first three Plans. This situation gives to the Plan a quite special fascination. Whether its objectives can be reached only time will show, and there are some big items of unfinished business to be settled before they can be, but whatever the outcome, what is being attempted is no mean thing. This can be seen by looking in turn at the production and social objectives of the Plan.

1 *The Production Objectives*

To take the production targets first, they are high, indeed higher in the aggregate than the rate achieved for any comparable length of time since the war, but they do not appear to be unreasonable.

Although the problem for the Fourth Plan is not simply one of channelling resources towards a limited number of priority sectors, its investment pattern is nonetheless modified by the Plan in a way which is favourable to growth. Thus the productive investment programmes in the public sector are geared, in a consistent way, to the chosen growth-rate and the unproductive, or more correctly, the less directly-productive public investments also. The same is true for other basic sectors, steel in particular, and the capital goods industries are receiving very positive encouragement from the authorities. In this way, a notable slice of total fixed capital formation is programmed so that it encourages the achievement of planned targets.

Moreover, as the work of the Planning Commissions and the comments made since by the business world indicate, the French entrepreneur is in an optimistic frame of mind and does not feel that what has been planned at the national, or branch, level is something foreign to his own personal experience. It would be a hard task to convince opinion in France that there is any valid reason why the future rate of growth of the economy should not come up, at least, to the best performance of the past.

Looking back over the ways the overall growth target was set, and the individual targets which compose it, there seems no reason to question the technical quality of the work that was done. Improvements could be made, the best proof of this is that the French planners themselves are not preparing the Fifth Plan in exactly the same way as they did the Fourth. All the outside observer can note is the very considerable amount of devoted work which went into the making of the Plan, and the intellectual ingenuity displayed in finding ways of dealing with awkward, and new, problems. If statistical data had been more abundant, if time had not been a scarce factor, and if the available talent had been more numerous, no doubt some results would have been different. But this is pie in the sky. If the Fourth Plan was not always as good a technical job as its authors themselves would have liked, it is not for want of the will to make it so, and the Fifth Plan will benefit from the experience of its predecessor.

Can the same be said of the policy decisions which inform the Plan at all its stages? By 'policy' we mean deciding between divergent opinions, or options, on the basis of the available information. A distinction is called for here between firm targets and forecasts. The impossibility for the technicians and the representatives of the motor-car industry to reach agreement does not prejudge the final outcome. The State is not taking measures to enforce its view and the acceleration of the auto-routes programme now under way seems to be designed rather to accommodate a faster growth in the number of motor-cars than was initially looked for. But, reading through the detailed Planning Commissions reports, one is struck by the consistency of the efforts made to found policy decisions upon an objective examination of the facts. Of course, it was not always possible to stand out against pressure in favour of particular sectors, although the determined resistance of the authorities to acceptance of the full-blown project for linking the Rhine and the Rhône was a notable example of this. Perhaps the basic policy decisions on agriculture remain among the most questionable of the chief options of the Fourth Plan, both in respect of the likelihood of the market forecasts being achieved and of their probable cost for the budget.

Agriculture is not the only sector whose output objectives are closely linked to foreign trade prospects. And it is in the nature of things that these estimates should be among the most uncertain in the Plan. Will it be possible to prevent French prices from rising faster than those of her major competitors? Can a return to excess demand conditions be avoided? Will French industry be able successfully to continue its adaptation to increasingly freer trading conditions?

To consider the last point only for the moment, it is certain that the French businessman's experience of stiff foreign competition, both at home and abroad, is still very recent. There are problems of changing production structures, of improving research facilities, of reinforcing marketing arrangements which will have to be solved, and which feature among the objectives of the Fourth Plan.

However, taking the first year of the Fourth Plan, 1962, and the forecasts being made for the second, results so far bear out the Plan's optimism despite a marked increase in demand pressures.

2 *The Social Objectives*

French planners were Galbraithians before the term acquired the resonance it has since come to possess. We have seen sufficiently the objectives of the Plan in this field. What are the essential problems connected with it? We leave aside the question of overall balance for the moment to examine the structure of consumption.

When the question is put in the form: what structure of consumption do you prefer? the answers are likely to fall into two groups. The first unites the advocates of free choice and the market, the second those who favour some conscious direction of demand, or production, or both. This is really a matter where each man should be prepared to stand up and be counted. On the whole the French planners were, and are, sincerely perturbed by the direction taken by the spontaneous growth of demand in the mass consumption society which is rapidly appearing in France.

The idea behind the Plan is substantially to increase consumption of collective goods and services. This in turn means, for example, paying more taxes and accepting a less substantial rise in disposable incomes than would have been the case otherwise. But the Plan does not set out to influence the structure of private consumption except very marginally, for example the consumption of alcohol. The forecasts of demand made were based upon the working out of present trends and, a point to which we return, upon the maintenance of the present structure of income distribution.

That this did not go far enough for some people was to be expected. But it is easier to regret the absence of stronger measures than to suggest what they should be. The motor-car is the most frequent example used to typify the 'gadget society' and it would be unfair to the Plan not to recognize that its authors did not go out of their way to favour the growth of its use. After all, petrol in France is still dearer than elsewhere on the Continent. But if it was intended actually to restrict the expansion of the industry by, let us say, heavy indirect taxation, problems would occur immediately. In the first place, it is far from clear that a majority of opinion would be inclined to accept such measures. Secondly, it might not be possible to implement them in the framework of the Common Market. Thirdly, it may be asked whether it is really desirable to organize shortages in order to be able to set up lists of priorities. Other ways must be sought for taming the affluent society.

The massive rise in public expenditure of a social character corresponds no doubt, in part, to the need for catching-up with the rapid growth of the urban population as the social and cultural amenities of the new housing estates had tended to be the poor relation in post-war building programmes. But the increases are more substantial than this minimum would call for and will probably strain the ability of some public departments, especially the Ministry of Education, to spend the credits they are now receiving.

It is not difficult either to appreciate the other reasons why it did not appear desirable to the authorities to push this aspect of the Plan even further for the time being. The temporary halt to the growth in living standards after 1958 did not render the climate of opinion favourable to a more ambitious programme. Also, the French fiscal system is not a very suitable instrument for implementing, in an equitable manner, a really marked extension of the existing programmes for social transfers.

A start has been made, however, and the past experience of the Plan shows how often major achievements have sprung out of small beginnings. The consequences of integrating firmly into the structure of the Plan these types of public expenditure could be far-reaching indeed. More modestly, if the Plan proves to be a means of securing a larger slice of the national cake for such purposes, this alone would be enough to justify its existence for many people.

The Plan has been criticized for excessive timidity in the field of income distribution. But here again it is necessary to be clear about the distinction between the Plan as a means and the ends it serves. There is at present in France no effective support for a radical redistribution of incomes. In these circumstances, the Plan had little option but to attempt to provide above all for a rapid rise in incomes in as harmonious a fashion as possible and to leave intact the present distribution of income and wealth. Even so, a significant departure is the stress being put upon the need to ensure that the incomes of some under-privileged groups grow rather faster than the national average. And this policy is being implemented with gratifying promptness. Unless, or until, a different constellation of social forces appears, any more radical change in this field is unlikely.

It does not follow from this that the chances of reaching a workable solution for the problem of an incomes policy are negligible also, although there are considerable difficulties to be overcome. Some are statistical and conceptual, and work is proceeding on them. Others are 'political' in a broad sense. What can be done about the relation between remunerations in the public and private sectors that does not impose an intolerable burden on the fiscal system, or render price stability more fragile? Can, and should, the rate of increase in incomes in the most progressive sectors be moderated? Are the trade unions in a position *vis-à-vis* their members, and the large majority of non-unionized workers, to implement an agreement on incomes? Is there a solution for agricultural incomes which would be acceptable to farmers and which would not call for income transfers on a massive scale, except perhaps speeding-up the movement from the land?

There are many positive elements in the present situation, though. If the Fourth Plan is allowed to proceed without any untoward event, such as a renewal of excess demand conditions, upsetting the achievement of its objectives, it will bring about a very notable rise in real incomes. This is something to make advocates of an 'all or nothing' approach to the problem of incomes pause. Also, the attempt made by the Fourth Plan to broaden the scope of the idea of an incomes policy so as to embrace the social objectives we referred to above, whilst removing the most evident anomalies associated with low-income groups, is an original one. The approach to the problem of the mass of incomes may seem excessively cautious and there is an evident danger in rounding-up some categories of incomes if nothing is done to moderate the rise in the others. But the dangers for the Plan, and the growth prospects themselves, which would be likely to be the only result of a head-on clash between the interested groups on this subject, would appear to justify the calculated risk implied by the more devious tactics used so far.

To discuss regional policy among the social objectives of the Plan may give rise to an abuse of language. Nevertheless, it remains that the re-activation of the French provinces is not something which will occur without active encouragement from the State. A stumbling block for regional development is invariably the difficulty met with in ensuring that the broad principles of the rational use of scarce resources are respected in the programmes. It is practically impossible to do this if the regional problem is not examined in the light of a coherent national development policy. It is interesting to see how all the pieces of the jigsaw fit into place once this basic principle has been laid down: town planning, infrastructure projects, agricultural improvement, social amenities, industrialization and so on.

As to the implementation of these programmes, establishing a link between them and the national medium-term Plan, through the annual procedure for operational tranches, on the one hand, and the long-term prospective studies, on the other, is a highly novel approach. It is a link which will not be forged in a day, however. There are conceptual problems to be overcome in this relatively little-explored field. Not less important are the practical administrative difficulties involved; the new local government structure which is emerging in France has yet to prove its vitality, and there are innumerable conflicts of responsibilities between the various public departments on the local level which have to be ironed out. Much of what is being attempted depends upon a radical change in traditional French attitudes, in the public administrations as well as in local opinion, towards matters of local government. But this theme is best seen in relation to the question: what is the Plan?

II. WHAT IS THE PLAN?

In the preceding paragraphs, we have sought to illustrate the character of the French Plan today in the light of the objectives it set out to achieve. These different strands can be drawn together in an omnibus definition which sacrifices brevity for the sake of comprehensiveness. *The Plan is a way of providing permanent arrangements for a collective and systematic reflection on the problems and prospects of the economy with a view to action.* It will help to clarify matters if each of the key words in this definition is examined in turn.

The Plan viewed as a *permanent* experiment is partly a question of institutions and partly one of people. The efficacy and appropriateness of its institutional structures are questions we shall look at later on. What concerns us here is the importance attached to the simple fact of the existence of a body such as the General Planning Commissariat. To be fully effective, long-term policy calls for continuity in studying, deciding and implementing it. In France, questions no doubt still get pigeon-holed, but there is value in the fact that the Commissariat, on big or small problems which it considers important, is a permanent force, capable of deploying with tenacity its talents for argument, persuasion and initiative in the ebb and flow of policy making. And where obstacles cannot be removed, they can sometimes be by-passed. The Commissariat stands at the cross-roads of so many currents that it is able to use its capacity as a collective memory of society to relate what would otherwise remain unconnected and to attenuate what would otherwise contradict or nullify policies decided elsewhere. It is not likely that this result could have been achieved by a body which was just another cog, albeit an important one, in the regular Government administration.

The Planning Commissions and organizations such as the Economic and Social Council and the High Planning Council, also provide a valuable link in this continuing process. Today the Commissions meet annually, but even before that, each Commission tended to follow-up problems from one Plan to another. The mandate of the two other bodies is also a permanent one. To a certain extent this system fulfils the functions of temporary special Commissions in use in many countries for the study of specific problems. When such special Commissions are set up in France, for example the two Commissions on Old Age and the Family in 1961, their work is often connected to the Plan. It could be argued that neither of them would have seen the light of day if the idea of a reinforcement of the incomes of under-privileged groups in the nation had not been in the air during the preparatory phase of the Fourth Plan. And their recommendations are much more likely to be implemented once they are incorporated in the Plan.

Continuity in personnel is a factor which, from many points of view, is as important as these permanent institutional arrangements. It is not only that the senior officials of the Plan have tended to change much less frequently than their political chiefs, although this has been important enough in post-war France. Of equal significance is the practice of co-habitation, over the years, in the same Councils, Commissions and working parties, of men drawn from all walks of life—civil servants from the different public departments, officials from the nationalized industries, businessmen, farmers, workers and technicians. Many men have been working for years in these conditions, a not inconsiderable number ever since the First Plan, that is, during a good slice of their working lives. It is impossible that problems should be seen in the same light by each individual after such an experience.

In this way we are led to consider the *collective* character of the French Plan which is among its most original features.

The claims made for the advantages of the concerted economy are sometimes pitched too high. But it remains that, if the two principles, of the maximum degree of autonomy of decision and of the participation in policy-making of those who will have to bear the brunt of the implementation of measures decided upon, are held to be valid guides, then some means of organizing this collective participation have to be found.

Concertation between the State and the private sector is facilitated by the structure of the French civil service, one of whose general features, which the Plan did not create, but which it has used profitably, is the ambivalence of senior officials—the Grands Corps de l'Etat[1]—sharing a common training, moving with ease from one section of the public sector—including the nationalized industries and the banking sector—to another, and occupying posts in the numerous boards of directors of semi-public and private enterprises where the State is represented. The 'business' and 'civil service' points of view exist in France as elsewhere but the French high official has perhaps a better chance than most of understanding business from the inside. And if he has not the direct experience himself, he can often be sure of finding a colleague, or ex-colleague, in the business world as his opposite number. The virtues of this system should not, of course, cause one to forget its possible dangers; there are times when a too highly-developed appreciation of the arguments of the other side can be harmful also.

The background of the officials of the General Planning Commissariat, and the technical planning bodies, is more varied still and is not based upon a strict adherence to civil service rules of recruitment and promotion. In this way, scarce talent has been used most effectively and contacts with the private sector have been facilitated.

More generally, it may be that greater uniformity in educational standards in France than in some countries contribute to reducing barriers based upon social class, or even accent, between men in different walks of life.

The procedure of the Planning Commissions, which was enlarged substantially with the Fourth Plan and now touches directly over 3,000 persons from all sectors of the public and private sectors, has sometimes been felt to be rather cumbersome. Judgments on this point depend upon what one considers to be the object of their work. As regards framing projections of demand, production, investments and trade, the technicians who collaborate directly with the General Planning Commissariat would probably have done nearly as good a job of work if the Commissions did not exist. Nearly, but not quite. The weight of past trends in influencing projections is not a danger to be shrugged off lightly. There is sufficient evidence to support the thesis that, even if large and unpredictable shifts in the structural

[1] *Conseil d'Etat, Inspection des Finances and Cour des Comptes.*

and technical relations between economic and social data are not frequent, the pace of change in modern conditions has accelerated. This makes it indispensable to endeavour to correct a bias due to the extrapolation of past trends. The development of prospective, very long-term studies, is one way of doing this. Another is to consult the man on the job, and the mechanism of the Planning Commissions seems to be a convenient and reasonable way of doing this. If the Planning Commissions did not exist they would have to be invented.

But a Plan is much more than a question of making projections; an understanding of the problems at issue and the will to solve them on the part of those who have to carry out the Plan are called for as well. The Planning Commissions provide a meeting place for discussions between groups of businessmen, civil servants and trade unionists who, otherwise, would never meet, or would do so in a limited and sporadic fashion on the occasion of some, probably, litigious debate. And they do so on the basis of problems which are defined as objectively as possible. There is considerable force in the suggestion that the work of the Commissions creates conditions which, on the one hand, favour a steady improvement in the technical competence of all concerned as to economic and social problems and, on the other hand, discourage demagogy. Not all divergencies of interests can be removed by just talking about them. Still the habit of discussing, inside a set of rules of the game, precludes arguments which cannot be substantiated by a reasonable show of facts and this is a first, but indispensable, step towards finding workable solutions.

The existence of the Commissions is also frequently a useful safety-valve for letting off steam. Their chairmen and rapporteurs try of course to make their reports as constructive as possible, and the General Planning Commissariat as well as the Government have the last word on what measures will be written into the Plan, or introduced by special legislation. But the practical usefulness of the periodic brain-storming done by the Commissions is by no means negligible either.

A new departure with the Fourth Plan is the widening of the collective aspect of the Plan to include Parliament and a number of consultative bodies in a much more consistent manner than up to now. The future of this experiment is among the most exciting features of the Plan today.

There is a specifically French aspect to the problem at issue. The tormented history of French political life since the war has led many people to pin their hopes upon the Plan as a catalyst for public opinion which will allow politics to take on a new lease of life at the national and local levels. But there is also a more general problem of the participation of the individual in the affairs of the State, which is relevant for other countries as well.

Clearly all will not be plain sailing in this connection. It is not difficult to conceive of a loss of efficiency corresponding to the gains in democracy. The organizational aspects of the proposed consultation procedures could become unwieldy and time-consuming. They could favour routine compromises rather than constructive ones. The technicians could find that they had less opportunity for throwing their weight on one side or the other in order to influence decisions, a tactic they have used very effectively in the past. On the other hand, the ambitions of the Plan today have a logic of their own which makes it necessary to seek an increased participation by the population at large.

The Plan seen as a *systematic* reflection on problems and prospects is a recent feature. Indeed, it could be argued that the Fourth Plan was the first to justify this epithet. There are two aspects to this. The Plan itself should be as systematic as possible, otherwise major options cannot be seen clearly. Secondly, the formulation of sectorial growth objectives in a common framework favours the choice of ambitious targets and increases the chance of their being carried out.

The choice of major options, or the acceptance of major constraints can only be made when all the relevant alternatives are made clear. We are becoming accustomed to this type of presentation for economic problems but the French Plan contains some original characteristics, which are not without their practical importance for the working out of the Plan either. Thus the link which is established between individual and collective consumption is a hope for all who would like to see in the Plan a way of raising the quality of life as well as the quantity of goods and services put on the market. It can also become a means of facilitating the adoption of measures to ensure that income distribution does not conflict with this, and other, objectives of the Plan. The experiment, which will take place with the Fifth Plan, of extending still further the scope of choice will imply, as we saw, a selection between coherent and balanced variants.

The simultaneous preparation of the Plan for all aspects of the economic and social life of the nation is a procedure which encourages growth in various ways. All branches work to the same hypothesis for the overall growth rate which is fixed by the Government. It is not unreasonable to suppose that this high rate is itself a general stimulant and that it is accepted with less reserve than would be the case if each branch, or firm, set up its own projections for the growth of the economy; projections, moreover, which would not necessarily be the same.

This procedure of 'generalized market research' also provides some guarantee that growth will be harmonious. The Planning Commissions, as we saw, communicate with each other and their individual development plans are influenced by this unique opportunity of knowing something of the intentions of the branches which purchase their products or those of their suppliers. This is particularly so for capital goods and raw and semi-finished materials. As to the consumer goods branches, it is important to have some idea, not only of the future rise in real disposable incomes, but of the likely geographical location of that rise.

The situation as regards the 'social' Commissions is similar. Thus the needs for infrastructure and housing are adjusted both globally, and by geographical location, in the light of the growth prospects for the economy as a whole. The same is true of research expenditure. And the work of these Commissions enables the State to facilitate and, in certain regions, actively to support the development of the private sector by anticipating future trends in demand.

A key element in the description of the Plan which was proposed earlier comes at the end—*with a view to action.* The more one considers the planning process, the more important this appears to be. Of course the Plan is a Plan for doing things, it may be objected, but what is so exceptional about that? Unfortunately, projects and plans do often serve to set objectives without much attention being paid to their achievement. Despite the mass of discussion and analysis which goes into drafting the Plan, it too could remain a dead letter if there were no adequate arrangements for its implementation. This is a first point. A second is the spur to initiative given by a widely-held belief that the objectives of the Plan stand a good chance of being translated into acts. This is indeed a field where nothing succeeds like success.

Any discussion of the arrangements for implementation must take account of the public sector itself. We have noted how long and arduous a process it was in France to gain acceptance here for the Plan. People have to be convinced, one is tempted to say 'converted', to the idea that the Plan is a worthwhile procedure which holds out an opportunity for achieving desirable ends. This implies, for example, that watertight compartments between the public departments have to be broken down, that the 'payers' and the 'spenders' habits of mind have to be modified and brought closer together. It means also that the black sheep have to be convinced of the error of their ways or, if that fails, called to order. Critics in France are not lacking who claim that this process has not gone far enough and that there is still no common concept of the rôle of the public sector in the Plan. This is no doubt true to some extent but the progress which has been achieved, notably with the Fourth Plan, should not be overlooked. The most striking victory in this field was the conversion of the Ministry of Finance and, simultaneously, the reduction in the mistrust of the rest of the public sector. It is likely that a more systematic co-ordination between credit policy and the Plan will be the next step in the same direction. Gradualism may be one of the facts of life when what has to be changed is mental habits as well as administrative routines.

The active nature of the Plan in relation to the private sector still gives rise to misconceptions, in France as well as abroad. There is room also for divergences of views here, as was noted earlier.

If one runs through the list of weapons used by the Plan for influencing the behaviour of the private sector, one is struck by the small rôle played by coercion. Between the carrot and the stick, the French authorities choose the carrot whenever possible. Even the offer of encouragements, however, seems often to be rather lightweight except in sensitive sectors and, increasingly, where regional development projects are concerned. This has not always been the case. The key sectors under the first two Plans really were given privileged treatment. But such measures are much less justified today when a harmonious growth of the economy is what is required. This is indeed a good example of the system of planning being modified to adapt it to changed policy ends. It is also surely the sort of result one would expect in a developed economy with a high, and rising, standard of living?

Enough has been said already about the objectives of the Plan for it to be unnecessary to justify the thesis that they have a normative character. But the objectives which really count include certain production targets only (transport services, energy supplies, a few products, such as steel and some chemicals, in the basic sectors of activity, and a range of new and specialized products in the capital goods industries). A large share of the industrial capacity involved here is under public ownership anyway and the steel industry's relations with the Plan are, and always have been, very close. The quasi-contract system is being used most in the capital goods sector. As regards all these activities, the Plan is very active indeed.

Elsewhere, its action is less direct and relies upon more general measures for stimulating production and securing flexibility in response to changing market conditions. It is here that the influence of the Plan in spreading attitudes favourable to growth and innovation is decisive, and this in turn obviates the need for more specific and direct intervention by the State. Tomorrow, of course, another Plan could set different objectives which would call for changes in the existing character of the Plan. But it is unlikely that these changes would mean a reversal of the present preference for decentralized decision-making which seems, and not only in France, to correspond to deep-seated tendencies in the evolution of industrial societies.

APPENDIX I

THE GOVERNMENT'S DIRECTIVES TO THE GENERAL PLANNING COMMISSARIAT FOR THE ELABORATION OF THE FOURTH PLAN

This document is intended to define the direction that the Government—in the light of surveys submitted to it by the General Planning Commissariat and by the Investment and Planning Section of the Economic Council—has decided to give to the work of elaborating the Fourth Plan (January 1, 1962/December 31, 1965). It will enable the General Planning Commissariat to furnish the Planning Commissions, responsible for working out the detailed programmes of the different branches, with a common view of the general lines of development within which their individual work will be contained and its coherence assured.

I. THE AIM OF THE FOURTH PLAN

The aim of the Fourth Plan is to develop the economic resources which France has at its disposal. For it to be continuous, the expansion of the French economy, which the Plan is thus designed to promote, must be effected in a stable monetary system.

On the extent to which its means are amply and progressively increased within the framework of the Plan will depend the growth of our country into a great industrial metropolis capable of accomplishing the tasks that fall to the nation and of improving the living conditions of its people whilst we continue to exercise our traditional responsibilities.

The Fulfilment of the Great National Tasks

Our country will need to quicken the agricultural, industrial and moral development of Algeria. The Constantine Plan, which constitutes an element of the Republic's Plan, will be incorporated in the Fourth Plan, with the necessary changes of dates. Similarly, the economic development of the DOM[1] and TOM,[2] which calls for increased effort, will be made the object of special plans to be included in the Fourth Plan.

In accordance with the obligations she has assumed, France will bring her aid and co-operation to the States of the (French) Communauté. By comparing the plans of these States with the Republic's Plan, the framework within which this action will take place will be determined.

Our country will have to pursue unceasingly the structural adaptation that will enable it to meet unharmed the competition of the other industrial countries of Europe and North America.

[1] *Départements d'Outre Mer.*
[2] *Territoires d'Outre Mer.*

At the same time, France will have to assure for herself broader outlets in countries making efforts like her own towards diminishing quotas and tariffs, in particular within the European Economic Community.

Finally, when account is taken of the evolution of the situation in Algeria, of the progressive reduction of the traditional armed forces and of the need to provide our forces with modern weapons, it is expected that the total expenditure on the fighting services in 1965 will be about equal to that of 1959.

Military strength, too, cannot be separated from economic strength. The latter constitutes, therefore, a dominant factor, which will become all the more important if international relations become less strained. There will then grow up between East and West peaceful but keen competition in which the essential trump-cards will be found in a nation's aptitude to promote the well-being of its people and to co-operate in developing the non-industrialized countries.

France will therefore have to combine the obligations of its national defence and the responsibilities arising from its entry into a network of special agreements in Europe and in Africa, whilst it shares with other industrial nations the task of promoting the economic and social growth of countries in the process of development.

THE IMPROVEMENT IN THE PEOPLE'S LIVING CONDITIONS

In spite of the 40 per cent increase experienced during the last ten years, the present standard of living in France cannot be considered adequate. Individual consumption remained unchanged between the middle of 1957 and the middle of 1959 because of the previous imbalance and the corrective measures that this necessitated. In many rural areas and in the working-class districts of the big towns, there exists real poverty which it behoves us to combat. Finally, the disparity of our standard of living and the present American standard is such that, assuming the best conditions, it will not be possible for us to bridge the gap until about 1975.

This means that the fear of over-providing for the needs of the people of France in a way that will involve a slowing down of economic growth must be considered to be without foundation, at least for the next two decades.

From all the foregoing, it follows that one of the fundamental results of the Fourth Plan must be to assure the full employment of the coming generations and to increase individual consumption by providing more and better food and clothing, by improving housing and by increasing the purchase of industrial goods that add to the comfort of the home and the ease of life.

But this overall increase of individual consumer income made possible by the growth of our economy runs the risk of being powerless, as the example of the United States shows, to ensure by itself the elimination of low standards of living whether they be tied to the economic situation in certain regions and to certain branches of activity, or whether they belong to certain groups of consumers—the poorly-housed, large families, those with small incomes, and old people. This elimination can be obtained only progressively by the action of public bodies in furthering professional training and creating centres of regional growth, action that will be rounded off by measures aimed at ensuring an adequate increase in the purchasing power of the family and in that of the lowest income group.

Moreover, the Fourth Plan will have to try to put an end to the present over-crowding in the homes, while at the same time, in anticipation of the Fifth Plan, it sets about renewing housing in town and country with all the demolition this will entail. This aim requires certain changes in the law of property and the passing of new measures to allow the most needy families to be reasonably well housed.

Finally, it seems necessary that the Plan should give more attention than has been given hitherto to needs met by collective investment—town planning, education, public health—in order to fill the serious gaps from which the country suffers, to combat social scourges (alcohol, etc.) to face up to the consequences of population growth and ultimately to complete progressively the quantitative rise in purchasing power by a qualitative improvement in the French way of life.

Indeed, whatever its positive advantages may be, there is no doubt that industrial civilization, when its effects are not balanced and humanized, produces numerous disadvantages which are felt more and more; noise, air pollution, lack of open-spaces, water-supply shortages, long daily journeys between home and workplace and difficulties in the use of leisure.

As far as towns are concerned, efforts agreed on with regard to housing will lead to the growth of investment for the improvement of sanitation, water-supply, communications and collective transports.

This development will need to be linked with the work of urban improvement that will ensure the progressive replanning of the large conurbations, especially that of Paris.

In this context, it will be necessary, in the interest of the physical health and psychological equilibrium of the population, to bring workplace and homes nearer to one another, and to improve the home more than has been done so far by social, recreational and cultural investments in parks, clinics, nurseries, sports fields, youth clubs, theatres, art galleries, libraries, etc.

Finally, if coherence in the growth of the motor-car industry and urban development is to be established in the end, through reciprocal adaptation to a degree yet to be defined, there is no doubt that in the next few years the doubling of the number of motor-cars between 1956 and 1965 will involve considerable effort in solving circulative and parking problems in the big centres, and in facilitating entry to and exit from the big towns by the making of fly-overs or motor roads.

As regards education, the Fourth Plan will have to prepare for the lengthening of compulsory school life to sixteen years of age, so that this may operate as planned, i.e. in 1967. But simply by this spontaneous increase in the span of compulsory school life, the total number of pupils will rise by 500,000 between 1961 and 1965. Now, the rapidity of growth has not enabled the 1,300,000 pupils by which the school population has increased between 1954 and 1961 to be given the same conditions in schools as existed for their predecessors. So the State is faced not only with the need to cater for the increase in the pupil-population, but to establish, in the various types of teaching, working conditions without which the pedagogic efficiency of the staff cannot produce the best results. Nevertheless, these different aims will not be achieved except by extremely costly efforts in providing staff and premises and if education, faced by the accumulation of knowledge, cannot on the one hand make the choices necessitated by its admission of the new sciences and techniques, and on the other the use of quicker modern teaching methods as provided by audio-visual aids. Considered from another point of view, the rapid evolution of techniques reinforces the necessity to develop types of education of a permanent kind which will ensure the indispensable bringing up-to-date of professional knowledge.

Much effort must be made to further research, whether it be fundamental research on which all progress is based, technical research or the application of the results of both to industrial and agricultural development.

Some concerted international effort, especially in Europe, would enhance the return to be gained from these researches.

In the field of public health, the rapidly increasing demand for expenditure on medicine, and the many out-dated hospitals will involve investment to facilitate the development of medical treatment, to accommodate the growth of medical knowledge, to provide for changes in the standard of living and the increase in the number of young and old people. Moreover, it will be necessary to give effect to reforms in medical education by establishing university medical schools.

THE RATE OF EXPANSION AGREED ON

The growth in the means at the disposal of the economy calls for a marked economic expansion. The Government has therefore decided that the Commissions should study the possibility of effecting, during the period of the Fourth Plan, in increase of about 22 per cent in Gross Internal Production, that is an annual average of 5 per cent.

Such an increase is greater than that experienced on the average during the last decade, as well as that envisaged when the Third Plan was made and that likely, in fact, to be achieved when account is taken of the Intermediate Plan. However, it seems possible to adopt it as a working hypothesis because of the improvement in the general economic situation of our country and the new prospects in foreign trade (notably a better supply of fuel products from the franc area).

In addition, the Government will examine, in the light of the work of the Planning Commissions, whether it is possible, without endangering the general balance of the economy, to prolong during this period of the Fourth Plan the rhythm of 5.5 per cent envisaged by the Intermediate Plan for the catching-up phase following the pause of 1958-59.

It has not been possible to accept the above figures for consideration except by excluding from the preliminary surveys exceptionally unfavourable political or economic eventualities, such as a serious crisis in the main economies of the West, or a return in the United States to a severer protectionist policy. Moreover, in any case, such a rapid expansion will only be possible if it is supported by everybody, producers and consumers alike, who, if they fail, will be faced by the threat of endangering monetary stability and giving rise again to inflation. In particular, when account is taken of the fact that the growth of the working population will be slow during the period of the Fourth Plan—the most sensitive effects of the post-war reversal in population trends will be felt only later—the rhythm of expansion envisaged above seems at present hardly in keeping with a general reduction in working hours, which should not be an aim of the Fourth Plan but the final criterion of its success. During the period 1962-65 on the contrary, a certain amount of immigration of manpower may well become necessary; moreover, in any case, special efforts towards increasing the rate of professional promotion are called for to meet the growing demands of highly qualified posts.

A marked increase of national production implies, on the other hand, the existence of a strong flow of imports and the realization of considerable investments. It therefore gives rise to problems of equilibrium in the balance of payments despite the progress of the first two years, and to problems concerning the needs for and the volume of saving. Consequently the Fourth Plan will achieve its aims only if, and at the same time, it helps to consolidate the recently acquired competitive hold of French production on international markets and to strengthen its weak sectors by certain specific measures. The investment effort will contribute towards this consolidation and strengthening, but alone it would be inadequate if it was not supported by a similar productivity effort and completed by a discipline of prices and wages to avoid reviving inflation by the distribution of unearned incomes.

THE SPECIAL LINES OF DEVELOPMENT IN DIFFERENT SECTORS OF ACTIVITY

Within the general framework of this survey of development, the Commissions will need to indicate by branch, and as often as possible by location, the detailed aims they set out to achieve. In this they will be guided by the lines of development suggested below for the principal sectors of activity.

1 *Agriculture*

In accordance with the points laid down in the 1960 Agricultural Bill, the surveys of the Agricultural Commission will need to try:

(a) to determine crop development, to fix production aims and to define the techniques and means of achieving these aims as well as the order of priority in investment;

(b) to establish in particular the elements of the new target prices applicable within the framework of an agricultural policy agreed on in the European Economic Community during the period of the Fourth Plan;

(c) to elaborate, taking account of national programmes, regional agricultural views that will have to be incorporated in regional plans of economic and social development;

(d) to look systematically for ways of increasing home and foreign outlets for agricultural production and of improving market conditions so as to obtain fair prices for the products of the land and thus exerting a favourable influence on farmers' incomes;

(e) to encourage the growth of agricultural incomes by improving the structure of family farms, by developing investment, technical research and agricultural training.

2 *Energy*

The experience of recent years has shown the importance of conjunctional fluctuations for an industry as rigid as the coal industry. In the years ahead, development will be dominated by the new oil supplies, notably from the Sahara. Then will come the problem of bringing to Europe natural gas from the Sahara. Still later, the market will be influenced by the progress of nuclear power stations towards competition. The surveys to be undertaken will endeavour to define the pace and stages desirable for the development of the different forms of energy as well as the steps to be taken eventually towards co-ordination, after allowing for various factors that will intervene, such as the more or less rapid success of new techniques, the speed of adaptation shown by the users, regional problems of equilibrium, security of supply, equilibrium in the balance of payments, European and international aspects of the policy relating to energy, and the need to ensure employment of miners or their transfer to other occupations.

3 *Industry*

The marked growth in industrial production from now until 1965 implies a great expansion of activity in nearly all sectors. The Commissions will seek to measure the investment needs of the various branches. A quicker pace in the establishment of the Common Market and the move towards the freeing of international trade will require, moreover, a growth in the volume of exports—hence a close scrutiny of selling possibilities abroad, and systematic research into the means of increasing the competitive strength of firms. Finally, to maintain full employment and equilibrium between areas, it will be necessary to study measures for the adaptation and conversion of branches that experience a reduction of their markets.

In a general way, for a certain number of activities such as the chemical, paper and cardboard-box industries and the making of plastic materials, the Fourth Plan will lead to sustained effort to expand along the lines of the results obtained in recent years.

Other branches, examined below, call for special comment because of their importance in the expansion of the general economy and because of the special difficulties that may be involved in the effort to achieve their aims.

Production in the *steel industry* in 1965 should reach 22.5 or 23 million tons; failing this, the rate of growth planned for the whole economy might not be achieved;

Production of *Aluminium* must follow the rapid development of demand, which raises the problem of the supply of cheap energy;

Development of *industries producing equipment goods* has been slower than that in most other branches, which makes French investment costly in foreign currency. Obviously, it is inappropriate to look for autarchy in this connection, but certain lines of production, selected for the breadth of their markets or the special suitability of French industry to supply them, should be developed so as not only to cover a considerable part of French needs, but also to provide a substantial flow of exports;

Agricultural and food industries—which do not yet provide agriculture with all the outlets they might—should increase their contribution to the export drive.

4 *Transport and Communication*

The achievement of the Fourth Plan aims implies an increase in the total capacity to transport goods and people, as well as more modernization and productivity leading to a reduction in costs.

The choice of operations will have to be made with care to ensure for the whole economy the best economic return from investments, account being taken of the general and regional aims of expansion and of the quality of the services to be provided.

In these surveys, it will be appropriate to take into account the results of the Common Market, and of the changes which have come about between France and Madagascar and the African States of the French Community.

In the field of telecommunications, vigorous efforts must be made to develop and modernize basic structures in order to meet, at one and the same time, the unsatisfied demands of the present and the new needs resulting from economic expansion.

5 *Commerce*

The modernization of commercial equipment will have to be undertaken at a pace that will ensure the general productivity of this sector being kept progressively in line with that of the industrial sector.

The means of following up and intensifying the efforts already made in this field will have to be used, first and foremost, to increase competition in the branches where it is still inadequate, and to adjust costs to the economic value of the function fulfilled—account being taken of the different levels in the quality of the service rendered to the consumer.

6 *Tourism*

Although tourism is an important element in the standard of living of the people of France as well as in the equilibrium of the balance of payments, it has so far been the object only of spasmodic efforts of development. But the revolution caused in transatlantic air transport by the advent of four-motor jet planes will lead to a considerable increase in the number of American tourists coming to Europe, and, in view of the rise in the standard of living, the growth observed in recent years in the number of French and European tourists will continue.

It is therefore vitally necessary for the Fourth Plan to envisage ways and means of ensuring the development of the whole field of tourist investment. In this effort, which should contribute appreciably to the policy of regional development, it will be appropriate to pay special attention to problems arising from the adaptation of hotel investment to the demands of this new clientèle.

CONDITIONS ESSENTIAL FOR FUNDAMENTAL EQUILIBRIUM

To reconcile economic expansion and monetary stability becomes all the more difficult as the rate of growth increases. Hence it will be more than ever necessary for the study of how to achieve expansion to go alongside research into equilibrium aims so as to allow these to be achieved without dangerous strain to employment, to foreign currency reserves, to price stability and to the State budget.

This investigation will be concerned first with the means that the Commissions intend to employ to achieve the detailed aims in the branches selected: choice of techniques, financing of investments, reform of certain regulations, procedures or practices. In this respect the Commissions will have to be able to exploit systematically the possibilities presented by the inquiries already made by the Committee created by the Decree of November 13, 1959, and responsible for examining the situations, existing in fact or in law, which constitute an unjustified obstacle to economic expansion.[1]

The Manpower, General Economic and Finance Commissions will have to be concerned, too, with the conditions necessary for achieving fundamental equilibrium as regards employment, saving, foreign exchange and regional economies.

Equilibrium of Employment. The Manpower Commission will have to study in particular the measures likely to assure:

the direction or re-direction of available manpower to the sectors and

[1] I.e. the Rueff-Armand Report.

occupations which will be short of it to achieve their production aims;

the development of professional training in all sectors of activity in which it is still insufficient and at all levels of qualifications, whether it is concerned with the education of the young, or with new training for workers to ensure their promotion, their adaptation to technical innovations or their conversion to other types of work;

the recourse to immigrant labour insofar as this will be found useful to counteract certain shortages that can be foreseen up to 1965.

Equilibrium of Foreign Exchange. The attention of the Commissions will have to be given especially to investment that will enable foreign currency to be economized or the mass of exportable products to grow rapidly, and to measures likely to widen foreign markets for French agricultural or industrial products.

Equilibrium of Sources of and Needs for Savings. To achieve rapid expansion in equilibrium requires the release of a volume of savings necessary for financing increased investments: their proportion in final demand will have to rise from 20.8 per cent in 1959 to about 23 per cent in 1965. It will be appropriate to define the conditions that will ensure the creation of an adequate volume of savings and its direction to sectors considered to have prior claims.

With this approach, it will be necessary to study steps to allow:

1. A progressive variation in the price of certain key products or certain services in accordance with real costs and the long-term aims fixed by the Plan.
2. An improved link between public action and private initiative, especially for market surveys of importance to insufficiently developed industries and for the achievement of corresponding investments.

Furthermore, it will be relevant to pay special attention to anti-cyclical policy destined to lessen economic fluctuations, notably by a policy of stock-piling, by evening out the rhythm of private investment and by the corrective use of the volume and distribution of public investment.

Regional equilibrium will have to be made the object of close examination by the Commission so as:

to enable industry and services to absorb the important excess of manpower coming either from normal population growth or from the transfers from agricultural to non-agricultural sectors.

to increase the steps already taken to lessen disequilibrium between the areas concentrating within them too many types of employment at too high a social cost, those with too much manpower which cannot be assured an adequate reward, and finally those which are being drained of workers although at times they are capable of welcoming economic forms of activity.

It is only in the light of the whole range of these surveys that the general and special aims of the Fourth Plan will be drawn up—after they have been made the object of an exercise of harmonizing and synthesizing which must be undertaken by the General Planning Commissariat in collaboration with the appropriate Commissions.

As it will need to obtain the advice of the Economic and Social Council and will wish to consult Parliament before putting the Fourth Plan into operation, the Government will have to be apprised of the proposals of the Commissaire General by the Autumn of 1961.

This programme implies that the Planning Commissions must be ready for action in the next few weeks, that a provisional synthesis of their work must be made by the beginning of 1961, and that their final reports must be drawn up during the summer of 1961.

APPENDIX II

SPEECH BY THE COMMISSAIRE GENERAL IN THE NATIONAL ASSEMBLY MAY 29, 1962[1]

Ladies and gentlemen, as I rise to address you here, I am deeply moved by the honour conferred upon me and well aware of the difficulty facing me. I will indeed try to be equal to both.

It is not for me, as Commissaire Général, to present, after the Minister of Finance and Economics, once again the Plan. Neither should I attempt any discussion of the terms of your reports. My task is more restricted. It is, I believe, an attempt to clarify the subject of debate. As the artisan of the Fourth Plan, I will try to show you just why it is what it is, and why certain choices have been made.

The Fourth Plan, based on the Third Plan, is an extension of it. I will therefore begin by an explanatory survey of the past before turning to prospects, the past serving to illuminate the future.

The Third Plan, as you know, began in the unfavourable conditions due to the deficit in the balance of payments and to the measures taken first in 1957, then at the end of 1958, to curb home demand. In 1959, the balance was restored.

And yet, the growth which followed was irregular. Production increased only half as fast as intended. Private consumption marked time, and essential investments alone advanced normally. Nevertheless, the restored balance offered general conditions favourable to lively re-expansion at the beginning of 1960. To launch this fresh effort, the Intermediate Plan was drawn up and published. Its chief aim was an 11 per cent increase in national production throughout the two years 1960 and 1961. This target was reached although the previous lag could not be fully made up.

A comparison of the results with the initial aims of the Third Plan shows that the export target was exceeded, the investment goal was reached, production lagged by about six months, but the consumption rate was about 10 months behind. Still, consumption was up 14 per cent on 1957, but merely 14 per cent instead of the 19 per cent anticipated by the Third Plan. Please bear this gap in mind.

The Third Plan was otherwise significant for the stress it laid on measures taken to help regional expansion. I will not dwell upon it here, as I shall revert to this subject.

I should now like to answer certain questions which might arise out of the Fourth Plan.

The first question refers to the choice of rates of expansion.

We know that the aim of the Fourth Plan is a national production

[1] Journal Officiel, *Débats Parlementaires,* Assemblée Nationale, May 30, 1962, p. 1354.

increase of 24 per cent in four years, i.e. an annual average of 5.5 per cent, given regular progress. It does not mean that 5.5 per cent will be reached each year, as variants of more or less can come from the risks we are subject to. Nevertheless, our appreciation of the rate must take this average rate as a basis.

Is it too high? Or too low? Or is it normal?

I will first point out that it is above the average rate of increase known since the progress in national accounts has enabled us to measure it. Still, it would not be unprecedented, for this rate has been reached and even slightly passed—by 0.2 per cent—during the four years of the Second Plan. But, in recent history, these are the only four consecutive years when this has been so. Moreover, this fast rate of expansion under the Second Plan was accompanied by considerable imbalance of our economy.

Considering everything, it can be claimed that to achieve an average rate of increase of 5.5 per cent during the six years covering the two years of the Intermediate Plan and the four years of the Fourth Plan—and without any foreign help or disturbance in the balance of payments—is certainly more difficult than reaching 5.7 per cent under the conditions that previously prevailed.

Hence, this rate of 5.5 per cent is ambitious, but not unduly so.

Why such ambition? I think we can take three points of view: firstly, we have to be ambitious; secondly, we are able to be ambitious; thirdly, we can if we will.

We have got to be ambitious, because that is our only way of reaching our high ambitions.

We can be ambitious, as is proved by the figures I have just quoted, and, even more conclusively, by the work of the Commissions of the rue de Martignac.[1]

But this possibility is not unconditional. It is up to us. And that leads me to my third and most important point: 'We can if we will.'

For us to keep on expanding in the desired rhythm, it is vital, in the first place, that overall demand should be great enough to stimulate production. I do not think we need fear any miscalculation in that direction unless an economic slump should hit the other European countries or the United States.

Next, for us to reach our goal, it is essential that supply can expand at the same rate, that is that new production capacity is created as planned. And this brings us to the question of finance. The fact that there must be no lack of manpower leads to the problem of employment. Finally it is necessary that our exports should allow us to pay for indispensable imports, which is a matter of competition.

Finance I will only mention briefly, as the Finance Minister and your Rapporteur-General have spoken on this. I will merely state that the possibilities of financial techniques should enable us to meet difficulties which are certainly real, but not insurmountable; and again, in reply to a point raised in the report of the Commission for Production and

[1] The address of the General Planning Commissariat.

Trade of the National Assembly, I will say that the question of financing the iron and steel industry is now being studied.

Secondly employment: in the first part of the Fourth Plan, the development of our economy will be hindered by lack of manpower, and especially by a shortage of technicians and rare specialists. This means that, during the first period of the Fourth Plan, a general reduction in working hours would be contrary to our most obvious interests by preventing economic development—I quote here the terms of the report—from following demographic development.

But gradually, things will change; the natural increase in population, the shortening of military service, immigration and repatriation from North Africa will create new sources. The labour market will tend to find a new balance, but the problem of transition will be a delicate one. Here we are on treacherous ground where we must beware of counting in too global terms. The problem will vary according to professions, qualifications and regions.

Then again our Algerian countrymen, after their painful ordeals, will often need a period of rehabilitation before they can be economically reintegrated, and our help must be no less effective than fraternal.

Thus professional training will remain, even more tomorrow than yesterday, the indispensable condition for the harmonious evolution of our economy—indeed of our society.

These hopes, and doubts too, give added significance, I think, to the part of the introduction to the Fourth Plan which deals with working hours, and I must re-read this to you textually.

'When major obstacles have been overcome, and the success of the Fourth Plan can be judged assured, shortened working hours can be weighed against other aims. Meanwhile a serious study will be made, not only of work-time, but of the distribution of labour over life, the year, the week and the day. Professional associations and trade unions will co-operate in this research.'

So I come to my third point, namely, competition.

The competitive power of our economy depends on both specific and general conditions.

The specific conditions are fundamentally the dynamism of our enterprises: we must encourage innovation and investment, improve organization, cut costs, explore foreign markets and establish commercial networks abroad.

But the most brilliant and worthy individual efforts would be valueless without a sound economy, that is to say, if French prices ceased to be competitive.

In this regard, the rise which occurred in the last months of 1961 is a danger signal which should be taken seriously. For although French industry on the whole has met brilliantly the first stage in the Rome Treaty, the second stage can in many respects prove more difficult.

These problems, you may be sure, have been thoroughly discussed by the Planning Commissions. The branches of industry have generally foreseen moderate imports and considerable exports. I was personally present at these meetings, and I must say that I was impressed by the spirit of enterprise and the confident action which these estimates inspired.

However, some mistakes are inevitable. That is why, after consulting the experts on foreign trade, we asked the Commissions to revise their early estimate to ensure a realistic overall result.

This part of the forecasts of the Plan is bound to contain many unknown elements, but the thought of defeat is inexcusable. We are determined to win through, but not, let us not forget, without a real effort on all fronts. This effort will certainly be strengthened by the implementation of the common agricultural policy of the Rome Treaty, and we can welcome the successful outcome of the Brussels agreements of January 14, 1962.

But although these agreements have caused certain passages of the Fourth Plan to be modified, especially with regard to price fixing and commitments *vis-à-vis* the Community, they have not fundamentally altered its balance.

And why have they not changed its balance? Because the Fourth Plan was made assuming the success of the common agricultural policy. If the Brussels agreements had indeed not been made, it is then that we should have had to make an 'agonizing reappraisal' of certain of our objectives.

It can be rightly admitted that, since January 14th, hypothesis has yielded to a reality which offers us more certain hopes of success in the future.

In short, the Fourth Plan proposes to speed up our economy, but without forcing.

This leads me to deal with the sharing of the fruits of expansion. I should like to reply briefly to the question: 'What is the Plan for?'

The first decision the authors of the Plan had to make was in the definition of the share of individual consumption in the fruits of expansion.

As the Prime Minister pointed out in his introductory speech, the Fourth Plan sees, with a growth of 24 per cent in production, an increase of 23 per cent in consumption. This difference of 1 per cent allows more investment in certain categories: +25 per cent for housing, +28 per cent for productive investments, +50 per cent for social objectives.

The three speeches which you heard at the opening of the debate, those of the Prime Minister, the Minister of Finance and of your Rapporteur-General of the Finance Commission, have given you the reasons, indeed the philosophy, underlying this choice.

I will add that this choice was approved by the Economic and Social Council who, in fact, requested it when consulted at the initial outline level.

The move towards a better balance between individual consumption goods and collective consumption, which constitutes an expression of national solidarity, won the approval of all those giving thought to the future of our society. But why stop at that? Why not take another 1 per cent off the increase in individual consumption? At this point in our evolution, any further effort in this direction seemed neither desirable, nor possible.

It did not seem desirable when we recall the lag in consumption during the Third Plan. I have stated that it increased by 14 per cent instead of 19 per cent. Hence, in this direction, there is pressure from needs.

It did not seem possible, either, because, for the last two years, consumption shows a distinct tendency to advance as rapidly as production, and the 1 per cent reduction anticipated by the Fourth Plan would require great restraint by everybody. I will return to this shortly. Consumer demand derives from incomes earned and spent freely. And strong forces are at work forcing up incomes: there is the scarcity premium for highly-skilled personnel, there is the general aspiration towards levelling up, there is the understandable wish for increased social allotments, there are the demands of equity for the underprivileged to which no one can be indifferent.

I think, therefore, that it was necessary to foresee a slight inclination towards collective consumption, but it would not have been realistic to switch over too suddenly.

Moreover, as I see it, the main thing is to put the problem clearly before the public and to encourage the appearance of a realization of what is at stake, which alone can be decisive. I believe that, as the Minister of Finance has already said, it is valid ideas which in the end prevail.

If this is granted, what considerations have guided us in defining the advance in the various categories of investment?

The rate of advance in productive investment—perhaps it would be better to say in directly productive investment—leaves no margin for choice if we intend to ensure, beyond the Fourth Plan, the expansion which we propose to realize within this Plan.

I emphasize that agricultural investments are included in the category of productive investments and that their increase is considerably greater than the average, as they almost double their figure in the Third Plan.

Amongst the other investments, special priority has been granted to education, health, research, culture and town-planning.

The different reports which you have received have stated clearly and firmly the reasons leading to considerable development of these programmes, as well as the reasons which impose some limit on them.

There are the demands of overall balance. There is, moreover, the fact that it is not possible for any activity to be speeded up too fast. The multiplying factor between one Plan and the next must not be too great. Besides the essentially economic and financial questions, there are, too, difficulties in administrative procedure, in the purchase of land sites, and the carrying out of plans which many of you know.

I don't mean that these difficulties have to be accepted in a conservative or resigned spirit. Quite to the contrary, we must make an effort to remove them, and for that we need not so much brilliant minds as clear thinkers.

In any case, it is safe to say that this is by far the greatest investment target ever agreed on for education, health, research, cultural and urban amenities.

In some cases, a complete change is envisaged; in others, such as education, the programme extends and enlarges the already great effort achieved in the past. Primary education has reached its maximum numbers although we still need to build schools in this category because of internal migration. In secondary education, the number of pupils has risen from 1,200,000 to 1,900,000 and it will reach 3,000,000 in ten years' time. Ten years ago, there were 140,000 students at our universities; today there are 240,000: there will be 500,000 in 1970.

These new figures illustrate what has been done, what remains to do, and the unprecedented wealth that our efforts will bring.

As regards housing, the Fourth Plan has foreseen an increase in investment of 25 per cent: 10 per cent in number and 15 per cent in size and quality. This corresponds to a goal of 350,000 dwellings in 1965. The demand for homes, as you know, has four sources: elimination of shortages, natural increase of the population, home and foreign migration and, finally, the renewal of our stock of houses.

In the long run, the first cause—shortage—will diminish, but the last, the replacement, on the contrary, will grow more extensive. But the renewal of our stock of houses is linked with the difficult problem of urban renovation. This problem must be solved if we are to clear present and future slums for, as the standard of living rises, the demand for light, wholesome and well-equipped homes rises also. But before embarking on this vast process of creative destruction we have thought fit to keep for the time being to the total of 350,000 dwellings.

The Fourth Plan has given no details as to the regional allotment of buildings nor of the annual march towards the final goal. I imagine that the detailed geographical allotment will inspire some useful discussions when the regional tranches are debated.

As for the annual progression, there we have on purpose left a certain latitude. When the Fourth Plan was drawn up we were faced with some Algerian doubts which today are beginning to be dispelled. If the current of repatriation continues to flow as strongly, we shall probably want to reach the final objective quickly.

Of course, all the aspects of the housing problem will be gone into with special attention in the event of an Intermediate Plan being drawn up.

The priorities which I have just presented to you have prevented us from pushing on as fast as we should have liked some other kinds of investments and especially the great infrastructures of transport. M. Marc Jacquet[1] objects that, in this field, the proposed policy of invest-

[1] The Rapporteur-General.

ment is not bold enough. 'The Fourth Plan,' he writes, 'remains indecisive.'

Our recognition of the order of priorities does not imply any lack of understanding of the importance of transport investments. But we are obliged to provide instruction for young people as soon as they enter our schools and universities. If the proposals put forward for necessary equipment were not accepted in time, this young generation would be placed under a lasting handicap and the nation would be wasting a valuable potential which offers one of its best hopes for the future.

The delay to which certain big infrastructures in transport are subject is certainly to be regretted, but it is not of the same human gravity.

In any case, ladies and gentlemen, a choice was inevitable.

A second reason in the same direction was, as the general report has stressed, that the choice of vast infrastructure operations must take a comprehensive view of the development of the national territory so as not to aggravate the present regional inequalities.

As I shall explain in a moment, development must be linked with a prospective geography of sectors of activity, not simply by isolating any particular infrastructure operation, but taking due account of any financial repercussions and economic consequences.

I shall add one last word on this chapter of choice.

Some reports express the regret that it has not been possible to retain in their entirety the aims proposed by certain Planning Commissions.

I should like to take this opportunity of thanking these Commissions for their responsible approach to this work, and for the help they have given me. They have enumerated, checked and classified all the needs expressed, but their proposals amounted to a total which could not possibly be integrated in the general balance. Some selection was necessary but the reports of the Planning Commissions provided judgments which were most valuable for the final decisions of the Government.

In fact it is quite likely that the priorities established by the Fourth Plan will be thought to be the best.

The Rapporteur-General has observed that fundamental changes would upset the unity of the Plan. That is true. And yet, even today, certain adjustments would still be possible, provided they took the form of transfers from one section to another, and not of additions incompatible with the overall balance.

And so I come now to a third type of question, the social aspects of the Plan.

The success of the Plan demands the 23 per cent increase in consumption which I have mentioned but no more. Now, as I said, consumption depends on incomes freely earned and spent. That is why it has been progressively realized that the Plan must follow closely an Incomes Policy.

This Incomes Policy is clearly necessary if consumption is not to encroach upon social investments; and it is also needed to ensure the desired redistribution of income in favour of the underprivileged groups such as aged persons, large families, workers earning the minimum legal wage, low-waged farm hands, persons physically handicapped, or repatriates from North Africa.

This second point is perhaps less obvious and is worthy of your further attention.

It might be thought, at first sight, that a redistribution of incomes effected within an unchanged total does not modify overall consumption either. This is not the case for, quite legitimately, it is in the underprivileged classes that the propensity to consume is highest and the propensity to save the lowest. Hence, any redistribution of a social nature augments total consumption unless the increase in the majority of incomes is not slowed down. In other words, if not by law, then certainly in practice, it can be said that social investments, social transfers and incomes policy are indissoluble and that they form the three aspects of one and the same reality and they should be seen simultaneously.

The Fourth Plan has not proposed in this field a programme of measures defined once and for all, but neither has it left things to work themselves out spontaneously. It has laid down contractual procedure for study in the framework of the Plan.

Why this attitude, some will say, wrongly, this lack of attitude?

The problem, you may be sure, has been thoroughly examined at the preparatory stage of the Fourth Plan, together with the representatives of all socio-professional groups. The exchange of views demonstrated how deeply each category was attached to the principle of freedom of negotiation, especially as regards wages, and the repugnance felt by all at the thought of any arbitrary control of incomes. It was seen to be psychologically impossible to put forward in this direction any suggestions which had not been accepted and even which would not perhaps have been understood. It therefore seemed vital in the first place to keep the study of incomes, not on an overall basis, but as detailed as our statistical knowledge allows.

This analysis will no doubt reveal some weak spots: an overall increase which I fear will be too fast, a lack of balance between the progressive and the backward sectors and regions of our economy, a discrepancy in the trends in the remunerations of highly qualified and those of unqualified workers.

Therefore, instead of imposing *a priori* standards difficult to establish and even more difficult to get accepted, the Government will ask the parties involved: 'Will you put up with these defects? Don't you think, on the contrary, that it would be a good thing, as much for social justice as for unbroken expansion, to try and correct the result of economic factors by a set of socially balanced measures?'

If an agreement is reached, it could be translated into the contractual or semi-contractual procedures mentioned in your general report.

And so I come to the fourth question: regional policy and development.

This policy has its pioneers who alerted the nation to the importance of the interests at stake. It was the subject of a first series of comprehensive measures which were published in the decrees of 1954 and 1955 but today it is the first time that regional action is incorporated organically in the National Development Plan.

The Fourth Plan, it is said in the Introduction, is significant for new departure as regards regional policy which is both an experiment and a hope. By their understatement the writers of this chapter tried to guard against the risk of raising in our provinces excessive expectations which would end in disillusionment. But I want to show you that matters will go, and have already gone, further than the words and I trust you will admit that if the Fourth Plan can, like any human work, embody some weaknesses, at least it does not make any pretences.

I will deal with this problem under four aspects: procedure, principles, application, development.

As regards procedure, for the first time the Planning Commissions were invited to forecast the location of their investments and employment needs. Thus it was possible to detect the fundamental imbalances. For the first time, too, the Fourth Plan anticipates the implementation of a decentralized procedure, regional operational tranches.

This procedure will not make it possible to call into question big infrastructure and other projects of national interest, such as the building of universities and auto-routes. But it will permit discussion at regional level of the individual location of a mass of regional investments, for example, of secondary schools, and of the collective location of many other investments, such as primary schools.

But I add that the decentralized procedure assumes its full importance when we note that it stands midway between the Fourth and Fifth Plans. Its applied value will be tried out in the Fourth Plan, but it will be valuable as a signpost in the Fifth. Its practical use will come late for the Fourth, it has been said, and I agree, but it will be in good time for the Fifth. I am tempted to believe that its chief importance lies there.

Secondly: the principles. There is a first line of action which seems tempting, but which unfortunately, is unrelated to reality. It might be called the policy of natural harmonies: let us develop all our regions to the full and we shall thus enable them all to contribute fully to the development of the whole country.

This theory would be right if we had endless resources. Such not being the case, we fell back, in this field as in all others, on the necessity of choosing or rather, of giving priority; for everything will be done, but all in good time.

Here, I think, it is necessary to be very clear and precise.

There is not, there cannot be, any difference in procedure and objective between the East and the West, between the South and the North. There does not, and cannot, exist—a term I read—any apanage in favour of this or that part of the national territory. But, in the nature of things, the common will for development must take account of a variety of regional activities. Taking a simplified view of the case, expressed in too general terms as 'strong zones' or 'weak zones', we are faced, in trying to lay down a Plan, with the dilemma whether to help the weak zones to remedy their weakness as soon as possible, or whether to help the strong zones to develop a general state of prosperity in which the weaker regions can be given assistance.

The Fourth Plan has refused this dilemma, for the weak regions do not really need aid to be granted to them; what they need is the encouragement which will stimulate self-help by means of their natural vocation and wealth in human talents. That at least is how we see development.

This leads on finally to a complementary policy for the strong regions and to a propulsive policy for the weak.

The complementary policy is on the whole a version of traditional economic rationality. The propulsive policy, on the contrary, goes beyond it. It admits point blank that economic calculations, even when made on the basis of national accounts can, in certain cases, be overridden to further a wider view of the future. This concept of development has, however, two limits. One is that it may lead to actions which anticipate notably future trends but which are not anti-economic in the end because they go against the current of technical change or the aptitudes of the regions concerned. The second is that it is necessary not to go too far in this direction. It is the sole means of avoiding an accumulation of expenditures which are not useless perhaps but which have no near possibility of yielding returns, which would be a drag on the entire economy and would end by going against the interests of the weak regions themselves. Who says a propulsive policy says that the State gives the lead but not that it is led. Giving up rationality does not imply giving up reason itself.

The subject is an arduous one. It will be the object of continued study. Gradually a jurisprudence will be created. I am convinced that the decentralized procedure for the regional tranches will furnish us with many useful elements of appreciation.

I come now to another aspect of the subject. The report of your Finance Commission criticizes the regional chapter of the Fourth Plan for attaching too much importance to the criterion of employment, stressing all the same that it is certainly one of the most commendable aspects of the Plan, a qualification which I appreciate highly.

I feel that there is no fundamental difference of opinion. There would be if the criterion of employment had been regarded by us as the only and final one. But such is not the case. This criterion occurs at a moment in our evolution when many young people are reaching working age. It seemed absolutely necessary for us to avoid, as far as possible, placing them in the dilemma of choosing between unemployment and migration. Of course we shall never succeed in completely eliminating inter-regional migration, but only in reducing it to a more reasonable rate. In spite of what I have just said, I do not think that the criterion of employment is as bad as all that for it serves to spotlight certain structural difficulties. Moreover, we intend to supplement it by other indices. Here again I await valuable data from the working of the decentralized procedures.

I cannot leave this subject without saying a few words about the intended reform of the freight rates of the railways, about which I was able to gauge the feelings of the Assembly in the discussion preceding this one.

The explanations I am about to give you are not meant to open a discussion; they are in a way preliminary to debate and even to reports. I am merely pointing out to you what has led us to inscribe what there is in this Plan.

The planned tariff reform of the SNCF has some positive aspects; it would improve the co-ordination of rail and road, it would favour the financial equilibrium of the railways, it would prevent wrong choices being made as regards industrial locations which would be all the more dangerous as they would be likely, by their cumulative effects, to have consequences not openly visible.

Even so, these positive aspects must certainly be weighed against the legitimate interests of our regions, and that is why I am treating this subject at this part of my speech devoted to regional action.

It seems necessary to me to introduce some compromises in the reform. It would be a grave error not to. Between 'complete reform' and 'no reform' there is a conceivable middle way.

And now for the practical application of regional action. I do not think that the Fourth Plan has made an error of judgment in stressing the industrialization of the West and I should like to recall briefly some of the big projects associated with this policy: a large motor-car factory at Rennes, a big electronics factory at Brest, a centre for space telecommunications at Lannion. And I am only mentioning here the most significant, for today the movement has begun.

These achievements bear witness to the fact that our means are able to solve very difficult problems. They do not however prove—I admit frankly—that the volume of operations under way is up to the volume of requirements. The Planning Commissariat sees clearly that we are engaged in a sort of race against time. We have therefore embarked upon an inventory which will allow us, should it become necessary, to attempt to accelerate our activities.

Even if the Fourth Plan has singled out the West, it has still not neglected the other regions of our territory. The Introduction quotes, namely: the North and the Pas-de-Calais, the Massif Central and its southern fringe, the whole of the South-West and its Atlantic coastline.

I do not want to exhaust the patience of the Assembly by prolonging too far this part of my address, but I think it is useful, without dealing exhaustively with everything, to mention two problems cited especially in the report of M. Marc Jacquet:[1] that is Alsace and the South-West.

I admit freely that, as regards Alsace, the Fourth Plan has tended in the direction of modesty rather than pride. Once a disputed province, then the outpost of our defence, Alsace has now become a link. The

[1] The Rapporteur-General of the Finance Commission.

Grand Alsace Canal—which I know very well, as I was most proud to play some part in its construction—has been a magnificent propulsive operation, all the more magnificent, I claim, as it has been paid for practically by the electricity it produces. Hence it has cost nothing, so to speak, and this canal definitely is, in the very words of your Rapporteur-General, 'a point of convergence for new industries', which seems to me to have a great future before it.

As for the South-West, it can certainly be said that it has not at present the place in the economy of France that it should have. The trouble is less severe than in the West, but it is of long standing. It is deeply entrenched in the economic structures of the region. There does not exist there, as in Brittany and the neighbouring départements, a clearly marked line of development which stands out at first sight. Several types of action need to be launched simultaneously. There is an industrial tissue and an urban tissue which needs reviving. There is a constellation of towns, the relative value of whose functions remains to be defined. There is agriculture which enjoys favourable natural conditions—sun and humidity—but whose yields are often mediocre.

Finally, to the old poles of development of Bordeaux and Toulouse, a third pole has come to be added, that of Lacq, which has not yet made its multiplier effects felt sufficiently.

Following up the example of what has been done for the West, we have just undertaken, in co-operation with highly qualified experts, the synthesis of all the studies made up to now. We shall thus propose some crash schemes, those that we are sure to be able to carry through infallibly and, a little later on, a comprehensive programme.

This is the first time that an economic experiment has been started bearing on fourteen départements and 10 per cent of the total population of France. This experiment is being directed by a committee including elements from the regions as well as from the central administrations.

I now come to development matters.

The four years of a Plan seem to be but a brief span compared with the evolution of the geographical aspects of a country. There it is indeed a matter, as Valéry said, of 'those tremendous phenomena which the slowness of their production makes imperceptible'.

And so I must agree with the Rapporteur-General as to the necessity of inserting the programmes for regional action in a long-term perspective for the harmonious development of the territory as a whole.

For the solution of this problem, there was one initial condition, namely that development questions should be placed on the highest level in the structure of the public departments, as it calls for the action of several Ministries.

This condition is fulfilled today. Unity has thus been established in the realm of both theory and practice. With your permission, I will only speak here of the theory, having no competence for the rest.

So far, in the realm of theory, there has existed a certain duality. There were four-year Plans for modernization and equipment, which have recently become Plans for economic and social development. There was, on the other hand, the prospect for a plan for territorial development put forward by the High Council of the Ministry of Reconstruction.

The development Plans, especially the Fourth Plan, have a universal character in the sense that they are a synthesis of all the aspects of evolution—technical, economic, geographical, social and cultural. But they are limited to a span of four years. The experiments in territorial development are, in a way, the reverse. They are far-seeing, but they favour and, to a certain extent, isolate the geographical aspect of development.

It remains for us to make a synthesis of the advantages and merits of these two types of studies, a prospective study embracing the overall and distant development of our country. More precisely, in the months ahead, it will be our task to set up a prospective geography of the activities of our country, with 1980 as a horizon, or perhaps 1985. And, first of all, we shall have to sort out from the mass of topical data the facts bearing on the future. Briefly I will quote a few of them.

The first is that materials weigh less and count less, because our manufacturing techniques are getting more refined and because expansion is based more and more on increasingly elaborated products and perfected machines. Thus the handicap of distant locations is being removed, at least for a whole range of light industries.

It is thus becoming possible to define a more volontarist geography around growth points giving industries a stimulating background and the employees an attractive way of life.

The second fact bearing on the future is that, with free and increased exchanges, we shall be led more and more to work with imported raw materials. In time we shall probably see the development of harbour industries, of which our modern refineries and petrochemicals, as well as the iron and steel combine of Dunkirk, are probably the first signs.

There lies in these prospects a chance of better territorial distribution that will not harm our industrial areas in the North and East, which are well placed for the Common Market. On the contrary the length of life of their mineral resources will be extended but the too exclusive concentration of industries may thus be stopped.

A third great fact, I think, must be the demand for a better framework of life as the standard of living goes up and as leisure plays a greater part in men's lives. One of your rapporteurs has drawn attention to this evolutionary tendency.

Better living conditions mean for citizens the renovation of their towns with more greenery and open spaces, less tiresome commuting and more means of escape. It means for country people easier access to the conveniences and comforts which are enjoyed, although still unequally, by town dwellers.

In conclusion, I will refer briefly to the growth of the Paris region, in the first place to forestall any misunderstanding. Indeed, it has often been said that 53 per cent of the investments of the Plan was allotted to the Paris region. But it is really a question of payments made by head offices of societies for undertakings which are actually carried out elsewhere. Certain projects in the Sahara, for example, are included in this 53 per cent. It is the same thing when Electricité de France orders alternators which are made in Belfort and then installed on the Rance.

But to get back to the crux of the problem, it is certainly true that the Fourth Plan does not aim at arresting the growth of the Paris region.

The reason is that, in four years only, such a scheme seemed unrealistic. But as the problem has been set, it will have to be examined in the inquiry into land utilization and be assured of a more certain place in the Fifth Plan.

Certain discriminations will certainly have to be made, for, even if it is necessary to rid the Parisian region of such industries as do not belong there, and make of it, in a way, the opposite of a Ruhr, yet it is important not to compromise the asset which Paris represents for France, seen in a European perspective. Péguy, Valéry, Jules Romains have said so, as well as many others.

So I now come to a problem of methodology.

In the speeches that you have heard, the Fifth Plan has often been mentioned. We can feel gratified at this for, as the Minister of Finance has said, we shall not control the future except by anticipating it. The services of the General Planning Commissariat feel the same concern and we are busy in the field of methods which is our speciality, in preparing this future.

I will first of all say a word about what we do not intend to do. We do not think that we should achieve any real progress by multiplying the number of the branches of activity for which targets are set.

If, indeed, the realization of precise targets is essential for the Plan as regards the basic investments such as steel and electricity, it becomes quite a different matter the more one approaches the tremendous diversity of consumer goods. If the change in cost prices and in the tastes of consumers cause more refrigerators to be bought and less washing machines, or more belts and less braces, one cannot say that the success of the Plan is compromised.

Quite to the contrary, the more detailed a Plan may be, the greater is the risk of it being belied by circumstances. The task of the planner would become too heavy with the bulk of the initial programme and the frequent need of revision. It would require much greater resources to get much more doubtful results.

Finally—and this is perhaps the chief point for it is the human aspect of this problem—we should thus rob the mass of individuals of the powerful element of interest afforded by decentralized decision-making. Here I will read a few lines taken from an article by M. Gélinier which appeared recently in the newspaper *Le Monde*:

'The coercive control imposed by the transmission of detailed orders to executants is contrary to economic productivity. But it is perhaps on the human plane that its effects are most disastrous.

'Ever since modern business enterprise has discovered the efficacy of decentralized initiative, it employs an increasing number of staffs and technicians; it raises the standard of its personnel; it directs not by imposing its orders, but by winning at all levels responsible co-operation. This "shared" direction at the heart of the business is not only a factor of productivity, but also of the welfare of personnel, of pleasure in work, of individual liberty and, let us say, of happiness.' The planned State economy should also achieve the sociological progress made by industry.

And by a curious coincidence, or rather by significant convergence, we find a similar tendency in the countries of Eastern Europe. This is what the Polish economist Oscar Lange writes on the subject:

'Active planning and effective direction are possible in economic development without going into such details. Worse still, the planning of such details hampers really effective guidance of the national economy. Indeed I think one can say that the introduction of this sort of detail in the national economic Plan'—and I apologize for introducing a little humour into this serious debate: Mr Lange quotes ironically as examples the production of salted cucumbers and the number of hares to be shot by sportsmen—'has really no connection with true planning. That falls rather within the competence of the centralized guided economy in day-to-day matters by means of administrative measures, which is quite different.'

After this Mr Lange gives the following definition of the fundamental contents of the Plan:

'The national economic plan which should control the development of the national economy must envisage at least two things. Firstly, the division of national revenue between investment and consumption. Secondly, the distribution of investment among the different sectors of the economy. The first determines the general rate of economic growth; the second determines the direction of that development.'

I shall not be going too far in stating that the French Plan reaches beyond this minimum.

There are, in fact, two other directions in which we hope to progress. They are first of all the prospective research I have already spoken of, and then, the inquiries into the democratic choice of our main lines of strategy.

The Fourth Plan, in its inspiration and form, has been more democratic than the preceding ones. It has been more democratic in the number of persons and organizations working at it, and because the Economic and Social Council has helped to choose the initial outline, and above all through being, for the first time, so freely open to public discussion as to the final ends of the Plan.

After which, it is clear that the Fifth Plan must be even more democratic than the Fourth. That is your expressed wish and the Prime Minister has shown the way in his preparatory declaration: namely by allowing fruitful discussion by parliamentary committees at the stage of the first outlines, as to the general direction of the Plan.

The mission of the General Commissariat follows clearly. The experts must succeed in presenting alternatives which are clear, yet precise, simple yet significant. The planners are men of coherence. It is then up to the nation to express its preferences through its representatives.

Alongside these studies, a plan for information is being provided. I am pleased to note the importance attached by M. Fréville[1] to statistical information. The adversaries of statistics, who are still too numerous, forget the amount and precision of information is one of the best guarantees of freedom of opinion.

Now, ladies and gentlemen, I should like to end this already overlong report by briefly expressing one wish. It is that, in your debates, you should make the distinction between the actual Plan under discussion and the idea of planning.

It is normal and democratic that this Plan, which corresponds to a moment of our economic evolution, should be the object of your remarks, suggestions and criticisms, and finally of your assent.

The French style of planning, on the other hand, which has come down to me from my predecessors, and which I am endeavouring to extend further, is something more lasting and precious than a plan. I hope that it will not be left impaired after your debates, for it is an asset for France, and the interest which it arouses in our neighbour countries constitutes one of the ways open at one and the same time to the spread of French thought and to a common conception of European development.

The Fourth Plan, I have said, is only one stage. It is, however, an essential stage, for it will enable France to emerge from what might be called the demographic defile. A more numerous generation will soon be reaching the age of employment. A rejuvenated France, strong in her greatest wealth—her men—will be ready to tackle the new tasks which will abound for them.

It is not that since the war we have spared our pains. On the contrary, by her production effort, France has reached a place among the leading Western nations. I have before me a British pamphlet which cannot be denied, and proves it. It affirms a success which belongs to all Frenchmen. It is their own work, and should be their pride. We have increased our production considerably with a static active population, whilst undertaking the education of an increased young generation, and we must still continue our thrust right to the end of the defile. In slackening our place today we should risk an incomparable chance and lose in missing the future much more than we could gain at present. By maintaining our effort, in all its forms, of course, we shall be making much more of the Fourth Plan than a limited stage on the way to a more dynamic economy and a more just society. It will become rather a springboard for new accomplishments.

[1] Rapporteur of the Commission of the National Assembly on Cultural, Family and Social Affairs.

APPENDIX III

LIST OF THE PLANNING COMMISSIONS AND THEIR MEMBERSHIP

HORIZONTAL COMMISSIONS

General Economic and Financial:
Chairman, Governor of the Bank of France; vice-Chairman, the director general of the Caisse des Dépôts et Consignations; general rapporteur, a senior member of the staff of the General Planning Commissariat; three rapporteurs; 40 members (four trade unionists). The Chairmen of the vertical sections attend when questions concerning their branch are discussed.

Manpower:
Chairman, a University professor and economist; vice-Chairman, a director of the Ministry of Labour; general rapporteur, a member of the staff of the Economic and Social Council; two rapporteurs; 13 *ex-officio* members; 26 members (four trade unionists).

National Productivity Committee:
Chairman *ex-officio,* the Commissaire General of the General Planning Commissariat; 14 members; eight observers.

Regional Planning:
Chairman, the deputy Commissaire of the General Planning Commissariat; vice-Chairman, a senior official of the Ministry of Construction; 13 members.

Scientific and Technical Research:
This Commission is in fact the permanent Consultative Committee of the same name with a certain number of additional members.

VERTICAL COMMISSIONS

Agriculture:
Chairman, a Counsellor of State and member of the Agricultural Academy; three vice-Chairmen, all senior civil servants; one general rapporteur, a senior civil servant, and six rapporteurs; 21 members *ex-officio*; 55 members of whom four are trade unionists.

Agricultural and Food Industries:
Chairman, a Counsellor of State; vice-Chairman, two senior civil servants; general rapporteur, an engineer, member of the General Plan-

ning Commissariat staff; two rapporteurs, 24 *ex-officio* members; 64 members (four trade unionists).

Artisans:
Chairman, a Professor of Economics at the University of Paris and member of the Economic and Social Council; vice-Chairman, a senior civil servant; two general rapporteurs, a professor of economics and a senior civil servant from the Ministry of Industry; 10 *ex-officio* members; 24 members (three trade unionists).

Building and Public Works:
Chairman, a Counsellor of State; vice-Chairman, a member of the professional association; general rapporteur, an engineer; 27 *ex-officio* members; 13 members (four trade unionists) of the first section (Building) and 13 members (four trade unionists) of the second (Public Works).

Chemicals:
Chairman, the Chairman of the Board of Directors of Kodak-Pathé Ltd. and vice-Chairman of the Union of Chemical Industries; two vice-Chairmen, senior civil servants from the Ministry of Industry and the Ministry of the Army; three general rapporteurs, the secretary-general of the Union of Chemical Industries, two senior civil servants from the Ministry of Industry; 10 *ex-officio* members; 35 members (four trade unionists).

Culture and Arts:
Chairman, a Counsellor of State; vice-Chairman, the director of the French archives; general rapporteur, a member of the Council of State; two rapporteurs; 19 *ex-officio* members; 54 members (four trade unionists).

Energy:
Chairman, a senior civil servant at the Ministry of Industry; vice-Chairman, two senior civil servants from the same ministry and a representative of the Atomic Energy Commissariat; general rapporteur, a mining engineer and five rapporteurs; nine *ex-officio* members; 32 members (eight trade unionists).

Housing:
Chairman, an Inspecteur des Finances; two vice-Chairmen, the governor of the Crédit Foncier de France and a director from the Ministry of Construction; general rapporteur, an engineer; 13 *ex-officio* members; 26 members (four trade unionists).

Non-ferrous Mines and Metals:
Chairman, the head of the Ecole Nationale Supérieure des Mines; vice-Chairman, a director at the Ministry of Industry; general rapporteur,

the deputy head of the Ecole Nationale Supérieure des Mines; nine *ex-officio* members; 20 members (four trade unionists).

Overseas Territories:
Chairman and general rapporteur, senior civil servants at the Ministry for Overseas Territories; vice-Chairman, an Inspecteur des Finances; a number of *ex-officio* members; 36 members (four trade unionists).

Petrol (collaborating with the Energy Commission):
Chairman, an engineer; vice-Chairman and general rapporteur, senior civil servants; 10 *ex-officio* members; 29 members (four trade unionists).

Post Office and Telecommunications:
Chairman, an engineer and senior post office official; vice-Chairman, the secretary-general of the Ministry of Posts and Telecommunications; rapporteur, a senior post office engineer; nine *ex-officio* members; 14 members (four trade unionists).

Radio and Television:
Chairman, an engineer; vice-Chairman, the director-general of the Radio Television Française; rapporteur, an engineer from the RTF; six *ex-officio* members; 14 members (four trade unionists).

Sanitary and Social Equipment (Public Health):
Chairman, a Counsellor of State; vice-Chairmen, the general directors of health and population of the Ministry of Health; general rapporteur, a member of the Council of State; 13 *ex-officio* members; 34 members (four trade unionists).

School, University and Sport Equipment:
Chairman, a Counsellor of State; vice-Chairman, a director of the Ministry of Education; general rapporteur, a member of the Council of State; 15 *ex-officio* members; 24 members (five trade unionists).

Sea Fisheries:
Chairman, a Counsellor of State; vice-Chairman, a director at the Ministry of Fisheries; rapporteurs, two senior civil servants; nine *ex-officio* members; 25 members (two trade unionists).

Steel:
Chairman, the Chairman of the board of the Société Métallurgique de Knutange Ltd; vice-Chairman, a senior official from the Ministry of Industry; general rapporteur, an engineer; eight rapporteurs; eight *ex-officio* members; 40 members (four trade unionists).

Trade:
Chairman, a Counsellor at the Court of Audit; vice-Chairman, a senior civil servant from the Ministry of Trade; general rapporteur, the Chair-

man of the Committee for Economic Expansion of Bourgogne; nine *ex-officio* members; 35 members (four trade unionists).

Transformation Industries:
Chairman, the Chairman of the board of directors of Papeteries Navarre Ltd.; two vice-Chairmen, directors at the Ministry of Industry; one general rapporteur, a senior civil servant at the Ministry of Industry and two deputies; nine *ex-officio* members; 61 members (eight trade unionists) divided into two sections—mechanical and electrical, and textiles and others.

Transport:
Chairman, an engineer and senior civil servant; six vice-Chairmen, senior officials representing aviation, railways, ports, roads, shipping, public works; two general rapporteurs, two engineers; nine *ex-officio* members; 70 members (12 trade unionists) divided into three sections (internal, sea, air transport).

Tourism:
Chairman, the chairman of the Crédit Populaire de France; vice-Chairman, a senior civil servant; general rapporteur, an Inspecteur des Finances; 16 *ex-officio* members; 30 members (four trade unionists).

Urban Equipment:
Chairman, the general director of the Caisse des Dépôts et Consignations; vice-Chairmen, two directors from the Ministries of the Interior and Construction; general rapporteur, an engineer member of the staff of the General Planning Commissariat; seven rapporteurs; 22 *ex-officio* members; 37 members (three trade unionists). This commission has a permanent mission.

BIBLIOGRAPHY

I. OFFICIAL DOCUMENTS

Agriculture:

Recueil des Textes officiels, Journal Officiel, No. 1166, 1962

Budget:

Loi Organique relative aux Lois de Finances, Journal Officiel, No. 59-5S, January 1959

Projet de Loi de Finances pour 1962, Imprimerie Nationale, No. 1436, 1961

Loi de Finances pour 1962, Journal Officiel, No. 61-224, December 1961

Décrets Nos 61-1450 à 61-1483 du 29 décembre 1961 portant Répartition des Crédits ouverts par la Loi de Finances pour 1962, Journal Officiel, December 30, 1961

Projet de Loi de Finances pour 1963, Rapport Economique et Financier, Imprimerie Nationale, October 1962

Comptes de la Nation pour 1959. Vol. II, *Méthodes,* Imprimerie Nationale, 1960

Comptes de la Nation pour 1960. Vol. II, *Méthodes,* Imprimerie Nationale, 1961

Departmental Equipment Commissions and Interdepartmental Conferences. *Circulaires du 18 décembre 1961, Journal Officiel,* December 18 and 19, 1961

Directives adressées par le Gouvernement au Commissaire Général du Plan en vue de l'Elaboration du 4ème Plan, June 8, 1960

Economic and Social Council:

Ordonnance No. 58-1360 du 29 décembre 1958 portant Loi Organique relative au Conseil Economique et Social, Journal Officiel, December 30, 1958

Décret No. 59-600 du 5 mai 1959 relatif à l'Organisation du Conseil Economique et Social, Journal Officiel, May 7, 1959

Décret No. 61-64 du 19 janvier 1961 relatif à l'Organisation du Conseil Economique et Social, Journal Officiel, January 20, 1961

Réglement Intérieur

Economic and Social Council: Principal Studies on the Plan

Before the Fourth Plan

Résolution du 23 décembre 1948. Journal Officiel, Avis et Rapports du Conseil Economique, No. 18, December 24, 1948

Résolution du 8 juin 1949. Journal Officiel, Avis et Rapports du Conseil Economique, No. 12, June 9, 1949

Résolution du 26 janvier 1950. Journal Officiel, Avis et Rapports du Conseil Economique, No. 1, January 27, 1950

Rapport en date des 24-25 janvier 1951 sur le Projet de Loi relatif au Développement des Dépenses d'Investissement pour l'Exercice 1951. Journal Officiel, Avis et Rapports du Conseil Economique, No. 1, January 27, 1951

Résolution en date du 20 mai 1952 sur la Réforme de la Structure du Ministère des Affaires Economiques. Journal Officiel, Avis et Rapports du Conseil Economique, No. 7, May 21, 1952

Rapport en date du 15 décembre 1952 sur le Projet de Loi relatif au Développement des Dépenses d'Investissement pour l'Exercice 1953. Journal Officiel, Avis et Rapports du Conseil Economique, No. 21, December 16, 1952

Rapport en date des 6, 7 et 8 juillet 1954 sur le 2ème Plan de Modernisation et d'Equipement, Journal Officiel, Avis et Rapports du Conseil Economique, No. 22, August 3, 1954

Motion en date des 21 et 22 décembre 1954 sur le Problème des Investissements pour l'Exercice 1955. Journal Officiel, Avis et Rapports du Conseil Economique, No. 29, December 25, 1954

Etude en date des 7 et 8 novembre 1956 sur l'Evolution de la Population rurale. Journal Officiel, Avis et Rapports du Conseil Economique, December 7, 1956.

Rapport en date du 3 février 1959 sur le 3ème Plan de Modernisation et d'Equipement. Journal Officiel, Avis et Rapports du Conseil Economique, No. 4, February 28, 1959

Rapport en date des 20 et 21 décembre 1960 sur la Réalisation de la première année du Plan intérimaire. Journal Officiel, Avis et Rapports du Conseil Economique et Social, February 14, 1961

The Fourth Plan

Etude présentée par la Section des Investissements et du Plan sur le Rapport de M. J. DELORS, *Evolution de la Consommation des Particuliers au cours des prochaines Années,* February 23, 1960

Etude présentée par la Section des Investissements et du Plan sur le Rapport de M. L. CHARVET, *Perspectives de l'Economie française pour 1965,* May 3, 1960

Avis adopté au cours de la Séance du 18 novembre 1961, 4ème Plan National de Développement. Journal Officiel, Avis et Rapports du Conseil Economique et Social, No. 26, December 12, 1961

Related Topics

Etude sur les Participations financières de l'Etat. Journal Officiel, Avis et Rapports du Conseil Economique, March 19, 1959

Problème du Financement du Développement économique régional. Journal Officiel, Avis et Rapports du Conseil Economique et Social, February 24, 1962

Problème de la neutralité fiscale et des Incitations fiscales destinées à faciliter la Réalisation des Objectifs prioritaires définis au 4ème Plan. Journal Officiel, Avis et Rapports du Conseil Economique et Social, August 9, 1962

Economic and Social Development Fund. *Rapport du Conseil de Direction pour 1961-62* (7th Report), Imprimerie Nationale, 1961

General Planning Commissariat:

Cinq Ans d'Exécution du Plan de Modernisation et d'Equipement de l'Union française (Réalisations 1947-51 et Programme 1952), 1952

Annual Reports on the Execution of the Plans (since 1952)

(with SEEF), *Les Perspectives de l'Economie française pour 1965,* 1956

L'Equilibre en 1961, Synthèse des Travaux du 3ème Plan, 1957

(with SEEF), *Les Perspectives à long Terme de l'Economie française,* 1959

(with SEEF and CREDOC), *Projection de la Consommation pour 1965,* November 19, 1959

(with SEEF), *Les Perspectives de l'Economie française pour 1965,* February 1960

Note aux Rapporteurs des Commissions de Modernisation, June 1960

Perspectives Economiques pour l'Année 1965 correspondant aux Directives du Gouvernement, June 9, 1960

Indications sur les Méthodes d'Elaboration du 4ème Plan, June 14, 1960

Programme triennal d'Equipement de la Région parisienne, July 1960

Note pour les Rapporteurs au sujet des Hypothèses d'Echanges avec l'Extérieur incluses dans le Compte provisoire 1965, October 1960

Note aux Rapporteurs des Commissions de Modernisation sur les Variations relatives de Prix, December 21, 1960

(with SEEF), *Rapport introductif aux Travaux du Groupe de l'Equilibre de la Commission de l'Economie Générale et du Financement du Plan,* December 1960

Note sur l'Organisation des Travaux de la Synthèse provisoire du 4ème Plan, January 5, 1961

Note générale d'Orientation des Travaux de la Commission de l'Agriculture, May 1961

(with SEEF), *Projet de Rapport du Groupe de l'Equilibre de la Commission de l'Economie générale et du Financement du Plan,* June 1961

Programmes généraux de Modernisation et d'Equipement des Agglomérations, October 1961

La Planification régionale, December 29, 1961

Rapport sur les Structures de la Commercialisation, February 26, 1962
Tranches opératoires régionales, Note pour les Conférences inter-départementales, March 30, 1962

General Planning Commissariat, Planning Commissions—Reports:
Horizontal Commissions:
Economie Générale et Financement, Imprimerie Nationale, 1961
Main d'Oeuvre, Imprimerie Nationale, 1961
Productivité, Imprimerie Nationale, 1961
Recherche Scientifique et Technique, Documentation Française, 1962
Vertical Commissions:
Agriculture, Centre National du Commerce Extérieur, 1961
Artisanat, Commissariat Général du Plan (roneotyped), 1961
Bâtiment et Travaux Publics, Moniteur des Travaux Publics et du Bâtiment, Supplément au No. 48, December 2, 1961
Carburants, Imprimerie Nationale, 1961
Chimie, Documentation Française, 1961
Commerce, Imprimerie Nationale, 1961
Départements d'Outre-Mer, Imprimerie Nationale, 1961
Energie, Imprimerie Nationale, 1961
Equipement Culturel et Patrimoine Artistique, Imprimerie Nationale, 1961
Equipement Sanitaire et Social, Imprimerie Nationale, 1961
Equipement Scolaire, Universitaire et Sportif, Imprimerie Nationale, 1961
Equipement Urbain, Imprimerie Nationale, 1961
Habitation, Moniteur des Travaux Publics et du Bâtiment, Supplément au No. 48, December 2, 1961
Industries Agricoles et Alimentaires, Imprimerie Nationale, 1961
Industries de Transformation, Imprimerie Nationale, 1961
Mines et Métaux non-Ferreux, Imprimerie Nationale, 1961
Pêches Maritimes, Commissariat Général du Plan (roneotyped), 1961
Postes et Télécommunications, Imprimerie Nationale, 1961
Radiodiffusion et Télévision, Imprimerie Nationale, 1961
Sidérurgie, Imprimerie Nationale, 1961
Tourisme, Imprimerie Nationale, 1961
Transports, Imprimerie Nationale, 1961

High Planning Council—*Décret No. 61-729 du 12 juillet 1961 instituant un Conseil Supérieur du Plan de Développement économique et Social, Journal Officiel*, July 13, 1961

Institut National de la Statistique et des Etudes Economiques. Imprimerie Nationale, 1961

Bibliography

Modernization and Equipment Plans:

Deuxième Plan de Modernisation et d'Equipement (1954-57). Loi No. 56-342, *Journal Officiel*, No. 1057, 1956

Troisième Plan de Modernisation et d'Equipement (1958-61). Décret 59-443 du 19 mars 1959, Journal Officiel, No. 1129, 1959

Plan Intérimaire (1960-61), Imprimerie Nationale, 1960

Quatrième Plan de Développement économique et social (1962-65). Cahiers annexés au Journal Officiel du 7 août 1962 (Annexe jointe à la Loi No. 62-900 du 4 août 1962, *Journal Officiel*, August 7, 1962)

National Assembly—Reports on Fourth Plan:

Avis présenté au Nom de la Commission de la Production et des Echanges sur le Projet de Loi portant Approbation du Plan de Développement Economique et Social, M. LEMAIRE et MM. BOSCARY-MONSSERVIN, DEVEMY, DUVILLARD, PILLET, No. 1707, Imprimerie de l'Assemblée Nationale, 2ème Session ordinaire de 1961-62

Rapport fait au Nom de la Commission des Finances, de l'Economie Générale et du Plan sur le Projet de Loi portant Approbation du Plan de Développement Economique et Social, M. JACQUET

Tome I, *Observations générales et Vues d'Ensemble sur les Objectifs et les Moyens du Plan*

Tome II, *Les Equipements sociaux, les Programmes par Secteur, les Départements et Territoires d'Outre-Mer*

No. 1712. Imprimerie de l'Assemblée Nationale, 2ème Session ordinaire de 1961-62

Avis présenté au Nom de la Commission des Affaires Culturelles, Familiales et Sociales sur le Projet de Loi portant Approbation du Plan de Développement Economique et Social

Tome I, *La Répartition du Revenu National*, M. FREVILLE

Tome II, *Problèmes Sociaux*, M. CHAPUIS

Tome III, *Les Aspects culturels du Plan*, J. R. DEBRAY

No. 1714, Imprimerie de l'Assemblée Nationale, 2ème Session ordinaire de 1961-62

National Assembly—Debates on Fourth Plan:

Journal Officiel, Débats Parlementaires, Assemblée Nationale, May 23, 24, 25, 30, 1962, June 7, 8, 15, 20, 21, 22, 1962

Organization for European Economic Development. *Fifth Report on Agricultural Policies in Europe and North America*, July 1961

Rapport sur la Situation financière, présenté à M. le Ministre des Finances et des Affaires Economiques en Exécution de la Décision du 30.9.58 (Rueff Report). Imprimerie Nationale, 1958

Rapport sur les Obstacles à l'Expansion économique (Rueff-Armand Report). Imprimerie Nationale, 1960

Senate—Reports on Fourth Plan:

Rapport fait au Nom de la Commission des Affaires Economiques et du Plan sur le Projet de Loi, adopté par l'Assemblée Nationale, portant Approbation du Plan de Développement Economique et Social

Tome I, *Ensemble du Projet*, H. LONGCHAMBON

Tome II, *Aménagement du Territoire et Economies régionales*, E. DAILLY

Tome III, *Habitation*, J. M. BOULOUX

Tome IV, *Agriculture et Industries agricoles et alimentaires*, R. BRUN

Tome V, *Energie*, H. CORNAT et G. BONNET

Tome VI, *Industries, Commerce et Artisanat*, R. JAGER

Tome VII, *Transports et Tourisme*, A. PINTON

Tome VIII, *Port Maritimes, Marine Marchande et Pêches Maritimes*, J. YVON

Tome IX, *Postes et Télécommunications*, J. BEAUJANNOT

Tome X, *Eau*, M. LALLOY

Tome XI, *Départements et Territoires d'Outre-Mer*, H. LAFLEUR

Tome XII, *Examen des Articles*, H. LONGCHAMBON, J. M. BOULOUX, R. BRUN, E. DAILLY et A. PINTON

No. 238, Imprimerie des *Journaux Officiels*, 2ème Session Ordinaire de 1961-62

Avis présenté au Nom de la Commission des Affaires Sociales sur le Projet de Loi, adopté par l'Assemblée Nationale, portant Approbation du Plan de Développement Economique et Social:

Tome I, *Aspects Sociaux du Plan*, R. MENU

Tome II, *L'Emploi*, A. CHAZALON

Tome III, *Les Equipements Sanitaires et Sociaux, la Vieillesse*, A. PLAIT

Tome IV, *Les Problèmes Sociaux dans les Départements d'Outre-Mer*, M. G. MARIE-ANNE

No. 243, Imprimerie des *Journaux Officiels*, 2ème Session Ordinaire de 1961-62

Avis présenté au nom de la Commission des Finances, du Contrôle budgétaire et des Comptes Economiques de la Nation sur le Projet de Loi, adopté par l'Assemblée Nationale, portant Approbation du Plan de Développement Economique et Social, A. ARMENGAUD, No. 247, Imprimerie des *Journaux Officiels*, 2ème Session Ordinaire de 1961-62

Senate—Debates on Fourth Plan:

Journal Officiel, Débats Parlementaires, Sénat, July 4, 5, 6, 7, 10, 11, 12, 13, 1962

II. BOOKS

AUBRY, M.: *Le Conseil Economique,* Librairie Générale de Droit et de Jurisprudence, October 1953

BAUCHET, P.: *L'Expérience française de Planification,* Editions du Seuil, 1958

BAUCHET, P.: *Propriété publique et Planification,* Editions Cujas, 1962

BAUCHET, P.: *La Planification française,* Editions du Seuil, 1962

BAUM, W. C.: *French Economy and the State,* Princeton, 1958

BELLEVILLE, P.: *Vérités sur la Viande,* Société des Editions Modernes, 1961

BENARD, J.: *Vues sur l'Economie et la Population de la France jusqu'en 1970,* INED, Paris, 1953

BLOCH-LAINE, F.: *A la Recherche d'une 'Economie concertée',* Editions de l'Epargne, 1959

CAZES, B.: *La Planification en France et le 4ème Plan,* Editions de l'Epargne, 1962

EHRMANN, H. W.: *Organized Business in France,* Princeton, 1957

FAUCHEUX, J.: *La Décentralisation industrielle,* Berger-Levrault, 1959

GASCUEL, A.: *Aspects du 4ème Plan,* Berger-Levrault, 1962

GRAVIER, J. F.: *Paris et le Désert français,* Flammarion, 1948

LAGACHE, M.: *L'Aide de l'Etat aux Investissements privés,* Editions Berger Levrault, 1959

MAILLET, S.: *Les Paysans contre le Passé,* Editions du Seuil, 1962

MALINVAUD, E.: *Initiation à la Comptabilité économique nationale,* Institut National de la Statistique et des Etudes Economiques, 2ème édition, 1960

MARCHAL, J.: *La Comptabilité Nationale,* Editions Cujas, 2ème édition, 1962

MASSE, P.: *Le Choix des Investissements,* Dunod, 1959

MENDES-FRANCE, P.: *La Science économique et l'Action,* Julliard, 1954

MENDES-FRANCE, P.: *La République Moderne,* Gallimard, 1962

CLUB JEAN MOULIN: *L'Etat et le Citoyen,* Edition du Seuil, 1961

PALLEZ, G.: *Finances publiques, les Cours de Droit,* 1961-62, Paris

PERROUX, F.: *Les Comptes de la Nation,* Presses Universitaires de France, 1949

PERROUX, F.: *Le 4ème Plan française,* Presses Universitaires de France, 1962

SAUVY, A.: *Le Plan Sauvy.* Commenté par P. Mendès-France, P. Le Brun, G. Levard, A. Malterre, J. Milhau, A. Philip, R. Richard, A. Verret, Collection 'Questions d'Actualité', Calmann-Lévy, 1960

STONE, R., and BROWN, A.: *A Computable Model of Economic Growth,* Chapman & Hall, 1962

Succès et Faiblesses de l'Effort française. Ouvrage collectif publié sous la direction de M. P. Laroque, Colin, 1961

TANNENBAUM, E. R.: *The New France,* Chicago, The University of Chicago Press, 1961

VASSEUR, M.: *Le Droit de la Réforme des Structures industrielles et des Economies régionales,* Librairie Générale de Droit et de Jurisprudence, 1959

WILSON, J. G. S.: *French Banking and Credit Structure,* G. Bell & Sons, 1957

III. ARTICLES

ALBERT, J.: 'L'Evolution de la Consommation en France de 1950 à 1960', *Consommation,* Nos. 3 et 4, 1961

ANTOINE, J.: 'La Prévision des Equipements résidentiels', *Revue Economique,* No. 1, 1961

ARON, R.: 'La Nouvelle Politique économique, les Régimes et les Partis', *Nef,* June 1959

AUBOURG, R.: 'Travaux de la Commission de la Distribution du Commissariat Général du Plan', *Co-opération,* March 1961

BAILEY, R.: '45 million Frenchmen', *Spectator,* April 29, 1960

Banque Nationale pour le Commerce et l'Industrie: 'L'Aménagement du Territoire', *Bulletin d'Information Economique,* No. 95, March 1962

BARJONET, A.: 'Un "Plan"—Pourquoi faire?', *Economie et Politique,* No. 87, October 1961

BARJONET, A.: 'Le 4ème Plan', *Economie et Politique,* December 1961

BAUCHET, P.: 'L'Organisation du Plan français', *Société belge d'Etude pour l'Expansion,* November-December 1958

BAUCHET, P.: 'Le 3ème Plan', *Droit Social,* June 1959

BENARD, J.: 'Problèmes et Instruments de Synthèse d'un Plan indicatif', *Cahiers de l'Institut de Science Economique Appliauée,* Série D, No. 10, 1958

BENARD, J.: 'Production et Dépenses intérieures de la France en 1970. Résultats et Méthodes', in *Europe's Future in Figures,* ed. R. C. Geary, North Holland Co., 1962

BERNARD, P.: 'La Planification régionale en France', *Revue de l'Action Populaire,* February 1961

BLANC, L.: 'Les Techniques d'Elaboration des Plans de Développement économique et social', *Service des Etudes Economiques et Financières,* January 1962

BLOCH-LAINE, F.: 'Economie concertée et Planification démocratique', *Bulletin de l'ACADI,* 2ème édition, 1961

BLOCH-LAINE, F.: 'Pouvoirs publics et Pouvoirs professionnels', *Revue Jeune Patron,* March 1961

BLOCH-LAINE, F.: 'Réflexions sur le Partage du Pouvoir économique', *Promotions,* No. 61, 1962

BLOCH-LAINE, F.: 'Economie concertée et Planification démocratique', *Cahiers de la République,* July 1962

BLOCH-LAINE, F.: 'Pour une politique de l'administration économique', *Revue Economique,* November 1962

BOISSONNAT, J.: 'La Planification indicative en France', *Revue de l'Action Populaire,* December 1958

BOITEUX, M.: 'La Politique tarifaire de l'Electricité de France', *Bulletin d'Information des Services Publics Communaux et Départementaux,* June 1961

BOITEUX, M.: 'La Planification dans une Industrie nationalisée (EDF)', Commissariat Général du Plan, April 2, 1962

BRETON, J. F.: La Place de la Co-opération dans le 4ème Plan, Confédération Générale des Co-opératives agricoles, 12ème Congrès national annuel, Colmar, May 7, 8, 9, 1962

Bulletin du CNPF: 'Le Financement du Plan Monnet, Epargne ou Inflation', December 5, 1952

Business Economists' Conference Planning Papers, Eyre & Spottiswoode, April 1962

BYE, M.: Rapport au Congrès MRP, May 1960, *Action Civique et Politique,* No. 16, June 1960

BYE, M., and VILLEY, D.: 'Quel avenir est réservé à l'Economie française?', *France-Forum,* February 1959

Cahiers du Communisme: 'L'Etat et le Pouvoir gaulliste', June 1959

Cahiers Français: 'Le Conseil Economique et Social', No. 49, April 1960

Cahiers Français: 'Le District et la Région de Paris', No. 59, 1961

Cahiers Français: 'Le Régime social agricole', No. 61, April 1961

Cahiers Français: 'Les Investissements de l'Electricité de France', No. 61, April 1961

Cahiers de la République: 'L'Agriculture, cette Inconnue', March, April, May, June, July, August, September 1960

Cahiers de la République: 'Quelques Problèmes posés par la Planification démocratique', No. 35, August 1961

DE CALAN, P.: 'Le Rôle des Organisations professionnelles et l'Exécution du Plan, Comité Européen pour le Progrès économique et social', June 1962

CASTLE, B.: 'Le Plan, Miracle or Myth?', *New Statesman,* September 29, 1961

CAZES, B.: 'Capitalisme et Planification sont-ils compatibles?', *Cahiers de l'Institut de Science Economique Appliquée, Recherches et Dialogues philosophiques et économiques,* No. 4, 1959

CAZES, B.: 'La Planification française', *Economie et Humanisme,* July-August 1960

CAZES, B.: 'Du Plan intérimaire au 4ème Plan', *Revue de l'Action Populaire*, December 1960

Central Planning Bureau: 'Scope and Methods of the Central Planning Bureau', The Hague, August 1956

Centre de Recherches et de Documentation sur la Consommation: 'La Consommation des Ménages français en 1956', *Consommation*, Nos 2 and 3, 1960

Centre de Recherches et de Documentation sur la Consommation: 'Etude Méthodologique sur les Programmes d'Equipements Urbains réalisés à ce jour', 1961

CHALANDON, A.: 'Pour une Economie concertée', *Le Monde*, June 8, 1960

CHALANDON, A.: 'Nouveau Plan, nouvelles Structures', *Vie française*, May 26, 1961

CHALANDON, A.: 'A la Recherche d'une Politique économique', *Le Monde*, May 30 and 31, 1962

Chambres d'Agriculture: 'Les Plans de Modernisation et d'Equipement', Supplément, December 15, 1957

CHAPEL, F.: 'Le Plan et les Industries de Transformation', Commissariat Général du Plan, January 1962

CHARVET, L.: 'Le choix du Taux d'Expansion, Clé d'une Planification', Association des Cadres dirigeants des Industries et des Banques, July-August 1960

CHASSENET, M.: 'Une Enquête sur les Dépenses médicales', *Consommation*, No. 1, 1961

CLAUDE, H.: 'Une Economie nationale-socialiste', *Nouvelle Critique*, November 1960

CLAUDE, H.: 'Qu'est-ce que l'Economie concertée?', *Economie et Politique*, September 1961

DE CLINCHAMPS, F.: 'Le Rôle de l'Entreprise privée dans la Préparation du Plan', Comité européen pour le Progrès économique et social, June 1962

CLOUGH, S. B.: 'France from Monnet to Hirsch', *Political Science Quarterly*, December 1956

Club Jean Moulin: 'Plan et Orientation de la Consommation', *Economie et Humanisme*, November-December 1961

Club Jean Moulin: 'Rapport sur la Nature et le Rôle du Plan dans une Démocratie', *Cahiers de la République*, December 1961 and January-February 1962

Colloquium on Democratic Planning: 'Pour une Planification démocratique', *Cahiers de la République*, June 1962

Communist Party: 'Le 4ème Plan', *France Nouvelle*, May 30-June 5, 1962

Confédération Française des Travailleurs Chrétiens: Rapport présenté par G. Declercq, 30th Congress, 1959

Confédération Française des Travailleurs Chrétiens: 31st Congress, Pour une Politique des Salaires, June 1960

Confédération Générale du Travail: Rapports au 33ème Congrès, May-June 1961

Confédération Générale du Travail-Force Ouvrière: Rapport présenté au 7ème Congrès Confédéral, Force Ouvrière Information, No. 108, 1961

COUSTE, P. B.: 'L'Economie concertée', *Jeune Patron,* December 1960

DESCAMPS, E.: 'Socialisme et Planification', *Cahiers du Centre d'Etudes Socialistes,* July 1962

DESSUS, G.: 'Un Plan pour quoi faire?', Association des Cadres dirigeants des Industries et des Banques, October 1960

DOW, J. C. R.: 'Fiscal Policy and Monetary Policy as Instruments of Economic Control', *Westminster Bank Review,* November 1960

DOW, J. C. R.: 'Problems of Economic Planning', *Westminster Bank Review,* November 1961

DUCAROY, G., FRACHON, B., GERMAIN, E., GONIN, M., and LOMBARD, F.: 'Planification socialiste et Démocratie, Perspectives Socialistes', *Revue mensuelle de Recherches Socialistes,* No. 45, February 1961

Economist: 'Five Years of the Monnet Plan', October 18, 1952

Economist: 'Planning like the French?', October 28, 1961

Economist: 'The French Government and Steel Prices', May 5, 1962

Economist: 'Britain's Five-Year Plan', May 12, 1962

Economie et Humanisme: 'Planification française et Démocratie', special number, November-December 1961

Economie et Humanisme: 'Secteur public industriel et Direction de L'Economie', September-October 1953

Engineering: 'Economic Planning's new-found Favour', October 13, 1961

Entreprise: 'Ce que les Industriels français pensent du 4ème Plan', December 30, 1961

FAURE, H.: 'Les Perspectives à long terme de la Demande de Textile', *Consommation,* No. 2, 1961

Fédération des Industries Mécaniques et Transformatrices des Métaux: 'Ce que signifie le 4ème Plan', *Industries Mécaniques,* No. 450, 1961

Financial Times: 'European Agriculture, The Rough and the Smooth', July 9, 1962

FOX, E. W.: 'The Failure of the Fourth Republic', *Current History,* May 1959

France-Forum: 'Qui dirige l'Economie française?', February 1957

France-Forum: 'La Planification en France', December 1959

FRISCH, R.: Preface to the Oslo Channel Model, 'A Survey of Types of Economic Forecasting and Programming', in *Europe's Future in Figures,* ed. R. C. Geary, North Holland Co., 1962

GASCUEL, A.: 'Le 4ème Plan—Analyse et Opinions', *Perspectives,* Supplément, March 24, 1962

GERMAIN, J.: 'Pouvoir économique et Pouvoir politique', *Revue Administrative*, September-October 1960

Grandes Ecoles: 'Originalité de la Planification en France', No. 53, April 1962

GRIMANELLI, P.: 'A propos de l'Agriculture—Essai de Prospective', *Prospective*, No. 6, November 1960

GRUSON, C.: 'Les Programmes en Chiffres', *Encyclopédie française*, Tome IX, l'Univers économique et social, Librairie Larousse, 1960

GRUSON, C.: 'Une Planification sans Rivages', *Cahiers de le République*, No. 29, 1961

GRUSON, C., and BLOCH-LAINE, F.: 'Information, Prévision et Planification', *Encyclopédie française*, Tome XX, le Monde en devenir, Librairie Larousse, 1960

GUINOT, J. P.: 'Le Taux d'Expansion économique', *Observation Economique Financière*, No. 153, November 1960

GUINOT, J. P.: 'Les Prévisions du Plan en Matière d'Enseignement', *Observation Economique Financière*, No. 159, May 1961

HACKETT, J. W.: 'Sur les Investissements dans un Plan indicatif, l'Exemple du 3ème Plan français', *Cahiers de l'ISEA*, Série D, No. 10, 1958

HALL, Sir Robert: *Rede Lecture on Planning*, Cambridge University Press, 1962

D'HEROUVILLE, H.: 'Le Plan intérimaire', *Cahiers de la République*, November-December 1960

HIRSCH, E.: 'Du ler au 2ème Plan', *Monde Nouveau*, July 1955

HIRSCH, E.: 'L'Exécution du Plan', *Annales de la Société des Ingénieurs Civils*, 1959

HIRSCH, E.: 'Les Méthodes françaises de Planification', *Société des Ingénieurs Civils de France*, March-April 1959

HIRSCH, E.: 'La Planification française', *Encyclopédie française*, Tome XX, le Monde en devenir, Librairie Larousse, 1960

HUVELIN, P.: 'Planning in France', *Review of the Federation of British Industries*, April 1962

HUVELIN, P.: Ce que les Chefs d'entreprises pensent du Plan, Comité Européen pour le Progrès économique et social, June 1962

JACQUES, R.: 'Pour une Approche syndicale du Plan', *Esprit*, July 1961

JACQUES, R.: 'Quelques Problèmes posés par la Planification démocratique', *Cahiers de la République*, August 1961

JEANNENEY, J. M.: 'Un Impératif Vital: devenir Solvable *vis-à-vis* de l'Etranger', *Entreprise*, February 21, 1959

JEANNENEY, J. M.: 'Espoirs et Difficultés d'une "Economie concertée" ', *Jeune Patron*, January 1961

Jeune Patron: 'Les Jeunes Patrons et la Démocratie économique', September-October 1956

KAHN, J.: 'Le 4ème Plan au Service exclusif des Monopoles', *Cahiers du Communisme*, June 1962

KLATZMAN, J.: 'Réflexions sur la Planification en Agriculture', *Economie Rurale*, No. 41, July-September 1959

LABASSE, J.: 'La Portée géographique des Programmes d'Action régionale française', *Annales de Géographie*, July-August 1960

LAGACHE, M.: 'Les Problèmes de l'Industrie chimique française', *Revue des Ingénieurs*, No. 125, February 1961

LAMBERT, G.: 'Le 4ème Plan doit corriger les Déficiences régionales', *Professions*, January 1961

LAMOUR, P.: 'Le Développement régional', *Revue Politique et Parlementaire*, August-September 1961

LANGLADE-DEMOYEN, C.: 'Du 3ème au 4ème Plan?', *Cahiers Agricoles*, Supplément, August 1-15, 1959

LASCAUD, A.: 'Le Pétrole dans le 4ème Plan, l'Industrie du Pétrole', *Chimie-Energies*, March 1961

LAURE, M.: 'Les Programmes de Modernisation et d'Equipement des Agglomérations', *Moniteur des Travaux Publics et du Bâtiment*, No. 15, April 9, 1960

LAURE, A.: 'Exposé sur les Programmes urbains', Commissariat Général du Plan, Stage de Planification, 1961

LAURE, A.: 'L'Equipement des Villes et le 4ème Plan', *Moniteur des Travaux Publics et du Bâtiment*, No. 49, December 9, 1961

LE BRUN, P.: 'Planification démocratique, Direction moderne et Marché Commun', *Le Monde*, August 17, 1962

LE GUAY, F.: 'Les Projections à long terme en France', Conférence Internationale de Genève sur 'Input-Output Techniques', September 1961

LERIDON, F.: 'Dix Ans d'Expérience de Prévision de l'Emploi', *Population*, No. 3, July-September 1961

LISLE, E.: 'L'Epargne et l'Epargnant', *Consommation*, No. 4, 1960

LISLE, E.: 'Les Prévisions de Consommation', *Revue Economique*, Nos. 1 and 2, 1961

LISLE, E.: 'Pour une Planification démocratique', *Signes du Temps*, No. 10, October 1961

LISLE, E.: 'Démocratie contre Inflation', *Signes du Temps*, March 1962

LISLE, E.: 'Les Perspectives de Consommation dans le 4ème Plan', *Consommation*, No. 2, April-June 1962

LISLE, E.: 'Planification Régionale et Développement urbain', Communication to the Conference on Economic Development, International Economic Association, Vienna, September 1962

LOMBARD, F.: 'Comment s'élaborent les Plans français', *Cahiers du Centre d'Etudes Socialistes*, July 1962

MALGRAIN, Y.: 'Données et Perspectives du 4ème Plan dans l'Agriculture', *Paysans*, February-March 1961

MASSE, P.: 'Prévision et Prospective', *Prospective*, No. 4, 1959

MASSE, P.: 'Une Approche de l'Idée de Plan', *Encyclopédie française*, Tome IX, l'Univers économique et social, Libraire Larousse, 1960

MASSE, P.: 'L'expansion, sa Nécessité, ses Contraintes, ses Moyens', *Moniteur Industriel et Commercial*, June 2, 1960

MASSE P.: 'Suggestions préliminaires pour un Essai de Programmation mathématique', Commissariat Général du Plan, October 1960

MASSE, P.: 'Productive Investment', in Series of Lectures on Economic Growth, University of Madrid, OEEC, Paris, 1961

MASSE, P.: 'La Préparation du 4ème Plan, Mémoires de la Société des Ingénieurs Civils de France', January 1961

MASSE, P.: 'Planification nationale et Programmes Professionnels', Assemblée annuelle du Syndicat de l'Industrie du Jute, March 22, 1961

MASSE, P.: 'La Pensée Moderne et l'Action économique', *Bulletin de l'Administration Centrale des Finances*, No. 11, April-May 1961, and *Cahiers* 'Reconstruction', May-June 1961

MASSE, P.: 'La Planification française, Problèmes Economiques', October 3, 1961

MASSE, P.: 'La Stratégie de l'Investissement', *Crédit Populaire*, October 1961

MASSE, P.: 'La Logique et l'Action', deux Conférences à l'Ecole des Hautes Etudes Commerciales, Paris, January 1962

MASSE, P.: 'La Planification française', Lecture at Dublin, April 1962

MASSE, P.: 'Situation et Perspectives de la Planification française', *Cahiers de la République*, June 1962

MASSE, P.: 'Discretionary and Formalised Planning', Communication to the Conference on Economic Development, International Economic Association, Vienna, September 1962

MATHIEU, G.: 'La Planification française, cette Adolescente', *Le Monde*, March 4, 5 and 6, 1962

MAYER, J.: 'La préparation des Budgets économiques', *Etudes de Comptabilité Nationale*, July 1961

Moniteur des Travaux Publics et du Bâtiment: Recueil des Textes Officiels sur l'Equipement du Territoire, July 1962

Mutualite de la Co-opération et du Credit Agricole: 44th Congress, Rapports sur l'Agriculture, May 1962

NATAF, M.: 'Le Modèle à moyen terme à Prix Variables', *Etudes de Comptabilité Nationale*, No. 3, Imprimerie Nationale, 1962

NIVEAU, M.: 'La Planification indicative en France et l'Equilibre des Paiements extérieurs', *Economie Appliquée*, Jan.-June 1962

Opinion Economique et Financière: 'Le Plan raisonnable de M. Massé', No. 23, June 8, 1961

D'ORMESSON, H.: 'Le Financement des Investissements de l'Electricité de France', *Revue Française de l'Energie*, November-December 1961

Parti Socialiste Unifié: Eléments de Programme élaborés par le Conseil National, Courrier du PSU, June-July-August 1962

Patronat Français: 'Autour des Problèmes de la Planification', July 1962

Patronat Français: 'Le Parlement et le 4ème Plan', September 8, 1962

DE LA PERRIERE, G.: 'Les Moyens d'Exécution du Plan', *Bulletin de l'Administration Centrale des Finances*, No. 12, July-August 1961

DE LA PERRIERE, G.: 'L'Exécution du Plan', Commissariat Général du Plan, 1961

PERROUX, F.: 'Le Plan Monnet et l'Avenir Economique de la France', *Banque*, April 1950

PERROUX, F.: 'Le Quatrième Plan Français, 1962-65—en quoi consiste Notre Planification Indicative, *Economie Appliquée*, January-June 1962

Perspectives: Le 4ème Plan, Analyse et Opinions, Supplément au No. 789, March 24, 1962

Perspectives Socialistes: 'Réalité et Perspectives de la Planification française', special numbers, January and February 1961

Pétrole Informations: 'L'Industrie française et le 4ème Plan', No. 311, July 5, 1961

PFLIMLIN, P.: 'Propositions pour un Plan européen', *Entreprise*, July 14, 1962

PISANI, E.: 'L'Agriculture française', Lecture at the Institut d'Etudes Politiques de Paris, Association des Anciens Elèves de la rue St-Guillaume, Bulletin 1962

Political and Economic Planning: *The Growing Economy*, October 17, 1960

Political and Economic Planning: *Economic Planning in France*, London, 1961

Reconstruction: 'Débat sur les Syndicalistes et le Plan', December 1961

Revue de l'Action Populaire: 'Démocratie et Plan', January 1963

Revue Socialiste: 'Planifier dans la Liberté', May 1962

ROCHE, E.: 'L'Activité du Conseil Economique (1954-57)', *Observation économique*, August and September 1957.

ROCHE, E.: 'L'Activité du Conseil Economique (1957-59)', *Observation économique*, September, October and November 1959

ROCHE, E.: 'Le Conseil Economique', *Revue Politique et Parlementaire*, August-September 1958

ROCHE, E.: 'Défense d'une Planification libérale', *Moniteur des Travaux Publics et du Bâtiment*, No. 18, May 6, 1961

ROTTIER, G.: 'Développement économique et Equipements urbains', *Consommation*, No. 1, 1960

SAUVY, A.: 'Quelques Aspects d'une Politique économiste progressiste', *Cahiers de la République*, May-June 1959

SCHEAHAN, J.: 'La Concurrence d'une Industrie nationalisée et les Réalisations de l'Industrie automobile française', *Bulletin* SEDEIS, No. 763, September 10, 1960

SCHEAHAN, J.: 'Problems and Possibilities of Industrial Price Control —Post-War French Experience', *American Economic Review,* June 1961

Socialist Party (SFIO): Programme fondamental, *Revue Socialiste,* July 1962

STONE, R., and BROWN, J. A. C.: 'A long-term Growth Model for the British Economy', in *Europe's Future in Figures,* ed. R. C. Geary, North Holland Co., 1962

VAN DEN PLAS, G.: 'Quinze Ans de Planification française', *Moniteur des Travaux Publics et du Bâtiment,* October 7, 1961

VENTEJOL, V.: 'Qu'est-ce que le Plan économique et social Force-Ouvrière?', *Perspectives,* March 24, 1962

VERGEOT, J.: 'Un Exemple de Programmation économique', *Revue du Conseil Economique Wallon,* November-December 1958

VERGEOT, J.: 'Regional Planning in European Productivity', OEEC, No. 38, Summer 1961

VILLIERS, G.: 'Un Pays moderne doit avoir une Economie en Expansion', *Jeune Patron,* February 1959

VILLIERS, G.: 'Notre Pays doit prendre Conscience des Possibilités et des Conditions de Progrès d'une Economie moderne', *Bulletin du Patronat Français,* November 1961

VINCENT, L. A.: 'La Prévision économique à long terme', Etudes et Conjoncture, September 1960

VIOT, P.: 'L'Organisation gouvernementale pour le Développement économique en France', Table Ronde de l'Institut International des Sciences Administratives, Lisbonne, September 1961

WELLISZ, S.: 'Economic Planning in the Netherlands, France and Italy', *Journal of Political Economy,* June 1960

WICKHAM, S.: Development of French Railways under the French Four-Year Plans, *Bulletin of the Oxford University Institute of Statistics,* February 1962

WOLFF, S.: 'Economic Planning in France', *Swiss Review of World Affairs,* July 1960

INDEX

For Product Safety Concerns and Information please contact our EU representative GPSR@taylorandfrancis.com Taylor & Francis Verlag GmbH, Kaufingerstraße 24, 80331 München, Germany